Not
The Whole Truth

By the same author

CONFESSION
MY FAITH
OUR FAITH
MY LORD AND MY GOD
COUNCIL AND CLERGY
WHAT IS HAPPENING IN THE CHURCH

With Rosemary Haughton:
DIALOGUE: THE STATE OF THE CHURCH TODAY

JOHN C. HEENAN

Archbishop of Westminster

Not
The Whole Truth

HODDER AND STOUGHTON
LONDON SYDNEY AUCKLAND TORONTO

Acknowledgements

The author wishes to thank the *Barking and Dagenham Advertiser*, the *Jewish Chronicle*, the *Catholic Herald* and the *Catholic Gazette* for permission to use extracts and articles quoted in this work.

ILLUSTRATIONS
between pages 160 and 161

Key to Acknowledgements

[1] *The Universe*
[2] *The Catholic Gazette*
[3] *Yorkshire Evening News*

WHY NOT THE WHOLE TRUTH?

After thirty years cabinet ministers are at liberty to reveal any secrets their colleagues may not have already disclosed in their memoirs. Ministers of Christ must keep confidences without limit of time. Whether or not they are of his flock, many people turn in confidence to the priest to discuss their intimate problems. This is one reason why I cannot give the whole truth. The priest is only a steward and it is required of a steward that he be trustworthy.

Nobody, I think, will feel betrayed by what is recorded here. It would have been possible to tell much more of the truth about myself but that would have required very great humility. I have not tried to emulate St. Augustine.

From time to time I have been approached by authors wanting to write my biography. I have always refused on the grounds that a balanced life story can be written only after a man's death. Hodder and Stoughton nevertheless sought leave to appoint a biographer. Nothing would be published until I was safely dead but meanwhile I was to grant the biographer frequent interviews. I decided that it would be less trouble to write this autobiography. It has occupied me during holidays and convalescence over the past two years. The first volume ends with my nomination as Bishop of Leeds.

Frequent mention is made of Dr. Doubleday who was Bishop of Brentwood from 1920 until 1951. He was a man of absolute integrity who thought it his duty to keep me down. I describe his treatment of me not in order to create an anti-hero but as an essential part of the account of the most formative influences in my life. The influence of Dr. Doubleday was wholly beneficial.

† JOHN CARDINAL HEENAN
Westminster, 12th March, 1971.
Feast of St. Gregory the Great
Apostle of England.

CHAPTER
ONE

THE MEMOIR OF CARDINAL HINSLEY WHICH I WROTE DURING THE SIX months following his death in 1943 begins with his funeral. This is in many ways more satisfactory than beginning with a man's birth. One baby is much like another. You cannot tell by looking in the cradle what kind of a person will emerge in later life. If you go to a man's funeral you can judge how important he became. It does not mean that if his funeral is well attended he must have been a popular man. The contrary may be true. Many people go to funerals not in sorrow but relief. Anyone holding a public position is bound to have a big funeral. When I was writing about Cardinal Hinsley I was able to show that many people at his funeral had no need to be there at all. I would prefer to begin this book with an account of my own funeral but that would obviously call for a more considerable gift of clairvoyance than I possess. I do not know what kind of a funeral I am going to have. If I die in my bed no doubt there will be a great gathering of my fellow bishops, clergy, laity, relatives, friends and deputations from the various organisations with which I have been connected. That is all I can safely predict about my funeral. On the other hand I may be blown to pieces. Every thinking person must have this possibility in mind since Hiroshima.

I cannot begin with my death and obviously I cannot remember my birth. I must therefore start with my earliest recollections. I shall not pretend to remember what people said to me when I was aged three and a half. There are phenomenal people who claim to remember with utmost clarity what happened to them in infancy. I am not one of them. My first clear recollection is of the day I started school. I was taken to school by my mother who had provided me with a slate and pencil. This was common practice. The pupil was going to school to learn how to write. That was the chief object of education. It was the first battle in the fight for literacy. The teacher in whose care I was placed was Mother Vincent. She was a Sister of the Ursuline Order. The name of the headmistress was Mother Dominic. I remember little about Mother Dominic except that she seemed extremely tall, graceful and gentle. Her pet name for me was Jackie Lantern. Naturally I have no idea why she called me that. I would like to think that it was because I was the light of the infants' class. It is more likely that I may have bumped my head against a lamp post and thus earned the sobriquet.

She used to appear in the classroom very rarely and always seemed to be carrying a handful of new boots. We are talking now of the year 1910—before there was any talk of the Welfare State. It was a time when the poor in England were really poor. The disabled and the unemployed survived largely on charity. It is true that health insurance had started but welfare schemes and social security were still largely the pipe dreams of politicians. These new boots were for the children who had none. I do not remember how many there were. There could not have been very many. Although I loved Mother Dominic very much I could not forgive her for passing me over when she was giving away these new boots. There was one boy in the class named Joe Barwick. He always managed to be given a pair of new boots. So did his sister Rose. What used to annoy me was that when these Barwicks put on their new boots they could walk with a lovely squeak. Having no new boots and certainly none that squeaked I disliked the Barwicks and liked Mother Dominic less for her meanness to me.

Mother Vincent, on the other hand, my first teacher, was lovely in every way. To console me when Mother Dominic had gone with boots still in her hands she would say that perhaps one day Mother Dominic would give me some new boots, too. It never occurred to me to be grateful that I had no need of Mother Dominic's boots.

The Ursulines left the school very soon after I entered it. I have no reason to believe that it was *post hoc ergo propter hoc*. The school was put in the hands of a man—Mr. Charles Saurin. This made very little difference to a boy of five. I must have noticed this man about the place but he did not bother me in any way. My attention was riveted on the lady who took the place of my beloved teacher Mother Vincent. She was Miss Kelly, destined to become a lifelong friend. When I saw her shortly before her death she was a grand-mother several times over. Even in old age she retained the same sweetness which had healed my heart broken by the loss of Mother Vincent. I can recall little about Miss Kelly's teaching beyond the fact that she taught us the names of all the colours. She had a wire frame on which beads of every hue and shade were fixed. We had to tell her which colour she was pointing to. It was easy enough to pick out the reds, blues, greens and yellows. Even the most stupid children could do that. It became much more difficult to pick out pink and mauve. We weren't allowed to call them pale purple. This was confusing but I was to discover during the next ten years or so that education can be very confusing indeed.

There was a bright girl in the class named Angela Lynch. She is now a nun and, in her turn, herself became a magnificent infants' teacher. No doubt she also fell in love with Miss Kelly and flattered her by imitation. Angela scored a great victory in class one day because she alone was able to tell the colour of a glass bead. This glass bead seemed completely colourless yet Miss Kelly wanted us to tell her what the colour was. It was not white. There were plenty of white beads. It was not even pale white. Nobody could tell her the colour of the glass bead. Then Angela Lynch put up her hand and said the colour was water-colour. The memory of that breathtaking act of genius remains with me as clearly today as sixty years ago.

I remember the names of most of the teachers who looked after me but there is little of interest I can say about most of them. There was a Miss Baker who taught us to sing. Miss O'Hare taught us to act. There was Miss Moffat who taught us geography in a most attractive way. She, I remember, instead of rolling out lists of places and telling us what they produced—the usual way of teaching geography in those days—put us aboard ship and off we steamed to the most remote corners of the globe. On our journey we learned what merchandise we were carrying, what the prevailing winds were and why they blew in that direction. She did not confuse us by talking of trade winds. We nevertheless came to know all about them—and anti-trade winds too. Miss Moffat was a teacher well in advance of her time. Many years later I was taught by a man who thought that history meant dates of the deaths of kings, the crowning of their successors and the principal battles they fought.

Miss Moffat's friend and colleague was Miss Shanahan who declared her intention of making us cultured boys and girls. Culture was always on her lips. We did not understand what she meant by the word. I confess that even today I often wonder what people mean by culture. She was the kind of person to make us ambitious to learn. She tried to give us a love of the English language. The educational fashion still required children to be taught spelling. She would encourage us and hold what we called spelling bees which we all found most exciting. She also encouraged us to learn poetry by heart. One Monday morning she offered a prize of sixpence to any child who would have learned to recite Gray's *Elegy* by the end of the week. Two of us accepted the challenge—Dan Hennessy and I. Poor Dan, a most brilliant boy, later decided to become a priest. He and I were destined to be class-fellows for many years both at this parochial school and later at the Jesuit grammar school in Stamford Hill. He was younger than I and had a better mind. When I left Stamford Hill to go to Ushaw College to start my studies for the priesthood Dan was to follow me. This, as we shall see later, led to his early death. He developed a gastric disease and died at the age of eighteen. He would have made a zealous priest and, perhaps, a considerable scholar.

Miss Guinevan stood out above all my teachers. She had a tremendous zeal for imparting knowledge but, above all, knowledge of the faith. She loved the Church with all her heart. She was devout in the most acceptable way. There was nothing sugary about her religion and she therefore had a greater influence on boys than on girls. I was very fond of her and it was her influence and inspiration which led me even as a boy to share her enthusiasm for the Church. She was hungry for the things of God but also had a love of learning for its own sake. I am not speaking of deep learning. She was an elementary school teacher whose scholarship was within the range of children. This remarkable woman made all of us want to learn more. She picked out Dan Hennessy and me for special tuition. She used to let us go to her house twice a week to learn French. She made us pay threepence a lesson. This, I was to learn afterwards, was not to enrich herself with fees from extra-curricular activities but to teach us to value the trouble she was taking. Miss Guinevan knew that Dan and I both hoped to become priests and this was an added reason for her care of us. She was also disposed to give us her spare time because we came from homes which gave us every encouragement to study.

There was one cultural venture of mine in which Dan did not share. This was learning to play the violin. My parents, like most simple people at that time, thought it important for their children to know how to play a musical instrument. At first—and at a very early age—I was sent with my sister to lessons in pianoforte. Our teacher was Mrs. Nicholson who lived across the road. My sister was successful but I was not. My trouble was my reluctance to practise. After a few months, in answer to my pleading my mother allowed me to abandon the piano and Mrs. Nicholson. But I had to pay a price. I had to exchange the piano for the violin. It happened that about that time a Mr. Storey had started to visit our school to give violin lessons once a week after the other lessons were over. I was duly enrolled in his group and I recall the lessons with a certain pleasure. Mr. Storey, we were told, was the son of the famous Professor Storey-Crofton. Why the professor was famous or what became of the Crofton part of his son's name we were never told and never had the curiosity to ask. We were also told that his wife and daughter who sometimes accompanied him to the music lessons (en route to the theatre of whose orchestra Mr. Storey was a member) were the champion lady fencers of England. I have no idea if this was true. Children are told and believe any kind of story about grown-ups. I remember distinctly that Mr. Storey had a stiff leg, that I disliked him very much, that he used to threaten me because I did not practise. He used to report me to the headmaster of the school for not practising. Mr. Saurin, the headmaster, would produce the cane and tell me that I would be beaten if I did not practise. Naturally he had no intention or, indeed, right to beat me for failure in out-of-school activities but between them these men killed any desire I might have had of becoming a virtuoso. It was not until many years later that I became really interested in the violin. When I went to Rome I took my violin with me and joined the orchestra. I might have continued to play the violin as a recreation had I not gone one Sunday afternoon to the Augusteo (then the Albert Hall of Rome) to hear Kreisler. I have never been able to bring myself to play the violin since hearing the maestro.

The great hero of my youth was Father Palmer the parish priest. A minister of religion in Ilford today would probably be little known. He would not be regarded as an important figure unless he had rare gifts. It was not so in the Ilford of my childhood. Father Palmer was

[11]

the best-known man in the little town. Other ministers of religion were also well known to people of every denomination and none. There was Dr. Vine the leader of the Free Churches. There was Eardley-Wilmot the Vicar of St. Mary's Anglican parish. Herbert Dunnico was, I think, the Congregationalist minister. He was also a member of Parliament and Deputy Speaker of the House of Commons. Father Palmer, however, was without doubt the religious leader of the town. He was a man of quite outstanding talent. His zeal and personality attracted hundreds to enquire about the Catholic faith. He had so many prospective converts that it was impossible for him to take them, as other priests did, in individual instruction classes. His church was half-filled every Monday evening with enquirers who came to hear his talks to non-Catholics. Thirty years later it became common for priests to give talks to non-Catholics. Father Palmer was the pioneer of this apostolate. Although the word ecumenism had not yet been coined this priest was a notable ecumenist. Nobody was surprised when vicars and ministers of other churches came to open the many bazaars and garden fêtes promoted by Father Palmer to pay the debt on his church and schools. He was a great believer in Christian Unity. For him this meant personal friendship with Protestants and non-Catholics of every description and a declared and unashamed intention of bringing them into the Catholic fold. This does not meet the definition of ecumenism but we are talking of a time when friendship between clergy of different denominations was rare. This priest was ecumenical according to the light then available.

One of the great events of the year in the parish of SS. Peter and Paul, Ilford, was the Whit Monday fête. It was a town event. Many who came may not have realised that it was a Catholic project. This garden fête was held in the grounds of the Territorial Army in Gordon Road. Father Palmer was renowned for his enterprise. We all took it for granted but looking back it seems to have been quite extraordinary. Each year there would be some breathtaking novelty. On one occasion he hired a balloon from which as a climax to the afternoon's entertainment a lady descended in a parachute. Parachute descents would not be considered remarkable today but before the first world war they were amazing. The garden fête also provided the occasion for a great sports day. The athletic events were of such high class that they were used by the A.A.A. (Amateur Athletic Association) as trials. One of the greatest of Father Palmer's enterprises (stunts?) was the Dunmow Flitch Trial. This event had been held in Dunmow, Essex during the Middle Ages. The idea was for a couple to prove that they had not had a cross word for a year and a day. If they succeeded in making good their claim they were awarded a flitch of bacon. Father Palmer knew that the trial had fallen into desuetude in Dunmow and decided to stage it in Ilford. He even managed to secure the historic stones upon which the couple had knelt in Dunmow when making their protestation of marital harmony.

I have good reason to remember the Dunmow Flitch Trial because on the first occasion it was held in Ilford my own parents were contenders for the flitch. It happened in this way. On Whit Monday morning there was a Mass at nine o'clock. It was the custom to have a late Mass on bank holidays and the church would be crowded with holiday-makers. My father on this Whit Monday was at the nine o'clock Mass—my mother having been, as was her custom, to the early Mass. After Mass Father Palmer called my father into the sacristy and told him to enter for the Dunmow Flitch. My father was aghast and said that it was out of the question. Nothing would induce my very shy mother to appear in public to make an exhibition of herself. Then Father Palmer revealed that there was only one pair of claimants for the flitch and that this couple, Mr. and Mrs. O'Mahony, had also been coerced into entering the lists. My father went home disconsolate to try to persuade my poor mother that it was the will of God—such was the prestige of the parish priest—that she should permit herself to be conscripted. At the time I was only a child. The story was given to me by my parents when I was older.

My father went into the witness box and declared brazenly that he and his wife had not had a cross word during the past year and a day or, indeed, throughout their married life. He claimed to be a very even-tempered man and declared that my mother was the most sweet-natured woman in the world. So far so good. Then my mother was brought to the witness stand. The first question was "When did you last have a quarrel with your husband?" "This morning," she replied "when he told me that I had to go in for this awful trial." It is not hard to imagine the reactions of the crowd. The laughter was so prolonged that it was virtually impossible for the trial to continue. I am not sure who was the judge on that occasion. The following year it was G.K. Chesterton. I have a picture of him with my father who by that time had been promoted to court usher, a position he held for many years. The jury hastily considered their verdict and wanted to award the flitch to my mother as a reward for her veracity. Justice, however, prevailed. The O'Mahonys won the flitch. Next day they sent half the flitch to the hungry Heenans.

Let me now say something of my father. He had the foresight to leave behind him an account of his family in the form of a letter to his children. The letter, dated February 1904, was from 2 Pretoria Terrace, Buckingham Road, Ilford. It continues for a hundred and ten pages. Then there was a break until 6th October of the same year when a new letter begins:

> 33 Ripley Road,
> Ilford, Essex.
>
> Dear Children,
>   We have today taken possession of this house which we now hope to call our home and your home for ever. It will undoubtedly be a big struggle at first but we trust in God to bless us with health and good luck to see the house purchased. There have been a great many unforeseen and incidental expenses to be met which leaves us with little or nothing.

There is yet another addition some three and a half months later:

> *Our little John Carmel*
> It is with the greatest gratitude to God I have to chronicle the birth of John Carmel Heenan on this day, the 26th January 1905 at 11 p.m. A fine little man, God bless him.

Because of the light they throw on the character of my parents I shall give some extracts from my father's letter. The first part of the letter gives at some length the history of the Heenan and Pilkington families. Like most family history it is fabulous. My forbears appear to have been mostly saints or giants. There follows an account of my father's search for work in London as a boy of nineteen. On page 87 he gives a description of his wife:

> Your dear mother Annie Pilkington was born and brought up next door to me in Clareen. We both attended the same school. Your mother was the eldest of a family of seven and she had to

leave school at the age of ten because of the death of her poor mother. I hope you will all remember this fact always. Your mother had to undertake at the age of ten years the duty of a mother and bring up five young children, the youngest not twelve months old. This little girl performed her arduous task so well that she was the talk of the whole parish. I shall always remember the sad afternoon when her mother died and the little baby at her breast three months old went with her to heaven. The sight of the mother and child dead together was awful and the five helpless children left motherless. But your mother stepped into the breach and brought them up better than many mothers. She sent them all to school for a longer term than any of the neighbours' children and saw that they were all put into respectable positions.

Ten years later her father died. This was also a very heavy blow. The mother died at the age of thirty-nine and the father was about forty-nine but by now the children were grown up. The boys were seventeen, eighteen and nineteen and excellent hard-working lads in every way. The whole family worked together in perfect harmony. The eldest boy, your Uncle Phil, worked like a real man on the farm. He was first with his crops every year and your mother, the eldest of the family, not only managed everything at home but also on the farm. All the children looked up to her as their guide and adviser. Whatever she said and wanted was law with all the boys. So they were a really happy family.

I went home to Ireland for my holidays in 1896 and to my delight I found your uncle Frank Pilkington from Chicago on holiday too. I always had the greatest admiration for his sister, Nan (your mother) but since she never even looked at a young man I always thought she never intended to get married. Cycling on one of our holiday trips I half jokingly said to Frank that I had really come home to look for an Irish girl that would have me and that I had only met one that I would like to marry but I was not at all certain if she cared a rap for me. Frank replied in his bluff Yankee style "Say Jim, if it was me I'd ask her." I told him that I hadn't the courage. Would he ask her for me? "Well," said Frank, "I might possibly say a word for you but I shall say two for myself. I'm not married either. Who is this wonderful girl?" When I told him that it was his sister, Nan, he looked straight at me and asked "Are you serious about this?" When he saw that I was he promised to intercede for me with your mother. To my joy she consented and soon after I returned to London I had a long letter to say that if I would return to Ireland in a year's time she would take me for better or worse. It happened that my father died just before I intended to return home so we had to put everything off until Easter 1898. We were married in the old church of St. Kieran, Clareen, on the 18th April 1898 at 6 a.m. It was a Monday morning and we left immediately driving six miles to the station in a lovely covered carriage drawn by two young horses. We span along the road and the people were out to greet us. Nearly the whole way there were people wishing us God speed.

My parents settled down in Fulham for the first four years of their married life. It was there that their first children, James and George, were born. My father gives a description of what happened on the night these twins were born.

Your poor mother nearly died at the birth of the twins, George (God be with this darling babe) and James. George died twelve hours after birth and eight hours after baptism. I was at the time recovering from an attack of rheumatic fever. I had been ill for seventeen weeks and during that time your poor mother nursed me night and day. It was due to her untiring attention that I recovered and it was the trouble and worry of my illness that brought about your mother's premature illness. When the doctor came to me at two o'clock in the morning—after having been eleven hours attending your mother—he told me that she was alive with two babies but he did not know which of the three would go to heaven first. I nearly fainted. The doctor was the best in Fulham. He was a Welshman named Edwards and a Catholic. He asked me if I was able to go for a priest. I said I was. I was not really able to walk without a stick and the priest's house was a mile and a half away but what could I do? I asked God to give me strength to get there and fetch the priest in time. I knew that the Holy Mother was looking down on us. When I reached the street I remembered that I had left the stick behind me in my hurry. I made a dash along the street and I think I never ran faster without pain or an ache. From that day to this I have never needed a stick to walk with, thank God. I rang the bell of the priest's house and told him my sad story. Fr. Galvin, a dashing Wicklow man, told me to go back home and said that he would be there as soon as me. I hurried back through the side roads, the shortest possible way, thinking every minute that the priest would catch me up. But there was no sign of him. As I neared home I was upset to think that he might have fallen asleep but when I got to the door and opened it I could hear his beautiful voice reading the words of baptism. He had very nearly finished by the time I reached home. He had come over on his bicycle evidently at terrific speed. He said to me "Georgie will soon be in heaven but Jim, you will stay with your mother, please God, to comfort her." His words turned out to be true. Little George was buried at Fulham cemetery and I hope that he will remember us in heaven.

Mine was a happy childhood. Looking back to the Ilford of the first quarter of the century I imagine—obviously wrongly—that all children must have been happy. Ilford at that period was a country town with several parks and no slums. Today it is a London borough, part of a great brick and concrete complex. When I was a boy there were cornfields less than a hundred yards from our front door. Friends from London would come to stay for a weekend in the country. A community of modest means, we were unpretentious but regarded ourselves as very respectable people. Our fathers did not go to work but to business. Nobody's mother went out to work. On Sundays we dressed uncomfortably. We did not play games, dig the garden or make a noise. That was the extent of the tribute our community paid to the Sabbath. My family and our Catholic neighbours, the Foleys, went to church at least twice on Sunday. Of the other hundred or so families four regularly attended a place of worship. Their names were Drever (Scots Presbyterians), Jones (Anglican), Abbot and Curtis (Chapel). The Bull family sometimes went to chapel. Both sons became Catholics in adolescence; the younger one, Alfred, was ordained priest in the diocese of Northampton. Neighbours, in our kind of area, were well acquainted and very friendly but rarely entered each other's houses. There were no feuds, no scandals. Children were well cared for and well behaved. Our parents loved us but kept us civilised less by kisses than by cuffs. In those days parents used endearments sparingly. They showed their love not in words but in making personal sacrifices to feed, clothe and educate us. I still remember the names of most of the children in the road but we naturally lost touch with each other when we grew up and went our various ways. Occasionally I hear from an old neighbour now in Australia and from another in Canada. Both are now Catholics. The faith must have been very strong in Ripley Road. Though quite a short road it produced a cardinal, a bishop and two parish priests. (The others are Bishop Foley of Lancaster, Father Bull and my brother Father Frank.)

Of all my small friends the boy I remember best is Rollie (Roland) Hughes. I was walking down a nearby street one Saturday morning when I came upon a crowd gathered round a motor lorry. A little boy had just been run over. I recognised the victim as Rollie Hughes and gave the policeman his name. The police must have been much less sophisticated in those days for I was immediately despatched to give the news to the Hughes family. "Break it gently," the policeman warned me. I ran with breathless speed back to Ripley Road and knocked at Mrs. Hughes' house. As soon as the poor woman opened the door I blurted: "There's been an accident, Mrs. Hughes, and Rollie's been killed." Rollie was an only child. His parents never recovered from the shock and eventually moved away from Ilford which spoke to them only of Rollie.

My great pal was Robin Aitken whose father was a soldier. Robin was self-consciously brave as was becoming in a soldier's son. He was always daring me to do the almost impossible feats which came easily to him. Afraid of danger but more afraid of being thought a coward I would climb dangerously high trees, jump wide brooks and raid orchards. The term juvenile delinquent had fortunately not yet been coined nor, I think, did juvenile courts exist. Mr. Aitken promised to take Robin and me to the boat race in 1913. For days we spoke of little else. The excitement mounted only to reach a tragic anti-climax. The day before the race Robin's father had a heart attack and died. It is not really strange that I am able to recall deaths with such clarity. Death is perhaps the greatest shock in the experience of childhood. This death was a personal blow because I not only missed the boat race but also lost Robin. On his father's death he was sent to the Duke of York's school for the sons of soldiers.

I was nine years old when the first world war broke out. The 4th August was a bank holiday and my recollections of that day remain vivid. My father was to take the family for a picnic in Epping forest. We walked to Seven Kings Station and arrived very early and had to wait for a train. While he was buying the tickets my father sent me across the road to buy a paper. Outside the newsagent's shop was a series of posters. I can still see the placard with the terrifying picture of a German soldier with a spiked helmet. My father asked me what the placard said. I had just learned to read big words and was proud to be able to tell him that it said: GERMANY CAPTURES FRANCE AND RUSSIA. The verb, of course, was not 'captures' but 'attacks'. My father laughed. "Johnny," he said, "that was quick work." Neither he nor anyone else was worried. Everybody regarded the attacks as bluff. England was mighty and the German cousins would soon be begging for peace. They did not become Huns until a few weeks later when, according to our papers, babies' heads were found in their knapsacks. We went off happily to our picnic in the forest.

It is hard to say exactly how long it took the public to realise that the war was not going to be only a brief encounter. As children we first experienced the evil of war through our stomachs. Sugar and potatoes were in particularly short supply. The government did not introduce official rationing for many months but the shopkeepers had their own methods of distributive justice. Men like my father who were unlikely to be called up—he was nearly fifty years of age when war broke out—rented plots of ground called allotments. I hated our allotment because my father expected his four children to share the work with him. None of us had been very eager to dig or weed our own little garden at home. We all showed marked lack of enthusiasm to dig for victory. My father was no tyrant and when he saw our reluctance he did not press us to dig. We were too foolish to realise that he was growing food to keep us alive. Children are thoughtless rather than selfish. My father was already engaged in war work. Civil servants too old for active service were expected to help other government departments after they had finished their normal work. My father was in the Patent Office in Chancery Lane. When his own office hours were over he had to go elsewhere in Whitehall. He was working on civil liabilities but I was never quite clear what the expression meant. I think it was something to do with compensation for civilians suffering loss through enemy action.

I suppose it was the air-raids which first brought home the horror of war to young children living in the London area. By comparison with the Nazi blitz in 1940 these were harmless firework displays but they terrified us. We were warned that a raid was imminent by bangs called maroons. The Zeppelins came over at a leisurely pace and in the early part of the war seemed invulnerable. The throbbing of their engines was especially sinister and frightened us almost as much as the bombs. Then came the wonderful night when one of the monsters was brought down in the nearby town of Billericay. A few nights later another was destroyed over Potters Bar. Then on one never-to-be-forgotten night a whole fleet of these fearsome dirigibles met their fate. The explanation current at the time was that they were attempting to avoid the harassment of the increasingly efficient Royal Flying Corps. They intended to arrive undetected. High above the North Sea they shut off their engines and floated silently to London. It was an exceptionally cold night and they were unable to restart many of their engines for the return journey. In the event some Zeppelins became easy targets for our men in their flimsy aircraft while others were forced to land in the sea or on the French coast. Whatever the explanation this was the last Zeppelin raid of the war. Thereafter German raids were made by aeroplanes—at first by small craft known as Taubes. Later, bigger planes called Gothas continued the bombardment from the air. These raids were unpleasant but lacked the power to terrify. I can recall no damage or casualties in Ilford apart from those caused by shrapnel or unexploded anti-aircraft shells.

Two wartime memories of school remain. The first was on the occasion of the only daylight air-raid. When the warning sounded none of the teachers knew what precautions ought to be taken. There were, of course, no air-raid shelters in those days. Combining piety with good psychology the headmaster decided that we should sing hymns to beg God's protection and keep out the noise of the anti-aircraft guns. At this point my friend Bobby Lawson burst into tears. We were all very ashamed of him (not one of the girls was crying) until he explained that he was crying because his father in London might be killed in the raid. At once he became a sort of hero and the rest of us felt pretty mean at being unable to summon up a few tears for our own fathers in London who were presumably in no less danger than his. Bobby was killed as a naval gunner in the second world war.

My second recollection is of the morning when a summons came for an altar boy to serve Mass for a sick priest who was going to say a late Mass. It was my turn to serve Mass and as soon as I saw the maid from the presbytery I gratefully and noisily closed my books and started for the door. Miss Guinevan the teacher regarded my taking leave without asking permission as an act of discourtesy. She sharply bade me sit down and told another boy to go in my place. The other boy incredibly enough was called Willie von Hebel. His family must have been foolish not to drop the 'von' at a time when to own a German dachshund was practically high treason. Willie was delighted to take my turn and surreptitiously poked out his tongue in derision. My outraged response was to call him a dirty German. The effect was disastrous. The headmaster, Mr. Saurin, was sent for and I was put over a bench and flogged. To me this was an act of gross injustice. It was, after all, my turn to serve Mass and the boy was a German. I could not understand the ferocity of the headmaster. During the second world war I heard a story which brought this boyhood incident back to mind. At Allied headquarters one evening an American colonel and an English major in their cups had a slanging match which ended in the colonel calling the major an English bastard. General Eisenhower, the Supreme Commander, sent the American home next day on a slow boat. "I don't object," he is alleged to have said, "to your calling him a bastard—he probably is. But in Allied Command you are not going to call him an English bastard."

The standards of an all-age parochial school could not possibly have been high. The pupils with ambitions (or ambitious parents) therefore sought other academic pastures before reaching the school-leaving age of fourteen years. Scholarships in those days were awarded to a pitifully small percentage of children. They were regarded more or less as geniuses and their names were recorded for posterity in golden letters on an impressive honours board. A school would rarely gain more than one scholarship a year. Unfortunately for my prospect there was in my class a brilliant boy named Ted Harding who in 1917 bore away the one available scholarship. He was an essayist of remarkable gifts while still only eleven years old. He once confided that his idea of heaven was to sit under a tree on a hot summer day with a packet of cigarettes and a book of Browning's poems. That, of course, was much later. He was by then nearly fifteen. He was predestined to be a journalist and later become a distinguished member of staff on more than one Fleet Street journal. That was to be in the remote future but meanwhile he had won the only scholarship. I was left to wonder how to achieve my now fixed resolve to become a priest.

My desire to become a priest was for many years a secret between my mother and me. We often discussed it. My mother indeed used it as a gentle form of blackmail. When I was late, ill-tempered, greedy, untidy or otherwise unbearable my mother would remind me that if I was to become a priest I had to be punctual, good-tempered, unselfish, tidy and, in general, insufferably virtuous. We both knew that the first step towards the priesthood was by way of higher education. Our first attempt to achieve this end was to seek a scholarship at—above all places—the Westminster Cathedral Choir School. I had a tuneful treble voice and, from my fruitless efforts to play the piano and violin, an elementary sense of melody and the ability to read a simple musical score. I now began to study what was called theory. This entailed learning mnemonics such as Every Good Boy Deserves Favour. I had already mastered the mysteries of crotchets, quavers and even semibreves.

Armed with this vast musical knowledge and several ballads— including 'The Last Rose of Summer' and 'Killarney'—I went to Westminster Cathedral with my mother to be tested by the Master of Music. At nine years of age I was excited as much by the trip to London as by the prospect of winning a musical scholarship. We were shown into a small room where my mother was told to wait while I was taken to the Master. Sir Richard Terry was seated at the piano smoking a cigarette. He did not greet me. He struck a few notes on the piano while I was wondering which of my songs he would ask me to sing. He looked up suddenly. To my horror I realised that I should have been listening. He told me to sing the notes he had been playing. I remained silent and he did not offer to play the notes again. I was now thoroughly frightened and wondered how I could please this cold angry man. Almost certainly he was not angry but bored by this most stupid of all the boys who had come that day to waste his time. I felt that I was losing my chances by remaining silent so I opened my mouth and emitted what Terry must have thought was a cry of pain. I was not asked to sing a scale much less 'The Last Rose of Summer'. I was very hurt that nobody had warned me of this trick of listening to a few notes and singing them. Songs and scales were all I had been taught in preparation for this ordeal.

My mother was then told to take me home to Essex. As we left the Choir School I could see that her face looked flushed and sad.

Always gentle she must have been wondering how to break the news of my failure. We went into a nearby ABC café and she gave me a glass of milk. I have often wondered where that café was. I was never able to discover it in later years. I know it was an ABC café because to postpone giving me news of my failure my mother explained the meaning of ABC. Apparently it had nothing to do with learning to read. The letters stood for Aerated Bread Company. My mother did not know what aerated bread was but supposed it was puffy bread. That brought her back to Sir Richard Terry. He had told her that my voice was metallic. Like aerated, this was a word not previously known to her. She said it meant that my voice was not like those of the boys in the Westminster Choir. I now realise that this was something of an understatement but at that time I was too downcast to worry about the meaning of metallic. But the word stuck in my memory. After a long silence and a few tears I put to her the only question that mattered: "Does this mean that I won't be able to be a priest?" Here was a question my mother was well able to answer. She knew nothing about metallic voices but a great deal about the ways of God. She assured me that if God wanted me to be a priest nothing in the world could prevent it.

The outlook, nevertheless, was not promising. First, I had failed to win a place in the Choir School and, secondly, Ted Harding had taken the only scholarship available in the summer of 1917. There was only one thing to do. I took to prayer. I still have the prayer book given to me on the day of my first Holy Communion by Mrs. Lynch, mother of Angela Lynch, genius in the babies' class who knew water-colour from white. I have described elsewhere* the Sunday in Lent 1913 when I made my first Holy Communion.

The church was SS. Peter and Paul's, Ilford, Essex. In those days Ilford was a country town. The parish was a family in which most people knew each other and all were known to the parish priest. I had been given a small prayer book with a white cover on which was a highly coloured picture of the Sacred Heart. It was the gift of Mrs. Lynch, a family friend, who many years later was to have three Jesuit sons and a daughter a Servite nun. I remember standing outside the church with my parents after Mass, feeling very holy and important. We children were soon called into the school hall adjoining the church but, much as I was looking forward to cake and custard for breakfast, I was

* *Dialogue* (with Rosemary Haughton) Chapmans, London, 1968.

reluctant to leave my family and friends. In the evening we had a procession of the Blesssed Sacrament for which we First Communicants wore red sashes to show how very special we were. I hope that no mistaken ecumenism will ever call for the abolition of First Communion Day in favour of Confirmation Day (or of a Solemn Communion on the French model) when children 'are old enough to understand what they are doing'. However long we live we can never fully understand the Holy Eucharist nor ever be more worthy to receive the Body of Christ than in the days of our innocence. First Communion Day, as I was to discover as parish priest, can be the most fruitful pastoral occasion in the life of a family and a parish.

The Thirty Days' Prayer was a common act of piety fifty years ago. It was—what novenas were later to become—a powerful way of making sure that if God did not grant a favour it would not be for lack of patience and persistence on our part. In the Sermon on the Mount Our Lord promised: "Ask and you will receive, seek and you will find, knock and it will be opened to you" (Matt. vii:7). Few know or remember that in the same sermon Christ had recommended living in the present without undue anxiety for the future: "Sufficient for the day is the evil thereof." (Matt. vi:34). To me as a child this meant that I must not keep worrying God to provide me with a new pair of football boots. Obviously it did not apply to spiritual favours. So from the age of ten or eleven every night I knelt wearily by my bedside to read the Thirty Days' Prayer. I cannot guess how many hundreds of times I read that long prayer. In *The Garden of the Soul*, which I still treasure, those pages are black and in one place actually worn away. When I came to study theology I realised that, whether or not my vocation to the priesthood was a direct answer to prayer, God had given one small boy the grace of understanding the importance of prayer. I also realised much later that my fidelity to prayer was more than a little tinged with superstition. If I did not go through my routine I might never become a priest. However tired after a hard game of football I would not go to bed without saying the Thirty Days' Prayer. By the time I was twelve my night prayers had been extended to include the litany of the Holy Name of Jesus and—almost incredibly—the litany for a happy death. Reading its gruesome description of the deathbed of a pious Christian would today provoke horror or, more likely, amusement. It is clear that I was determined to put my vocation firmly in the hands of God and leave nothing to chance. With the faith and directness of a child I asked God to make me a priest here and a saint hereafter. Thomas Hood's jingle expresses my feelings as I recollect the intensity of my prayer as a twelve-year-old:

> I remember, I remember
> The fir trees dark and high;.
> I used to think their slender tops
> Were close against the sky:
> It was a childish ignorance,
> But now 'tis little joy
> To know I'm farther off from Heaven
> Than when I was a boy.

Providentially—the direct answer to the Thirty Days' Prayer?—all my difficulties were suddenly overcome. Ted Harding, whose scholarship had taken him to St. Ignatius' College, the Jesuit school in Stamford Hill, was withdrawn by his parents half-way through the year and sent away to a boarding school. At this very time—this is where Providence seemed manifest—a remarkable Jesuit, Father Edmund Lester, was preaching at our parish church of SS. Peter and Paul, Ilford. Father Lester, a convert to the faith, had made it his life's work to 'save' vocations. His interest lay mainly in late vocations, that is, those who had felt no call to the priesthood until after they had begun to follow a worldly career. He opened a house at Osterley to give these young men the rudiments of the humanities in preparation for the seminary or novitiate. He sentimentally called his men 'Our Lady's young priests'. This was probably nauseating to them but it appealed to many old ladies who sold their jewellery to become 'godmothers' to these young 'priests'. There have already been over a thousand priests ordained as a result of Father Lester's work which was continued and greatly extended by his successor, Father Clement Tigar.

Father Palmer explained my predicament to Father Lester. I had no hope of being educated by the Jesuits without a scholarship and the only available scholarship was, so to speak, lying fallow. He produced a school report from Miss Guinevan who knew that both Dan Hennessy and I wanted to be priests. By a quirk of memory I remember the exact words of the teacher's recommendation: "John is a thoroughly good Catholic boy who is always eager to learn and to make progress." It fascinates me that this fairly humdrum testimonial should have so impressed itself on my mind. The explanation, I suppose, is that it was to prove to be my passport to higher studies. Armed with Father Palmer's opinion that I had a vocation to the priesthood and Miss Guinevan's assurance that I was keen to learn, Father Lester approached his Jesuit colleagues at Stamford Hill. I was transferred without waiting for the beginning of a new scholastic year. I left SS. Peter and Paul's parochial school for St. Ignatius' Grammar School in April 1918.

Stamford Hill was a fine school. The masters were mostly young Jesuits of whom many were not yet priests. They were called scholastics and were, in fact, ticket-of-leave undergraduates pausing between their courses of philosophy and theology. Two I remember with special affection. They were my first form masters—Mr. Weaver and Mr. Bickerstaff. Both were soccer and cricket enthusiasts but I have no recollection of their academic ability. I was put into form 2b (Remove) on my arrival but as the year was more than half over there was little I could do but follow blindly in the tracks of those with two terms of French and Latin behind them. Mr. Weaver ran a magazine for 2b which he unimaginatively called *Twobilia*. At the time of my arrival he was drawing near the end of a poetic alphabet in which he had contrived to include the names of everybody in the form. The letter H had long been dealt with (Hammil and Hawkins had been duly saluted) but I was nevertheless found a place. It was the first occasion on which my name had appeared in print. This doubtless is why I recall the glowing phrases—

Q is a question
To be answered by Heenan
Who pays no attention.

Not a perfect rhyme but, I am sure, a sound piece of history.

Mr. Weaver's chief claim to fame as a schoolmaster was to have inaugurated a football team he called the Bantams. These, as the term implies, were lightweights who were not old enough (or heavy enough) to find a place in the first or second eleven. The bantams became the legacy of Mr. Weaver to Mr. Bickerstaff who replaced him as form master of 2b at the end of my first term. 'Bickie' was the most beloved of masters. He was a Lancashire youth with a baby face and schoolgirl complexion. In fact he was every inch a man and a superb performer on both football and cricket fields. He was coach when I received my bantam spurs (if that does not make our sport sound too much like cock-fighting). Football, it seemed to us, was his main interest in life. This, of course, was an illusion of boys who themselves thought of little else. Bickie was not a gifted teacher. Being no scholar he was over-sensitive to the reactions of the boys in his class. He could not explain things well. Probably he did not know a great deal about the subjects he was teaching. In those days few of the young Jesuit teachers had been trained as teachers. Few, indeed, had taken a university degree. The cultured Jesuits were mostly writers at Farm Street or professors in the Jesuit seminary at Stonyhurst. From time to time Mr. Bickerstaff's schoolgirl complexion would change from pink to purple. Thunderbolts would be hurled in every direction. Many boys in the class would be ordered to receive the ferula. The Oxford dictionary describes this as 'a flat ruler with widened pierced end for punishing boys'. The ferula used by the Jesuits was considerably more menacing than a flat ruler. It was, I believe, made of gutta-percha and caused a very painful swelling. The delinquent was ordered to receive three, six, nine, twelve or, for exceptionally serious offences, eighteen (called, for some reason, twice-nine). He was allowed twenty-four hours in which to request punishment from one of two tolley masters assigned to the duty of beating the boys. I do not know the origin of the word tolley. I suppose it to be a derivative of toll which is the measured stroke of a bell. It was an excellent system which forbade a master who ordered punishment to be the executioner. No boy was ever struck a blow in anger.

When Mr. Bickerstaff lost his temper—these rare but terrible occasions were liable to arise when the bantams were going through a bad patch—a large number of boys in the class would be ordered six or nine ferulas. None of the victims was unduly disturbed because everyone knew that Bickie never let the sun go down on his wrath. At the end of the day when the purple had gone from his cheeks and the anger from his soul he would declare a general amnesty. Coughing with confusion and going a bright pink he would say: "I'm afraid I rather lost my temper this morning and I'm very sorry. And-er-by the way—those boys I ordered needn't get their ferulas." We would have loved this man even had he not almost invariably forborne to punish us. Even tough boys can recognise humility. It made Bickie doubly dear to us.

It would be self-indulgent to prolong the story of my days at

Stamford Hill. By modern standards it was a small school. The masters and boys all knew each other. There were not more than two or three lay masters and these were not accorded the same respect as the Jesuits. The boys wrongly regarded them as second-class citizens in the academic world. This was through no fault of these splendid laymen—it was simply the result of the negative attribute of not being Jesuits. (Fifty years later at the Second Vatican Council I was to realise that the Church has no definition of a layman. He is merely a non-cleric. This was recognised to be ecumenically disastrous so the notion of the People of God was resurrected to give both *laos* and *cleros* an honoured place.) We were made to work hard at school and at home. The homework occupied two or three hours each night with a proportionate increase at the weekend. Like most schools of the period Stamford Hill employed corporal punishment as a normal sanction against a boy's poor performance. The ferula was not used excessively. I was not in any way exemplary and during all my years at Stamford Hill I was not punished half-a-dozen times—that is, not even once a year. Modern educational practice discountenances any use of corporal punishment. I am not convinced that bullying and violence should not be counteracted by the infliction of physical pain. I am quite sure, however, that no boy should be beaten for academic failure. Stupid boys in those days were beaten in every type of school almost as a matter of routine. The customary picture of the teacher presiding over his class with cane in hand was not altogether a caricature. Corporal punishment and capital punishment are both to some extent relics of less civilised days.

I remained at Stamford Hill until, at the age of seventeen, I was sent to Ushaw College, Durham. I had thought very little about the future during the stimulating years at the Jesuit School. I had made my decision to be a priest at about the time of my first Holy Communion. It was not for me a question needing reconsideration. I cannot remember exactly how many of my school friends apart from Dan Hennessy knew that I was leaving to study for the priesthood. We had long ago shared the secret of our common desire to become priests. Of the rest I told only my closest friends, Leslie Gordon who went into the City, Herbert Ross, later a lawyer, and George Blinman the brightest boy in the class, a near neighbour in Ilford, who after a brief spell in Barclays Bank took a permanent commission in the Royal Air force. It was by no means uncommon for Stamford Hill boys to enter a seminary or the novitiate of a religious order. The school had something of a reputation among Jesuit schools as a nursery of vocations. In my own circle Austin Delaney became a Benedictine, Jack Lynch, T.B. Murray, Bernard Latchford and Terence O'Brien joined the Jesuits, Basil L'Estrange went to the Dominicans, Edward (Tank) O'Brien to the Redemptorists, Tom Keane became a White Father (African Missionary) while Denis Twohey, Denis McCarthy, John Mills, W. Philpott, Joe Scholles and I went from Stamford Hill to diocesan seminaries.

I have often wondered why Stamford Hill was so prolific in priestly vocations. One reason may be that in those days the very presence of a boy in such a school usually meant that his parents were making great sacrifices to keep him there. About half the boys had been awarded scholarships. The rest were charged about four guineas a term (that would now represent a little over a hundred pounds a year). There were no government allowances. A scholarship provided only tuition fees. Books, fares, food and clothes were the parents' responsibility. The Welfare State was not yet even on the horizon. Most Catholic parents were poor and found difficulty in supplying all these extras. Most adolescents were helping to support the home with their modest wages.

Only if parents were willing to make sacrifices could their children hope for any higher education. No matter how clever the child, if his parents could not afford to provide decent clothes, sportswear, dinner money and fares he would have no chance of further schooling. Only exceptional parents among the poor allowed their children to take up scholarships. Boys who were permitted to do so were often withdrawn at the age of fourteen to become wage earners. Local authorities had a system of fines for parents failing to leave scholarship children for the full course but these fines were rarely exacted. Parents of Stamford Hill boys had to make greater sacrifices because most of them lived at a great distance from the school. Because they valued Catholic education they were prepared to send their sons half-way across London instead of to local grammar schools. The hardship of travellers was greater then than now. In this era of smoke-free zones fog usually causes problems only for aircraft. In the London of fifty years ago fog was a hazard throughout the autumn and winter. Foreign visitors may still expect to find London blanketed by fog. In my childhood it was not unusual for a London fog to be so dense as to make the pavement on which we walked invisible.

I was particularly fond of fog. To reach Stamford Hill I had to use two railways. The first was the Great Eastern Railway which took me from Seven Kings to Forest Gate. Thence I walked a few hundred yards to Wanstead Park station on the Midland Railway. On foggy days I thus had a double chance of delay. With average luck on foggy mornings my train from Seven Kings would arrive too late at Forest Gate for me to catch my connexion at Wanstead Park. On many a morning I arrived happily at school a whole hour late with an innocent face and impregnable defence. I was one of the few who lived at the Seven Kings end of Ilford. The only others were the Rowntree boys who lived almost opposite the station. Ernie and Frank Rowntree were often my companions in crime. They were splendid boys but neither reached manhood. Ernie was drowned in a bathing accident when he was a midshipman. Frank died after an operation while he was a student for the priesthood. In a letter to his parents which arrived after his death Ernie announced his intention of leaving the sea and commencing studies for the priesthood. Although neither boy lived to be ordained, two of their sisters became Ursuline nuns. The other Ilford boys avoided the Great Eastern Railway (thus saving the expense of a second season ticket) by taking the Midland train from Woodgrange Park which was only a penny bus ride from Ilford Broadway. I was thus reasonably sure that my stories of catastrophic delays due to fog could not be gainsaid by the witness of those unhappy boys from Ilford whose mothers roused them from sleep on foggy mornings to catch an early train.

Before resuming my reflections on the extraordinary number of recruits for the priesthood from Stamford Hill let me add a word about the 'train boys'. We came from many parts of Essex and deservedly had an unwholesome reputation. The priest in charge of discipline was Father Arthur D'Arcy, S.J. I came to know him properly only after I had grown up. I was surprised to find him a shy and soft-spoken man with a North Country accent. We all liked Father D'Arcy and greatly respected him, but with his completely bald head and florid complexion he was slightly forbidding. Occasionally the whole school was lined up for Father D'Arcy to address us on some point of discipline. Uncomfortably often the villains of his homily were the train boys. Local station masters must have spent much of their time writing letters of complaint about our behaviour. Father D'Arcy always apologised in the name of the school and promised to speak to us severely. Hence the homilies. So far as I can judge dispassionately I would say that we were not what are now called juvenile delinquents. We were cheeky and mischievous but not, I think, criminal.

It was our habit to goad one station master simply by smoking in the station waiting room. We were not regular smokers because we were mostly keen athletes. We smoked to show how grown-up we were and, of course, to annoy the station master. He would have been wiser to ignore us but his sense of duty and outrage was strong. Occasionally there would be what Father D'Arcy in a subsequent homily would describe as fisticuffs between the railway porters and ourselves. We were full of initiative. The boys who used the Midland Railway formed their own football team—the Midlanians—for those not good enough for the school elevens. They had their own colours, made their own fixtures and acquitted themselves remarkably well. These boys were, for some reason, more law-abiding than the rest of us. It would be flattering but false to suggest that we were more manly and adventurous. One of our escapades (invariably leading to an official complaint to the school) was to change compartments between stations. This involved climbing out of our compartments and walking along the footboards. It can be dangerous even to lean out of a window. Continental trains used to carry a notice to this effect in three languages—*Nicht Hinauslehnen! Pericoloso Sporgersi! Ne se pencher en dehors!* We foolish boys were unaware of the potentially suicidal aspect of our exploit—misadventure is never very far from youthful adventures. We were delighted to shock the adult passengers. We were not malicious. It was only that we were too immature to appreciate that it was not clever to alarm our elders.

One day I had a brush with the station master of Seven Kings station which nearly resulted in the termination of my schooldays. By then I was quite a big boy of nearly seventeen years. It was a Saturday morning and, as was my custom, I had taken this one chance in the week to serve Mass. Mass had started late and I arrived at the station just as the train was due to start. I dashed down the staircase but the train had begun to move and was gathering speed. I sprinted along the platform and was about to jump on the now fast-moving train when I was intercepted by the station master. He was a small man. Rushing madly with bag in hand I bumped into him but—alas!—this took a precious two seconds and the train was lost. I was furious. I was captain of the eleven and that morning's game was against Latimer County School, one of our most formidable opponents. I was almost crying with disappointment and rage. There followed a dramatic scene on the platform. The station master had clearly been within his rights to prevent my boarding a train moving at speed. He was also protecting me from a possibly serious accident. I see that clearly now but I did not see it then. I was furious because he had made me miss the train. He was even more furious because I had practically knocked him down. He demanded my name and address but did not believe me when I gave them to him. By this time a small crowd had gathered. They had rightly supported the station master but did not like to hear him call me a liar. The station master demanded my season ticket. I refused to give it to him. He said that he only wanted to read my name for himself and that he would return the ticket immediately. I replied that I, in turn, did not believe him ('tit for tat' said someone in the crowd—thus encouraging me to show off still more disgracefully). I would hold the ticket, I told him, while he read the name. To this he reluctantly agreed and was astonished to find that I had not given a fictitious name. At this point another train arrived and I hastily took leave of the still angry station master.

I arrived in time for the match, told my success story with suitable embellishments and the whole incident soon passed from my mind. But not for long. Two or three weeks later I came home from school to find my father and mother sitting over the tea-cups with grave faces. My father asked me why I had assaulted the local station master, disgraced Stamford Hill and dragged the good name of the family in the mud. (Naturally I do not recall my father's exact words. He may, for all I know, have accused me of betraying my country and dishonouring the Church of God.) He pointed to the mantelpiece where I saw an envelope addressed to the Rev. A. D'Arcy, S.J. It had not been sealed and I was invited to read the contents. They were predictable. My father's letter briefly stated the nature of my offence and begged pardon that a son of his should have brought shame on the Jesuits. He concluded by assuring the good father that Stamford Hill would not be further embarrassed by my presence. It was a splendid letter. I felt fairly sure, however, that my father had no intention of posting it. Otherwise he would not have left it there for me to read. There was clearly room for manoeuvre. I felt flushed and unhappy. I asked my father what he wanted me to do. He told me that I was to have my tea and then post the letter. (There was, I noticed, no stamp on the envelope. This was a good omen. My father, I reflected, was too sensible to waste a stamp on a letter he did not intend to send.) Soon afterwards my father left the room and I was left alone with my mother. This, I now assume, had been planned between them. My mother told me the story in detail. She said that my father was well known to the station master by sight though not by name. My father had always greeted him and passed rather more than the time of day with him. The station master had been horrified to learn that such a gentleman as my father could have sired so desperate a monster. These were not my mother's actual words but this was their import.

The station master had consulted the railway authorities and decided to forfeit my season ticket and forbid me ever again to use the Great Eastern Railway. This, he thought, would be condign punishment because it would make it virtually impossible for me to continue my studies. My father in his letter to Father D'Arcy had given this as the reason why I must be withdrawn forthwith from Stamford Hill. My mother explained all this and said sadly that this was not only the end of school but the end of any hope of my becoming a priest. At that I became really alarmed. My mother then gently suggested that if I were to apologise at once to the station master all might yet be well and the letter to Father D'Arcy not sent. Thus the crisis ended. I meekly apologised to the station master who, true to character, accepted it with the utmost ungraciousness. He told me that he accepted my apology only for the sake of my father ('a very nice gentleman') who deserved a better fate than to have a future criminal for a son. This time I kept my temper—and my season ticket which symbolically had become my passport to the seminary.

This account of a misdemeanour hardly explains why Stamford Hill produced so many priests. It does however answer the question many people raise about the type of boy who early in life sets his mind on the priesthood. Such boys are not necessarily the most pious or best behaved. A call to the priesthood has little to do with virtue. Contemplative nuns are frequently ex-tomboys. This pheno-menon is to be explained on the grounds that only a girl full of spirits could possibly endure the silence and restrictions of a cloister. The boy wanting to be a priest is often a rascal but almost certainly loves his prayers. Most priests first felt the stirrings of their vocation as altar servers. To the eyes of faith the summit of human ambition is to stand at the altar to offer the Sacrifice of the Mass. Only in that sense is the Catholic priesthood a career. The word preferment is virtually unknown in Catholic circles.

Today it is customary to leave candidates for the priesthood at home or at boarding school until they have completed their humanities. They are sent to the seminary to begin professional studies. Since the Second Vatican Council there has been wide experimentation in the course of studies. Some believe that bright pupils should go to university immediately on leaving school. The study of philosophy and theology, it is said, can be more profitably undertaken when a young man is intellectually more developed. Fifty years ago the outlook in the Church was different. It was thought unwise to leave the future cleric too long with those preparing for worldly careers. For this reason I was removed from Stamford Hill when at the age of seventeen I was about to enter the sixth form. I was sent to Ushaw, a large seminary near Durham under the direction of the northern bishops.

The small diocese of Brentwood to which I belonged had been cut off from the mother diocese of Westminster during the first world war. The first Bishop of Brentwood was the historian Bernard Ward who at the time of his appointment was president of St. Edmund's, Ware. It might have been expected that Church students from Brentwood would be sent to St. Edmund's the Westminster seminary. This did not happen for a curious reason. It appears that Monsignor Ward as president of St. Edmund's had conscientious objections to Church students being members of the O.T.C. (Officers' Training Corps) which was then a feature of all boarding schools. Cardinal Bourne, Archbishop of Westminster, regarded St. Edmund's as part seminary and part public school. He insisted for patriotic motives that all boys, clerical and lay, should join the Corps. While Ward was president he was willing to carry out the policy of his archbishop but now that he himself had episcopal responsibility he relieved Brentwood students of military obligations. When Cardinal Bourne refused to differentiate between Westminster boys and those belonging to the new diocese Ward withdrew his students. My own brother, Frank, then at St. Edmund's was transferred to Oscott (the Birmingham seminary) thence to France and, after ordination, to Cambridge. This controversy took place some years before the time came for a seminary to be chosen for me. Bishop Ward by that time was dead. He lived less than three years after his nomination to Brentwood. It was his successor Bishop Doubleday who sent me to Ushaw.

CHAPTER
TWO

NOBODY IN LONDON SEEMED TO HAVE HEARD OF USHAW IN THE FAR distant North. When my father put me on the train at St. Pancras I might almost have been emigrating. I felt elated yet apprehensive. Another boy was also being seen off by his father and they kissed on parting. My father looked at me uneasily and asked me if I wanted him to kiss me. Though most reluctant he was evidently prepared for any sacrifice to give me a good start in my new life. He was relieved to see that I wanted only to shake hands. We had not kissed since I was a small boy. I remember the journey well. The first and depressing experience was to observe that one of the new boys was reading the *Children's Newspaper*. This was then a fairly new venture and I considered it as far beneath me as the *Magnet* and *Gem* which I had outgrown at the age of ten or eleven. I hoped that being a Church student did not involve behaving like a child. The kissing episode and the *Children's Newspaper* were unnerving. I was making an uncertain start in my clerical career.

All I can remember of the journey is that we had to change at York. At Durham the station was crowded with boys and students of divinity who had come in mainly from Northumberland, Lancashire and Yorkshire. I had not previously met any Northerners and found them rather rough. Nobody took any notice of the three new boys from the South. We kept close together for comfort and protection. A bus took us to the college where a welcoming atmosphere greeted us. On the notice board we found our names but discovered to our dismay that we were to be in different classes (called 'schools' at

Ushaw) and different houses (called 'bounds') and different dormitories (called, oddly enough, dormitories). I rarely saw the others again during my two years at Ushaw. We were completely separated because we were in different bounds. These bounds were arranged according to age groups. Boys in different bounds were not allowed to speak to each other. This was baffling to a boy from a day school, but segregation according to age seems always to have been the rule in Catholic boarding schools for reasons which in those days I could neither have guessed nor understood. Now that I understand the reasons I am not sure that they are valid. Repulsive small boys can become attractive when put in purdah.

Friends at home had predicted that as a new boy (the Ushaw term is 'new-cod') I would have my leg pulled soon after arrival. I did not have long to wait. After I had washed I came downstairs and rather diffidently joined a group of my own age. They were all veterans ('old-cods' at Ushaw). Feeling hungry after my journey I asked my new chums if the food was plentiful and good. They told me that for supper at Ushaw I would be given a piece of bread, one pat of butter and a cup of tea from an urn. I laughed heartily. A boy from London was not going to be fooled by these Northern oafs. I knew that after my long journey there was bound to be a substantial hot meal awaiting me. Alas! my leg was not being pulled. That night and every night I spent at Ushaw I was given for supper some bread, a pat of butter and a cup of tea.

The food at Ushaw was dangerously inadequate in those early post-war years. I was at the college only two years and most of that time I was hungry. When over thirty years later I became one of the governors of the school my first enquiries were about the food. I discovered that it had improved beyond measure. In my day for breakfast we had bread, butter and coffee from an urn. At one o'clock we had meat, potatoes and gravy. Then pudding (the most common variety was called 'pod' at Ushaw). The food at this main meal was plentiful and tasty and almost all home-produced. The college had its own crops, dairy farm and slaughterhouse. It even had its own gas works. Dinner was the last meal until the bread-and-butter supper. There was no tea-time at Ushaw. One boy whose uncle was a prison governor assured us that even convicted criminals are given tea. We were permitted to go to the refectory for bread and water at five o'clock but only the young boys—who were, if possible, even hungrier than the adolescents—followed this practice. We

[36]

thought it beneath our dignity. We preferred the pangs of hunger. In the interests of truth I must record that never have I enjoyed meals more than those bread-and-butter suppers of Ushaw days. There is no better appetiser than hunger.

Looking back on those post-war Ushaw days I wonder why our health did not suffer more. The diet was as unbalanced as culinary incompetence could contrive. There were virtually no vegetables except potatoes. People did not speak much of vitamins in those days. Perhaps they had not yet been discovered. It was taken for granted that starvation was a preparation for the self-sacrifice of the priesthood. Lay boys were allowed such extras as bacon for breakfast and, I think, treacle. There were very few lay boys in Poetry and Rhetoric. (The boys in these two classes were in Ushaw language Big Lads.) The lay boys were lower down in Syntax and Grammar (Little Lads) or still in the prep school which was called with Ushaw's customary singularity the seminary. Naturally most of the lay boys were to be found in the seminary. The breakfast bacon-eaters were lay boys. No distinction was made between lay and church boys for the other meals of the day. Starvation was evidently considered suitable for producing apostolic laymen as well as zealous clergy.

I assume that we were fed largely on starch. It was said that all priests in the North (the Ushaw term was 'old voccers'—presumably a reference to vocation) had ulcers as a result of their years of malnutrition. This is what we were told by old boys of Ushaw but it may have been only grisly humour. The health hazards were nevertheless considerable.

Since health is the context I must anticipate events in order to refer to my childhood friend Dan Hennessy with whom I had been at school in Ilford, in Stamford Hill and in my second year also in Ushaw. He was not only hungry but permanently ravenous. I was to stay only two years at Ushaw but Dan remained for another three years before it was decided to transfer him to Rome where once again we would have been fellow students. He was destined never to reach Rome. He died at Ushaw still, I think, in his teens. His father, a senior civil servant, was convinced that the Ushaw food had killed his son. I was already in Rome at the time of Dan's death but when I returned his father told me of his intention as a matter of conscience to call for a medical commission to investigate conditions at Ushaw. He was persuaded that his son had contracted a disease of the same family as beri-beri, a nutritional disease found in India, China and

South America. I never heard the upshot of this investigation but the food improved enormously after a team of doctors and dieticians had reported. By that time I had been at the English College in Rome for some years. I therefore had no experience of the fat years but the headmaster (at Ushaw called the prefect of studies) sent me a letter on the day tea was served to the students for the first time. "Dear John," he wrote, "The great days are over. Mollycoddled boys who eat bread and butter and drink tea each afternoon have replaced the great Ushaw men of yore." Yore was a favourite word of his. He borrowed it from the school song.

Food was not my sole interest at Ushaw. It was merely my chief preoccupation. By the end of the first term I could eat anything put before me. I had also learned to eat at speed so that after consuming my food (Ushaw word 'portion') I could wave my hand for more (at Ushaw 'seconds'). When I returned home for my first holiday my mother, having spoiled her youngest and most finical child, was astonished to see me fall on bread and butter as if it were pâté. There is no better place for a pampered boy than a boarding school. A spell in the services presumably has a similarly therapeutic effect. Since national service has been abandoned the majority of boys must enter manhood comparatively undisciplined. A poor boy never experiences anything like the rigours of most boarding schools.

I was put into the class of poetry on arrival at Ushaw. The scholastic programme was markedly classical. Boys entering poetry would normally have matriculated. In contemporary terms that would represent something between O and A levels. In poetry in those days such unimportant subjects as mathematics, physics, chemistry, biology, history and geography had been dropped from the syllabus. Latin, Greek, French, English and logic occupied every hour of the curriculum on weekdays. On Sunday morning there was a scripture lesson and on Sunday evening a class called antiquities. This was devoted to the study of Greek and Latin mythology. I was able to keep up with the rest of the class in Latin and French but of Greek I had learned little more than the alphabet at Stamford Hill. The rest of the class were reading Thucydides. I was not expected nor even invited to chase them. During the long Greek lessons I read Tacitus, Cicero, Vergil and, for relief, such elementary Greek texts as Xenophon. The one subject I really relished was logic.

Our textbook of logic was one of the Stonyhurst series of philosophy edited by George Joyce, S.J. It was a splendid book which I still consider superior to any textbook of logic then available. The logic course included part of what we were later to call epistemology. I found it fascinating. This was due in part to the influence of Syd Kelly, one of my many non-Catholic cousins. He was a peripatetic civil servant who at that time was personal assistant to the Under-Secretary for Education. I am not quite sure that this was the title. In those days there was no Minister of Education but only a President of the Board of Education. What we now call county schools were then known as board schools. My cousin was interested in religion but not, I think, at that time an active member of any church. I am not sure whether he would have described himself as a Protestant or agnostic. It was he who introduced me to the writings of Bertrand Russell. For this I have always been grateful, not because Russell is likely to be regarded by future generations as a great philosopher (though, of course, he was one of the clearest writers of this century) but because he taught me to question everything. This proved a great asset in later years when I began to read seriously.

Bertrand Russell might have become an exemplary Christian had his father, a monumental bigot, not robbed him of the chance to learn about God. Russell senior was a militant atheist. His hatred of religion must have been pathological. Although he did not live to affect his children personally—Bertrand was two years old when his father died—his will laid down the strict injunction that his children must receive no religious instruction of any kind. To make sure that his last wishes would be carried out he appointed as executors two atheists. Bertrand Russell therefore inherited unbelief as an Irish or Polish child inherits the Catholic faith or an Arab the creed of the Prophet. Apart from his views on sexual morality he was an example of *homo naturaliter christianus*. He had a genuine and self-sacrificing love for the suffering and persecuted. He also had a kind of arrogant humility which led him more than once to change his views on fundamental issues such as the use of force. I was introduced to his writings before he had conceived any of his second thoughts.

My two years at Ushaw were academically boring and wasteful. Latin nearly all day long is not enough to satisfy the inquisitive mind of a youth in his late teens. This regime, on the other hand, had the effect of testing my vocation. Boredom is far harder to withstand than shot and shell. Although I made small progress in the humanities I learned much about the spiritual life. I arrived at Ushaw with a missal and a prayer book but obviously I was a stranger to asceticism. The exercise they called meditation was a new experience. It seemed extraordinary to have to rise at half-past six to kneel for half-an-hour before Mass. Nobody told me how to occupy the time. At first I used to read my prayer book but the old cods said this was not the way to pass the time. I must meditate. The method was to read a few verses of the Gospel until the imagination caught fire. The theory was that this would lead to spontaneous prayer. I was never very good at it. My prayer routine soon became a fight against sleep and distractions. The only hints on prayer were given by priests who came to preach retreats. No master was appointed as spiritual director. The young in those days being rugged and independent, a full-time spiritual director would have been underemployed. Fifty years later a priest in charge of young people in a seminary, college or university could be overemployed by a generation of young people wanting reassurance at all hours of the day and night. We did not want to be loved by our masters. We preferred to be ignored.

Almost everything at Ushaw was the fruit of tradition. The college was immensely conscious of being descended from the English College in Douai. During the Elizabethan persecution William Allen, an Oxford convert, founded a college in France for the training of priests for the English mission. These seminary priests, as they came to be called, kept the faith alive during the years of persecution. Many of them were put to death for offering the sacrifice of the Mass. This was an act of high treason. It is the memory of these heroes of the faith which makes Ushaw men so tenacious of tradition. I have no idea which of the many Ushaw traditions actually came from Douai. I suspect that many are of much later vintage but all were guarded jealously. Askings-Down were days when the censor (a senior philosopher) invited the prefect of studies (by tradition unable to refuse) to make the half play day (Tuesday or Thursday) a full play day. There was Greek play-day, President's Feast and other occasions when the censor requested the president to grant a holiday. There was a play day on the first day the ice on the pond was thick enough to bear the whole house. To give a list of the Ushaw traditions would be tedious but they were all known and cherished by the students. There is at least a psychological link between loyalty and respect for tradition. Whether or not Waterloo was won on the playing fields of Eton, I am sure that many priests were strengthened in their later spiritual combats through their steadfast upholding of tradition in the ambulacra of Ushaw.

Tradition was so highly regarded that the only truly genuine Ushaw man ('cat and pod man') is one who had started in the junior house ('sem') and ended as one of the fourth year divines ('Divs'—theological students). Cat is the Ushaw game. Not unlike baseball it is probably more historic. Balls and sticks were made by the boys. The balls were as hard as concrete and quite lethal. Pod is the Ushaw pudding. It was a species of suet pudding but on special occasions when full of fruit it tasted like Christmas pudding. To play cat and eat pod were marks of a true Ushaw man. Even late starters became acceptable if they developed these accomplishments and became sympathetic to the Ushaw traditions. My short time at Ushaw was full of interest and joy. I soon came to appreciate the qualities of the rough-spoken Northerners (short a's and broad o's to a Southerner sounded rough if not actually uncouth). The warmth of the friendships formed in those days remains undiminished.

At Ushaw I learned the meaning of self-discipline. At my Jesuit school there had been no spiritual significance in rules. They were purely penal. If you broke rules and were foolish enough to be caught you were punished. When I went to Ushaw I did not realise that seminary rules form an important part of training for the priesthood. In company with most of my companions I observed only those rules which I found convenient. We were not allowed to smoke. On our walks we were forbidden to visit restaurants. These rules were widely disregarded. This was not because the students of the time were particularly lax. The explanation has nothing to do with spirituality. The fact is that everyone was still recovering from the effect of the first war.

Before the war, rules in seminaries were by modern standards strict to the point of harshness. Relaxation was confined to the sports field, play room and library. Not even senior students nearing ordination were allowed to smoke. They were allowed to take snuff and that is why the typical nineteenth century cleric was pictured snuff-box in hand with a cassock made unsightly by brown stains down the front. In 1919 students returned from their war service. It was no more possible in seminaries than universities for war veterans to accept the restrictions of pre-war days. These men had faced death and grown old far beyond their years. The cigarette had often been their only consolation in the trenches. Seminary rules had to be revised to accommodate them.

In this relaxed atmosphere we who were not returned warriors also took an indulgent view of rules. Unfortunately the superiors were not disposed to be similarly indulgent towards us. A few weeks after I arrived at Ushaw several of my friends were caught leaving a café and were forthwith expelled. This spread considerable despondency among Big Lads. If such savage reprisals were to be taken against rule-breakers we must obviously be more careful. This did not mean careful to keep the rules but to break them with greater caution. The restaurants we visited were now to be further afield. We took more precautions when we smoked our cigarettes. At that time it simply had not occurred to me that there might be some spiritual significance in keeping rules. The connexion between discipline and fitness for the priesthood had not entered my mind. One day I read an article on vocations in an old copy of the college magazine which altered my outlook on keeping rules. Indeed it changed my whole life.

The article was by Father Forkin, a former prefect of studies. Its purpose was to show how to discern a true vocation. Two firm indications of the absence of a true vocation were given. One was a refusal to obey seminary rules and the other was persistent questioning of the truths of philosophy and theology. This, the article said, betokened a twisted mind. I was much disturbed by what I read. At that time I was ignoring most of the rules and pestering the priests who taught logic and scripture with arguments I had picked up from Bertrand Russell or my non-Catholic cousin. This article, I thought, could have been written to describe me. There was only one thing to do. In all honesty I must leave Ushaw and give up all thought of the priesthood. This was the dilemma. I still wanted to be a priest but I had not realised the importance of keeping rules. As for the objections I voiced in class these were the outpourings of a southern extrovert showing off in front of his northern chums. The scepticism did not represent my real mentality. I was remarkably well able to hold my own in the company of my cousin and his agnostic friends. In something of a panic I approached Dr. McCormack whose hapless task it was to teach me logic. He was one of the targets of my immature questioning. He would be aware of my twisted mind.

I told Dr. McCormack that I had no vocation but did not know how to go about explaining this to Monsignor Browne, the President. He asked me why I was suddenly so sure that I ought to leave. I explained my twofold disqualification which I had discovered by reading the article on vocation. He was not worried about my awkward questions in class because, of course, this experienced man had realised that, like the sneezing boy in *Alice*, I only did it to annoy because I knew it teased him. Rule-breaking, however, was something serious. When he heard that I kept only such rules as I found convenient he agreed that the seminary was no place for me. He told me to tell the President next day that I had no vocation. There would be no need to recite my misdemeanours. This was a slight relief. I thanked him most kindly as I rose to leave. I walked to the door but as I was about to open it Dr. McCormack called me back. "John," he said, "have you any idea what rules are for? Sit down again and let me tell you."

In a few sentences the priest explained that rules are intended to train the will. Priests are called to observe a high standard of discipline. They must be at the service of their people day and night. The diocesan priest has nobody to see that he fulfils his task. The life of a monk is regulated by the bell. He has superiors to give him orders. The priest in a parish is his own master. He can be either zealous or slothful. It depends, Dr. McCormack said, on whether a man has learned discipline in the seminary.

Having given the reason for rules he now asked if I would be willing to keep them in order to save my vocation. He told me to concentrate on the Ushaw games—cat, keeping-up and handball. If I mastered them I would have no inclination to smoke or frequent restaurants. This was the most important day of my life at Ushaw.

My time at Ushaw was short but these were formative years. It is said that today's children mature much more quickly than those of fifty years ago. Without question boys and girls now mature physically much faster. This presumably is the result of improved diet and hygiene in the West. In Africa and Asia there has not been such an astonishing acceleration of maturity. It is difficult to know to what extent mental and emotional maturity has kept pace with physical growth. I left Ushaw at the age of nineteen. For two years I had withstood the burden of a school curriculum devoid of variety. I had forced myself to keep the rules. I had become confidently independent of home and family friends. Above all I had begun to learn how to pray. My enthusiasm for the priesthood had enormously increased. The more I thought of possible alternatives the greater my conviction that no life could be more worthwhile than one consecrated like that of Christ to the salvation of souls. Nothing was ever to shake that conviction.

Many years later a friend and fellow student of mine in Rome was already making his final retreat for the priesthood when for the very first time he began to examine his suitability. The invitations to his ordination had been issued but before the week's retreat was ended he returned home. It was a wise and courageous act. The temptation to go on must have been almost irresistible. Most students for the priesthood make their great decision in their late teens or early twenties. My own self-questioning took place during my years at Ushaw. I remember the battle for my vocation in painful detail. I imagine that most priests must have gone through a similar crisis of indecision at some period of their training.

Mine came as an indirect result of sickness. One morning I noticed when washing that skin was peeling from my hands. I was not alarmed because I attributed the phenomenon to the rigours of the northern winter. A few days later the skin was peeling off in great strips and I thought it wise to report myself to the infirmarian. He sent for the doctor who decided that I was in the late stages of scarlet fever. I was removed to an isolated building known as the sanatorium which had not been occupied since a fever epidemic a few years earlier. I was not confined to bed and spent my time playing golf or walking round the Durham countryside. After a few weeks I was allowed to go away to convalesce. One of the students arranged for me to stay with his family in Newcastle-on-Tyne. Relishing the experience of being away from domestic authority for the first time in my life I spent a glorious month in freedom. I experienced for the first time the warmth of Tynesiders.

Returning to Ushaw I felt miserable. I had to begin the fight for survival all over again. For several weeks I had been pampered and now school life seemed unbearably hard. I had also met a charming girl of about my own age. Thinking of her constantly made the seminary seem like a prison. I felt unable to endure the separation. I spoke to nobody of my anguish and could find no comfort in prayer. The Mass which had been the chief source of my strength and joy now became a penance. There was only one thing to do. I must decide whether or not I had a vocation. Was I strong enough to make the sacrifices required of a candidate for the priesthood? Could I ever be happy without my beloved? I well understood the seriousness of renouncing the right to become a husband and father. On the next play day instead of going for a walk I spent the afternoon in the deserted school chapel. For hours I wrestled with my problem. Light did not come at once but by early evening I became increasingly convinced that I had no vocation to the priesthood. Now quite calm I visited the shrine of Our Lady on my way out of chapel. I knelt before her altar to say a prayer of thanksgiving that my mind was made up. I was thankful too soon for at once all my doubts flooded back. I opened my eyes and read the words embroidered on the altar cloth. *Monstra te esse matrem*—show yourself a mother. Then with almost blinding clarity I saw my problem in simple terms. I realised that in fact I had no problem. There was no real doubt in my mind about my vocation. God was calling me to become one of his priests but I was shrinking from accepting the invitation. I was not prepared to give up comfort and the delights of human love to follow Him. Self-questioning began again. Did I put good food before the priesthood? Was the friendship of this girl more valuable than the sharing of the priesthood of Christ? My real trouble was nostalgia. I was hungry and homesick. I needed my mother. That afternoon I found her. Never again in the long years of my preparation was I to be troubled by doubts about my vocation.

During May the whole school used to march into the chapel of Our Lady of Help (the Ushaw Madonna) singing the Magnificat. It was an Ushaw tradition to foster in the alumni a manly devotion to the Mother of God. Far removed from sentimentality it is a source of spiritual strength to a priest. Manliness was characteristic of most of the typically Ushaw virtues. We lived hard but for a male community we were astonishingly well mannered. The toughest boy would open a door for his companion to pass through before him. Courtesy is the mark of mutual respect. Years later I was to learn of the Ushaw custom also founded on respect and what today—but most certainly not in those days—might be called love. On the annual school reunions all expenses were shared. Thus coming from London I was no worse off than those who had only to take a twopenny bus. This sharing of expenses was designed to enable the poorest or most remote member of the school to attend the reunion without embarrassment.

My two years were valuable not only for what they taught me but also for the lifelong friendships they enabled me to form. I had expected to remain at Ushaw for the whole of my course, that is, for two years of philosophy and four of theology. It happened almost by chance that I was to be sent instead to the English College in Rome. Mgr. Browne, the President, was a member of a venerable society known as the Old Brotherhood. This select and self-perpetuating society is the successor to the valiant priests who ruled the Catholic Church in England before the restoration of the hierarchy. The Brethren still meet regularly but their business is now mainly the allocation of funds to various charities. In 1922 the Brethren were considering what use to make of a legacy left by one of their number, Canon Keatinge, author of *The priest, his character and work*. They decided to found a bursary to train a student at the English College in Rome. The bursary was to be offered to a poor diocese—Brentwood was then the youngest and poorest diocese in England. Mgr. Browne was able to tell the Brethren that he had at Ushaw a student just about to start philosophy. I do not know if the President recommended me because he regarded me as an undesirable influence or because he thought me likely to profit from a university course in Rome. He was probably not sorry to be rid of me. It is true that I had become a law-abiding student but I had been responsible for some original activities among the Big Lads which though harmless were certainly not traditional. At Ushaw untraditional activities were regarded with marked disfavour. The President may have thought that I would benefit both myself and Ushaw by exchanging Durham for Rome.

Before leaving the Ushaw part of my story I must relate two amusing events which I recall with special joy. The first occurred on the occasion of the visit of Admiral Charlton who was at the time the most distinguished lay Ushavian. In charge of the demolition of enemy armaments at the end of the war, he had presented to the museum a huge German mine. A few weeks before the admiral's arrival the museum was tidied up and the famous mine given a fresh coat of grey paint. On the morning of the visit we woke to find that the divines (most of whom were ex-servicemen—some from the Royal Navy) had chalked arrows on every corridor wall. Above the arrows was the caption TO THE MINE. In the museum itself all other exhibits had been pushed aside and around the mine chairs were ranged in great depth. It was to be obvious to the admiral that his mine was the greatest attraction at Ushaw.

For the other incident the ex-servicemen were also responsible. There had been much talk since 1918 of a memorial to the former students, both priests and laymen, who had lost their lives during the war. So far there had been many proposals but no plans. One day Monsignor Broadhead, the procurator, had a big stone put at the end of a grass verge to prevent lorries from cutting the corner. The same evening the divines raided the professors' garden and carried off a large number of flowers which were strewn round the big stone together with a large notice: USHAW WAR MEMORIAL. The next day Mgr. Broadhead sent for the senior divine and making no reference to the war memorial complained that flowers had been taken from the professors' garden. He said that if they were not returned the divines would forfeit some of their privileges. The next day the flowers were removed. An even larger notice now replaced the old one: USHAW WAR MEMORIAL—NO FLOWERS BY REQUEST.

I left Ushaw a few days before the end of term to attend the ordination of my brother Frank who had studied for the priesthood in France. The only Englishman in the grand seminaire of Arras he had become a fluent French speaker. After ordination he went to Cambridge to study modern languages. With a brilliant mind went an independence of spirit which his superiors regarded as insubordination. While at Cambridge he was expected to do duty also as curate in the parish of Chelmsford. This taste of pastoral action drained his academic ambitions. He had little to learn of the French language and felt that he was wasting his time at the university. He left after his first year. When he was much older and a parish priest he regretted his impatience and, largely for his own satisfaction, took an external degree in modern languages at London University. Though rarely at peace with those in authority he was popular with his fellow clergy and much loved by his parishioners. He became parish priest of Frinton and on the outbreak of war volunteered to be an army chaplain.

Towards the end of October 1924 I left England for the English College in Rome. I had been instructed to travel direct to Rome without breaking my journey. My only recollection of the journey is the half-hour stop at Modane where I succeeded in making myself understood in French at the bookstall. I also bought some postcards but could not remember the word for stamps and had to resort to sign language. The postcard I sent to my parents failed to arrive. This, as we shall see, had repercussions. I arrived in Rome travel-worn and light-headed. Students from the English College met the train and I soon forgot my fatigue as the taxi rushed through narrow Roman streets to the Via Monserrato where the college stands. Its drab exterior is not attractive but the welcome awaiting me within was most reassuring. The next morning I was taken by three veteran students to St. Peter's. As we walked across the piazza I was warned—as all new men are warned—that the proportions of the basilica are so perfect that no impression of its size is given. It nevertheless seemed pretty big to me. Inside St. Peter's I was bewildered by the crowds and overwhelmed by the singing of what turned out to be the Sistine Choir. High Mass was in progress and the celebrant was Cardinal Merry del Val, the arch-priest.

My companions took me out of the basilica by way of the Porta Santa Marta so that we might watch the procession of prelates make its way to the arch-priest's house. The other students were dressed in cassock, soprano (gown) and black beaver sombrero. I, of course, was still in lay clothes. We stood watching the colourful procession when to my astonishment the cardinal halted it and came over to our group. Seeing that I was not in the college dress he asked if I were a new man and where I had been at school. When I told him that I was from Ushaw he was delighted. "I am also an Ushaw man," he said, "and I am going to give you some good advice." To my surprise his advice was not to work too hard in my first year. It took time, he told me, to become acclimatised to the air in Rome after the cold pure air of the North. I would be in Rome for seven years and would have plenty of time to settle down to study after I had explored the city and grown used to the food and climate. Finally he told me not to hesitate to let him know if he could be of service to me. As this was only my first day in Rome I did not appreciate the honour that had been done me by Cardinal Merry del Val. I assumed that students in Rome frequently rubbed shoulders with high prelates. It was, in fact, several years before I spoke to another cardinal.

That afternoon a student called George Ford who was an enthusiastic amateur archaeologist took me to the Forum. By now my head was throbbing. The heat and the glare of the sun on the ancient monuments made the tour of the Forum agonising. Before the night was out I was in bed with a raging fever. For some days I was able to take no food or drink beyond sips of lemonade. Nobody in Rome drank water. Water was eschewed even if it came from a tap marked *aqua potabile*. It was a week before I was able to join the rest of the community in the retreat which had begun in preparation for the work of the scholastic year. As soon as the retreat was over I was sent for by Monsignor Hinsley, the rector. He looked very grave and held in his hand a letter in what I recognised as my father's handwriting. I nearly fainted with apprehension that he was about to give me terrible news—perhaps my mother was dead?

My alarm was soon set at rest. My postcard from Modane had not arrived nor had the letter I wrote home as soon as my temperature had subsided. My parents had become anxious. These were still the early Mussolini days and my father must have feared that I was being held incommunicado by the brutal Fascists. I do not know what my father wrote but among his papers after his death I found Mgr. Hinsley's reply:

Venerable English College,
Rome.
10.xi.1924.

My dear Mr. Heenan,

I hasten to reassure you about your son. It is true he caught a slight chill on the journey, and had a sore throat. I kept him in bed for several days, and now he is himself again, bright, happy and ruddy with health. He has a good appetite, and seems in excellent spirits. I will see that he writes to you at once. I did not write, because there was no reason for alarm. A long journey, especially with night travelling, always means the danger of a cold, unless care is taken; and you know that boys are not always careful of themselves. I got out of him the information that he sat next to the open window and facing the engine—all the way from Genoa, and that he did not put on his topcoat or cover himself with a rug. It was raining most of the way, and the damp must have driven right on to him. Small wonder he took a chill! But boys are boys, and need a careful eye. I promise to keep my eye on him, and see that he takes care of himself; he is now able to finish his bottle of wine at dinner and supper, and he takes all he can get. He is a very dear lad, bright, frank and earnest: he should do very well here, and make a good priest someday. The course is long, and requires hard work and patience: but the end is worth the struggle along the road. So we must just have courage, and trust in God's goodness and blessing.

With kindest regards and renewed assurances about your boy's health and happiness,

I remain,
Yours very sincerely,
A. HINSLEY.

The English College (commonly called 'the Venerabile' by reason of its official description—*Venerabile Collegium Anglorum de Urbe*) was founded during penal days. With Douai and other continental seminaries it prepared Englishmen for ordination at a time when a price was set on the head of every priest. Men from these schools abroad returned to England in the knowledge that not only was it unfashionable and dangerous to call oneself a Catholic, but to perform the functions of the Catholic priesthood was high treason. The Venerabile is, of course, much older than four hundred years. As an institution it antedates the Middle Ages. Originally the building in Via Monserrato was a hostel where English pilgrims could claim lodging.

As soon as I knew that the Venerabile was to be my future home I wrote to the rector to tell him how much I looked forward to studying in Rome. I have no record of my letter but I still have Mgr. Hinsley's reply:

Venerable English College,
Rome.
10.vi.1924.

My dear Mr. Heenan,

Your letter of the 5th June was very welcome to me as showing that you are coming to Rome with the right spirit. I am glad to say that the President of Ushaw has given me an excellent account of you. The medical report is satisfactory also.

So I can depend on having a man who is sound in mind and body, and who is prepared to face the difficulties of a Roman course, as well as to enjoy its advantages and its joys. Of course there are difficulties, here as elsewhere, and a man who means to be a priest is ready to face them. To begin with, the climate is not that of England, and for the first year or so you must be prepared for some inconveniences. Too much is often made of these little annoyances, and great deal too much is said about health in Rome. It is as healthy a place as there is in Europe, if only reasonable care is taken. Then there is difficulty about study. Latin is not too well known—i.e. in a practical way so as to follow the lectures and to answer questions; and this causes some difficulty, especially at the beginning. All the Professors tell me that our men do not make the best of themselves at the University, because they have not sufficient practice in Latin. They are, as one of them expressed it, tongue-tied though they know their work! This difficulty too will call for patience and hard work. But Rome will repay your trouble and enthusiasm.

Now for business. As for the journey, you will get all particulars as regards route, fares, time-table from the ordinary tourist agencies. Your passport can also be obtained through them. Do not put off the affair of your passport till the last few days. Get it made out for you not later than August. The day on which all must be in the College will be Saturday, October 25th at a proper hour, i.e. not later than 8 o'clock! Of course we will welcome you at an earlier hour on that day, i.e. anytime in the morning, say, in time for dinner at 12.30. But we do not want you on any day before October 25th, because till then we shall be out at the Villa, our country house, on Lake Albano—and there we have no room for newcomers!

Your best plan, for the journey, will be to get into touch with some of the students who are going to England for the summer holidays. You could fix up with some of them to join hands on the way. I give you a list with addresses, and you could write and agree to meet them at some appointed place—say, Victoria, London, etc. These could also give you hints about Rome and Roman life.

Lastly as to clothes: You ought to have with you two pairs of strong boots, and two pairs of house shoes. You will need six pairs of *long black* stockings. The cassock is worn indoors and outside the house, and *long stockings*. It would be useful to bring a cassock with you, and also clerical stock and collars, and a biretta. For the winter you need good warm underclothing—e.g., 'mutande' or knickerbockers (something like golf knickers, of strong warm material), woollen vests (4) and shirts (4) and drawers (4)—for summer you will need much lighter things, and

I would recommend 6 shirts and 6 'mutande' of cellular material.

We can sometimes get football and cricket and tennis, and swimming. About this ask some of the students to whom you write for hints. Bring very few books—only your prayer book and one or two favourites. You can get plenty here. Bring only one suit for travelling: you will not need 'civilians' for three years after your arrival, and it is no use having trousers, coat, waistcoat, etc., stored up for the benefit of the moths!

I think I have told you all that is necessary. Of course you will not forget handkerchiefs and toilette requisites.

> With kindest regards,
> Yours sincerely,
> A. HINSLEY.

It is almost impossible to give a convincing description of the happy and full life of students of the Venerabile fifty years ago. By modern standards I suppose we were extremely mature. Mgr. Hinsley used to say that the English College was not a seminary but a half-way house to the mission. I am not quite sure what those words mean but we were all quite sure what the Boss—our name for Hinsley—meant when he used them. He wanted us to think of ourselves as men and for his part he wanted to treat us as men. Since the Second Vatican Council the theory is that such maturity can come through the abolition of rules. In this way the students will learn to exercise initiative. There is a great deal of good sense in this view of seminary training but its dangers are obvious. A man precisely because he is young may lack the initiative to train himself in self-discipline. He may throw away his vocation. It is facile to contend that such a vocation is well lost since a man of this kind would have made a shipwreck of his priesthood after ordination. The whole purpose of seminaries is to teach young men how to correct their faults of character. Through the years of seminary discipline many a self-centred man makes Christ the centre of his whole life.

Mgr. Hinsley, while treating his students as men, maintained firm discipline. He trusted them so long as he regarded them as trustworthy. A man of moods, he was liable to become unduly depressed by occasional transgressors. He was, on the other hand, excessively elated if an English student scored an outstanding success at the university. Because he was the most humane of disciplinarians the students loved him and made allowance for his occasional moodiness. He formed his men less by the rules he laid down than through the patently high ideals which he set himself. No number of books on prayer could convey the importance of prayer so clearly as the daily example of the rector at prayer. Giving God the first fruits of the day was fundamental in the *pietas* which Hinsley preached by example as well as word. To miss or be late for morning prayer was the only student failing to which the rector was never indulgent. It was his conviction that men who could not rise promptly to give the best hour of the day to God while in training were not likely to become holy and zealous priests. This great lesson was learned by most men of the Hinsley regime.

Nobody in the Rome of 1925 expected that one day the rector would become a figure of international renown as Cardinal Hinsley. He was a rectorial Mr. Chips. You could not imagine him anywhere else than in a college for the training of priests. But the rector did achieve fame and in due course his influence was extended far beyond the Venerabile. By that time he had been given experience as an apostolic visitor to Africa and later as a papal delegate. Like most men he became more tolerant with age. There were few signs of the old disciplinarian left when he became Archbishop of Westminster. It is therefore easy to forget the Hinsley of the Venerabile. He was admirable, lovable and, above all, unpredictable. His character and style of rectorship is described in the memoir I published a year after his death:

Let it be frankly admitted that it was only because Mgr. Hinsley was a man of powerful character that his habit of treating students almost as equals did not ruin his authority. Not many men can preserve dignity and control without a certain uncommunicativeness suggestive of wisdom. Mgr. Hinsley was unique. His informal equalitarian attitude, in moments of relaxation, was possible only because of his self-evident holiness. As rector he had one ambition—to train future priests to be worthy of their office and of the Church. As men he wanted to teach them to be frank. At all times he hated intrigue. If he had any complaints against his students he did not dissemble. He expected from them a similar spontaneity. If the house were restive because of his actions, whether in matters of general policy or regarding his treatment of individual students, he would want to be told. He could not tolerate murmuring or the nursing of grievances. In his family there must be no grumblers. The students were encouraged to call public meetings to thrash out any point which was disturbing them. The same evening he would receive the senior student to hear the result. It might easily happen that the senior student would be curtly dismissed without any satisfaction. More often the rector would either explain why his own action was right or, not uncommonly, see the student's point of view and countermand his previous instructions.

This policy had a twofold effect, one good and the other dangerous. The obvious advantage was that, except during the rector's infrequent moods of depression (caused almost always by the shortcomings of the students but sometimes the result of financial worries), the Venerabile was a contented house. There was complete understanding between rector and students. Public spirit stifled any disloyalty that might occasionally be provoked by a disaffected and usually unsuitable type of student. The serenity of the Venerabile atmosphere can be credited only by those who have tasted its joy. But the disadvantage is equally obvious. To be able to question unpopular decisions of the rector might lead the less intelligent students to believe that reasonable obedience means obeying only when authority gives its reasons. That view is mischievous and un-Catholic. Any extended residence in the Venerabile would certainly have corrected any such idea. Mgr. Hinsley not seldom issued instructions which, however restrictive and unpopular, had to be obeyed without discussion or delay. It is important to know that Hinsley, not the students, decided when argument was permissible. This may explain the apparent paradox of a college at once democratic and disciplined. It also explains why Mgr. Hinsley's unorthodoxy produced a magnificent priestly training. It may be said, however, that Hinsley methods without Hinsley would probably prove disastrous.*

Twelve young men began the Roman course in October 1924, of whom seven were eventually ordained. Five out of twelve was in those days about the average fall-out of senior students. The majority of seniors used to be products of junior seminaries. So few today are

* *Cardinal Hinsley,* Burns & Oates, 1943.

able to stay the whole course of humanities and divinity in one institution that bishops now question the wisdom of maintaining junior seminaries. For many reasons it is probably more desirable to segregate church students only when their general education (including university) has been completed. There is indeed a school of thought which questions segregation even during the years of divinity. These ideas had not been ventilated fifty years ago. The seminary as the name implies was the seed bed of vocations. It was no hot-house but for centuries the Church had held that seminaries were necessary to provide an atmosphere removed from worldly excitement, in which a young man can learn to study and to pray.

In the Rome of 1924 seminary routine in the national colleges was more or less of a pattern. The noisy cosmopolitan city with its ecclesiastical life centred on the Vatican was considered to provide all that was necessary for our social development. The Gregorian University, a Jesuit institution, provided the best priestly intellectual formation then available. In retrospect it seems that it must have been inadequate, but in a period when the anti-modernist spirit was all-pervasive the broad outlook of today's Gregorian would have been unthinkable. Those who have read the *Journey of a Soul* will see what Pope John regarded as the proper intellectual formation for future priests. Narrow and uninspiring as it was it produced the best-known and the best-loved pope of modern times. Here I wish not to discuss but merely to record the style of Roman seminary life in my student days.

Even at the time many of us regarded the system as anachronistic. Lectures (which were not optional) began at eight o'clock in the morning. There could be as many as three or four a day. To sit through three hours of lectures in Latin each morning and to have to return again in the afternoon was obviously an exercise in patient endurance but of little cultural value. The standard of the lectures was surprisingly low. Apart from Vermeersch, the celebrated Belgian moralist, Paul Geny, the philosopher from France, and the German theologian Lennerz I cannot recall a lecturer who was really worth hearing. Most of them lectured by reading without comment the notes which were published as textbooks soon after delivery. It seemed to us pointless to have to listen to a recital of words which we could later read in the quiet of our rooms. The examinations were also conducted in Latin. It would therefore have been useful to attend a few lectures to familiarise ourselves with spoken Latin but this consideration did little to reconcile us to compulsory attendance. Most of us learned to study or write during lectures but the voice of the lecturer was a distraction. I look back on most Gregorian lectures as a series of wasted hours.

The Gregorian gave us only part of our intellectual formation. Although there were no lectures in the college it was here that our real training took place. There was ample time for study. We rose at twenty-five past five each morning and retired at ten o'clock at night. It was a long day. I have already spoken of the value the rector placed on our being punctually in our places in chapel for meditation. Morning prayers and Mass were the daily duties first in importance as well as in time. The frugal continental-style breakfast was at seven o'clock. At a quarter to eight we left for the university. We returned at various times according to the number of lectures. At a quarter to twelve we assembled in the chapel for spiritual reading. At midday we recited the Angelus followed by the prayers for the conversion of England which had been introduced by Cardinal Wiseman when he was rector of the Venerabile. We then had an excellent lunch followed by a siesta which was official during the hot months and unofficial for the rest of the year. Each student had a bed-sitting room and there were three libraries to which we had access at any time. Most of us were fully taxed by the textbooks themselves and repaired to the libraries mainly to check the references to the works of the Fathers. Migne's *Patrology* was the most useful of all the tomes since even in pre-conciliar days books of theology went quickly out of date. Most theological libraries are replete with volumes which were once required reading and have now become obsolete. Franzelin, de Lugo, Buccerone and even Billot had already served their turn fifty years ago.

Lectures at the Gregorian were in Latin. A common language was obviously an immense advantage in an international university but both professors and students suffered through being tied to the Latin medium. A wag has described lectures as the mysterious process by which the notes of the professor are transmitted to the notebook of the student without passing through the mind of either. Scholastic Latin possesses a treasury of jargon which is virtually untranslatable. The pastoral disadvantage of having studied theology in Latin is felt as soon as a priest begins to preach in English. The Latinised language that sometimes does duty for English in the pulpit leaves the congregation unenlightened. The breaks between lectures were brief.

Most people, exhausted after an hour in a crowded lecture hall—always crowded because lectures were compulsory—would walk round the small cortile (yard) to regain their breath. The more enterprising students formed partnerships with men of other races to learn languages. The most common partnerships made by English students were with the Germans. I doubt if any great advance in knowledge of German resulted from these encounters. After the initial questions (*"Wie viele Katholiken sind in Deutschland?"*) we tended to fall back on Italian as the lingua franca. After an hour or two in a stuffy lecture hall most of us were too tired to learn new German words or teach English to our German friends. There would be more opportunity of learning languages in the long vacation· which we spent at Palazzuola in the Alban Hills.

In those days most national colleges had a summer house away from the heat of Rome. Mgr. Hinsley had acquired the astonishingly beautiful villa of Palazzuola soon after the war. Overhanging Lake Albano it is only a few hundred yards from Monte Cavo and refreshingly cool even in August. Life at the villa was relaxing. No day was officially without study but this was interpreted in a wide sense to mean that the morning must be devoted to serious reading. The rector's rule was that nobody might read fiction before afternoon. After the few days immediately following examinations the students would hive off in groups with kindred interests. There was a Dante club, various language groups, musical people and a large section of altruistic and muscular men who built stairways from the villa garden to the playing fields, dug into the rocky ground to make a swimming pool, levelled the uneven fields to provide a small golf-course. Everyone was happy and busy. To spend three months of the year in Palazzuolo was recognised to be a luxury. It was also very obviously part of the Roman course. Being young and home-loving, most of us, given the choice, would probably have preferred to spend the summer holiday with our families and friends in England. In fact the rule was to have only one break in the seven years course. Everyone went home after the three years of philosophy. Most students were heartily glad to return to Rome. In those days the custom of seeking employment during vacations had not become common among students. At home for the long vacation, students in their twenties found that except for the August holiday period most men of their age were at work every day. For a man who had arrived home in early June time was hanging heavily by the end of August. There were still two months to go and he was likely to think nostalgically of Palazzuolo. The modern system of spending a time at home and a time at the villa is probably a most sensible compromise. It has become possible because the journey between England and Rome is no longer regarded as exclusively costly. There can be no doubt about the value of those quiet hours when students had leisure to increase the range of their reading and knowledge without the unattractive incentive of examinations.

I recall so much about my years in Rome that without effort I could devote several chapters to this part of my life. The result would doubtless fascinate my contemporaries but might bore younger readers. We were—what students always will be—supremely conscious of our maturity and wisdom. We really did feel grown up. We also felt superior to the Italians who were then going through their early Fascist phase. We had no little contempt for the idolatry of the Duce and for the obvious fear of every Italian to criticise the regime or express an opinion critical of Fascism. We did not at that time realise that the docile citizens of totalitarian regimes are not necessarily sub-human. In our ignorance we had written off the Slavs as victims of Communist terror. We had yet to hear the name Hitler. Within a decade of leaving Rome we were to see most of the world threatened by some form of dictatorship and engaging in war ostensibly concerned not with conquest but with ideology. The Italians, in fact, were less docile than the Germans. Their cult of the Duce was less emotional and heartfelt than the almost universal adulation of the Germans for their Fuehrer. We had no understanding of the strain of self-imposed silence which the highly intelligent Italians must have suffered. Many years later I was to catch a glimpse of the hatred of cultured Germans for Hitler. This will be recounted in its place. I now have no doubt that among the Italians, whom in our ignorance we despised for being supine, there must have been thousands who shared our contempt for Fascism but not our ignorance of the realities of life under a political dictatorship.

The years in Rome passed happily and profitably. I was much more attracted by philosophy than theology. In the days before the Vatican Council theology was a discipline. The chief objective of the theologian was to discover the teaching of the Church and demonstrate its truth. This is not much of an oversimplification. The theological method then in vogue was to search first for documents of the Church. If the Church had pronounced that was the end of the matter. All that remained was to determine the emphasis with which the Church propounded any proposition. It was of the greatest importance to know what note to award a thesis. A note is the technical expression of approval or disapproval attaching to a theological statement as a result of a papal or conciliar pronouncement. A proposition may be a matter of faith, a matter of defined faith, or simply a commonly held theological opinion. On the other hand an opinion could be wrong in a confusing variety of ways. The theological note may dismiss it as heretical or near-heretical. An opinion may be erroneous, foolhardy or offensive to pious ears. Notes of this kind were to a large extent ephemeral. What is offensive to pious ears today may become tomorrow's most cherished theological fashion. Only after the student discovered the theological note was he encouraged to search the scriptures and the fathers for light and inspiration. That is why I did not find the study of theology so enthralling as the study of philosophy.

There has been a radical alteration of outlook on theology in the years following the Second Vatican Council. I am thinking not of the content of theology but of the attitudes of theologians. Today much theology can be called exciting in the same way that daring new designs are said by architects to be exciting. It is the result not so much of the Council as of the conscious turning away from authority in the years following the Council—a phenomenon not exclusively religious. This attitude of mind was common to illiterates and academics alike after the middle sixties. It involved a rejection of authority but was not primarily anarchic. It was, however, self-assertive and tended to be violent. Beatles, provos (Holland), hippies, death-of-God theologians, student demonstrators, skin-heads and the sex-obsessed were all children of their time. Whatever had once been cherished must be wrong since change can be only for the better. Only a cretin can prefer Mozart to pop. The popular theologian need take little notice of what popes have said. Insights are the modern guide and, as everyone knows, scripture can be quarried to find texts for any opinion. Charismatic theologians are fun but they are not always safe guides to the faith. Speculation which used to be largely restricted to philosophy now acknowledges no theological limits.

Fifty years ago the study of theology was largely a matter of memory. (I refer, of course, to the theological foothills in which young students walked. The theology of men like Billot and de la

Taille, who were both alive in the twenties, was full of metaphysics.)
It held no great charm for me. The three years of philosophy, on the
other hand, were a delight. It is now the custom to deride metaphysics. One modern philosopher has dismissed it as nonsense. I
thought it fascinating and found sheer joy in wrestling with ideas. I
cannot imagine any other subject which leaves the student so free to
think. No formulae, no dates, no names, nothing to commit to
memory, just the contemplation of ideas—even music is a hard
discipline by comparison. Every new branch of philosophy meant an
advance in primary knowledge. I had already conceived a passion for
logic as a boy at Ushaw and now here were new fields for unfettered
speculation. I do not know how good our professors were but
coming from so many nations they were bound to enrich the mental
experience of a young Englishman. Paul Geny (epistemology) was
from Paris. Hoenen (cosmology) was a Dutchman. Munzi (natural
theology) was Italian, Elter (ethics) was Polish. The professor of
general metaphysics was Charles Boyer a Frenchman. History of
philosophy was taught by a Prussian, Lehman, a magnificent lecturer
but a deadly examiner.

One of my chief recollections of the Gregorian University is of my
final examination in philosophy. It was an experience which persuaded me that older people are not necessarily stupid and vindictive.
In those days a Ph.D. was obtainable after only three years'
specialised study. After a written test which was of slight importance
an hour-long oral examination was held by four professors sitting
together. It was a formidable experience not made any easier by the
fact that the dialogue was in Latin. Some months before the viva
examination a so-called thesis list was published. This contained a
hundred theses which were cunningly contrived to cover the whole
philosophical course. The procedure was for the candidate to sit at
the table and wait to be told which thesis to defend. When I sat
down I was asked to defend the shortest thesis in the list: *Deus habet
influxum immediatum in omni actione humana* (No human action
takes place without God's direct collaboration). This is Thomistic
doctrine but some philosophers, including Suarez, disagree with the
word 'direct'. The point at issue may be of small interest or
importance today but it was of great moment to me on that hot June
morning in 1927. I declined the thesis on the grounds that it was
indefensible. I rose to go away unexamined but the professors bade
me stay while they conferred. After a few moments the presiding

examiner said: "We would not ask a young man to defend a thesis against his own convictions. We therefore want you to take a thesis of your own choice." There was obviously no brain-washing of students in those unenlightened days. I was awarded a doctorate *cum laude.*

Students at college abroad are bound to come closer to each other than those at home and their friendships tend to last longer. As exiles we were much more constantly together than students in England who return home several times a year. I shall not speak much of my companions who are still alive and at work in the vineyard. There was one student who influenced me greatly and remained a close friend until the day of his death. This was Val Elwes, a man of quite exceptional spirituality. He took me under his wing a day or two after I entered the college. It may have been because I was unwell that he adopted a protective attitude towards me in those early days. We were together as students for less than a year but the effect of his personality was so great that despite constant separations we were to remain intimate friends until the end. Val Elwes' gifts were spiritual and social rather than intellectual. He had not inherited any special musical talent from his famous father the tenor Gervase Elwes. His personality was warm and his zeal infectious. He had been given a remarkable call to the priesthood. Destined for the Royal Navy, he was a midshipman at the outbreak of the first world war. During the battle of Jutland he was on a destroyer which was severely shelled. Around him the senior officers were all wounded or killed. He was no more and no less frightened than any other young sailor but Jutland gave him his vocation to the priesthood. He thought it likely that he would be killed in the battle. He was quite calm about the prospect but bitterly conscious that if he died he would have achieved little in life.

This, of course, was not true but it was the beginning of his overpowering desire to consecrate his life entirely to the salvation of souls. For the rest of the war—during which he became a lieutenant— he gave himself to spiritual exercises. He was anxious to become a priest but was so aware of his unworthiness that he resolved to make a long preparation before offering himself as a candidate. As soon as the war was over he resigned his commission and went to Oxford. At the university he was the centre of a rather gay set and scored no great academic successes. He did not tell his new friends of his desire to become a priest and at the end of his course they were astounded to hear that he was about to enter a seminary. To at least two of his close friends his determination to renounce a worldly career was not only a disappointment but a deep personal sorrow. By the time I arrived in Rome Val was far advanced in asceticism.

The spiritual director of the Venerabile was a quite remarkable Jesuit, Father Welsby, assistant general of the Society of Jesus in charge of his order's affairs in most of the English-speaking world. He was therefore an exceptionally busy man. He nevertheless came to the college twice a week to hear the confessions of the students and give guidance to the many who asked him to give them a rule of life. Although he never volunteered advice he was always ready to give detailed instructions to those who sought his help. There was nothing soft about his direction. A man of stern discipline, he was ready to lead young men to the heights. Bodily mortification, including the use of the discipline, was for him an obvious means for a future priest to prepare himself for the following of Christ the Eternal Priest. Prayer, of course, came first. By penance and prayer he led many of the young men to a genuine desire for perfection.

Inevitably some felt that they were called to a life of contemplation. Early in my course three of my fellow students left Rome to try their vocation as Carthusian monks. Bill Park, Eustace Malone and Val Elwes all took the road to Parkminster and solitude. All three eventually left the cloister and were ordained as diocesan priests. Val remained a monk for several years but eventually he contracted tuberculosis and was forced to leave and be nursed back to health. After a break of some years he completed his studies at Fribourg and was ordained for the diocese of Northampton. His priestly work was destined to take him to Westminster as Cardinal Hinsley's secretary, back to the Royal Navy as chaplain, and once more to Oxford to take charge of the chaplaincy. He died as a much beloved parish priest in his native village of Great Billing. It would be difficult to exaggerate his influence on me as a young man.

Students probably learned more from each other than from their official mentors. Unlike a regional seminary the Venerabile admitted students from all parts of England. This in itself was a means of education. People from the South, the Midlands and the North sometimes regard each other almost as foreigners. In Rome we became familiar with the tribal customs and accents of all English natives. There was also a fair variety according to age and ability. Many were from school or junior seminary. A number were ex-servicemen. These included former Lance-Corporal Masterson who died as Archbishop of Birmingham and the one-time Sergeant Griffin who became Archbishop of Westminster.

There was little resemblance between a seminary at home and an English college abroad. The students in Lisbon, Valladolid (Spain) and Rome were much more isolated fifty years ago than they are today. Air travel was still in its infancy. The time and distance separating students from home made for a family spirit which is difficult to achieve in a community which breaks up for vacations three times a year. The centres of social life were the chapel and the common room. All recreation was taken together and was compulsory. This sounds more sinister than in fact it was. Nobody needed to be compelled to consort with his fellow students after dinner and supper. The college rule forbade students to visit each other's rooms. This, I imagine, was to promote what is now called a sense of community. In those days we did not use the expression but we assiduously practised the virtue. It may seem strange that men not destined, like monks, for community life after ordination should be bound to it during training. The explanation is that diocesan priests who must be at the service of all sorts and conditions of men and women need to learn how to make friends of the whole community. It is easier to live in isolation in a monastic community than with one or two priests in a parish presbytery. We had the custom of taking our daily walks with whatever companions chanced to reach the front door at the same time. Similarly in the common room we would take any vacant chair. There was such a strong public spirit against exclusive sets that it was almost impossible to be lonely at the Venerabile. Today in colleges there is much talk about community but common rooms are deserted. The old camaraderie is bound to return. This is highly desirable. In his parish a priest will not be able to associate only with kindred spirits. He must be "all things to all men" (1 Cor:ix).

Towards the end of my sixth year in Rome I was busy making preparation for ordination. Some bishops called their students home for ordination but most men were ordained in Rome. I had always wanted to be ordained, like my brother Frank, in the parish church in Ilford where I had been baptised and received my first Holy Communion. At the beginning of 1930 my mother fell ill and it became clear that even if she recovered it would not be possible for her to make the journey to Rome. I therefore asked my bishop to ordain me at home. It was necessary to obtain a dispensation to be ordained in July. Canon Law required the student to have already begun his final year of theology. The regular day for ordinations was the last Sunday in October, the feast of Christ the King. For some reason which I am now unable to recall the secretary of the Sacred Congregation of Studies, Monsignor (later Cardinal) Ruffini, had begun to make difficulties over granting leave for summer ordinations. The customary application by the bishop backed by the rector was now being refused. Monsignor (later Cardinal) Cicognani, a frequent visitor to the English College, suggested that the most certain way of obtaining the consent of Mgr. Ruffini would be for the cardinal protector of the college to support the request. Here, at last, was the opportunity of accepting the cardinal's gracious offer of help which, it will be recalled, he made six years earlier outside St. Peter's on my first Sunday in Rome.

A petition was drawn up by Mgr. Cicognani and the rector was asked to add the following recommendation: *Questo alunno e esemplare nello studio e nella virtu* (This student is exemplary in his studies and behaviour). Mgr. Hinsley looked at the words and asked me if I wanted him to endanger his immortal soul. Nevertheless, he signed. Mgr. Cicognani took the document to the cardinal protector who promised to add his own recommendation and send it to Mgr. Ruffini. Weeks went by without any word coming from the Congregation of Studies. Baffled by this delay Mgr. Cicognani called again on Cardinal Merry del Val to suggest that he might send a reminder. The cardinal was embarrassed. He confessed that he had left the document on his desk and forgotten it. To make amends he said that he would now not merely write his recommendation but would himself take it to the office of the Congregation and make a personal request for an immediate answer. He was as good as his word. The next day he walked to the office, saw Mgr. Ruffini and before the day was out secured the necessary permission. This was an example of the humility of this great prelate. Lesser men in his position would not have gone to such trouble to make amends for the sake of a young student. This act of charity was one of the cardinal's last acts. A few days later he underwent an emergency operation. The operation was not serious but a careless or inexperienced anaesthetist caused the cardinal's death. He died on the operating table. This so played on the mind of the doctor responsible that he became deranged and committed suicide.

CHAPTER
THREE

AT THE END OF JUNE I LEFT ROME FOR ENGLAND WHERE I MADE A
week's retreat at the Jesuit house in Roehampton. On 6th July I was
ordained in the parish church at Ilford by Dr. Doubleday, Bishop of
Brentwood. It is not surprising that I remember every detail of my
ordination day. It was a day for which I had longed for nearly
twenty years. Yet it was not an altogether happy day. The ordination
ceremony itself was and has remained the greatest spiritual experience of my life. Receiving consecration as a bishop, being enthroned
in no less than three dioceses in succession (Leeds, Liverpool and
Westminster) and receiving the cardinal's scarlet biretta from the
Pope were by contrast minor events. The priesthood itself is
incomparably greater than any increase of rank within the priesthood. Bishop Doubleday was a lover of the liturgy. The ordination
rite was carried out with marked dignity and reverence. When Mass
was over I gave the customary new priest's blessing to my family and
friends. In the biblical phrase 'my cup was overflowing'. I had never
been more full of joy.

Then I was chastened by a series of events which in retrospect
seem trivial but which at the time disturbed me unduly. Looking
back I realise that I was physically tired and tense. I had only just
finished a year of hard study leading up to the examination for the
licentiate of theology just over a week earlier. I had been unable to
sleep the night before ordination and had spent many hours in
prayer. In those days the rules for the Eucharistic fast were rigorous.
The ceremony ended long after midday and I had not had so much as

a glass of water. These were the factors which made me so vulnerable to the petty annoyances to which during the day I was to be subjected. The first occurred immediately after the conclusion of the ceremony. I went to kneel in the now empty church to thank God for the unbelievable grace of being a priest at last. I had scarcely begun to pray when a priest interrupted me to tell me rather ungraciously—no doubt he was unconscious of the effect of his jocular words—that I had made a bad start. I must not indulge in the luxury of private prayer while the bishop and clergy were fainting with hunger. Guiltily I hurried from the church resolving to return as soon as possible to continue my colloquy. At the meal which followed, Canon Palmer, the parish priest who had baptised me twenty-five years before, was the presiding host. The bishop was on his right and I on his left. At the end of the meal Canon Palmer proposed a simple toast. He spoke only a few words but I remember their substance even now because they were to become my albatross. Speaking with emotion he said that this was a great day in his life because I was the first child he had baptised to be ordained a priest. Turning to the bishop he then said: "My Lord, today you have ordained your successor."

The bishop was very displeased. It was not, I think, that he objected to being reminded of his mortality (he lived for another twenty years) but he rightly thought that it was foolish to give a young priest exaggerated ideas of his own importance. The meal ended rather abruptly. I thought myself free to resume my prayers of thanksgiving. But again I was rather bluntly advised not to keep thinking of myself. Instead of returning to church I was told to go home where my family and numerous friends were awaiting me. It was a perfect summer day and when I reached home I found many friends sitting in the garden while even more were distributed through the house. My nerves were now fairly on edge. Never had I felt less inclined to be sociable. I wished that I had been ordained in Rome where it would have been easy to slip away to the college chapel and pray to my heart's content. There was still a long ordeal before me. As the day lengthened to evening the number of visitors increased. Priest friends of the family, old teachers and their families (the Saurins and Guinevans were there) relatives and neighbours, both Catholic and Protestant, came crowding in. I felt an almost frantic need for some respite. It did not come. Courtesy required me to stay until the last guest had gone. At last I escaped to my room. When my mother came to say goodnight I felt a surge of self-pity which almost brought me to tears. My mother had always shared the secret of my ambition to become a priest. Yet here we were at the end of my ordination day and we had not even had the chance of a word together or of thanking God. My self-pity received no encouragement from my mother. She understood my feelings but gently rebuked me for giving way to them. She said it was an added grace to have learned on my very first day as a priest that I must no longer consult my own interest or preference. Having given me this wise counsel she kissed me and asked me to bless her. Then at last we knelt together with full hearts to thank God for making the dream of my childhood come true.

I spent a restless night thinking not of the day with all its joy and disappointment but of the tremendous event to take place the following morning. Technically a priest's first Mass is offered at his ordination when he concelebrates with the bishop. In fact everyone regards the next day's Mass, which the priest celebrates alone, as his first Mass. St. Ignatius, the founder of the Jesuit order, waited a whole year after ordination before offering Mass. St. Francis of Assisi, founder of the Grey Friars, was so dismayed at the thought of his own unworthiness to offer the Holy Sacrifice that he refused to take the next step after he had been ordained deacon. These saints were vividly present to my mind that Sunday evening. The night passed slowly. At times I thought that dawn would never break. I was like a child before a treat. But, of course, I was no longer a child and I was approaching the greatest experience known to man. I was going to change bread and wine into the Body and Blood of Christ. To those without the faith this is romantic nonsense but to Christians it is reality. How was it possible to sleep as the hour drew closer when I would put on my vestments and carry the bread and wine to the altar for consecration? I rose early and walked alone to the church. For the first time I knew what is meant by the expression 'walking on air'. It really did seem too good to be true. After all the years of preparation I was to take the bread and wine into my hands—now anointed hands—and say the words of consecration.

It has become the fashion in certain circles to make little of the priesthood. Today some priests cast it aside as a layman throws up his job. What I have written may therefore sound unreal. It must be remembered that the year was 1930. All Catholics then held that after the faith the greatest grace a man can be given is a call to the priesthood. No priest experienced what is now called a crisis of identity. Neither priest nor layman doubted that to offer the sacrifice of the Mass is the most sublime privilege on earth. Belief in the supreme value of the Mass was still as firm in Catholic circles as in the household of St. Thomas More. So I made my way to church and prepared for my first Mass. To say that offering Mass came up to expectations is banal. It was an incredibly wonderful experience. As I took off my vestments the wonder grew. I thought then—as I have thought constantly since—that all the toil of preparation would have been worthwhile for the privilege of offering only one Mass. All during the day I kept telling myself that I should have the same joy the next day and every day. It seemed too good to be true. My thoughts on that day in 1930 seem more obviously true after forty years. God is prodigal in generosity to his priests. They at least know what He meant by describing the reward of an apostle as a hundredfold in this life.

I returned to Rome in October to complete my studies for the doctorate. In those days it was possible to take the examination after only four years of theology. Since I was not destined to teach—there was no seminary in Brentwood diocese—I was not interested in a post-graduate course of theology. I was happy to leave Rome to start parish work. During my last year in Rome my health had not been robust and I was glad to take the opportunity of a long holiday in the United States before taking up my first appointment. This trip was paid for by my cousin Anne Blyth, a generous and devoted friend. We had met on one of her European tours and she was determined to provide an occasion for me to meet my many American relatives.

My first appointment was as curate in the parish of St. Ethelburga in Barking, Essex. I was due to take up residence during the week of celebrations for the granting of a charter to Barking as a borough. Each night there was an historical pageant in Barking park. Local teachers played the chief characters—Ethelburga, Erkenwald and the many minor saints attached to Barking Abbey in the days of Ethelburga, the first abbess, and her brother Erkenwald, Bishop of London. The large cast of monks and nuns was chosen from the parishioners of the local churches. Although Barking is contiguous to Ilford I had scarcely ever visited it and had to ask my way to Linton

Road where the Catholic church is situated. Not knowing that a pageant was in progress I was bewildered by the crowds of monks and nuns thronging the streets. I was nonplussed, to say the least, as I walked down Linton Road to see monks and nuns arm in arm, some of them smoking, others eating fish and chips or licking icecream. My apostolate would evidently call for a Savonarola to deal with this emancipated religious community. I was immensely relieved on arriving in the presbytery to be assured that the local scene need cause me no alarm. Within minutes I had put on my cassock and gone to the church to hear confessions. Since I had now learned the true facts I was not disturbed to find that most of my prospective penitents were wearing religious habits.

Most of the Barking parishioners in those days were poor. In 1931 the country was still suffering from the effect of the great depression. The Welfare State had not yet emerged. It was still the era of the means test. Barking was an almost perfect parish for a priest's apprenticeship. There were virtually no social distractions. Long before ordination I had resolved never to dine in the homes of parishioners. I had more than one reason for this policy. Poor people cannot invite their priests to dinner. It would therefore be easy to belong to the better-off section of the parish by indulging in social visiting. For the sake of easy relationship it was sometimes useful to accept a cup of tea (which was as often offered by the poor as the better off). There was another good reason for this self-denying strategy which was to prove as valid for me as cardinal as it had been for the young curate. It has always seemed better not to be under any social obligation to those under my spiritual care. To preserve the proper professional attitude (that is, to be best able to help those under my care) there had to be a certain reserve. In Barking there were a few professional and business families in a position to entertain me but being educated people they readily understood why I avoided social entanglement.

When I went to Barking there was no parish priest. Canon Van Meenan, the former parish priest, and his curates had simultaneously been given new appointments. The new parish priest, Canon Cameron, and the senior curate, Father Carthy, were not due in Barking for some time after my arrival. For the first few days I had with me an Irish priest temporarily working in the diocese. The word ecumenism was scarcely known outside Protestant theological circles and joint religious services were rare and unpopular. Anglicans and Free Churchmen occasionally held united services but the Catholic scruple against taking part in combined acts of worship was respected. In those days embarrassment was caused to all parties when Catholic officials were obliged to absent themselves from religious functions. Their custom allowed Catholics to attend weddings and funerals of non-Catholic friends but made no exception for civic or national occasions. The present tolerance arose during the second world war when all citizens were on active service. Thrown together in peril of life, sharing the misery of loneliness and privation, people learned not only to suffer but to pray together. The Vatican Council merely ratified what events throughout Europe had already brought about.

Barking in 1931 was not exceptional in being unecumenical. The pageant was to end with an outdoor act of worship after a march through the town of a procession with the Salvation Army band at its head and the Anglican Bishop of Barking in cope and mitre in the place of honour. Many Catholics felt it wrong to take part in this religious finale. It fell to me as the priest-in-charge—the Irish priest said it was no business of his—to decide if it was permissible for our people to join the procession and take part in the united service. First of all I spoke on the telephone to Canon Cameron. He said there would be no harm if our people took part in a procession but they must not join in a united service. When I told him about the Salvation Army band and the Anglican clergy he changed his mind. It had originally been decided that only actors in the pageant would take part in the procession. Since the bishops, abbots and prioresses were only make-believe dignitaries no theological problem would have arisen. A live bishop of the Established Church was a different matter. Catholics were forbidden to take part. Even in those pre-ecumenical days some of the Catholics (St. Ethelburga and St. Erkenwald, the chief characters, were both Catholics) were most indignant at not being allowed to take part in the glorious finale. But all accepted the decision and stayed away. The fact that the priest in charge of the parish was a young man with exactly one week's pastoral experience was not regarded by anyone as a reason for not obeying. That sense of discipline may remain to this day in places like Barking but elsewhere the *ipse dixit* of a priest would no longer suffice. Since the Second Vatican Council more democratic methods prevail. The reformed parochial system requires the priest to consult representatives of the people in those matters which are their proper concern. The frustration at the conclusion of the Barking pageant could not occur today. One of the manifold fruits of the work for unity is that

Christians now worship together on suitable occasions without any sense of surrender or compromise.

The years of preparation did not seem to have been too many when I began to face pastoral problems. At some time or other I found use for everything I had been taught. Even philosophy proved to be of practical use. It was amazing to feel the training in logic and epistemology affecting every kind of activity. Sermons, lectures, articles and, the ability to read critically all reflected the years of study. Yet, on the other hand, the seminary had taught me nothing very practical. I learned more about human relations in the first few months in Barking than in seven years in Rome. This may well have been inevitable. I suppose the young doctor learns more from dealing with patients than from all his books and lectures. It is now widely alleged that his training did not fit a priest for a cure of souls. Some very desirable changes in seminary training have taken place since the Vatican Council—for example, deacons are now sent to parishes in their final year to gain experience and, incidentally, to test their suitability for the priesthood. But the virtual abolition of seminary rules on the grounds that they are destructive of initiative cannot be proved right until we have seen the effects of relaxation. There are two possible reactions to having been made to pray at set times—to abandon all regularity when pressure is released or to continue the habits of prayer and discipline formed in the seminary. Time alone will show us which method produces more zealous pastors of souls.

I knew surprisingly little about people before ordination. Hence my first few months in Barking brought many surprises. The first traumatic discovery I made was that the poor are not always close to God. I had always thought of the poor as God's poor. It is easier, according to the Gospel, for a camel to pass through the eye of a needle than for a rich man to enter the kingdom of heaven. I had assumed that the converse was also true and that a poor man would have no difficulty. I had never realised that being rich or poor is a question less of possessions than of attitudes. A poor man can be a miser and a rich man the soul of charity. Until I began to visit the homes of the poor I did not know that poverty is not lack of goods but a state of ignorance. The wages coming into the homes of the 'poor' were sometimes higher than those of 'respectable' parishioners. In homes without books or ambition life itself is impoverished. I was to learn for the first time that the mentally poor are usually also spiritually poor. I had known before becoming a priest that some Catholics miss Mass. Thoughtlessly I had imagined such Catholics had been choked by riches. I now found that poverty is a greater spiritual hazard than wealth. In other words I discovered the tragic apostasy of the poor. This is not remotely akin to the apostasy of the workers which I had already met in my travels abroad. It had no ingredient of anti-clericalism. The Barking poor loved their Church and their priests. I was welcome in every home. My parishioners were all my friends and came to me for every kind of help. They would do anything I asked—except perform their spiritual duties. I now think that most of these lapsed Catholics had lost the faith or, more probably, had never had it. As a young priest I assumed that those who are proud to call themselves Catholics must be strong in faith. I am less sure now.

The Mass-missers were almost always feckless in everything they did or, rather, failed to do. Those whose homes were dirty, whose children were neglected, were rarely practising Catholics. The lapsed were usually also in arrears with their rent and hire purchase payments. They were pathetic, friendly people. They were for me a source of disillusionment. These people were the 'God's poor' I had dreamed about. I did not realise what is obvious to me now—that many calling themselves Catholics are not believers. Experience has taught me that even priests can go through the motions of the ministry after faith has been lost. In recent years priests have been known to continue to offer Mass while awaiting a convenient moment to renounce the priesthood. When I was young it was unimaginable that a priest could lose the faith. We knew that it was theoretically possible but we heard only of the priests who lost their chastity. These were the poor fellows who threw away their priestly vocation through self-indulgence. Failed priests (whose number was remarkably small) surprised and shocked me less than poor Catholics who were completely dead to the things of God. I neither palliate nor excuse my ignorance of the widespread neglect of religion among the poor. I merely record that until I went to Barking I was under the impression that poverty and religion went together. I was to learn that intelligent people—with or without education—are the most likely to be dutiful Catholics. I have made much of my surprise at finding faithless Catholics among the poor but this does not mean that only a few poor people practised the faith. On the contrary most Barking parishioners were artisans or unskilled labourers. In those days of high unemployment the social services were by modern standards rudimentary. Most of the congregation were poor. The men worked on buildings, on roads and in various factories around Barking Creek. Of the Irish most had come to Barking when Ford's factory was transferred from Cork to Dagenham. Many of our girls were employed making tin boxes or in the asbestos factory—some, indeed, contracted the fearful disease asbestosis. These parishioners were mostly enthusiastic Catholics. A remarkable number came every morning to Mass and Holy Communion. The men's and women's guilds met each week and were extremely well attended.

Barking was an ideal place for a young priest's apprenticeship. There were two Catholic schools, a hospital and a number of old and sick parishioners. There was also social variety. One part of the parish (called New Barking) was purely residential. It was here that the people lived who later came to be called commuters. They were typical of the white-collared working class usually referred to as lower middle class. The Catholics in this part of the town were nearly all exemplary. They first showed me—what I was to see repeated throughout my ministry in every part of England—that people who take pride in their homes, make sacrifices for their children's education and pay their debts are usually also the most dutiful Catholics. Barking was blessed in having an up-to-date junior school in a beautiful setting. More important still, St. Joseph's School had in Miss Lyons a head teacher of exceptional quality who had gathered round her a superb staff. The spiritual health of a parish is often dependent on its primary school. Since all normal parents are interested in their children's welfare good teachers reach parents through their children. The priest can easily come close to families with small children in his school. The priests at Barking certainly regarded St. Joseph's School as the hub of the parish. Scarcely a day passed without one or other of us visiting the school. On Sunday St. Joseph's was used as a chapel of ease for that part of the parish. As a raw curate I learned much pastoral theology from Miss Lyons and her staff. To show, as the saying goes, that the world is small the teacher of the infants' class at St. Joseph's was Maureen Cremen who twenty years earlier had been my companion in the parochial school in Ilford.

I learned not only from the teachers but from parishioners. Their living faith and generosity to neighbours in trouble were a constant lesson. Here, at least, I found meaning in the old phrase 'God's poor'. In the North of England Southerners have the reputation of being reserved and unfriendly. This is certainly not true of those who live in the East End of London. When trouble strikes a family the neighbours organise help without delay. The poor are reputedly improvident but the people in Barking planned for the future by means of innumerable clubs. In addition to Christmas clubs they had clothes clubs and sick clubs. They paid doctors small weekly sums as an unofficial form of insurance. The Welfare State presumably removed the need for many of these provident clubs but I imagine that the comradely spirit remains. I grew close to the people of Barking. Their love and reverence for the priest was a constant lesson. To an outsider it might appear dangerous for sinful men who happen to be priests to be treated with a respect little short of adoration. In fact the effect on the priest is salutary. The attitude of the people is a constant reminder of the standards expected of him. Unless a man is more than usually insensitive he is not likely to grow proud if, with the eyes of faith, his people see Christ in him. Their view of the priesthood tends to make him humble.

I learned not only from the pious but from the less worthy. I remember a persuasive lady who claimed a disproportionate share of my small resources. Had I been more worldly wise I would have realised that my contributions were used mainly to quench her thirst. One day I called to see her husband who was dying. He was not a Catholic but I knew him well. Whenever he went to a church it was to ours. I was not surprised when he asked me to receive him into the Church and give him the last rites. When this was done the lady astounded me by asking to be married so that he would die happy. Without further enquiry I asked two neighbours to be witnesses and performed the marriage ceremony. The man seemed very happy indeed to have received so many sacraments in so short a time. He died peacefully a few hours later. After the funeral the widow came to the presbytery for her marriage lines in order to apply for the widow's pension. I had taken for granted that the couple were civilly married and merely wanted me to give the marriage the Church's blessing. I explained to the widow that although married in the eyes of God she was not married in the eyes of the State. She was therefore not entitled to a pension. I told her that she need not worry because I would continue to help her.

I told the president of the Society of St. Vincent de Paul (a lay organisation devoted to the welfare of the poor) that it would be necessary to give regular help in default of a widow's pension.

Unfortunately I went on to explain that what I had done was against the law. A marriage may not be performed outside a place of worship licensed for marriages except by special dispensation of the Archbishop of Canterbury (an ordinance coming down from the pre-Reformation times). The president undertook to look after the widow. He was as good as and better than his word. He promised her a regular allowance but added that I had acted illegally and would be in serious trouble if she was not discreet. Without delay the lady appeared at the presbytery door demanding money with menaces. If I did not give her money she would go at once to the registrar and 'get me into trouble'. There had been nothing in my textbooks to tell me how to deal with such a case. At least it was clear that if I gave way to blackmail I would never have any peace. I told her to go to the registrar and, to show her that I was not afraid (I was, in fact, terrified) undertook to telephone the registrar to say that she was on her way. I told the registrar what I had done for the sake of the dying man and begged him not to tell the widow that she had not been properly married. He promised to explain to the poor woman that of course she had been properly married but not according to English law. She was therefore not entitled to a pension. It did not occur to him that I had committed a misdemeanour (or, maybe, a felony). I had no more trouble with the widow but when she sought the consolation of another companion she brought him to church to be married. This time everything was legal. I had to pay the fee and buy the ring but I thought this less costly than the fine I might have incurred through my indiscretion.

I knew few priests of the diocese of Brentwood before coming to Barking. I met Canon Cameron for the first time when, a few days after the pageant, he took up residence as parish priest. First impressions were not favourable on either side. The Canon was extremely shy. To cover his embarrassment he was apt to bluster but since he weighed nearly twenty stones this only made him appear pompous. I did not then know that the well-meaning Canon Palmer had already predisposed the Canon against me. Meeting Cameron a few days earlier he had congratulated him on his good fortune in having such a wonderful young priest as his curate. It is hard to imagine a more unfortunate introduction. Canon Cameron, as I was to discover, was not of a brilliant cast of mind. He did not appreciate that I could not be blamed if the old priest was blinded by affection. This was the same Canon Palmer who a year before had proposed my toast so tactlessly in the presence of the bishop. It took Canon Cameron a long time to lay aside his misgivings. The first three months at Barking was a time of great trial. Happy with the people and devoted to Father Carthy, my fellow curate, I was rarely able to please my parish priest. He was distant and sometimes uncivil. He called Father Carthy (whom he had brought with him from Grays) by his Christian name but always addressed me formally as 'Dr. Heenan'. After we had become close friends he told me that this unpleasantness was occasioned by his fear that, deceived by Canon Palmer, I might regard myself as a paragon. There was an additional factor. I came to Barking just before the arrival of Canon Cameron and Father Carthy. This proved unfortunate. The pageant involved me in negotiations with teachers, officials and leading parishioners from the beginning. Of the new trio of priests I was the first to be established. In the early days people wanting to see a priest usually asked for Father Heenan because mine was the only name they knew. This was not the best way for a young curate to win the heart of a new parish priest.

It is said that it takes two to make a quarrel. This is not invariably true but it was verified in the Barking situation. Had I been more docile, life in the presbytery would have been more harmonious. I was still young and had not yet learned that one may disagree without contradicting older people and insisting on putting them right. Sometimes it is advisable to lose an argument and thus provide an opponent with the opportunity of being magnanimous. I made this dramatic discovery towards the end of December 1931 when life in the presbytery had become almost unbearable. This was to be my first Christmas in England since 1923. I had been sentimentally looking forward to a grand family reunion. As Christmas drew near I began to have misgivings. I wondered if it was really right for me to go to my parents' home for my Christmas dinner. Canon Cameron had no close relative and Father Carthy's family lived in 'Ireland. Reluctantly I came to the decision that it would be caddish to leave the other priests to eat Christmas dinner on their own. The presbytery, after all, was our home. When Christmas came I stayed in Barking and felt heroic. Our Christmas dinner was not a success. During its early stages I referred to a senior priest by his unadorned surname and this put the canon into a royal rage. He called me a whippersnapper and warned me not to speak of my seniors without proper respect in his presence. I had a worse experience a day or two later when he attacked me in the presence of several priests in a neighbouring presbytery. This was resented by our host almost as much as by myself and led to a climax in my relations with Canon Cameron.

On 7th July, 1930, the day following my ordination, I had written to thank the bishop for ordaining me. My letter quite simply asked his Lordship to regard my promise of obedience in the most literal sense. I was prepared not only to obey but to accept any unattractive task that nobody else wanted to do. This letter had not been written on a wave of emotion. During my years of training I had clearly realised that I would find peace of mind only by doing God's will instead of my own. In this crisis with Canon Cameron I remembered the letter. It ruled out the possibility of asking the bishop to remove me from Barking. To ask for a change so soon would make mockery of my promise of obedience—not to mention my special request for unattractive tasks. I therefore decided to solve the problem of Canon Cameron on my own. With consummate self-deception I told myself that it was praiseworthy to resist a bully. However willing to bear the burden with humility I owed it to my fellow curates everywhere to stand up for our rights. All, of course, must be done prayerfully. I resolved to offer Mass next morning for God's guidance in my confrontation with the Canon. I prayed with great sincerity—or so, at least, I thought. I did not yet know the difference between listening and talking to God. In my so-called prayer I brooded on my grievances, hoping thus to sanctify what I had already made up my mind to do. Thus I had the comforting feeling that I was not acting without God's guidance.

God answered my prayer in a way I could not possibly have anticipated. After Mass I went to my room to rehearse the exact words I wanted to say to my parish priest. He had spent most of his life teaching junior boys at St. Edmund's College. His chief mistake was to treat me as if I were still a schoolboy. My plan was to speak to him firmly but without anger. "The time has come, Canon"—these are the words I rehearsed and still remember—"for plain speaking. You are no longer a teacher in a seminary and I am not a boy. We are fellow priests." That is how I proposed to begin. If he objected to my attitude he could have me moved to another parish. I did not have much hope that the interview would do any good. Leopards do not change their spots. (The canon, of course, was the leopard.) But at least he would know that I was no longer prepared to tolerate his incivilities and, above all, his offensive remarks in front of other priests. The Mass and my prayers had made clear that there was no self-seeking in what I was about to do. I listened nervously for the footsteps of the canon on his way to his room. While waiting I casually picked up a book to occupy my mind. It happened to open at a passage which compared our complacency over offences against God with our sense of outrage when a 'punctilio'—yes, that was the word—of the honour due to us is withheld. I heard the Canon's footsteps and hastily shut the book. "Punctilio," I thought. It was a good thing I had prayed. Thank God I knew that I was not acting from petty motives.

I walked to the canon's door and knocked firmly. I was word perfect in my prepared speech. I went straight up to him. Then I heard myself say "I have come, Canon, to apologise for the way I have treated you since we came to Barking." I could hardly believe my own voice. What happened next was even more astounding. The canon stood up and seized my hand. "John," he said (using my Christian name for the first time), "what a lot of nonsense you are talking. You have nothing to apologise for. I am the one to apologise." He then said that we would have a bottle of wine that night to drink each other's health. I have reason to remember every detail of that interview because it changed my life. Hitherto I could do nothing to please the canon but henceforth I could do no wrong. He trusted me and gave me every possible encouragement in my work. He had been left too long teaching small boys the rudiments of French and Latin to become an effective parish priest. He kept the accounts and saw callers while Father Carthy and I were out on our rounds. Apart from that he did little but read. There are some in authority who do nothing and allow nobody to make good their deficiencies. Canon Cameron was not of this type. Once confidence was established he became an enthusiastic if non-playing captain of the pastoral team.

Father Carthy, the son of a regular soldier, was born in India. Slow-spoken, he gave the impression of being dull. He was, in fact, brilliant at mathematics and could make calculations in his head which most of us found difficult on paper. He delighted in problems brought to him by teachers and fellow mathematicians. But his chief quality was zeal for souls. The people in his part of the parish—it was divided between us—knew him as a thoroughly priestly man. He was a poor preacher but with those troubled in body or mind he was superb. In Barking, as in all working-class parishes of the thirties, the people looked to the priest before anyone else in all their troubles. Neither they nor the clergy would have thought it unbecoming for the priest to be a welfare officer as well as a spiritual father. Then as now, no clearly marked boundaries between spiritual, moral and material welfare were discernible. The priest was still regarded and regarded himself as the father of his people. Paternalism had not yet found a place in sociological jargon. Father Carthy with his soft Irish voice and happy disposition was a true father to the people of Barking during the suffering years of the economic depression.

Once peace had been made with Canon Cameron life in Barking became blissful. The people were notably responsive to the spiritual leadership of the clergy. The numbers at Mass were large and always increasing. Mass on weekdays, Sunday evening services and the meetings of the men's and women's guilds were well attended. One important result of the enthusiasm in the parish was that young men and women came forward to offer themselves for the priesthood or religious life. There was no stampede to join seminaries and convents but there was a steady flow of recruits from a poor parish which hitherto had produced scarcely any religious vocations. Our difficulty was to persuade the bishop to accept candidates for the priesthood. He suffered from the delusion that the diocese could not afford the cost of training. I was not well placed to sponsor candidates because the bishop still held against me the remarks made on the day of my ordination. I had to divert some of our best young men to Westminster diocese. Thirty years later the bread cast on the waters was gratefully recovered when, as Archbishop of Westminster, I found some splendid priests who had been rejected by the diocese of Brentwood. I had been unable to persuade Bishop Doubleday to accept them. He almost always rebuffed me but not, I think, out of animosity. He was afraid that pride might ruin my priestly work. I am not sure that he was wrong.

My first misunderstandings with the bishop were over small impersonal matters. As often as not my applications for dispensations would be returned for trivial reasons—perhaps a date had been omitted or a signature not placed on the right line. Small things lead young men to a sense of frustration and even of persecution. I happened to meet the bishop one day about a year after I had come to Barking. I asked him to tell me frankly what was wrong. I had reached the stage when any communication with Bishop's House was almost certain to be unsatisfactory. I asked him to tell me what was wrong so that I might try to put it right. Bishop Doubleday, essentially a kindly man, at first denied that anything was wrong but I pressed him strongly. Unless he told me where I was at fault, I pointed out, the situation could never be rectified. He then revealed that my real trouble was being swollen-headed and self-opinionated. I must stop acting as if I were the bishop and begin to learn my place. I thanked him for his frankness and we parted on excellent terms. The improvement in our relations was unfortunately only temporary.

The following year Monsignor Cicognani, whom I as a student had often helped in Rome with his English correspondence, was appointed Apostolic Delegate to the United States of America. He invited me to Rome for his consecration as bishop soon after Easter. I was reluctant to apply to the bishop for permission to accept his invitation because he might take it as another proof of my self-importance. I therefore wrote for permission to take my annual holiday early. The bishop's secretary replied that his Lordship wished to inform me (the usual formula used at Bishop's House, Brentwood in those days) that as a curate I had no right to a holiday and that, in any case, I needed my parish priest's permission before applying to the bishop. On receiving this refusal I wanted to write to Mgr. Cicognani to decline his invitation but Canon Cameron would not hear of it. He said that a trip back to Rome and the English College would do me good and he promised to help me with the fare. He made me write to the bishop giving the whole story. To this letter the bishop replied personally. He upbraided me for not giving him the facts in the first place but agreed to let me go.

I was only at the beginning of an extended series of disputes with my bishop. One of our first clashes was over birth control. In the nineteen-thirties nobody thought of over-population as a world danger. The world, of course, meant the western world. We in England knew nothing of the birth rate in Asia, Africa and South America, which even then must have been high. In the West we talked not of over-population but of race suicide. The birth rate in France and England had fallen below replacement level. All the social and economic literature of the time was preoccupied with the perils of the shrinking birth rate. The fear of race suicide reached its climax just before the war. The facts were proclaimed in a centre-page article in the *Observer* for Sunday, 16th October, 1938. For readers not disposed to read the two thousand words of Sir Arnold Wilson M.P. the headlines told the story:

BIRTHS AND POLITICS

THE HAND THAT ROCKS THE CRADLE

CONQUEST BY FERTILITY

AN IMMINENT CRISIS

What light do birth-rate trends throw on the future? The figures are disconcerting to Western parliamentary democracies, which are, without exception, at the bottom of the list and below the danger line. Making full allowance for improved survival rates, a minimum of 200 births annually per 10,000 living is needed to maintain the population. Sweden, Norway, Belgium, Denmark, Switzerland, and Holland are all below this limit. Austria, at 131, was the lowest in Europe. Czecho-Slovakia had fallen from 271 in 1921-25 to 174 in 1936—a record drop. France has fallen to 150, the United Kingdom to 153 ... A nation which cannot perpetuate itself has lost the biological title-deed to the soil on which it lives, for though numbers are not the sole index of national strength, they are, in the ultimate resort, the only valid claim to hold land ... No diplomatic shifts, no rearmament, no international conferences can long mask the effects of a shrinking adult able-bodied population. If we cannot solve this problem, appeals to Christian principles will fall upon deaf, because unborn, ears ... A dwindling population does not cure but aggravates unemployment: it does not make war less but more likely: it does not help to raise but to depress the standard of living: it does not increase but diminishes the value of savings. It does not promote peace, but invites aggression. To demonstrate these truths and to bring them home to the well-to-do who, in this as in other matters, have greater need of education than weekly wage-earners, is a task which might well absorb the energies of public-spirited English women for the next generation. Thus only can we make the world safe for our children.

At the close of the decade the second world war broke out and France was overrun. Marshal Petain pointed to the empty cradle as the major cause of France's capitulation. At that time contraception was considered by most people to be not only unethical but unpatriotic.

Dr. Marie Stopes addressed a meeting in the Baths Hall, Barking, on 14th February, 1935. To this meeting most of the town councillors accepted invitations. As a result of this meeting it was proposed to build a birth control clinic to be maintained with public funds. Today it would cause little surprise if public abortoria were built and maintained by the state. It may therefore be difficult to credit that so short a time ago a birth control clinic would give rise to bitter public controversy. The Catholic community was outraged by the proposal. It was only six years since the publication of Pope Pius XI's encyclical *Casti Connubii.* This document had reiterated in unusually solemn terms the Church's well-known condemnation of artificial methods of birth control. In those days we had no liberal theologians or emancipated laymen to tell us that a celibate pope could know nothing about love and marriage. In Barking priests and people were united in opposition to the proposed clinic. So were most of the professing Christians in the town.

One of the most worried men was Dr. O'Connell, the deputy medical officer of health for the borough of Barking. His chief, Dr. Williams, now nearing retirement did little active work. It would therefore have fallen to Dr. O'Connell to operate the clinic. He was prepared to resign rather than do so. Dr. O'Connell was a Tynesider. Apart from being a doctor of medicine—oddly enough an unusually high qualification for a medical practitioner—he was a virtuoso pianist. The prospect of a Marie Stopes clinic in his area was traumatic to this man of refinement. He decided that if the plan went through he would retire from the health service to take up music as a career or go into general practice. He was anxious for a protest meeting to be held but as a public servant he could not sponsor it. It was left for me to take action. I booked the Baths Hall for the evening of Lady Day, 25th March. It was the Monday preceding the council meeting to decide about opening a birth control clinic. I asked the redoubtable Dr. O'Donovan, M.P., of Harley Street to be the principal speaker and invited Bishop Doubleday to take the chair. From Dr. O'Donovan I received an enthusiastic acceptance but from the bishop came not only a refusal but a veto.

He was not prepared to come to Barking to address a handful of parishioners. He was apprehensive lest at such short notice it prove impossible to attract an impressive crowd. From his experience he knew that a half-empty hall would play into the hands of Marie Stopes by convincing the councillors that there was no formidable opposition to be feared. He therefore forbade me to hold any meeting.

My dilemma was resolved by Dr. O'Connell. He knew of a body called the League of National Life. The League which was non-sectarian and non-political had been founded principally to fight race suicide. Its officers although non-Catholics shared the Catholic attitude to contraception. Without delay I telephoned the secretary to ask if the League would be prepared to sponsor the meeting. She said the notice was too short for the League to undertake the expense and organisation. I was happy to assure her that the League need provide nothing but its name. The hall had been paid for and the speakers booked. The League was asked simply to send a representative to say why it so strongly opposed contraception. The League gladly agreed to accept responsibility and the free advertisement. I wrote to the bishop to tell him that the League of National Life having taken over our meeting had asked me to preside. During the next few days I urged the members of the men's and women's confraternities to bring all their friends to the meeting. I also wrote to the councillors informing them that seats would be reserved for them. Since it was my first experiment in what has now come to be called public relations my letter to councillors may be of interest.

> The Catholic Church,
> Linton Road,
> Barking.
> 21st March 1935.

Sir,

The League of National Life which, as you are no doubt aware, is not a Catholic organisation but non-sectarian and non-political, has asked my co-operation in bringing to your notice the meeting advertised in the enclosure.

After consultation with my Bishop I feel it to be my duty as the priest for the moment in charge, to inform you of the very definite opposition the Catholic Church has always shown towards contraception.

Every man is of course a keeper of his own conscience. It might therefore seem impertinent on my part to acquaint you with the restrictions imposed by a Catholic conscience. But I do so for a very practical reason. Catholics do not oppose contraception upon narrow or denominational grounds, but upon a point of ethics, and although it is not for them to press their views on their non-Catholic fellow townsmen, as ratepayers they have every right to resent the spending of their money upon contraceptional instruction and as citizens have a right to voice their opinion on questions of public morality.

It is only fair therefore in view of the possibility of the question coming before the Borough Council, to inform you that you will forfeit any reasonable expectation of a Catholic vote at the next election if you assist the passage of any motion to further what Catholics regard as morally and socially unsound.

I quite understand that the position of those who oppose contraception is difficult to appreciate unless it is clearly stated. I trust therefore that you will accept the invitation of the League of National Life, so that you may judge for yourself whether this attitude, which is also the attitude of the Catholic Church, is reasonable.

In the firm belief that frank discussion will not impair the good relationship which has existed between your party and the Catholic Church,

I am,
Yours sincerely,
JOHN C. HEENAN.

I offered local doctors a seat on the platform. Dr. O'Connell decided to take his place on the platform so that the councillors—by whom he was much respected—would know of his opposition. With him were several doctors, both Catholic and non-Catholic, from neighbouring areas. The only Catholic doctor in practice in the town, Dr. John Foran, was also on the platform. He was a tall, impressive young man who was destined to spend his whole professional life in the service of the people of Barking.

There was not an empty seat in the Baths Hall. Whether or not they were impressed by the oratory, the councillors must have noted how many hundreds of ratepayers—not all Catholics—felt strongly on the subject of contraception. Some reluctant members of the audience felt that my invitation had been an act of blackmail. My letter was admittedly the crude work of a young man without experience. At question time I was strongly attacked for threatening that Catholics would use the power of the polls. I contended—honestly enough but naively—that a candidate opposed to the Catholic view of ethics is not entitled to the vote of a Catholic citizen. I was well able to withstand personal attacks but I was much embarrassed by the contraceptionists who cited the recent Lambeth Conference in their support. I avoided attacking the Anglican bishops but I could hardly defend them. The day after the meeting I wrote to the League of National Life to express the hope that I had not failed them (all the leading members of the League were Anglicans). In a gracious reply the secretary reassured me:

> Please do not be troubled as to the line that the opposition took. We did not in the least think that it was either your wish or your intention. It is one of the unfortunate results of Resolution 15 of the 1930 Lambeth Conference that it places such a weapon in the hands of our opponents. We wish that it had been possible to stress that the great bulk of the resolutions on this subject at that Conference were entirely in agreement with the traditional standards, and that the offending resolution itself was by no means an unqualified approval of contraception, as our opponents like to assume, and that there were no less than sixty-three Bishops who were directly opposed to that resolution. But there it is and we cannot get away from it. So please do not think that we in any way criticised what happened at Barking.

The local press gave a full account of the meeting. The following is an extract from the *Barking Advertiser* of 29th March, 1935:

THE PROPOSED CLINIC FOR BARKING
Resolution of strong disapproval

A meeting promoted by the League of National Life was held at the Baths Hall, Barking, on Monday to—in the words of the announcement—'examine the real issues of Birth Control'.

It will be remembered that a public meeting was recently held in the Hall, arranged by the Society for Constructive Birth

Control and Racial Progress, at which, on the motion of Dr. Marie Stopes, a resolution was passed urging the Barking Town Council and the Medical Officer of Health to use the powers given by the Ministry of Health to establish a Birth Control clinic.

Roman Catholic Views

Rev., J.C. Heenan presided, and was supported by Dr. W. O'Donovan, M.P.; Dr. Alfred Piney, pathologist, St. Mary's Hospital; Mrs. Stanton of the League of National Life; and members of the clergy and medical faculty. There was a very large audience.

The Chairman said the object of the meeting was to give some sort of resolution to the Town Council of Barking to help them in their deliberations with regard to the proposal for a centre of contraceptional instruction. The League of National Life was formed to uphold the honour and blessing of parenthood; to combat the theory and practice of contraception; and to oppose any form of State or municipal assistance for the promotion of contraception . . .

Because certain good followed from the practice of contraception, it most certainly did not follow that contraception was therefore a good thing. In other words, the end, whatever might be said to the contrary, did not justify the means. If he were to propose to the Borough Council that they should give a small dose of poison to everyone who was a burden on the rates, definitely incurable, and unemployable, he would suggest a solution to a social problem with definite and good results, but he did not thereby make out any case for the administration of poison. What they had to decide was not whether the results were good, but whether the means by which they were expected to obtain those results were in keeping with the moral law. Those who were religiously inclined had viewed for some long time with trepidation—to use no stronger word—the tendency of legislation. There were politicians whose pens were dripping with the ink of pseudo-reform . . . The League opposed contraception because it preached a doctrine opposed to human nature, stripped woman of her dignity, and destroyed the fundamental ideal of the family. Men were waiting to put upon the Statute Book methods of progress which were going to write paid to the account of

Christianity of this country. The Church was in a very difficult position . . . Either it was interfering with what did not concern it, or condemned for a guilty silence.

Dr. O'Donovan, in his address, urged that the wealth of the country rested not in gold, machinery, or crops, but depended on its people. The things they were considering were big and solemn things. They were starting on a slope that would alter the whole balance of population in this country. He also referred to the schools closed by the London County Council because they had not the children to fill them. There was no justification for saying that the economic condition of the country justified the abolition of the poor. They had to alter the conditions and look to the future with hope and confidence. They were not fighting a movement or a people, but for the right to live of the English poor . . .

At the close, Alderman D.G. Hardwick (not a Catholic) proposed a hearty vote of thanks to the speakers and said he felt greatly indebted for what he had heard. As a Christian man he felt they had given good counsel. He was there as a Christian candidate and if this matter came before the Council he would vote against it on Christian grounds. He had no ties on the Council, and was free to vote as he thought fit. He looked upon the practice which had been referred to as the breaking of God's laws.

The motion was carried with acclamation.

From every point of view the meeting had been a great success. The only reservation I had was the possible reaction of the bishop. He had told me that the Catholic community must drop the meeting. I did not yet know what he would think of our active co-operation with the League of National Life. What would he think of my taking the chair? I wrote after the council meeting had taken place to inform him that the clinic proposal had been defeated. I subsequently sent him this clipping from the local paper:

THE SUGGESTED BIRTH CONTROL CLINIC

The Public Health and Maternity Committee recommended that consideration of the question of the provision of a birth control clinic be deferred *sine die*. Alderman Edwards in presenting the report, said the words '*sine die*' did not accurately convey their decision . . . The question of birth control was not discussed, and as regarded morality and expediency they were not discussed. Inasmuch, however, as the rate had only just been made on expenditure put before the Committees, none of them thought it fair to introduce something of which they did not know the cost and for which no provision had been made in the estimates. It was, therefore, postponed for that particular reason.

Councillor Craig: *Sine die* was not ours, Mr. Mayor. (Laughter.) Alderman Hearn asked if it was possible to have a vote on the question of birth control.

The Mayor suggested that in the circumstances the only way to get a vote upon it was to move that a birth control clinic be established. (Laughter.) The report was adopted.

The matter was closed in the nicest possible way by a charming letter from the bishop. It was an illustration of the truism that nothing succeeds like success.

Bishop's House,
Brentwood.
Mar. 27 1935.

My dear Dr. Heenan,

I am glad to hear that the meeting was such a success and has most likely scotched the proposal. You are to be thanked and congratulated for your part in the effort. I should like to see any report of the speeches at the meeting, if available.

Wishing you every blessing
Yours devotedly,

† ARTHUR
Bp. of Brentwood.

Canon Cameron was inspector of schools in the Brentwood diocese and I was his assistant. The canon was not well qualified for the post. He had been appointed because he had assisted Canon Norris before the diocese of Brentwood had been created. In those days a religious inspector was an external examiner. A school was warned two or three months in advance that the examiners were coming and from that moment the children were subjected to intense pressure to make them word perfect in the answers to the catechism. Following the ordeal of examination the children were free for the rest of the day and the brighter pupils were given magnificent medals or certificates. If requiring children to learn catechism is right there is obviously some merit in having school examiners but it is not the present educational fashion to learn anything by rote. Spelling, arithmetic, geographical and historical statistics are now acquired not learned. In the nineteen-thirties everything—including Christian doctrine—had to be learned.

I was never able to see much value in the old-style religious examination. When I began the work I had to abide by the system but later I sought the advice of the chief inspector of the Board of Education. I explained that I was a junior religious inspector without training or experience and asked if I might be granted an interview with one of His Majesty's Inspectors of religious knowledge. I was very courteously received in Whitehall and given a great deal of helpful advice. I was told that the most useful function of an inspector in any subject is to encourage teachers. A stranger coming into a school once every year or so cannot hope to have a great or lasting influence on the pupils. Like a bee collecting pollen the good inspector should gather ideas and carry them from one school and teacher to another. This and much more I learned in one day at Whitehall. Later in the week I received a typed account of my interview. It is conventional to joke about civil servants but everyone is impressed by their integrity and efficiency. As a result of this and other meetings with government inspectors my examinations gradually became inspections. Towards the end of my years as religious inspector I rarely questioned the children. Whenever possible I encouraged the teacher to give a lesson and offered comments and suggestions after the children had been dismissed. Sometimes we had a staff meeting to discuss methods of religious instruction. This routine is commonplace today but in the nineteen-thirties it was new. It was therefore regarded by some of the older teachers with the hostility and suspicion accorded to all original ideas.

It was during my Barking days that I began to take a serious interest in writing. It began almost by chance. A pamphlet was published in 1933 by the C.T.S. (Catholic Truth Society) under the title *Pitfalls of the Confessional*. It was written by Father Arthur Day, S.J., one of the two Jesuit sons of a famous judge. The father was said to be responsible, with another Catholic judge, Mr. Justice Walton, for putting a stop to the prevalent dockside crime of garotting by recourse to the cat-o'-nine-tails. Mr. Justice Day was known to criminals as Judgement Day. The pamphlet annoyed Wilfred Eyre, a friend of mine, (to whom I shall refer again) and he begged me to write a new pamphlet as an antidote. This I did with great assiduity but without success. When I submitted the manuscript I was informed that it was against the policy of the C.T.S. to publish a second pamphlet on the same subject. But in correcting Father Day's errors I had come to see how much help could be given by showing the laity the exact function of the priest in the confessional. I therefore decided to discard the pamphlet and write a book. This time I did not set to work without hope that my work would subsequently be published. I went to see Frank Sheed of Sheed and Ward and was accorded ready co-operation. Most of my spare time during 1935 was devoted to writing the book which was published in 1936 under the title of *Priest and Penitent*.

One of the chief delights of young priests is to train altar servers. I made up my mind not to refuse to train any boy willing to serve Mass. My plan was to make boys enthusiastic about the liturgy and through them to attract the interest of their families and friends. My object was purely pastoral—from the liturgical point of view it would have been much more effective to train half-a-dozen boys selected from zealous Catholic families. Recruits for training were so numerous that we had to have two altar staffs to serve during alternate weeks. We had rehearsals every week and eventually the liturgy was carried out almost faultlessly. Very small boys can be taught to speak and act with dignity—as every infants' teacher knows. The altar boys wore robes modelled on those of the altar servers in Oberammergau. In 1934 my friend Val Elwes and I went to the Passion Play. I was leading a group of pilgrims which included my mother. Out of respect for them I could not play truant, but I found the Passion Play so boring that after the luncheon interval I returned with the greatest reluctance. Much more exciting than the Passion Play was the Mass in which the whole village took part. These were the days of the Latin Mass and visitors from all over the world joined the villagers in the singing of the Gloria and Credo. Every kind of musical instrument found a place in the orchestra but it was the dress of the altar servers which chiefly caught my attention. Instead of the usual cassock and surplice they wore a white linen tunic over a red skirt and round their necks a collar of the same material. Val, who had a genius for improvisation, went into the sacristy after Mass and cut a pattern out of a newspaper. On my return to Barking I gave the pattern to my women's confraternity and within a few months they produced forty robes of various sizes in royal purple serge lined with pale blue satin. Thus splendidly attired the boys took an even greater pride in their task. Today this might be condemned as triumphalism. I am sure that the self-respect and the sense of occasion which their robes created did the boys no lasting harm. English people, after all, still relish the changing of the guard without feeling the smallest nostalgia for the days of imperialism. The Vatican has abolished papal trumpets but nothing will be allowed to interfere with the glorious pageantry of Westminster Abbey.

Experience in Barking taught me the need to visit families regularly if I was to be useful to them as a priest. Apart from a few nominally Catholic families in whom the faith was quite dead they were greatly encouraged by the priest's visits. The custom of the East End of London required the priest to call on all families for the outdoor collection. Originally this collection was to pay teachers at a time when they received no salary from the state. During the nineteenth century Catholic teachers had to be confessors of the faith as well as instructors. It was professional ruin to teach in a Catholic school because it meant the sacrifice of salary, prospects and pension. In the large towns the Catholic body was pitifully poor (immigrants from Ireland and the continent). The Sisters taught without hope of earthly reward but lay teachers with domestic responsibilities had to be supported. The outdoor collection was intended to guarantee them a regular pittance. By the time I was going the rounds in Barking the outdoor collection had lost its original purpose. Teachers in Catholic schools had been treated for two generations in the same way as their colleagues in the state schools.

On Sunday I might be saying the early Mass at the parish church or in St. Joseph's at the other end of the parish. At eleven o'clock I would either be singing Mass or looking after the choir (despite my musical limitations I was choirmaster). After the last Mass I attended the weekly meeting of the Society of St. Vincent de Paul. A wise priest always works closely with these zealous men who make regular visits to poor families and destitute old people. After the S.V.P. meeting came breakfast and the outdoor collection which lasted until it was time to return home to take the children's service and baptise babies. In the evening Father Carthy and I took turns to preach the sermon or give Benediction. We then sat down for the first real meal of the day. If the canon was in good mood he gave the curates a half-bottle of wine. Sunday in Barking was busy and happy—except for the outdoor collection. I resented having to take money from lapsed Catholics. After a year or so I refused their contributions and told them to bring their offerings to church. Lapsed Catholics were not happy to have their money refused. They thought it 'unlucky not to pay the priest'. They may have lost the faith but they had not shed all superstition. The outdoor collection survives in few parishes today mainly because it is thought unbecoming for a priest's visit to be associated with collecting money. Since the disappearance of the outdoor collection some families complain that they are rarely visited by their priests. Despite the grievous loss to souls in parishes where homes are unvisited it would nevertheless be wrong to reintroduce the outdoor collection as a means of inducing the shepherd to tend his flock.

My apprenticeship in Barking nearly came to an end in the year 1935. When Bishop Hinsley became Apostolic Delegate in Africa his place as rector of the Venerabile had been taken by Dr. Godfrey, professor of theology at Ushaw. Although already a priest I was still a student in Rome when Dr. Godfrey came as rector. I had known him very well at Ushaw but we had not kept in touch. Nor had I kept in touch with him after leaving Rome. I was therefore surprised nearly four years later to receive from Dr. Godfrey a letter marked urgent in which he told me that he had been given a new appointment which he wished to discuss with me. He was about to come to England and wanted to meet me in York where the annual meeting of the Roman Association (former students of the Venerabile) was to be held the following week. He had arranged for me to stay with him at the Bar Convent, York. It seemed strange that he should want to consult a young man about his new post. I assumed that he was already feeling out of touch with his contemporaries in England. That must be the reason for falling back on one of his disciples. When I arrived at the Bar Convent Dr. Godfrey told me that once more he was to succeed Mgr. Hinsley—this time as Apostolic Delegate to Africa. He wanted me to accompany him as secretary but would not allow me to give an answer until we had both said Mass next day.

When I went to his room after Mass my mind was made up. I had no desire of any kind for a quasi-diplomatic post. I was extremely happy in Barking and felt no urge to become a missionary. It seemed to me that my native land was sufficiently pagan to challenge what evangelical zeal I had. Since I had no desire whatever to accompany Dr. Godfrey to Africa it seemed clearly right to accept. Although still young I had sufficient experience of the spiritual life to accept a superior's request provided that for my part it was completely unsolicited. My philosophy was to trust a man in authority on the grounds that if he were stupid or misguided somebody higher up would eventually put him—and me—right. Dr. Godfrey warned me to tell my plans to nobody except the doctor who must pass me as fit for service in Africa. Mgr. Godfrey had also been told to have a medical examination. To reduce the number of people to be consulted I arranged for Dr. O'Connell to examine us both in Barking. He certified us fit for tropical service. I was then instructed to write a formal letter expressing willingness to join the staff of the Apostolic Delegate in Mombasa. I was not to write to my bishop. He would be informed in due course by the Holy See. He was never, in fact, informed because to my relief no more was ever heard of the project. On 5th June, Mgr. Godfrey suffered sunstroke while attending the laying of the foundation stone of the Metropolitan Cathedral of Christ the King in Liverpool. The sanctuary of the vast outdoor altar (designed by Lutyens) was encased in glass. The sun's rays beat upon the head of Mgr. Godfrey and caused the mishap. It was in reality no mishap for Mgr. Godfrey or for me. He was eventually able to use his talent for diplomacy to much greater purpose as the first Apostolic Delegate to Great Britain. Having no desire to enter the diplomatic service or to leave parish work I was delighted to be left in Barking. I have often reflected how the hot sun of that June morning altered the history of the Church in Liverpool. Twenty years later as Archbishop of Liverpool Dr. Godfrey commissioned Adrian Scott to modify the Lutyens design. Still later as Archbishop of Liverpool I rejected this compromise plan and put the design out to open competition. But for the sunstroke we would both have gone to Africa and, almost certainly, neither would have returned to Liverpool as archbishop.

With immense relief I turned once more to pastoral work in the parish of Barking. Daily I learned more about human folly and wisdom, weakness and strength. I saw how inextricable are the strands of heredity and environment in closed communities. Inter-marriage between near neighbours was common in Barking. Three inbred families in particular seemed to be ubiquitous and would have provided a full study of sociology in themselves. None of them—not even the children at school—attended Mass or received the sacraments. The fathers and, in due course, the sons were frequently 'inside' (the poor man's word for prison). They were not so much criminals as loiterers, pilferers and heavy drinkers. The women of the tribe were never in trouble with the police. They were devoted mothers, enthusiastic about such special occasions as their children's First Communion Day but devoid of serious religious convictions. They were, however, pertinaciously Catholic. When the children were five years old nothing but the Catholic school would do. They were the kind of people whom crime reporters are wont to describe as 'devout Roman Catholics'. In the journalists' world all Catholics are devout and all Protestants staunch (escapers, for some reason, are all escapees).

When the male members of such families grew up they were so clearly destined to be at war with society that as a young priest I might have become a determinist. Nothing the priest or teacher might say would deter them from the path of petty crime. The balance of my judgement was preserved by the children born into equally poor and religiously indifferent homes who were totally transformed by the school. Such boys and girls, usually of above average intelligence, learned to love the faith. They were eager to practise their religion. These children were apostles in their own homes and were often able to re-kindle in them the lamp of faith. I recall two girls from religiously indifferent homes who were close friends and daily communicants. When they reached the age of twenty-one they both became nuns. Two swallows do not make a summer but I saw enough children who were able to overcome adversity to convince me that environment is not all-powerful. It is, of course, true that a bad upbringing can diminish responsibility to vanishing point, but equally an excellent home may produce a ne'er-do-well. As curate in Barking I saw the power of grace to save the weak and raise up the strong. None may ever be canonised like St. Ethelburga the town's patron but there were many saints among the parishioners of Barking.

One old saint lived in the road adjoining the presbytery. I saw her every day because I could not bear to pass by her house. Mary Lake was nearly a hundred years old when she died. She was blind and bedridden long before I arrived in Barking. Her whole life had been spent in the service of the Church. In the hungry days of the nineteenth century she used to starve herself to feed those poorer than herself. Everyone in Barking called her Gran. She listened to each one's problem and gave wise advice. Her only complaint was that she had to wait so long to die. "Where's my little Father?" she would ask stretching out her arms to me. Then taking my hands she would say: "Ask the good God [pronounced Gawd] to take me." Gran was one kind of saint but there were many in the parish whose lives gave unostentatious example of Christian perfection. Finding the strength in the sacraments, like St. Paul's just man they lived by faith. The customary excuse given by those who neglect their religious duties is that they are 'just as good as those who go'. Churchgoers by implication are hypocrites who say prayers but refuse the calls of charity. In Barking I found that the most devout were also the most generous to those in need. The priests had no long search when good samaritans were needed by sick or needy neighbours.

On the last day of the year 1934 Cardinal Bourne died after a long illness. The see of Westminster was left vacant for an unusually long time. In my memoir of Cardinal Hinsley I have described the astonishment with which his nomination was received:

> The appointment to the Archdiocese of Westminster of Monsignor Hinsley, a retired and ailing missionary, was not received by all English Catholics as a sign of great wisdom in the Holy See. That the spirit breatheth where he will nobody could doubt. But many of the clergy thought that this was too much. Those accustomed to show the finger of God to others in distress often have a less elevated vision when seeking interpretation of their own misfortunes. Some pious priests were doubtless content to praise the Holy Ghost for the Hinsley appointment. Many others equally pious were more inclined to blame what they took to be an ill-informed Consistorial Congregation.
>
> It would be wrong to suggest that there was any personal

hostility to the new archbishop. You must know a man before you dislike him. Monsignor Hinsley was almost unknown. Far from having to suffer opposition the incoming archbishop received all the sympathy which his clergy could spare from themselves. Looking back it is curious to remember that the greatest human consolation of many clergy was the thought that a man broken by years in the tropics could not be expected to have a long reign. It is curious because the same priests eight years later were fervently begging Almighty God to spare the cardinal for their own sakes as well as for the Church of God in England and the whole world.

On April 29th, 1935, Archbishop Hinsley was enthroned in Westminster Cathedral. The contrast between this ceremony and that of his Requiem Mass is more notable for the sentiments of the congregation than for the vastly more impressive gathering on the later occasion. What thoughts were in the minds of those who assisted at the enthronement of the unknown archbishop? The uppermost thought was probably the same in the minds of Shepherd and flock—a puzzled interrogation. "Why send this old man?" many, at least among the clergy, were wondering. "Why this old man?" was the echoing thought of the humble archbishop. He was bewildered. He had been mentally numb ever since the Holy Father had imposed upon him the burden of this office. He honestly considered himself to be unequal to the burden. As we now know it was precisely because, like the Curé of Ars, he relied more and more upon Almighty God to supply his deficiencies that he became so distinguished a figure in an already distinguished line of succession.

A Brentwood priest normally has little contact with the Archbishop of Westminster but Mgr. Hinsley's appointment greatly affected me and my work. When Cardinal Bourne, a great believer in the Sulpician method of training, wanted to send a student to study abroad he was likely to choose St. Sulpice in Paris or the Procure of St. Sulpice in Rome. There had not been a single Westminster student in Hinsley's Venerabile. So it was not long before I was invited to visit Archbishop's House, Westminster. Val Elwes, the new private secretary, was a very special friend and also not being a Westminster priest he felt as isolated as the new archbishop. It was natural that Val and the archbishop should turn to me for companionship. They never discussed the affairs of the diocese (of which, in any case, I knew nothing), but increasingly I was asked to help in drafting speeches and articles for the archbishop to whom much of the contemporary English scene was foreign. The fact is that he had left his heart in Africa. It was not until the war that he found himself fully at home in his native land. He has been compared with Churchill as an example of a man whose real greatness might never have been revealed but for the war. In his early days in Westminster the archbishop had to deal with educational matters with which he had been out of touch for nearly twenty years. Fascism and Nazism were also beginning to create social problems. In the years immediately preceding the war the British public became politically conscious in an unprecedented way. Looking back after the second world war we forget the upheavals of the thirties during the heyday of the dictators. Hitler came to power in 1933, Franco made his bid for the control of Spain in 1936, Mussolini had been consolidating his regime since the twenties. Stalin had tyrannised the U.S.S.R. for much longer. The restlessness of the public during the thirties increased with each passing year. Anthony Eden and Winston Churchill trusted none of the dictators. Oswald Mosley and serious political figures like Harold Nicolson thought that the salvation of England might lie in some sort of alliance with the international forces opposed to communism. Political feelings rose so high that processions had to be banned to prevent clashes in the East End of London between Mosley's black-shirts and anti-Fascists. It is not easy for us to recapture the atmosphere of those days. Even at the time it was difficult for Arthur Hinsley who had been out of the country since 1917 to interpret the new and uncharacteristic mood of the British public.

At the time most of the press—with the exception of the Beaverbrook newspapers—was critical of Italy. The castor-oil administered by the Duce to his enemies, the alleged papal blessing of Italian troops setting out to conquer Abyssinia with poison gas, the victory bells pealing from St. Peter's, Rome, were widely reported. Little was said of the Soviet dictatorship. Mussolini was regarded as a more immediate menace. The government and the service chiefs were not yet troubled by the potential threat from Germany and Japan (which in 1932 had withdrawn from the League of Nations after the condemnation of its annexation of Manchuria). In the eyes of most people Fascism was the great threat to peace and

they were prepared to buy peace at almost any price. Pacifism was nevertheless not a popular creed—people preferred to talk of collective security or disarmament. The League of Nations Union organised a house-to-house canvass in what came to be called the Peace Ballot. The result was almost beyond belief. Nearly twenty million citizens responded. Apart from children and illiterates this represented the vast majority of the nation. The questions on the ballot were phrased, as is the way with ballots, to elicit the answer desired by the organisers. More than ten million answered positively to every question except the one which asked if an aggressor should be stopped by war? To this query only six million answered 'yes'.

When in 1935 Mussolini attacked Abyssinia the League of Nations once again proved ineffective. The United Kingdom felt itself disgraced by the Hoare-Laval plan which had been devised by Sir Samuel Hoare, the foreign secretary, to placate Mussolini and save Abyssinia from total defeat. The explosion of public opinion was probably the loudest of this century. Hoare had to resign. The public mood was bitterly anti-Fascist and sanctions against Italy were gleefully supported.

It was about this time that Archbishop Hinsley made a blunder which possibly arose from his having been so long out of touch. Preaching at St. Edward's, Golders Green, in October 1935 he attempted to answer a question being asked by many in England. They wanted to know why the Pope did not condemn Mussolini. The beginning of his long sermon was attuned to the spirit of the times. He condemned exploitation of Africa and Africans. He went on to deny that the bells of St. Peter's had been rung to celebrate an Italian military occasion ("I am authorised by the Holy See to let it be known that this assertion is absolutely false"). He answered the objection to chaplains accompanying the Italian soldiers on their campaign ("The poor soldiers of the Italian army, mostly conscripts or forcible volunteers, are not to blame. Their souls are the object of God's loving care in or out of war").

Now came the offending passage in his sermon:

> What can the Pope do to prevent this or any other war? He is a helpless old man with a small police force to guard himself, to guard the priceless art treasures of the Vatican, to protect his diminutive State . . . He could excommunicate [Mussolini] and place [Italy] under an interdict. Thus he would make war with his

dictator neighbour inevitable besides upsetting the peace and consciences of the great majority of Italians ... The Pope is not an arbitrator. He was expressly excluded by the secret Pact of London in 1915 from future deliberations in the Councils of Peace.

The archbishop was attacked on all sides. The religious press was as yet untouched by the spirit of ecumenism. The *Church Times* published a leading article exuding horror and delight: "The Pope is 'a helpless old man with a small police force to guard himself and the priceless treasures of the Vatican'. Here, indeed, is the Nemesis of temporal power—Christ's Vice-regent on earth, a timid old man fearful of his life and his treasure, terrorised into silence by wickedness in high places." Nor was that redoubtable warrior Pius XI very pleased with the reported remarks of the Archbishop of Westminster. He was very far from being afraid of the Duce. His encyclical letter *Non Abbiamo Bisogno* in condemnation of the excesses of Fascism suggests that 'helpless old man' was an infelicitous description of the Pope.

Looking back to this period—less than four years before the outbreak of the second world war—it would be easy to condemn the shortsightedness of the British government and people. Italian Fascists now look petty criminals by contrast with those responsible for the concentration camps and mass murders in Hitler's Germany and Stalin's Russia. But in 1935 the events which shook this country awake had not yet happened. The reoccupation of the demilitarised Rhineland did not take place until March 1936. The Spanish civil war which gave Nazis and Soviets the chance to try out their strategy and weapons did not break out until 1936. A year later came the Anschluss in which Hitler peacefully occupied Austria. The tragedy of Czechoslovakia was still far distant. Small wonder that in England only few could see any other enemy but Fascism. Fear of Fascism became a national obsession. Vaughan Williams, the composer, exemplified the public mood. He gave up writing folk music to devote himself to composing anti-Fascist symphonies. Stanley Baldwin, the prime minister, and Neville Chamberlain who succeeded him in 1937, knew that Fascism was not the sole nor the most powerful enemy of Great Britain. The Spanish civil war when it came proved revealing. It showed the growing power of both Nazis and Soviets. It disillusioned many who had made idols of their ideological heroes.

More than two thousand British went to the aid of the republicans. Many of them were unemployed miners from the North. They were idealists. Arrived in Spain they found the communists and, in particular, the Russian communists in control of the republicans. These volunteers were not, in the main, communists. At the start of the civil war many party members—including 'intellectuals' (the communist word for non-manual workers)—saw active service but most of them returned home in the early stages of the war. To the more discerning the Spanish civil war was the beginning of a world struggle between ideologies. This reached its first peak on 22nd June 1941 when Hitler invaded Soviet Russia. Its summit may be reached in nuclear confrontation between China and the West.

This apparent digression will be seen to be part of my personal story. The middle thirties were a period of unwonted political consciousness. Despite economic depression, mass unemployment, hunger marches and the means test the workers (and the workless) remained remarkably docile. Led by such law-abiding men as Ernie Bevin and Walter Citrine the unions were the reverse of militant. The twenties had produced the greatest strike in the history of British industry but there was no great strike throughout the thirties. Among the literate, however, political ferment was rising. There was an outcry against poverty in the midst of plenty. Auden, Day Lewis and Spender gave poetic expression to this protest. Marxism was becoming fashionable—German Marxism in deadly conflict with rising National Socialism supplied the spur. But more significant than German Marxists were the British supporters of Soviet Russia which in 1928 had started a series of five-year plans to break the power of capitalist anarchy. By the middle of the nineteen-thirties public discontent remained. Love was still on the dole. That was bad enough but there was something worse—the spectre of world war had reappeared.

Dr. Hinsley now began to feel the need for advisers close enough to be able to keep him more in touch with opinion. Monsignor Elwes, his only intimate friend, did not feel capable of giving the old man—Hinsley was seventy years of age when he came to Westminster—the guidance needed in those days of rapid social change. The archbishop asked Val Elwes to sound me about coming to Westminster as second secretary. The proposal was for Elwes to continue to look after the archbishop's personal and private affairs while I helped with his speeches and writings. I was to become what we would now call an ecclesiastical P.R.O. My reaction was decidedly negative. Having providentially escaped a diplomatic career I was most reluctant to consider giving up the parochial work which I found so congenial. Apart from my personal disinclination to become the archbishop's secretary there was another and more valid objection. A new bishop even if appointed from outside a diocese always chooses his secretary from among the diocesan clergy. In view of his age and long absence from England few objected when Hinsley invited Val Elwes, a former disciple of Venerabile days, to take leave of absence from Northampton diocese to serve temporarily in Westminster. To have appointed another secretary from outside the diocese would, I felt, have been to risk alienating the Westminster priests. I pointed out that I could continue to draft speeches and provide memoranda on current affairs without moving from Barking. So, for the moment, I was left in peace. In 1937 the archbishop was to reopen the question with much more insistence but with no more success. On the second occasion, as will be told in its place, Bishop Doubleday was my saviour.

CHAPTER
FOUR

SOON AFTER ORDINATION I CONCEIVED A STRONG DESIRE TO VISIT THE U.S.S.R. At first I was moved mainly by curiosity but after a few years in Barking my motive changed. I began to feel a need for first-hand information about conditions in Soviet Russia. It was increasingly coming to be accepted as the workers' paradise but I had no doubt from my reading and reflections that Marxism in any of its manifestations must lead to tyranny. But study and theory were not enough. People were losing faith in the ability of anyone but the Soviets to solve economic problems without recourse to war. The dictators (Italy and Germany) were clearly war-minded. The men in Whitehall were neither trusted nor believed by the working class. In 1934 the Chancellor of the Exchequer (Chamberlain) had assured the country that the story of Bleak House was finished and Great Expectations had begun. He spoke against the background of mass unemployment. The whole male population of many villages in Lancashire, Durham and South Wales was out of work. Two thirds of the men in Jarrow were idle. Four regions were officially declared Depressed Areas. Later they were disingenuously renamed Special Areas but they remained depressed. It is not surprising in such circumstances that those opposed to capitalism were able to turn the gaze of citizens from England's green and unpleasant land to a country where all were said to be content, well fed and fully employed. Through communism they had achieved peace and prosperity. The workers, in the famous phrase, had lost only their chains.

Communist influence was widely and skilfully spread by a non-

Marxist intellectual who was full of genuine compassion. A man of culture he was guided more by his emotions than his mind. Victor Gollancz was a good businessman and must have made a modest fortune from the Left Book Club which he founded. Teachers, students and all with intellectual ambition read the club's publications. The books were selected by Victor Gollancz who did not yet suspect that betrayal could come as easily from the Left as from the Right. His associates in the enterprise were John Strachey and Harold Laski. Strachey was a man of intense political feeling. He had been a candidate for Mosley's New Party at the general election of 1931. The following year he published *The Coming Struggle for Power* which is a stylish apologia for communism. Laski had a brilliant mind. Like all left-wing intellectuals he had been influenced by the Fabians. Shaw and the Webbs had discovered in Soviet Russia a civilisation which fulfilled their socialist dreams. The club had an actual membership of over fifty thousand but it was spread among political groups throughout the country. Gollancz published a periodical called *The Left Book Club News* aimed at school teachers and the more literate workers. It provided a series of communist tracts for the times which few school teachers would have read had they borne the imprimatur of communist headquarters in King Street. Until the eve of the second world war the economic depression and left-wing writing combined to make the British public think kindly of Soviet communism. If few people in Britain believed rumours of the persecution of Jews in Hitler's concentration camps there were not many more to give credit to the stories of Stalin's slave camps and his liquidation of hundreds of thousands of fellow Russians. Victor Gollancz realised too late—after the Nazi Soviet Pact of 1939—that he had guilelessly served as an agent of propaganda for a system which was no less abhorrent than any dictatorship of the right.

I made several unsuccessful plans to penetrate the still mysterious U.S.S.R. My first—and completely straightforward—attempt was to accompany a group of students from London University on an educational tour. To my application no answer was ever received. The second effort was made with more circumspection. I sought advice from Sir Philip Gibbs, the novelist who became famous for his dispatches during the 1914-18 war. Soon after the war he gave the world the most harrowing reports of the Russian famine. Presuming on a very slight acquaintance with his wife (as a boy at Stamford Hill

I had attended retreats in the chapel of her house near the college) I wrote to Sir Philip requesting an interview. He invited me to take tea with him at the R.A.C. club. By this time I had the notion of visiting Russia as a reporter. I hoped that this intrepid journalist would encourage me. Alas! with great courtesy he gave me nothing but discouragement. He thought it would not be difficult for me to find a way in but doubted if I would ever find my way out of the Soviet Union. If my identity as a priest were to be discovered it was unlikely that I would be arrested and put on trial. He thought it more likely that I would merely meet with an accident. His firm advice was to drop the whole idea.

Though crestfallen I was by no means crushed by my interview with Philip Gibbs. My friend Wilfred Eyre was, among other things, a playwright. He was never short of ideas. He suggested an approach to a newspaper proprietor who might sponsor my trip to the U.S.S.R. as a special correspondent. Wilfred invited Cecil Harmsworth to dinner in his house at Hampstead. Young Harmsworth—he was about my own age—was more than helpful. He felt that as editor of one of the Harmsworth group of papers he might be able to arrange for me to be sent to Russia as a reporter. The idea so fascinated Harmsworth that he said he would like to come with me. I was delighted. To achieve my aim of seeing what was going on inside the Soviet Union I would have been ready to go as Cecil Harmsworth's valet. It now seemed that it would be comparatively easy to find a newspaper willing to collaborate. Harmsworth promised to meet me during the following week to arrange further details. I never saw him again. He sent a friendly note saying that if things went wrong it might cause international complications for a Harmsworth to be found in my company. So I decided to follow the journalistic track alone. It did not take me very far. The last application I made to a newspaper was to the *Daily Express*. I managed to secure an interview with a senior member of the editorial staff. He listened with interest but did not rate my chances of survival very high. It must be noted that unlike the general public some of the leading press men were aware of the current rise in the rate of liquidation in Stalin's Russia. The great purge had already started. My interview took place after the trial of the Vickers Engineers. Although no British citizens were put to death the case revealed something of the xenophobia prevailing in Moscow. The *Express* man said that he personally could not take the responsibility of letting me act as a special correspondent. The matter would have to be put before the proprietors. I reminded him that I was asking for no money from the *Express* and needed only to be put nominally on its staff. He promised to telephone and asked for my number. I told him it was Rippleway 2849. He smiled sadly. "That means," he said, "that I dial RIP. I hope it's not an omen." He never did phone but wrote to say that my application for employment had been turned down. He wished me the best of luck.

In Barking there was a factory belonging to the Acme Floor Paving Company. Tom Fitzgerald whom I knew very well—his children attended St. Joseph's school—was the manager. The floor paving of Acme was done, at least in those days, entirely in wood. This gave me my next idea. I asked Acme to send me to the U.S.S.R. to buy wood. I was willing to promise that I would not actually buy any timber. I would merely look at forests, visit saw-mills and bring back a report. I emphasised that I would pay my own fare. I wanted from them nothing but the use of the Acme name. Tom promised to put my proposition to his directors. At first they appeared cooperative. They felt that they had nothing to lose. On reflection, however, they must have decided that one day they might be very glad of the good will (and wood) of the Soviets. Once again I had failed to find a sponsor for my journey.

In the nineteen-thirties psychology for priests with normal intellectual interests was what social anthropology became in the nineteen-sixties. It was a subject of which a slender grasp could be acquired with little effort. Between the wars great things were claimed for what psychologists called deep analysis. Under American influence this has now largely given place to group therapy. This or any form of probing is dangerous. A doctor is marginally less likely than a lay practitioner to cause damage but all psychological experimentation is hazardous. With the exception of sociology, a comparative newcomer, there is no more fertile field than psychology for the charlatan. This was true even in the nineteen-thirties. While still in Rome I had begun to take an interest in what was called experimental psychology. A young Italian professor, Gaetani, first aroused my interest. He spoke Italian so musically that he would probably have made his subject sound exciting if it had been calculus. On my return to England I read the psychological literature which publishers at that time were finding profitable. Psychology had the attraction of novelty and solemn judges still listened respectfully to the totally contradictory opinions of psychiatric consultants. McDougall in America was writing textbooks of psychology which were completely free of jargon. A young man can soon learn to talk knowledgeably on a subject in which there are few experts and no infallible doctrines. One evening in 1935 I gave a lecture to the Guild of St. Luke, a society of Catholic doctors, on Freud. Fortunately I have not preserved the text of my address. It was composed almost entirely of extracts from contemporary psychological literature, much of which I was not equipped to understand. I remember that some searching questions were put by Alfred Piney a well-known pathologist of those days. Debate after the lecture revealed that the distinction between inhibitions and repressions had escaped me. The self-assurance of youth is astonishing but at the time I was unaware of the depth of my ignorance.

It was nevertheless probably through this lecture that I came to the notice of Dr. Eric Strauss, director of the London Institute of Psychology. A Jewish convert, Strauss was at this time the best-known psychiatrist in London. He had studied under Freud in Vienna and was a great authority on Rudolf Allers whom he had translated into English.* At his invitation I went to Oxford to attend a meeting of Catholics interested in psychology. The fifty people present were mostly psychiatrists, lecturers or psychiatric social workers. The rest were doctors in general practice and clerical frequenters of conferences mostly jesuits, benedictines and dominicans. By an almost unanimous vote taken soon after the start of the meeting it was decided to found an organisation to be called the Catholic Psychological Society with the object of promoting study of the pastoral implications of the new psychology. ('New' later gave way to 'progressive' as a label of approval.) I recall only two points of the discussion. One was the question of a heavenly patron. St. Paul began as hot favourite but eventually it was agreed that although a sound psychologist he was probably overburdened with patronage of other societies in the Church. St. Thomas More received wide support on the strength of his knowledge of human nature revealed in *Utopia*. The palm eventually was carried off by St. Thomas Aquinas after some powerful pleading by a dominican priest who claimed to be a patient of Dr. Strauss. The other subject discussed was the sacrament of penance. Great harm to souls was said to have resulted from ignorance among priests of elementary psychological principles. Doctors gave harrowing examples of the damage sustained

* *The Psychology of Character*, R. Allers, Sheed and Ward 1931.

by their patients through unwise advice given in the confessional. A benedictine priest declared that until he had undergone deep analysis he had been a completely inadequate father confessor. He proposed a resolution to be forwarded to the hierarchy that no priest be granted faculties to hear confessions until he had been psychoanalysed. The motion failed.

A few days later I received an invitation from Eric Strauss to serve on a committee formed to draw up the constitution of the Catholic Psychological Society. Since my contribution to the Oxford discussions must have indicated how slight was my acquaintance with the subject I was surprised to be asked to serve on the committee. In my simplicity I attributed my nomination to the spirited intervention I had made on the question of psychological tests for confessors. At that time I was completing my book *Priest and Penitent*. Doubtless I had given the audience the fruits of my research on the relative roles of confessors and psychologists. In the book I had made clear that the penitent's prie-dieu had little in common with the psychiatrist's couch. I was certainly mistaken in thinking that I had been chosen on the strength of my contribution to the discussions. The reason was, of course, my contact with Archbishop Hinsley. It was necessary for the new society to have, in addition to a heavenly patron, an earthly supporter among the bishops. Dr. Strauss and his friends doubtless thought that having me as a member of the committee would help towards this end. I had been so little impressed by the Oxford meeting that I did not agree to serve. Dr. Strauss was disappointed at my refusal and asked me to reconsider my decision.

It was now that I conceived my final and, as it turned out, successful plan for gaining entry to the U.S.S.R. I decided to enlist the help of Dr. Strauss. I told him that I felt it my duty to obtain first-hand evidence of conditions under the Soviet dictatorship. Communism was gaining converts, I thought, only because its true nature was unknown. Marxist propaganda could not be refuted merely by theoretical counter-argument. That was why I proposed to visit the U.S.S.R. I felt it would be easy to pose as a psychologist. I asked Dr. Strauss if he would be willing to write to the Soviet government requesting facilities for his colleague Dr. Heenan. Eric Strauss agreed without hesitation. He saw at once the advantage of having reliable information about the war on religious freedom and the rights of man in Soviet Russia. He sent me a suitable recommendation to use at the appropriate time.

I spent the next few months planning my strategy. In 1936 an intending visitor to Russia had no difficulty in securing a visa unless he were a known critic of the Soviet regime. Then and at all times the Soviet government rarely refused a visa to intending tourists. If an applicant were regarded as undesirable he would simply be left without an answer to his application. At that time it would have been futile for a Catholic priest to have applied for a visa. I gave a great deal of thought to the question of changing my name. In the end I decided that it would be too great a risk to use a fictitious name. It was not difficult to obtain a fresh passport which gave my profession as lecturer in philosophy. To give false personal details is, of course, illegal but I was about to embark on a series of rather more serious deceptions. Looking ahead to my stay in Russia I had to take into account the possibility of an emergency in which my credentials would be questioned. In a delicate or dangerous situation I might become confused and forget my assumed name. I therefore decided to use my correct name when making my first approach to Intourist, the sole agency authorised to handle travel arrangements in the U.S.S.R. There was no problem about an address. All my communications to Intourist were on writing paper carrying an adopted address and telephone number. I felt fairly sure that the Russians would not bother to investigate if they had only to pick up a telephone to check my bona fides. My name did not appear in any telephone directory. I thought it unlikely that the Russians would connect me with the Rev. J.C. Heenan of Barking in the unlikely event of their examining the electoral roll. Meanwhile I operated from Reddington Road, Hampstead, the address of my friend Wilfred Eyre. Everyone in his house was instructed in the event of a call from Intourist to say that I had gone out but would telephone Intourist as soon as I returned home. As I had anticipated no call ever came.

I thought it prudent nevertheless to give Intourist little excuse for ringing the Hampstead number. To this end I made frequent visits to the Intourist offices in Bush House, Aldwych. These calls had no object other than to make me a familiar figure to the Intourist staff. Since I was so available there would be no need for them to make enquiries. I used to be driven up to London by Jim Graffy, a Barking parishioner who had retired young from the building trade and was delighted to be of service to any of the priests. He asked no questions but assumed that I had some good reason for supping with the devil. In the absence of a long spoon I used to exchange my clerical collar for a soft collar and tie each time the car drew near Bush House. For reasons of security I told the smallest possible number of people of my impending visit to the Soviet Union. I always kept in mind the possibility of being arrested in Russia. Stalin's great purge was reaching its height in 1936. In a macabre way the purge worked to my advantage. During the Stalin reign of terror Soviet citizens were watching each other much more closely than foreigners. It sounds melodramatic now but it seemed prudent at the time to picture myself in prison with nobody belonging to me aware that I was in Russia. I had a vague feeling that this might give me a better chance of bluffing my way out of trouble. To provide an alibi I wrote a series of postcards to my parents, Canon Cameron and other friends. I arranged for these to be posted in France and Italy at intervals during October 1936 when I expected to be inside the U.S.S.R. I imagined that if these postcards from Father Heenan could be produced the Soviets would release Mr. John Heenan in Moscow. It is just as well that my theory was never put to the test. I was, indeed, briefly in custody in Moscow but this was in circumstances which had nothing to do with my clerical status.

Cardinal Hinsley had been aware of my intention to visit Russia since my first fruitless efforts. He had approved the journey and given me permission to leave my Roman collar and breviary at home. I was canonically out of order in not consulting my own bishop but the cardinal agreed that this would be unwise. The cardinal gave me his blessing and promised to explain everything to my bishop when I was safely out of Russia. Today it is no more difficult to visit Russia than the U.S.A. or India but the Russia of Stalin was like the China of Mao Tse Tung. Fears now sound superfluous but in 1936 the Bolsheviks were still associated with cloaks and daggers. John Dixey, an enthusiastic convert and most discreet solicitor, was also kept informed of my plans. If anything went wrong he was to telephone my family and Canon Cameron (who by that time would have received my postcards). There were no other precautions I could take. I was puzzled over one small detail. I did not know how to pay Intourist for my tickets. I was afraid if I paid by cheque that their suspicions might be aroused. They might wonder why my bank was in Barking if I lived in Hampstead. If Wilfred Eyre were to write a Hampstead cheque in exchange for my Barking one this equally might create suspicion. Would not a psychologist possess a cheque book of his own? I solved the problem by making yet another needless visit to Bush House. I paid the bill in pound notes. The astonished clerk asked why I had not sent a cheque. I replied that I had been told that the Soviet government would not accept cheques from foreigners. He gave me a sharp look and told me not to believe silly stories about Soviet Russia.

In addition to boat and rail tickets I was given a book of service vouchers. This contained a coupon for every meal I was to eat during the coming weeks in the Soviet Union. After the war this would not have seemed strange but in 1936 it was very odd. There were three for each day—breakfast, dinner and supper. In addition there was a daily sightseeing coupon which entitled the bearer to transport and an Intourist guide. The client was informed that no guide, waiter or hotel servant required or expected tips. There was no need to take any cash but if roubles were needed during my stay I would be able to change money at my hotel. There was not—nor is there to this day—any quotation for the rouble on the international market. The official rate of exchange in Moscow is fictitious—in 1936 it was twenty-five roubles to the pound sterling. (I was to discover in Moscow that resident foreigners had little difficulty in finding a black market rate of exchange which represented real values.) Once I had my tickets and vouchers I felt that I had entered a strange world. On any other journey I would already have been in touch with my destination. I would have chosen hotels and planned itineraries. About to set out for Russia I did not even know the names of the hotels at which I would be staying. My passport would have to be surrendered and would not be returned to me until I was about to leave Soviet territory. I felt that I was setting out for a very alien land.

The few days before my departure were full of small but vexing problems. I did not want to give Canon Cameron or the housekeeper in the presbytery reason for doubting that I was about to leave for Italy. I could not therefore buy my lay clothes until the last moment. Just before leaving I bought 'off the peg' a natty gent's suit in slate blue twill. Ties and socks of a suitably striking but matching shade were locked away with the suit so that the housekeeper's curiosity would not lead to awkward questions. Already I was finding it hard to parry the Canon's enquiries about the details of my journey. I was afraid almost to the last moment that in his hospitable way he might offer to give me a meal in London before seeing me off on the continental train from Victoria station. I was able to avoid this complication by telling him that I would be spending the first day of my holiday with Marney and Wilfred Eyre. This, indeed, was true. As part of our plan of campaign a day had been set aside for a rehearsal of my masquerade as a layman. The Eyres were to watch closely to see if by word or mannerism I was likely to betray my clerical identity. The programme for the day had been worked out with no little thought by Wilfred.

Early in the morning of 6th October the faithful Jim Graffy arrived at the presbytery in his little car. He took me to the house of Vivian Stevens, an old friend from school days, who lived in Snaresbrook, Essex. Like John Dixey he was a lawyer in whose discretion I had full confidence. I needed a half-way house because I could not leave Barking in lay clothes. Transformed into a layman I took a train from Snaresbrook to London where Wilfred Eyre awaited me. We went to his club which I had not previously visited. He introduced me to one or two people presumably to see if I could remember how a layman conducts himself. He was afraid I might question them on their beliefs or ask the Catholics if they had been to Mass last Sunday. In fact I had no temptation to resume pastoral work. After lunch we met Marney who insisted on taking me shopping in case I had forgotten anything necessary to a layman's wardrobe. This was typical of a woman's practical outlook. There were, of course, a number of purchases to be made. Marney then produced a most useful gift for my journey. It was a midget camera in an unobtrusive case like a tobacco pouch. The similarity was so close that in Russia I usually carried a pipe with the camera. I did not take pictures of any lasting value but the camera proved its worth on more than one occasion.

I had made up my mind to travel to the U.S.S.R. on a Soviet boat. I wanted to become accustomed to a Soviet atmosphere before arriving in Russia. For three weeks I was going to be an actor in a play. Three or four days on the boat would give me time to practise playing the character of a layman. I took for granted that my fellow passengers would be mostly Russian. I also had an idea that I might be able to detect on board whether the Communists had pierced my disguise. If I thought from the demeanour of the crew that I was suspect it might be possible to jump ship as we passed through the Kiel canal. In retrospect these fears seem exaggerated but as the time came nearer the whole enterprise began to appear foolhardy. Wilfred Eyre had organised the day in London so that there was little time for brooding. When we had finished shopping he took me to the Palladium music hall. I do not recall the title of the revue but for those days it was a daring kind of show. Wilfred Eyre had decided that my metamorphosis would be accelerated by the Palladium's bright bill of fare. I remember little of the performance beyond the fact that the stage became the deck of a battleship. The actors were in fancy dress naval uniforms. The chorus was decent by modern standards but more scantily clad than fashion permitted when I had been a theatregoer. I have kept a letter which Wilfred sent me on 11th October c/o Intourist Moscow. It was a reply to my thank-you note posted at Kiel. Here is an extract which recaptures the mood of that day:

> The day after you left Marney and I went to a performance of a very different nature to the one we attended with you. It was Oedipus Rex at Covent Garden. We had felt it a positive duty to do this since a tragedy by Sophocles is not (fortunately) a thing one can see every day of the week. I'm afraid the show at the Palladium was not of a very elevating character but I did think it was very suitable indeed that the scenes depicting episodes in the history of the Senior Service should have been balanced by that amazing navel·(sic) display in the other half of the programme. Anyway we all had some good laughs and the whole day in London was vastly entertaining if rather exhausting.

At about 11 p.m. the Eyres took me to Hayes Wharf. It was ill-lit and the Russian boat looked as gloomy as the ships which were not preparing to sail. A sailor scrutinised my ticket and checked my name with a list held by a civilian whom I recognised as one of the men from Bush House. They did not have about them any air of this-is-the-man-we-have-been-waiting-for. It seemed reassuringly clear that to them I was just another passenger. The Eyres were not allowed to accompany me on board. There was none of the party spirit which I associate with Southampton or New York at a sailing. My friends having been dismissed I found myself feeling very much alone but it was obvious even if the Soviets had discovered I was a priest that nothing would happen until we had arrived within Russian territorial waters. I therefore went without fear to my cabin and was asleep before midnight.

Next morning for the first time in my life I had caviar for breakfast. There were about twenty passengers of whom only one other was English. He was Mr. Parkinson, consultant engineer of a firm building a bridge for the Soviet government. The rest of my fellow passengers, all American citizens, were Russian Jews on their way home to visit relatives. The Russians, most of whom were enthusiastic communists, behaved like Moslems on pilgrimage to Mecca. During their few hours in London instead of seeing the Houses of Parliament, Buckingham Palace or even Madame Tussauds they had gone down to the East End. Their object had not been to visit Jewish friends in Whitechapel but to see the degradation of the poor under British imperialism. Communism was their sole interest. The first day at sea I spent learning further lists of Russian words which I thought might prove useful. I had already learned the Russian alphabet and a few stock phrases. Without being able to read Russian words a visitor is at a serious disadvantage in the Soviet Union. It is impossible for example, to read the name of a street.

In the afternoon we took on a German pilot to guide us through the Kiel canal. I spent about an hour on the bridge talking to him before one of the ship's officers decided that I was breaking the rules and ordered me to leave the bridge. It would not have entered my head to invade the bridge of an English or American ship. I suppose it is the prerogative of foreigners everywhere to break rules. I have penetrated many forbidden places abroad by displaying a foreigner's ignorance. We must entertain many innocents from abroad who invade secret places to which we would not dare to go. The only thing I learned from the German pilot—except his contempt for the Soviets—is, I suppose, known to most schoolboys. He gave all instructions to the Russian seamen in English and the engine room answered in the same language. I had not known that English is still the language of the sea. When we stopped in the canal we were offered duty-free tobacco and spirits. I bought three bottles of whisky for one pound. It was not only a remarkably good bargain but a most valuable investment. When I managed at last to establish some rapport with the Russian passengers I invited the men to my cabin. Encouraged by the excellent Scotch whisky they became friendly and talkative.

There were two in particular who interested me greatly. Jack Ross, gentle and sad, was in business in Chicago. A year earlier his wife had died of cancer in a hospital run by nuns and he was still suffering her loss keenly. Without being aware of my religious beliefs he spoke in terms of highest praise of the Catholic Sisters. He said that although a Jew he had to describe them as Christlike. Those who, like his companions on board, attacked religion did not understand what they condemned. He was going to Moscow with an open mind. Unlike the rest of his party who were on their way to their promised land he was prepared for both pleasant and unpleasant experiences. I did not cross-examine him but guessed that he had information about conditions inside the Soviet Union of which his fellow travellers were unaware. He already sensed the stress under which Soviet citizens were living. His family had emigrated from Russia in 1913 to escape the endemic Russian anti-semitism. In the time of the Czars no Jew was allowed to live in St. Petersburg (Leningrad). I told him I was anxious to discover the facts about life in Moscow. He promised to keep in touch with me after we had landed and to give me whatever information he might pick up. His family's Jewish name had been changed to Ross for business reasons. Two weeks later I was to meet some of the Rosenbergs in their own homes. By that time Ross and I had become trusted friends. He was one of the most intelligent and compassionate men I have ever met.

The other man with whom I became acquainted on board was a young dentist from New York called Sam Levett. He was a crusading communist. He kept giving me books and pamphlets about the glories of the Soviet Union. He and his pretty companion Rosie had made up their minds to apply for Soviet citizenship. Sam had brought with him a great quantity of gold to use for bridge-work, a dental art in which he said Americans excel. He had an astonishing knowledge of communist history and literature. A first-class apologist, he reminded me of the trained controversialists with whom I had worked as an adolescent in the Catholic Evidence Guild. There was no question to which they could not give answers which were at least plausible. This man being patently honest obviously suffered mental torture. As a Jew he wanted to be proud of Trotsky but as an orthodox communist he was bound to vilify him. Sipping whisky in my cabin he would tell me almost tearfully what a tragedy it had been for Trotsky to have missed Lenin's funeral. In a fit of pique or pride he had refused to put himself out to be with Lenin at the end. Had he attended the funeral there would have been no Stalin succession and therefore no feud between the heirs of Lenin. He did not, of course, say a word in criticism of Stalin. As a good apologist he was able to find explanations for all Stalin's actions. Even the slaughter of the peasants, though less desirable than the liquidation of the Kulaks, could be justified. He, like Jack Ross, agreed to meet me after we had spent some time in Moscow. He felt sure that after a few days he would have gathered sufficient proof of Soviet progress to convert me. In the event it was poor Levett who became the convert. When we met two weeks later he had become, as we shall see, quite disillusioned. Neither he nor Rosie was destined to apply for Soviet citizenship.

Apart from continuing to add to my smattering of Russian I made good use of the time on board by talking to Levett and reading communist literature including the life of Stalin by Henri Barbousse. What fascinated me about Levett was his ability to rationalise everything Stalin had ever said and done. This convinced me that for the real enthusiast communism is a religion. Levett would react to criticism of Stalin as an intelligent Catholic might react to an attack on the Pope. Stalin, he explained, being only human could not always achieve perfection but the system itself was infallibly right. When I pointed out inconsistencies in the Soviet system, its inequalities and its crimes against human dignity, Sam only smiled. Neither he nor anyone in Soviet Russia pretended that communism had yet arrived. The U.S.S.R. was in transit to the ideal world. It was not possible in one generation to undo all the evils of capitalism. Because self-interest remained the State sometimes had to act violently to protect the proletariat. Stalin's new economic policy (N.E.P.) was in no way a reversion to capitalist methods. It was a policy dictated by prudent statesmanship—an example of *reculer pour mieux sauter*.

Communists did not pretend that all men are equal in talent but only that all men have an equal right to develop their talents and enjoy the fruits of their own labour. No man had the right to exploit another. State ownership of the means of production was the essential basis from which socialism must be built. Socialism itself is only a stage in social progress on the way to true and full communism. The next step of the abolition of class would be the establishment of complete equality in providing for the needs of all citizens. Unfortunately the party had to employ police (including secret police) to combat capitalists and saboteurs. The state must punish the selfish but sanctions would eventually become unnecessary and the state itself would wither away. It was obvious that Sam believed all this as firmly as Christians believe that we have here no lasting city but seek one which is to come. What theologians call the eschatological outlook is common to all religions. The difference is that communists look for a lasting city here below. They scorn the pie in the sky of believers. Talking to this young man I realised that a communist has greater need for childlike faith than any Christian.

I did not intend to engage in religious arguments inside the Soviet Union so I was glad to have this preview of a Russian communist's outlook on religion. I had always assumed that the Czarist Orthodox Church, so notoriously Erastian, was a more powerful incentive to anti-religious feeling than the Leninist dogma that religion is the opium of the people. It seems that I was wrong. Levett had an angry contempt for personal religion of any kind. To him religion was part of the capitalist system which had to be destroyed as a matter of routine. He found it repulsive that a man should degrade human actions with religious motives. Far from being impressed he was outraged by the Sisters who had nursed the dying Mrs. Ross. They should have been ready to look after Jack's wife, he said, from love of humanity not for love of a mythical God. Persecution of religion was necessary for the salvation of the people. Now that only the old were believers there would be less need to continue the anti-religious crusade in Soviet Russia.

Levett used one argument against religion that was new to me although thirty years later the argument was to become common. He contended that the U.S.S.R. was the only peace-loving nation on earth. Russia needed peace in order to achieve stability. All war, he said, is based on economic factors. Through artificial scarcity capitalists create demand and make their fortunes (the notorious destruction of thirty-two million bags of Brazilian coffee was adduced as proof). The alternative way of making money was through war. Stalin would never willingly wage war. "We do not want a foot of anyone else's land but we will not yield an inch of our own." That, according to Levett, was Stalin's slogan. Now came the nub of the argument. Religion is a way not of peace but of unhealthy pacifism. Both Christ and Gandhi betrayed the cause of peace. Christ told the people to turn the other cheek while Gandhi preached non-violent resistance. Both betrayed the masses. Progress can come only through revolution and demands a relentless struggle against the existing world order. Religion prevents progress because by opposing violence it teaches acquiescence in evil. That is why Marxism must destroy religion in whatever guise it may appear.

By the time the voyage was nearing its end I had become so interested in my new acquaintances that I was sorry the party was about to break up. I realised that my decision to take the boat instead of the train to Russia would pay an uncovenanted bonus. My

Russian friends with relatives in Moscow might become my eyes and ears. I did not know if Levett would trust me sufficiently to give me an account of his conversations with his family but I was certain that Ross would pass on whatever he learned. Talking to foreign residents in Moscow later I heard how impossible it was for them to make contact with Soviet citizens apart from their servants (appointed by the state) and the officials with whom they did business. Few of them had been inside a worker's home. The only houses they were invited to visit were official residences or the dachas (country cottages) of party officials and senior executives. To become socially involved with Soviet citizens was inadvisable for people in the diplomatic service or on business missions. For the citizens it would have been positively dangerous. It was my good fortune on the boat to make friends with Russians who were no longer Russian citizens.

On the last night of the voyage the captain made his first appearance in the dining room. He sat at the table which Parkinson and I shared. It was not a very lively social occasion. Mr. Parkinson and I had little in common. Our conversation at meals went little beyond the usual English routine condemnation of the weather and the government. He did not speak of his affairs nor I of mine. By the end of the journey we had formed the habit of eating our meals at great speed and almost in silence. The captain did not prove to be a dazzling conversationalist. He offered no comments beyond apologies for leaving it until the last night to visit his guests. In answer to a question he said that he was not a Russian but a Latvian. I noticed that unlike the other officers his uniform carried no little red flag on the epaulet. I asked if this was because of his rank. He replied that the clash of red, gold and blue offended him aesthetically. He added that he liked good cloth and had his uniforms made in London. It is quite likely that as a Latvian he also detested the Soviets. The captain did not eat with us because he had already eaten his supper. After a few minutes a sailor came—no doubt by arrangement—to say that the captain's presence was urgently requested on the bridge. The captain heard this without surprise but with evident gratification. He told us that we should be docking in a few hours. He hoped that we had enjoyed the trip. We arrived at the pierhead in Leningrad at 10.30 p.m. on the night of Sunday 11th October, 1936.

I am always suspicious of memoirs which reproduce in direct speech conversations alleged to have been held thirty years earlier. I am referring to the accounts of what his grandfather said to the author then aged ten. I shall not make any attempt to reproduce the exact words of those who spoke to me during my stay in the U.S.S.R. except on those occasions when I was able to make notes within a short time of the actual encounter. I shall relate in its proper place that for some time I had the services of a trained stenographer. This American lady acted as my unoffical secretary and took shorthand notes of some conversations. I was thus able to keep the account of my journey which enables me to reproduce details of what was said and done. For my experiences in Leningrad I have only the notes I compiled each night. I did not meet the stenographer until I reached Moscow.

I made my way from the boat with some trepidation. It might soon be revealed that my identity as a priest was already known to the Soviet authorities. I felt reassured when the customs officers dealt with me courteously and quickly. They carried out only a perfunctory examination of my luggage. Mr. Parkinson's baggage received the same treatment. Our Jewish friends from the United States were not so favoured. They were made to turn out every suitcase and answer a litany of questions. I could not help noticing the astonished chagrin of poor Levett. He had not expected a red carpet or even red flags but he had taken for granted that a son returning to Mother Russia would be accorded a rather warmer and more gracious welcome. He had particular trouble over the gold he had so unselfishly brought for his dental work. The customs men were clearly suspicious of his motives. The gold apparently marked him down as a capitalist. It was past midnight before our small group was taken to a hotel.

To my amazement the hotel dining room was crowded with people queuing for tables. This was my introduction to Soviet—or, perhaps, merely Russian—social customs. In London a restaurant at midnight is like an empty tomb. I learned that the following day (Monday) was Rest Day. Since they would not have to be up early next morning clients did not mind waiting half the night for food. Since this was my first view of Russians in the mass I spent a fascinating two hours just watching. There was no smart-set look about them though they were obviously dressed in their Sunday (Rest Day?) best. What struck me most was their patience. The service in this hotel was the slowest I had ever seen. This was not in any sense a personal complaint—everywhere I went in Russia foreigners were given preferential service. Whether this is part of the undoubted Russian charm or a dictate of Soviet policy it makes travellers feel that they are honoured guests. I retired at 2 a.m. Mr. Parkinson, who did not go to bed until 4 o'clock, told me next day that the crowds had not dispersed when he departed.

The next day being Rest Day we were spared any sightseeing tours. This suited me well because I felt it wise to follow the Intourist programme at first in order not to draw attention to myself. In the absence of a tour I was able to spend this first day walking round the streets trying to capture the Soviet atmosphere. Leningrad, though by now a run-down city, remained elegant by virtue of its beautiful wide streets. Literally palatial buildings were in a state of decay because the whole economic emphasis was still on heavy industry. The Soviets had not yet begun to pay any attention to amenities. During my tour of the city I found a drabness not wholly due to the sameness of dress. People looked expressionless but obviously I could not tell if this was only because Russians being Slavs have oriental impassivity in their faces. The children out walking with their parents were as gay, noisy and neatly dressed as any in London. I walked down side streets and found that like side streets in any western city they were less clean and attractive. I was surprised to find a market where women up from the country were selling fruit and vegetables. I had been under the impression that even such modest private trading had been abolished. I learned later that such commerce though tolerated is not encouraged.

I passed no less than two Catholic churches both of which were closed. I learned later that one Catholic church in Leningrad is allowed to function but a priest is not always available. I did not see any Orthodox church but if I had walked down the right streets—as I did before leaving Leningrad—I would have discovered them and also found them open. In the afternoon I strolled down the magnificent Nevski Prospekt where all tourists go. Here I was given my second surprise of the day when two urchins aged about twelve accosted me asking for cigarettes. They knew I was a foreigner by my clothes and addressed me in German. Their learner's vocabulary just about matched my own. After cigarettes they asked me for money since being English I must be rich. They had been taught in school that in England everyone is rich except the workers and they are unemployed. "*Hier*," said one of the small boys, "*haben wir Arbeit aber kein Gelt; im England haben sie keine Arbeit aber viel Gelt*"

(Here we have work and no money; in England you have plenty of money but no work). I had no intention of giving them money but, in any case, there was no opportunity to do so. At this moment two men approached and the children fled. Begging is against the law in Russia as in most countries. This unattractive law is better observed in the Soviet Union than elsewhere in Europe.

In the evening I went to a ballet which though splendid I found uncomfortably long. In Russia love of the ballet is rivalled only by love of chess. This is more a Russian than a communist trait. In Czarist days the workers and peasants could not afford tickets for the ballet but they knew the music. Tickets are expensive but most of the audience watching *Esmeralda* that night had the faces of workers. In those days in Russia nobody dressed up to go to the theatre. Knowing that wages were low I wondered how it was possible for so many workers to buy tickets for the ballet. The Intourist guide told me that factories buy blocks of seats for the most deserving workers. During the next two weeks I learned a great deal about the genuine thirst for culture among the workers. I could not imagine many of my parishioners in Barking jumping for joy on receiving a ticket for Sadlers Wells in lieu of a cash bonus. Here people were anxious to fit themselves to enjoy the cultural amenities which for centuries had been the monopoly of the rich. The word 'culture' was to be heard everywhere. Even the recreation grounds were given the title 'parks of rest and culture'. (I was told that wags refer to them as parks of rest from culture.)

After the ballet I had a long talk with one of the receptionists in the hotel. Business was slack and she was studying. It happened that her subject was English and she gladly availed herself of my help. She had been set the task of writing a letter to an imaginary pen friend in England. The task was quickly accomplished and we talked of family life in the Soviet Union. She was a very intelligent young woman. Russia, she said, was going through a phase which eventually would come to every country. It was the conflict between young and old. By this she meant much more than what a quarter of a century later we called the generation gap. There has always been mutual intolerance between the young and old. The Russian phenomenon, according to this young lady, had a deeper significance. Children in school and adolescents in club or party meetings were indoctrinated with atheism. This led to angry discussions in the home. The older generation (people over forty), even if they were no longer believers, objected to the anarchy of young people. In her view about half the people in Russia were still believers. The proportion was much higher among moujiks (peasants) than workers.

The following morning I continued to follow the Intourist trail. We visited the Hermitage and the Winter Garden. However decayed its buildings there was no doubt about the loving care Leningrad lavished on its works of art. We enjoyed a feast of painting. Rembrandt, Van Dyck, Raphael and Murillo were all there. The glories of old St. Petersburg have not all faded. It would have been pleasant to spend all day in the galleries but I had to keep my objective always before my mind. In the afternoon I abandoned sightseeing to begin to play my role of psychologist. I went to the Leningrad clinic of experimental medicine. I carried with me the official chit assuring me of co-operation in my research. I was fortunate in being allowed to visit Pavlov's laboratories. When I first read his studies of conditioned reflexes I had not thought that one day his animals would be demonstrated for my benefit. The professor who had taken Pavlov's place must have been almost as old as his master. Pavlov himself had died only a few weeks before my visit. The son of a priest, Pavlov had not taken kindly to communism. For years he had refused to collaborate. He returned to work in his old laboratory only in 1933 when he was already eighty-four years old. (The old man now in charge looked so like Pavlov that for years I was under the impression that it was Pavlov I had seen. It is the Russian way not to release bad news quickly. Hence while I was in Russia Pavlov's death had not yet been announced.) I was fascinated by the old professor—more by the man than by his pigeons, mice and dogs. His long white beard gave him the appearance of a patriarch. He looked and sounded so unutterably bored that I wondered if he was staying on at the institute because he lacked resources to live in retirement. It was very difficult to follow his patter. This was partly because he spoke French into his beard with a thick Russian accent and partly because I ostentatiously paid scant attention to his explanations in order to give the impression of being completely familiar with conditioned reflexes. I regret to say that my French did not stand up well to the strain of discussing psychology with a Pavlovian practitioner. I had read a little psychology in Italian but none at all in French. I did not even know the French for 'reflex'. (On returning to England I consulted a dictionary to discover that the French for reflex is *reflexe*.) The man from Intourist appointed to accompany me was happily unaware of my poor showing. The professor attributed it—as I intended—to the language difficulty.

Before leaving Leningrad I also visited the Institute of Psychiatry. This I did less in search of knowledge than to impress Intourist. Assuming that reports on clients were sent to the Soviet Home Office I thought it wise to establish my bona fides fully in Leningrad. That would leave me free to go where I wished during my two weeks in Moscow. There was nothing of note to be seen in the Institute. It was, in fact, a rather old-fashioned lunatic asylum. I saw the director and showed him the letter of Dr. Strauss (of whom he had heard). He told me that they do not believe in psychoanalysis in Soviet Russia. They had no belief in such methods but relied on blood tests and the study of conditioned reflexes. He took me to the wards and left me alone with the patients. I felt nervous. Before tranquillising drugs were used in psychological medicine it was difficult enough to control patients speaking one's own language. My few weeks with Hugo's Rapid Russian Course had scarcely equipped me to control Russian lunatics. I did not, of course, display any anxiety because mental patients react in some ways like young children. Smiles, handshakes and friendly gestures readily win their approval and keep them calm. So it proved with these poor patients. I had no cause for alarm. (The only occasion on which I ever felt actual fear in a psychiatric ward was some years later when at the famous Johns Hopkins Hospital in Baltimore I found myself in a room with three homicidal maniacs one of whom had killed a man a few days earlier.)

The next day I visited the Catholic church. I found about twenty old or middle-aged people praying before the altar where the Blessed Sacrament was reserved. When I revisited the Soviet Union thirty years later I found rather more people praying in churches. They were still mostly old or middle-aged—doubtless the children of the people I had seen in 1936. Evidently the Soviet theory that religion would die with the older generation had not proved true. But it is not surprising that the communists were so confident of their ability to stamp out religion. Even young mothers had to work in factories or clean the streets (in 1936 there were no male road-sweepers in the U.S.S.R.) while their children were looked after in creches. In their scant leisure hours parents had to undergo political education. It would have been difficult to find time for studying religion or going to church and, in any case, the abolition of Sundays in favour of

Rest Days virtually killed Mass attendance in the towns. I was told that in the country peasants often ignored the official Rest Day and continued to observe Sunday as the day of rest. When I returned to the Soviet Union after the second world war Sunday had once more become the official day of rest.

One day I went to an Orthodox church. It must have been an Orthodox feast day because the crowds were so great that it was hard to squeeze into the building. In the afternoon I took a tram (quite an adventure because of overcrowding) and returned to the same church in the hope of being able to talk to the priests. I had seen them at Mass in the morning but obviously could not approach them. There were still many people in church mostly grouped round shrines or ikons. I approached two or three priests but none could speak any language but Russian. I tried English, French and my rudimentary German. I thought it imprudent in the circumstances to try them in Latin. In return for my efforts I received a piece of blessed bread but no information. At the time I attributed this to their ignorance of any language but their own. I assumed that the Russian Church found it impossible to recruit educated men to the ranks of the clergy. It was only in Moscow that I learned what risks Soviet citizens ran by having communication of any kind with foreigners. These priests may have had to pretend to be unable to speak to me. Even in church they were under the surveillance of the secret police. (In 1964 I was a guest in Zagorsk monastery near Moscow and found little difficulty in carrying on conversation with the monks. At Zagorsk dozens of monks, young and old, spoke French or English.)

Returning from church I decided to look up my Jewish friends who were staying at the Hotel Europa. I found Levett and Rosie sitting at a table near the hotel entrance. Their expressions were so lugubrious that I knew before asking any questions that they were disappointed in their Promised Land. Levett told me that far from being welcomed by his Soviet colleagues he had been practically insulted. They regarded him not as an ally but a rival. This Yankee, they evidently felt, had come to teach these backward moujiks. Furthermore they were suspicious that a man with all that gold wanted to throw in his lot with them. He was unlikely to be satisfied to live in one room like the rest of them. As for Rosie her reception had been even less heart-warming. Her interviewers had observed her with the critical disdain of women scrutinising a woman. Rosie was dressed in a stylish fur coat. By Soviet standards she was simply a svelte upper-class foreigner. She had nothing to offer the Soviets since typists in the U.S.S.R. were in greater supply than typewriters. As Sam was describing her experiences poor Rosie burst into tears and ran out of the hotel. I never saw her or Sam again. Soon after arriving in Moscow they had paid a visit to their relatives and, glad not to have surrendered their American citizenship, hurried gratefully home to capitalist New York.

That evening Jack Ross and I went to a performance of *La Tosca*. In this opera, as in the ballet two nights previously, the villain was a bishop. This could happen anywhere today but in 1936 prelates were still highly regarded in the West. Ross explained that the old plays, operas and ballets had all been re-geared for purposes of propaganda. Heroes were no longer brave soldiers or beautiful princesses but commissars or Stakhanovites (i.e. factory hands who produced more than their allotted norm.) Villains were capitalists, Trotskyites or clerics. The playing, singing and acting were superb. Wherever else the revolution may have failed it had not allowed Russian artistic standards to fall. The only branch of art in which the Soviets seemed to have produced nothing of quality is painting. Whether this is due to lack of inspiration or to the absence of any national tradition I could not say. Despite the quality of costumes and scenery the opera house lacked atmosphere. The audience was appreciative and critical —they thought the soprano too shrill and accorded her only modified applause. But there was none of the elegance of patrons of opera in the West. Near me in the grand circle some young women were eating bread. The poor girls had probably come to the theatre straight from the factory.

The next morning I spent in a school. The director (head teacher) was an Esthonian. He received us courteously but without enthusiasm. One or two of the best schools are doubtless selected for inspection by tourists and this unfortunate man was probably subjected to constant invasions. There were few differences between this school and the pre-war English all-age mixed school. Since that time there have been radical changes in the educational system both in England and the Soviet Union. One has to be reminded that in 1936 what we took for granted in England the Russians found excitingly new. Probably the greatest achievement of the Soviets has been the abolition of illiteracy. Before the revolution there were less than eight million children in school. By 1936 there were over thirty million. This figure may still appear unimpressive for such a vast country but it was not reached without brave improvisation. The use of school buildings was doubled by making them provide for two sets of scholars. The shift system of factories was simply transferred to schools. Education in every grade was free. Academically gifted children—at least in the cities—pass from high school to university. Those not considered fit to follow university courses are withdrawn from their places of work for a certain number of hours each week for further education. There are no small boys selling newspapers or working as page boys as in England. If all Soviet enterprise had achieved such social justice there would not have been so much misery in Stalin's Russia.

I asked the director the purpose of the 'Lenin corners' I noticed in each department of the school. He told me they were for purposes of culture and reflection. They were not unlike shrines in Catholic schools. In place of white linen a red cloth; in place of the crucifix a picture of Marx, Lenin, Engels or Stalin. Communism in Soviet schools performs the same kind of function as religion in a church school in this country. No doubt many Soviet parents complain that too much time is wasted on political education. No doubt they find it deplorable that communism gives a slant to every subject in the curriculum. Communist youth are regimented from infancy until far beyond adolescence. From the age of four a child with the right family background (not of bourgeois or Kulak stock) becomes an Octobret (the name commemorates the October revolution). At the age of nine children graduate to the Pioneers. When they are sixteen they are made members of the Komsomol. They retain this status—provided they keep up their political studies—until after their twenty-sixth birthday when they become eligible for party membership. I had seen the same pattern of youth regimentation during my years in Italy where infants joined the Balilla, proceeded to the ranks of the Giovanni Fascisti and eventually acquired full party membership.

Two features of school life were especially noteworthy. Firstly, girls as well as boys were instructed in woodwork and elementary engineering. Secondly, a woman doctor was employed full time in every school. She had to examine each child every term as well as provide first aid in emergencies. The regulations for all Soviet schools require the director to see each pupil privately at least once a quarter. Much of what I saw has now gone from the Soviet educational system. Schools in modern Russia are bigger and rarely co-educational. Experience has shown that girls suffered from not being trained in specifically womanly arts. It was also thought that mixed schools had a bad effect on the academic work of the boys.

We took the evening train to Moscow. I was resolved to waste no time visiting psychiatric clinics. My Intourist credentials said: "Mr. Heenan is particularly interested in psychological clinics and we shall be obliged if you will give him special facilities for visiting these." I felt that I had established myself sufficiently by touring the Leningrad clinics. I could now set aside all fears that my identity had been discovered. With two weeks before me I intended not to waste a minute. I would begin by making the tourist rounds to disarm suspicion still further. After a couple of days sightseeing I would concentrate on seeking information. I was especially anxious to discover the extent of religious persecution and the suppression of freedom. Unfortunately I had no clear idea of how to go about my search. I had no names, no addresses, no letters of introduction. My only lead (it turned out to be false) was to the French embassy. I had once been told that an old bishop, Mgr. Neveu, was living there in retirement (he had disappeared years before).

In the twenties a priest was alleged to have gone from Rome to live in Moscow. The Bolsheviks had granted permission in recognition of the fact that the Holy See had ordered the sale of chalices and other religious objects for the relief of victims of the Russian famine which followed the first world war. According to the story I had heard while a student in Rome this priest broke his journey in Berlin where he stayed with the Papal Nuncio. The following morning in his private chapel the Nuncio had consecrated him bishop so that while he was in the U.S.S.R. he, in turn, could consecrate bishops from among the dwindling number of priests. Thus it was hoped to preserve the priesthood for the scattered Catholic flock at a time when life and liberty were precarious for clergy. It was my recollection that the only surviving bishop had been offered asylum by the French embassy. This whole story may have been fictitious and in any case I did not know if the bishop were still alive and in Moscow. Clearly I had no reliable source of information awaiting me in the Soviet capital.

CHAPTER
FIVE

THE JOURNEY FROM LENINGRAD TO MOSCOW WAS COMFORTABLE AND uneventful. The only odd incident took place at bed-time. In those days the Soviet authorities allotted bunks to men and women indiscriminately. This was not to promote promiscuity but simply the failure of one of the world's most incompetent bureaucracies to solve the simple problem of sorting out passengers according to sex when allotting sleeping compartments. There were three men and one woman in our compartment. We were all English. A much-travelled young man with red hair who was on his way to the Far East advised the lady against lodging a protest. A celebrated woman traveller, he said, had once complained, only to be told that if she could share a tent with male elephants in the desert she had no grounds for complaint at having male humans in her compartment. We solved our problem by vacating the compartment while the lady was undressing and waiting until she was asleep (or at least had her eyes closed) before going to bed ourselves. I do not recall what happened the next morning. The much-travelled young man with red hair bade us farewell at Moscow station and begged us not to miss *And Quiet flows the Don* at the Bolshoi theatre. I was taken to the rather smart National Hotel and after breakfast I joined a sightseeing tour. The Kremlin was our first stop. In Stalin's day nobody was allowed into the Kremlin except on business. We had to be content with a view of its rather grim exterior. (Thirty years later when the Kremlin was open to visitors I saw what treasures I had missed that day in 1936.) We were taken to a sports stadium and to a park of rest and culture. These unremarkable places were a source of pride to Russian citizens because they represented the first fruits of what they took to be democracy. They had not yet appreciated that the so-called dictatorship of the proletariat was in fact the dictatorship of one man over the proletariat. It is nevertheless true that the peasants and workers had become the chief beneficiaries of most of the new social legislation. A stadium for the people's games was a sufficient novelty in Russia to be worth putting on show. The greatest showpiece of all was the metro. Its stations have dazzling walls of marble and the spotless trains run smoothly. The psychological value of the metro must have been immense as a glimpse of the glory to come. Muscovite workers might be crowded into one-roomed apartments but riding on the metro they could dream of the days when they would dwell in marble halls.

In the afternoon we visited the tomb of Lenin outside the Kremlin. It was strangely touching to see the poor Russian pilgrims at the shrine of their Little Father. There can be no doubt about the religious significance of this mausoleum—a few peasants blessed themselves as they passed the corpse. In Italy I would have expected them to touch the glass case with their rosaries. A loud-voiced American behind me explained to his friends that this was exactly like the holy sepulchre in Jerusalem. Christians, he explained, have Christ and the communists have Lenin. Personally he worshipped neither because he felt no need for religion. For him socialism was enough and he wanted nobody to confuse his motives with religious motives. Pilgrims at Lenin's tomb were made to keep moving so that thousands could file swiftly past the body during the two hours or so the mausoleum was open to the public. As foreigners we did not have to take our place in the waiting line. I think this is an example of Russian courtesy rather than propaganda.

No criticism of anything Lenin did or said is tolerated in the Soviet Union. This policy was probably fostered by Stalin to establish his own omniscience and infallibility. The cult of Stalin within the Kremlin was no less obvious than the cult of Lenin in his tomb outside. It was possible to gather this from the whole attitude of the people as reported in the papers. While I was in Moscow the draft Constitution of the Union of Soviet Socialist Republics had just been published. The citizens were encouraged to study it and make suggestions for its improvement but apparently they all agreed that not a word of the draft needed to be altered. The papers were full of praises of Stalin whose genius had conceived the constitution. While I was in Moscow the papers were publishing votes of thanks to Stalin from workers at various factories. On 13th October, while I was actually in the city, the Military Academy of Leningrad discussed the Constitution and approved it with one amendment: "that it be inserted in the Constitution that the genius behind this new charter of the proletariat and its creator is Comrade Stalin" (*Pravda* 14 Oct., 1936). I had grown accustomed to the sycophancy of Italians addressing the Duce. I noted from *Pravda* some of the equally inflated epithets evoked by the Stalin cult: 'leader of the world revolution', 'Defender of the oppressed peoples of the world'. On more domestic occasions Stalin was addressed simply as *'Nash otets'* (our father). In Germany and Italy pictures of the Fuehrer or Duce were everywhere on display. Stalin's portrait was, if possible, in even greater evidence in Russia. He stared from the wall of the principal room in every hotel, hospital and public building. His face was even incorporated as an architectural feature in civic buildings. (Under Kruschev the process of de-Stalinisation involved the elimination of Stalin's effigies and such buildings were an intractable problem.)

It was in Moscow that my friendship with the Russians on board ship began to pay dividends. Jack Ross invited me to accompany him on a visit to his niece and her family in a Moscow suburb. We went on foot and on the way Jack gave me some of the impressions he had gathered from talking with Russians. The characteristic common to all was a very real fear. People were frightened of strangers and of each other. They were frightened even of their own children who, schooled to be intolerant of old ideas, were encouraged to report their parents' conversations. Young citizens must fight all class enemies including their own parents. It is difficult to convey such domestic fear to those without experience of life in a totalitarian country. Dictatorship in Italy and Spain was always mild in comparison with the German and Russian versions. The Nazi system was milder than Soviet-style dictatorship because despite its despotism (which later I had an opportunity of seeing at close quarters) it rarely interfered with the non-political citizen—unless he had committed the unforgivable crime of having been born a Jew. In Soviet Russia nobody—Jew or gentile—felt safe. A spiteful neighbour might send anonymous complaints to the local Soviet with fateful results. Millions in Stalin's Russia were tormented every night by fear that the secret police would carry them off to prison before morning.

During Stalin's long and terrible purge it was the constant hazard of citizens simply to disappear. It must be remembered that I was in Moscow at the height of Stalin's reign of terror.

Before describing my meeting with the relatives of Jack Ross I must explain that fear was felt by Jewish citizens with particular anguish. The ancient germ of Russian anti-semitism had been fortified by a virulent communist strain. From conversations with non-Jewish Russians I gathered something of the specifically communist anti-semitism. To some extent it was a legacy from Trotsky. The defeated Red Army leader had not been content merely to depart but had continued until his assassination to sponsor anti-Stalinist groups among communists in Europe and South America. He thus provided a pretext for hostile action against all Jews. This was not, of course, the complete explanation of Soviet anti-semitism. Jews had been prominent among the Bolsheviks from the beginning and had never shown indulgence towards their Jewish brethren. Communist Jews were, in fact, the most vicious persecutors of believing Jews. The revolution had been welcomed by Jews as a liberation from Czarist tyranny and anti-semitism (though this word is of later coinage). Having been victimised for generations they had every reason for hailing the red dawn which was to end racial persecution. They had gratefully and eagerly put their considerable talents at the disposal of the new rulers.

This may have been the chief cause of their downfall. Through sheer ability they soon found themselves in positions of authority. Clannish by nature (the inevitable result of past ill-treatment at the hands of gentiles) they tended to trust—and promote—only their fellow Jews. This has always been and must always be the way with minority groups. Where they are a minority Catholics are like Jews in their clannishness. If an Anglican becomes captain of England or wins a Nobel prize his co-religionists do not regard his religious affiliation as worthy of mention. To Jews and Catholics his religion would be the most significant feature of their own champions. Clannishness, however, provokes hostility and Soviet Russia was no exception. By the time I arrived in Russia many Jews had risen to key positions. Yagoda (Jehuda) was head of the secret police (G.P.U. changed from O.G.P.U.). His official title was Commissar of Home Affairs. The foreign secretary was Litvinoff. The third powerful Jewish figure was Lazarus Kagonovitch, Stalin's father-in-law. During my first few days in Moscow I was to hear a great deal of the jealousy and hard feeling against Jews. In a Moscow factory a worker complained that he was one of twenty gentiles all earning less than a hundred and fifty roubles a month. His Jewish foreman was paid five hundred roubles and the Jewish deputy director of the factory six hundred roubles. This man alleged that neither had previously been factory workers. He was convinced that both had been appointed because they were Jews. In all probability they had been appointed because they were competent but the twenty gentiles would never accept such an obvious explanation. Similarly people rejected at interviews are apt to complain that the selection board was composed of freemasons.

My friend Ross was aware of the anti-Jewish feeling in the Soviet Union but would probably not have heard the anti-Jewish stories in circulation at the time of our visit. A young university student not personally anti-Jewish (her best friend to whom she introduced me was a Jew) told me of the growing anti-semitism. Stalin, in the course of a speech to introduce his third five-year plan, said to the audience "Life has become more happy." The wags changed the first word to Dzhid (Yid): "The Jew has become more happy." But anti-semitism was more than a joking matter. Since the murder of Kirov the Jews had been suffering a veritable pogrom. (It is significant that the word pogrom is Russian.) In the summer of 1936 Zinoviev and Kamenev, the senior Jewish members of the Central Committee of the Supreme Soviet, had been sentenced to death. Soon afterwards Yagoda was shot. While I was in Moscow Karl Radek, the Jewish leader writer on *Izvestyia* was awaiting trial. A few months later he was sentenced to ten years' hard labour and has never been heard of since. He had been a popular figure because of his political jokes—in Soviet Russia, Fascist Italy and Nazi Germany citizens were addicted to this form of humour. Political humour makes little appeal to us but no doubt acts as a safety valve for those living under tyranny.

Here are two examples of Radek's jokes retailed to me by Russians. A man is about to drown himself in the Moscow river. A politician pleads with him: "Don't commit suicide, tovaritch, after the next five-year plan Russia will be a paradise." The man is not impressed. "My friend," he replies, "after the next five-year plan there won't be any water left in the Moscow river." The other story is also about the famous five-year plans. An enthusiast is trying to impress Radek. "The first five-year plan was completed in four years. The second is nearly finished. Just wait for the third five-year plan and you will see the greatness of the Soviet Union." To which Radek replies, "My dear fellow, you know nothing about the criminal law of the U.S.S.R. There can never be a third five-year plan. The maximum punishment is ten years." Stalin, the story goes, was angry when these jokes were repeated to him. He sent for Radek. "Karl," he remonstrated, "you know I am your friend. I always laugh at your jokes but I won't tolerate any jokes about the five-year plan." To which Radek replied, "Joseph, the five-year plan is your joke not mine." From these stories it will be seen that while I was in Moscow there was a great deal of talk about the five-year plans.

The shadow of the anti-Jewish drive fell deeply on the household of Jack Ross's niece. We found the young woman at home with her son, a pale-faced boy of about twelve years. I was surprised that Jack had taken me with him on his very first visit to his family. I had not realised that he had never met his niece and, feeling a stranger, was, in fact, glad to have my company. The family had only one private room. They shared a kitchen with two other families. The lavatories were communal for the block of flats. The woman cried a great deal as she told her uncle about her hardships. At one time the family had been in comfortable circumstances. Her husband's wages had been high and they were living in a three-roomed apartment—the height of luxury in Moscow. In the early hours of one morning he had been arrested. He had been receiving letters from relatives in U.S.A. and the secret police had swooped on him. Since they could not prove him guilty of espionage or even of sabotage he was fortunate enough to be released. But he lost his responsible post and his apartment. He might have lost his freedom but his services as a highly skilled engineer were too valuable to lose. The poor woman was obviously relieved to have this chance of pouring out the story of her troubles to her uncle. It would have been dangerous to speak so openly to her neighbours. They shared their misery but prudence forbade them to share their complaints.

We were engrossed in the woman's tale of misfortune when the door opened and her husband arrived home from work. He was a short, thick-set man of about forty years of age. He greeted Ross without warmth and was obviously displeased to see me. He asked Ross immediately who I was and why he had brought me. He told Ross very bluntly that it was foolish and dangerous to have brought an unknown foreigner to his home. Ross tried to reassure him by saying that we had known each other before coming to the U.S.S.R.

He promised that I would not repeat anything I heard. (They were speaking in Yiddish. I could sometimes understand the general drift of the conversation because many Yiddish words are similar to their German or English equivalents. On our way home Jack gave me a detailed account of all that had been said.) The husband remained unconvinced and was far from happy. When his wife continued her jeremiad he grew more and more restive. He shook her and told her to keep her voice low. He was clearly worried about what the neighbours might have overheard before he had come in. I felt uncomfortable and Jack was most embarrassed. After a few minutes of this whispered conversation it was time for us to go. As we stood up Jack handed his niece an envelope containing five hundred dollars. Her husband at once snatched it from her and gave it back to Ross. He thought it bad enough to have entertained foreigners without accepting foreign currency. So we departed. I felt that I had learned more about Soviet communism that evening than if I had read the whole Lenin library.

As we walked back to the hotel Jack Ross was very downcast. It seemed incredible that one of his own family had refused to take a gift from him. I suggested that it was my presence which caused the difficulty. The little boy we had just seen was obviously very sick. He had sat white-faced and silent during the whole of our stay. Jack would have liked to buy him food, toys and sweets but realised that to return would only cause further embarrassment. When we reached the New Moscow Hotel a message awaited Ross from another niece. She proposed to bring her family to see him at nine o'clock. Jack at once suggested that I should stay for dinner at the New Moscow instead of returning to the National. We both realised that this niece's family must be very different from the one we had just visited—otherwise they would certainly not have taken the risk of visiting foreigners. Promptly at nine o'clock Jack's niece, her husband and a grown-up son and daughter arrived. They were well dressed, self-confident and cheerful. Fortunately they were in no way resentful of my presence. The young man was twenty years old, his sister a year or two older. Both spoke adequate English and were glad of the chance to practise on an Englishman. They were apparently not interested in their parents' conversation (in Yiddish) with their uncle. When addressing their parents I noticed that they invariably spoke Russian. I learned later that the younger generation of Jew is anxious to be just as Russian as Soviet gentiles. Many are resentful of their own Jewish family and traditions. Whether to repudiate the faith of their fathers or from fear of anti-semitism many young Jews at that time were changing their names. Lists of these changes were given each day in *Pravda* and *Izvestiya*. From *Izvestiya* of 23rd October 1936 I copied a typical announcement:

> Rebecca Vaselievna Chekolaivna of Moscow wishes to change her name to Marguerita Vaselievna Chekolaivna.

Anti-semitism was officially discouraged. The proposed new Constitution forbade racial discrimination in article 123:

> The equality of the rights of citizens of the U.S.S.R. irrespective of their nationality or race, in all spheres of economic, state, cultural, social and political life is an immutable law. Any direct or indirect restriction of these rights, or conversely, any establishment of direct or indirect privileges for citizens on account of their racial nationality, as well as any propagation of racial or national exclusiveness or hatred or contempt, is punishable by law.

Many Jews nevertheless thought it prudent to remove any Jewish taint.

The young man was an ardent member of the Komsomol. A crusading communist, he had nothing but pity for those of us who lacked the benefits of Soviet citizenship. He knew all about the slavery of the workers in capitalist society. He had special contempt for England where fathers were deprived of employment and given only five shillings (roubles) a week to keep their families. Nothing could shake his conviction that he knew exactly what was happening in the West. His professor had given him the facts which as an Englishman I would have to deny for purposes of propaganda. He took me to task for the persecution of Ingersoll, condemned for believing in evolution. It was vain to tell him that Ingersoll lived a long time ago and not in England. He was contemptuous of a class system which allowed only the rich to follow a profession. He had a passionate love for his country and in due course would enter the Red Army Academy to train as an officer. Both he and his sister were studying English and German at the academy of languages. They were given one hundred roubles a month for maintenance. His sister would later study medicine. They both wished to give their lives to the service of the U.S.S.R. He had a poor opinion of foreigners and of the old (I was English and thirty-one years old). Happily he appreciated that I could not be blamed for the place or date of my birth. He was supremely content with the prospects for youth in the Soviet Union. He was a boy who accepted every article of Soviet faith. He would have been quite unaware of the anti-Jewish campaign that his hero Stalin had just begun to unleash.

Jack Ross told me later what had passed between him and the parents. Although they were both convinced communists they were very upset because their son and daughter wanted to marry gentiles. The parents were utterly opposed to mixed marriages of this kind. Jack regarded this as proof that race remained for a Jew a more powerful incentive than Marxism. He was cynical about this quarrel between dedicated communists. It reminded him of the family disputes common in the U.S.A. when children of orthodox Jews want to marry Christians. He concluded that communism was only skin deep in his niece and her husband. At about midnight the party broke up. I was anxious to see where and how this evidently prosperous family was living. I therefore suggested that since the night was fine Jack and I might accompany his guests on their way home. I walked ahead with the young man and we continued our discussion. I walked at a lively pace with the object of being out of range if the parents called a halt before we reached their home. I hoped that the well-known Russian hospitality would compel them to invite us to come inside for a cup—or, to be exact, a glass—of tea. In this I was disappointed. They kept us chatting on the door-step for nearly half-an-hour. We were not invited in for a night-cap.

On the way back to the hotel I took careful note of streets and landmarks so that I could retrace my steps the following day. I was determined to compare the homes of the two families we had met. The next afternoon I once more took the route of the night before. Everything looked different in daylight but my memory served me well. I found the house without great difficulty. Having pushed open the front door I found myself to my consternation inside a huge apartment house. The building was markedly superior to the wretched block of flats we had visited the day before. At the entrance a board gave the names of the residents. My dilemma was the greater because I did not know the family name. I thought I would have to admit defeat—but not without a struggle. Although I knew no Russian beyond the few phrases I had picked up from the Hugo booklet, having learned the characters of the Russian alphabet I could read the names on the board. By great good fortune all but one name was typically Russian. The exception was a family on the fifth floor. The name was Steinberg. It was literally one chance in twenty but I took courage and knocked at the Steinbergs' door. It was opened by the young Red Army cadet. He was not overjoyed to see me. Remembering that I had not been asked into the house the night before I did not await an invitation to enter. I walked inside and found myself in a three-roomed apartment beautifully furnished. In the carpeted living room I saw armchairs, bookcases and a piano. There were also a radio and a telephone. It was clear that this family was in a good position. I told the young man that I had come to continue our interesting conversation of the previous night. He said that he had an appointment and must leave at once. He had to go to a meeting at the Pioneers club. I offered to accompany him but he said that he would need to arrange my visit. He would talk to the director and call for me next evening to take me to the club. I was back in the street within two minutes. As a social call my visit had not been a success. But I had achieved my purpose. I had seen the home of a prosperous party member. The same evening the Steinbergs telephoned Jack Ross to say that on no account must either of us call again. Contact with foreigners might lead to trouble. Their son would not be taking me to the Pioneers club. We never saw any of them again.

Meanwhile I was undecided about visiting the French embassy in search of a bishop. I was fairly certain that I would be wasting my time. My information was, after all, about ten years out of date. For the moment I decided to content myself with the sightseeing provided by Intourist. The following morning we went to a creche which was, in fact, a babies' home. Ten per cent of the children were foundlings, just over ten per cent were being looked after while their mothers were in hospital, while the vast majority were orphans. The children were spotless and the nurses devoted to their charges. In view of the casual nature of celebrating marriages and the ease of divorce I was not surprised to find so many children 'in care' (as we would say in England).

We were driven by coach to a factory. The usual port of call for tourists was the Kagonovitch ball-bearing factory but we were taken to a lathe factory. On the coach tourists were divided into language groups—French, German and English. A guide lectured each group and answered questions. I joined the French group. It was not difficult to follow the gist of the French while overhearing what the English-speaking guide was telling her group. I knew that the guides were well trained but I was curious to see if there would be any inconsistencies. In the English group a man kept asking hostile questions in a loud voice. His English was excellent but I could detect a slightly Dutch or German accent. He was wearing a fawn trilby with wide brim and a grey feather. Arrived at the factory I followed the group for about a quarter of an hour until I managed to lose them by the old ruse of stopping to tie my shoelaces. When I stood up the group was satisfactorily out of sight. I had no clear idea of what to look for. It was just an impulse to see the parts of the factory not on show. I walked purposefully in the wrong direction because it is fatal for the furtive to walk furtively. Turning sharply into an opening between two machines I practically fell over a man bending down to examine the markings on the base of a machine. To my astonishment it was the feathered foreigner from the coach. He naturally assumed that I had been shadowing him. He was not at all pleased and asked who I was and why I had broken off from the rest of the party. I replied that I might as well ask him the same questions. For good measure I enquired why he had posed as an Englishman on the coach. It was obvious that we were both, so to speak, in the same line of business. We shook hands. His name was Karl Wilhelm. He told me that he owned a large factory in Dresden.

Under Wilhelm's guidance I continued the tour of inspection. He was critical of everything. He pointed to women working over hot machines and said that in Germany a factory manager would be imprisoned for allowing this to happen. All sorts of technical details which meant little to me earned his censure. We had been told by the guides in the coach that this factory employed four thousand workers of whom a thousand were women. Under Stalin's five-year plan five hundred and eighty machine-making factories had been constructed. Under the Czars, the guide said unblinkingly, no machinery had been made but now in this factory alone there was machinery worthy forty-eight million roubles. Herr Wilhelm and I eventually rejoined our group and heard the customary recital of the astonishingly high average wages. This device, simple as it is, deceived most visitors. An average wage is, of course, a figment. It does not exist in any actual wage packet. Wilhelm asked how much was paid to the women we had seen cleaning engines. The guides did not know. They knew the wages of the prize workers, the Stakhanovites. (Stakhanov was a worker who distinguished himself by doubling his output.) We were introduced to Comrade Goodoff, a miracle man who could produce no less than fourteen times his norm. His reward, apart from high wages, was to have his photograph fixed to his machine. We spoke also to a girl of seventeen who produced two hundred per cent more than her norm and was rewarded by six hundred roubles a month. Her picture also adorned her machine. The idea of an incentive bonus is familiar in capitalist societies but is not in tune with communist idealism. It is, in fact, a denial of the socialist principle: 'From each according to his ability, to each according to his needs.' In the new constitution a novel version of socialism is promulgated. Article 12 says " . . . In the U.S.S.R. the principle of socialism is realised: 'From each according to his ability, to each according *to his work*'."

It is not only the tyranny of good example which is used to incite workers to greater efforts. Every factory has its wall newspapers. Against the names of successful workers are pictures of aeroplanes and ships in full steam. The names of the laggards are also there to provide a kind of dishonour board. Their names are illustrated with the picture of mules, snails and tortoises. There is a section in the factory newspaper for foreign workers. The language is French and German. (Herr Wilhelm ascertained that sixty German communists had come to work in this factory.) I copied from the newspaper an appeal by the editor of the German section: "The two worker comrades Wickenberg and Schmitt said that they would hand in last week an article on Political Life for this magazine. We are still waiting. We are wondering when the swine will wake up and do their duty."

When we returned to the hotel Wilhelm confided that his trip was really a trial run. I suspect that he had received instructions from the German government to visit Moscow and was looking for excuses for not doing business with the Soviets. An enthusiastic Nazi, he was rabidly anti-communist. He begged me to stay with him in Dresden on my way home from Russia because he was anxious for me to compare the efficiency of Nazi Germany with that of the Soviet Union. I accepted his invitation. To me dictatorship whether communist or fascist was equally abhorrent. I was delighted at the prospect of taking a close look at the Nazi brand of terror. My visit to Dresden will form part of the account of my adventures on the return journey from Moscow to London.

A chance meeting with another type of tourist now opened up for me an entirely new line of enquiry. It also ended my hesitation about visiting the French embassy. On the Saturday afternoon I called at the New Moscow Hotel to see Jack Ross. He had just gone out but was expected back shortly. I sat down in the lounge to await his return. Suddenly I heard an American voice raised in anger. A young woman was in hot dispute with an Intourist girl in the foyer of the hotel. I went over to ask if I could be of assistance. It appeared that some of the American's meal tickets were missing. She alleged that at lunchtime a waiter had removed a whole page instead of a single ticket from her book of vouchers. Both ladies were highly excited but a little manly common sense soon calmed them down. The American was grateful for my intervention and stayed to talk to me while I waited for my friend. Ross did not, in fact, return so our conversation was prolonged. The young woman began by criticising the Soviet bureaucracy. She was on a trip round the world and complained that she had encountered more difficulties in the U.S.S.R. than in any other country. Like myself she had seen evidence of the fear gripping the Russian people. I did not ask what was her profession but surmised—wrongly as it happens—that she was a journalist. She spoke of the 'contacts' she had in Moscow and offered to share them with me if I would let her share mine. Her name, she said, was Alice but her friends—among whom I must now include myself—called her Allie. I said that she might call me John.

It was easy enough to exchange names but I was embarrassingly aware that when it comes to 'contacts' I had nothing to offer. It was then that I decided to make use of the French embassy. It would serve as a 'contact'. I took out my street map of Moscow and we set out to find our way. On the way I confessed to Allie that I was not sure if the person I wanted to see was still living in the embassy. (I was to discover that the good bishop had departed many years earlier.) I told Allie that if I met the bishop I might go to Confession and she would then have to leave me alone with him. I could think of no other way of making sure of a private talk with the bishop—if, indeed, there was a bishop to talk to. At the embassy I asked to see Monseigneur. I deliberately did not use any name in case I was told that Mgr. Neveu was not and never had been at the embassy. To my joy we were invited in at once. If we would wait a few minutes Père Braun would be free to see us. Father Braun, an American of French family, did not keep us waiting long. He asked how he could be of service. It might have made Allie suspicious if I had asked Father Braun at once to hear my confession. I therefore replied that we had come to enquire the place and time of Mass. Allie gratuitously remarked that never in her life had she missed Mass on a Sunday. The priest was most gracious and invited us to his room for a chat. He told me later that he was afraid that all reception rooms in the embassy were 'bugged'. He was reasonably sure of the security of his own room. We chatted for half-an-hour and then I asked if I might go to Confession. Tactfully Allie stood up and Father Braun took her back to the reception room.

When he returned I told the incredulous Father Braun that I was a priest. I discovered much later that after five years in the Soviet Union Father Braun had become pathologically suspicious. His nerves were so damaged that soon afterwards his superiors had to recall him to his Augustinian monastery. To reassure the priest I began to speak in Latin. I told him that I had come to Russia with the blessing of Cardinal Hinsley. I was also able to tell him of my friendship with Mgr. Cicognani, the Apostolic Delegate in the United States. We soon discovered that we had mutual friends and his doubts were removed. He took a very poor view of my chances of survival if the communists were to discover my identity. On no account must I tell anyone else that I was a priest. I asked if there were no Catholics in the diplomatic service to whom I might entrust my secret. He said that Mr. Bostock, the British vice-consul, was an excellent Catholic who would be sure to help me in any emergency. He advised me nevertheless not to take even a diplomat into my confidence. I then asked if I could use his church to say Mass early in the morning before it was open to the public. The very thought terrified him. There were always police on duty outside churches and they would become suspicious if they saw me enter the sacristan's lodge. He might then be questioned and put under pressure. Since it was obvious that more than my own safety was involved I withdrew my request and had to be satisfied with attending the Mass each morning and receiving Holy Communion.

For the next two days I battled with the temptation to call on Mr. Bostock. In the end I succumbed. I felt that with his assistance I would be able to make far greater use of my limited time in Moscow.

While not wishing to disregard Father Braun's advice I did not believe that it would be dangerous to confide in a British diplomat. In the end I reached a compromise. I decided to visit the vice-consul but appeal to him as a fellow Catholic without revealing my priesthood. I called at the consulate and was shown into the library where Mr. Bostock was working. After shaking his hand I asked if he would take me to a room where we could talk privately. He assured me that the library provided all possible privacy. I nodded towards a desk where a man was writing. "That," said Mr. Bostock icily, "happens to be the consul."

Garry Bostock told me later than when I had refused to talk to him in the presence of the consul he thought I was probably insane. He decided to humour me and took me to his apartments adjoining the consulate. He sat me down at a table and asked irritably what I wanted. I told him that I was a Catholic who had come to Russia to study the religious situation. Bostock said that the motives of my visit were no concern of his. I mentioned that I knew from Father Braun that he also was a Catholic. Bostock's comment did him credit but was of no help to me. He was in Moscow, he wished to inform me, not as a Catholic but as a British citizen in the service of his Majesty. His manner was as pompous as his words. He then asked to see my papers and studied them carefully. He rose, and said quite kindly that if I found myself in trouble as a result of my investigations he would give me any assistance in his power. I felt defeated. I had achieved precisely nothing. Mr. Bostock nevertheless had impressed me by his attitude. Here was a man of integrity. He would not let his religious beliefs affect his position as the King's servant. He was obviously a man to be trusted. Despite the wise advice of Father Braun I decided to tell all.

"Mr. Bostock," I said, "I'm a Catholic priest in disguise."

Bostock smiled. "That's different," he said, "what will you have to drink, Father?"

I told Garry Bostock why I had come to Russia and what I had so far seen. He was most enthusiastic about my mission. He told me that being on duty in Soviet Russia was like being in an ice box. There were no social contacts with citizens as in the diplomatic service elsewhere. They saw only colleagues in other embassies and Soviet officials. Other Russians were terrified of contact with foreigners. The purge had been going on for some time secretly but, in Bostock's view, was going to spread and become a reign of terror.

He thought that if I were reasonably careful I would not be unmasked because the Russians were so intent on watching each other. It is now public knowledge that Stalin's great purge had already begun in 1934. Many foreigners in 1936 would undoubtedly have regarded Bostock's views as alarmist but, of course, he was justified by events. Within the next few months the list of famous citizens to be liquidated was formidable. Piatakoff, Muralov, Ratachak, Yagoda, Bukharin, Krestinsky, Rykolf, Rakovsky, Orloff, Tukachevsky were all shot. So were former presidents, ambassadors, commissars, police chiefs, admirals and, above all, generals. Within less than a year of Bostock's prediction of a reign of terror ten of the eleven constituent Republics of the U.S.S.R. had lost either president, premier or both. Having given me a dramatic account of what the future might hold for Soviet citizens, Bostock said that I must collect as much information as possible and return to England to give the true facts to the gullible admirers of Stalin at home. He then introduced me to Hilda, his charming and intelligent wife. She at once invited me to return that evening for dinner. Bostock arranged for his car to pick me up at my hotel at 7 p.m.

The Bostocks had invited their friend Bob Hubbard to meet me at dinner. He was also an enthusiastic Catholic and ready to give me every help. Both put their cars at my disposal. It was an immense advantage for the rest of my stay to have a car and chauffeur always at hand. One or other of the cars was available whenever I needed transport. I remember the conversation at the dinner table that night very vividly because it might easily have led to my undoing. Young Hubbard was a keen convert and wanted to talk theology all the time. I would have preferred to listen to Bostock's views on the Soviet Union. He had lived in Russia for many years and before joining the diplomatic service had lectured in Moscow University. During dinner Hubbard had his way and we talked theology. The subject which above all others he found fascinating was Confession. The particular aspect he fastened on that evening was the seal of secrecy which binds the father confessor. His contention was that since priests are weak sinful men there must have been thousands of occasions on which the confessional seal was broken. Almost the last thing I had done before leaving Barking was to post to the publishers the manuscript of my book on Confession. My knowledge was therefore very up-to-date. I was able to deal with Hubbard's questions with uncanny accuracy. This almost brought me low. The next day Hubbard suspected that the whole conversation might have been too good to be true. Perhaps I was some kind of double agent posing as a priest. My conversation at dinner might have been a contrived performance. Perhaps I had subtly steered the discussion to Confession after having learned the facts by heart. So Bob decided to send a telegram to the Air Ministry (he was on the staff of the air attaché) asking for my credentials to be checked. Before sending the wire he called by God's grace to ask Father Braun's advice. The good priest, though astonished that I had disregarded his advice to be cautious, felt that it was, so to speak, my own funeral. He had no difficulty in assuring Hubbard that my priestly orders were valid. The telegram mercifully was never sent.

At the dinner party I managed at last to turn the conversation from religion back to Stalinism. I wanted to learn all I could from Garry Bostock (his real name was Harry but Russians have difficulty with the *h* sound so Garry it had become). He said that party members and their friends lived very well in Moscow. In terms of actual cash they were not well off but they were provided with so many amenities that life was made very comfortable. Most of them had country cottages (*dachas*) as well as apartments in town. Transport and hospitality were also provided. In Garry's view only fear, Russian indolence and fatalism saved Communist Russia from revolt. If *manana* illustrates the Spanish attitude to life, *zaftra* (tomorrow) might as suitably be the Russian slogan. The word *nichevo*, he said, was expressive of an outlook common in Russia. *Nichevo* means 'it doesn't matter' ('*ça ne fait rien*': '*non fa niente*'). After dinner he took me to see some of the better-off citizens in their moments of relaxation. We visited places which could not be called night clubs because of the sinister connotation of the term— the Soviets are puritanical in matters of sexual morality. Our interest was not in the cabaret but the audience. The patrons were well dressed and among them were several Red Army officers. The most popular of the places we visited was the Kavkaski restaurant in the Oulitza Gorki. As the name implies it specialises in Caucasian food and entertainment. As anywhere in the West some couples were sitting at tables sipping drinks while others were dancing. The dances would seem very old fashioned today—one-steps and fox-trots. Occasionally there would be an act by professional Cossack dancers.

I was surprised to see jazz bands in these places. On the next Rest Day I saw them also in the big hotels. Before coming to Russia I had understood that bourgeois entertainment was forbidden. Garry told me that officially jazz is discountenanced and strict party members would not listen to it. The few young people who could afford them were keen on western style in clothes as well as music. The authorities found it wise to be tolerant over such trivial matters. I wondered what the waiters thought of the people frequenting the Kavkaski who would have looked equally at home in a Paris café or London bar. Garry said he would ask one of the waiters on our way out. He gave the waiter helping him on with his overcoat a generous tip (tips are officially unacceptable) and asked him in a semi-alcoholic kind of way what he thought of 'this bourgeois lot'. Garry translated the man's reply which I wrote down as soon as I returned to my hotel: "They're the same as the bourgeois in your country. What do you expect? Russia is no different from anywhere else. It's the same the world over. People say one thing and do another."

Allie was very impressed by the motor cars with C.D. number plates which used to come to pick me up. She was too intelligent to ask questions but she must have thought that I was in the employ of the British government. Allie had come to Mass on the Sunday and to my surprise continued to attend Father Braun's Mass each day. The church of St. Louis was kept open by courtesy of the diplomatic corps and the congregation at Mass on Sunday came in the main from embassies. Father Braun told me that the native members of the congregation were mostly of Polish descent. They were truly confessors of the faith. It needed heroic virtue for Soviet citizens to be active members of any church. (Soon after the outbreak of the second war Stalin decided that the church of St. Louis must close. The man who secured its reprieve was the British ambassador, Sir Stafford Cripps. Although not a Catholic he was determined to save the church. He assembled an impressive list of names of foreigners who would be so seriously affected by the closure of St. Louis that they would ask to be recalled. This would entail a great deal of unwelcome publicity for Stalin because the communist persecution of religion would once again become world news. Not surprisingly Stalin relented. All this, of course, was in the future.) In 1936 the rules governing freedom of worship were clear and strictly enforced. Nobody would have suspected from a casual reading of the Soviet Constitution that the persecution of religion was as much part of the modern Soviet way of life as in the time of Lenin and the first savage Bolsheviks.

Article 124 of the Constitution which became law three weeks after my departure from Russia (25th November, 1936) reads: "In order to ensure its citizens freedom of conscience the Church in the U.S.S.R. is separate from the State, and the school from the Church. Freedom of religious worship and freedom of anti-religious propaganda is recognised for all citizens." It is impossible not to admire the cunning of these words. Article 124 means, in effect, that you may say your prayers but not spread the teachings of Christ. That would be a criminal offence. Anti-religious propaganda is alone permitted by Soviet law. Evangelisation (religious propaganda) is forbidden by law. There is not even paper freedom for believers. Bezbozhnik, the league of the godless, was one of the most active departments of government in the months preceding the promulgation of the new constitution. Its chairman when I was in Russia was Lukachevsky. In his speeches he made it clear that people were free to practise religion only if it did not interfere with their duty as citizens. Some comrades, he complained, had been seen to leave the fields on Sunday morning to attend church. This was sabotage. Will God look after the crops while comrades are in church? Will God take the punishment if the crops fail? Let churchgoing comrades not abuse their freedom.

During September 1936, Krylenko, the notorious People's Commissar for Justice (the same man who led the prosecution of Archbishop Cieplak in the first bloodbath of the Bolshevik persecution of religion), gave a series of explanatory lectures on the new constitution. According to the report in the Moscow press of one of his speeches he declared:

> Every comrade may engage in any religious ceremony he pleases. He may baptise his babies though it may be dangerous to their health. He may bury his dead. Similarly he may bury his potatoes with a religious ceremony, so long as they grow and provide the norm demanded by the State.

The actual rules governing churches made the new constitution meaningless in practice. To be left open a church must be the responsibility of a committee of twenty (*dywatsatka*). It is not difficult to imagine the pressure on members of the committee. Understandably few Soviet citizens would risk their security by putting themselves forward. Old people with nothing to lose were the only likely candidates for membership of a dywatsatka—except, of course, foreigners who need not fear reprisals. It was no easy task to maintain a church once it was saved from closure. It was heavily taxed and the public utility services were charged for at prohibitive rates. Thus in 1936 a householder was charged four kopeks per kilowatt for electricity. The church committee had to pay forty kopeks. The result was that the churches were rarely heated. Services were held in daylight and, when light was required, candles were used.

To impress foreigners the Soviet government, despite its declared intention of destroying religion, has always tried to avoid overt acts of persecution. If economic warfare did not succeed in putting a church out of business (it was automatically liquidated if it was unable to pay its taxes) the local communist party could organise a sobranya (public meeting) to call for the closure of a church to meet the alleged wishes of the proletariat. The people of the area might wish, for example, to use the building for a club. Churches in towns to which tourists rarely go were the most likely casualties. In Samara in 1936 a sobranya was called by a group of Jews whose parents had emigrated from Poland. Polish Jews, having suffered at the hands of Christians, handed down a legacy of hatred to their children. These had become fanatical communists at a time when they still believed that the Soviets would suppress anti-semitism and racial discrimination of every kind. A meeting was arranged by the local party but not a single Christian dared to attend. By a unanimous vote the workers of Samara were declared to be in favour of an anti-religious museum in place of the church. This was given to me by a foreign resident in Moscow as typical of the communist drive against religion. I had no opportunity of visiting Samara to test the truth of the story. I did, of course, see churches which had been turned into museums in Leningrad and Moscow. In the countryside museums were not wanted but many churches were derelict. The surprising thing was that there were any priests left to man the churches remaining open. Officially regarded as political enemies they were not at that time accorded normal civilian rights. (During the most critical period of the war attacks on the Church were relaxed— Mother Russia was in peril, people were mourning their dead and seeking the consolation of religion—from that time priests were no longer regarded as outlaws.) Their personal documents (*duokovni*) were stamped with a red arrow which marked them as unemployable.

They were in the same category as vagabonds. Despite the penalty for aiding such people (a fine of twenty-five roubles) the flock saw that their pastors did not die of starvation. The drama of Christian resistance in Soviet Russia will one day take its place in religious literature. The heroes will be the orthodox clergy and people but, for sheer courage, the Baptists and members of various sects including the Jehovah's Witnesses will deserve the highest honour.

I made good use of the cars which were put so kindly at my service. I was able to travel many miles out of Moscow without the company of Intourist guides. One day I went with Bob Hubbard on a long drive during which I saw the political prisoners at work on the Volga-Moscow canal. They were guarded by armed soldiers. I took a picture of these unfortunate people over the shoulder of our driver. Nobody had any idea of the number of Stalin's victims who had escaped death only to spend the best years of their lives doing forced labour. Our route took us past the house of Prince Yousupoff, the reputed assassin of the notorious Rasputin. This splendid country house had been kept in excellent repair to serve as a rest home for Red Army staff officers. We continued to the village of Petrovskoe Selo where the estates of the former Prince Galitzine had been turned into a state farm (*sofkhoz*). The difference between a sofkhoz and a kholkoz lies in its being an exclusively national soviet enterprise. The peasant in the collective farm known as a kholkoz has a certain independence. Members of the kholkoz are free, once they have produced the norm appointed by the state, to work for themselves. They had to be careful, however, not to become kulaks. The rough rule laid down by Stalin was that their private enterprise should not exceed the limit of one acre, one cow, a pig and a few chickens. I tried unsuccessfully to discover what happened to the calves and piglets. Without the bucolic equivalent of Herr Wilhelm as companion and guide I could not judge the efficiency of the agricultural methods of the Soviets. This journey was memorable chiefly because I nearly contracted frostbite. At Alexandrovsk we left the car in a pine wood and walked past some of the dachas belonging to various Soviet personalities. I took a photograph of Stalin's dacha but in my excitement forgot to turn the film before taking the next picture. Walking around in the snow I began to lose the use of my legs. We returned hurriedly to Bob Hubbard's house in Moscow. It took several electric fires and a number of toddies to restore circulation to my limbs. For the first time since coming to Russia I really was alarmed. The prospect of spending weeks in a Moscow hospital was daunting.

I had fully recovered by morning when Garry Bostock's car arrived at the hotel. I had asked Garry if I might take Allie on my next outing. Allie was due to produce one of her 'contacts'. I had begun to believe that her contacts were only slightly less bogus than my own. She had, in fact, only one contact. He was Henry Ware, an American communist studying political economy at Moscow University. She had never met him but she had been given a letter of introduction. I suggested that we should drive to the university and pick up Henry Ware. He might direct us to places more exciting than those on the route which Bostock had written down for his driver to follow. So we went to the university. Allie thought she knew where to find Henry but after wandering through the students' quarters we could not trace him. We would have reconciled ourselves to not finding Henry Ware but we could not establish contact with a student of any kind. I suggested to Allie that she might act the damsel in distress. When I had explained the act to her Allie was more than ready to play the damsel. She let out a series of shrieks. Within seconds two women students rushed from their rooms to the rescue. Drying her tears Allie explained that she was lost. Her friend Henry Ware had failed to meet her and she felt deserted. One of the girls whose English was fluent said that she knew Henry Ware. She told us that there was little purpose in hunting for him in this vast building. We chatted for some time and thanked her for her kindness. She was most courteous and insisted on seeing us to our car. As we were saying goodbye I asked on an impulse if she would care to come for a drive. After only a moment's hesitation she accepted and told us to drive round the corner out of sight of the porter's lodge. In a few minutes she rushed up breathlessly and jumped into the car. This was Lola.

Lola, twenty years of age, came from the Caucasus. Her grandfather having been a successful architect, she was of bourgeois background and therefore fortunate to have been given a place in the university. I did not realise at the time what courage it took for Lola to drive with two foreigners. Soon I was to have proof that Lola was a girl of exceptional courage, intelligence and sensitivity. As we drove through the city Lola pointed out the chief buildings and described the life of a Soviet student. She enjoyed being at the university but like students everywhere regarded most lectures as a boring waste of time. Social life was rugged and she suffered a great deal from lack of privacy. Her outlook was that of any cultured young woman. She refrained from discussing anything remotely touching politics but when we were well into the country a derelict church we were passing gave me an excuse to ask her views on religion. She replied, as if speaking by rote, that no educated person in Russia believed in religion. When the old people had died off religion would disappear with them. Scientific evolution had disposed of God. Watching her closely I began to feel that she was not speaking from conviction. It was hard to reconcile deceit with such a charming girl but she seemed too intelligent to be an atheist. It suddenly struck me that Lola was afraid of revealing her true mind in the presence of the Russian driver.

Lola was sitting between Allie and me on the back seat. I assured her that there was no need to be afraid of speaking in front of the driver because he could not understand English. She smiled and shook her head. She evidently regarded me as ingenuous. All these people, she whispered, are in the employ of the G.P.U. This man would have to report every conversation he heard in the car. I then began to whisper like a conspirator. I told her that the embassy people had satisfied themselves that this man did not understand an English conversation. Since Lola was still unconvinced I called out: "The engine's caught fire!" The Russian drove on unperturbed. It was obvious that he had no idea what I had said. This impressed the doubting Lola. She confessed that until now she had carefully weighed her words having the driver in mind. She had not realised when she agreed to come for a drive that there would be a Russian in the driver's seat: Now that she could speak without fear. Lola's personality opened up like a flower. She returned at once to the question of religion.

Lola then informed us that she was in fact a believer. In her view nobody could deny the existence of God. "I did not make myself," Lola said, and evidently thought that little more need be said by way of argument. She did however give birds and flowers as further examples of life which could be explained only by the existence of a creator. She said that she had to pretend to be an atheist to stay in the university. If she were known to be a believer she would not pass her examinations. She would be sent home as being intellectually unfit for higher studies. I asked if she thought there were many secret believers at the university. She replied that like herself they would keep quiet about their religious beliefs. People who at home might kneel by their beds at night would not dare to say prayers in front of their comrades. Each night in the room which she shared with four girls she covered her head with the sheet, blessed herself and said her prayers. In this way she felt at one with her family and with Christians everywhere. I found this confession of faith most moving. Soon we came to another abandoned church surrounded by a graveyard. We left the car to visit the church but found the door locked. She asked me to take her photograph standing in front of the church.

The next morning I went as usual to Mass in the church of St. Louis. On the way I had to pass the Lubyanka prison. I had my camera with me and for no very good reason decided to take a picture of the viaduct between the two main buildings. This is known to local cognoscenti as the Bridge of Sighs because prisoners have to cross it when being taken from their cells to the administrative block for questioning. I had noticed each morning that the sentries followed a pattern of movement which was Prussian in its regularity. Each marched from the Bridge of Sighs to the corner of the block he was guarding, marked time and marched back to the Bridge. Once again they marked time, turned back-to-back and without looking to left or right marched again to the end of the building. A few seconds after the back-to-back manoeuvre I took my picture. This was a pointless and foolhardy action but it had no unfortunate consequences. On a later occasion, however, my camera did lead me into trouble. On that morning I was able to continue on my way to Mass unmolested. As always there was a policeman on duty at the church door. So far as I knew the police, posted at the door of every church, never interfered with those wishing to enter. I can only assume that their presence was regarded by the Soviets as a vague deterrent. Doubtless they would report to their superiors if the number of regular worshippers were to increase. Except on Sundays there were never more than half-a-dozen people at Mass at Father Braun's church.

Allie also went to Mass each morning. I have no reason to think that she was moved to do so out of devotion. At no time did I question her about her religious beliefs. It is likely that she found church the most convenient place to meet me to discuss the day's strategy. This morning I had scarcely had time to begin my prayers when I heard footsteps approaching. I paid no attention until I felt someone kneel down by my side. It was Lola. For the next half-hour my thoughts were far from the Mass. I was seriously worried on Lola's behalf. If her fellow students knew that she had gone to church the result might be serious. She might be reported and lose her place in the university. As soon as Mass was over I asked Lola why she had come. She told me that our conversation the day before had made her desperately unhappy. Hearing that Allie and I went to Mass each morning had made her envious. She had not been inside a church since coming to Moscow. All night long she had been unable to sleep. She reproached herself for not having had the courage to go to church. She thought—quite wrongly—that Allie and I must be brave to attend Mass in Moscow. She had made up her mind to tell her room-mates that she had a headache and would go for a walk in the morning air. To keep the fiction she intended to go back to bed and feign sickness for the rest of the day.

The three of us held a council of war in church. What worried the practical Allie was that Lola would have had nothing to eat when she went back to bed. We decided that it would be best for her to keep to her plan of pretending to be sick but meanwhile she must have some breakfast. At that hour there were no shops open so we took Lola back to my hotel. To avoid awkward questions being asked in the hotel restaurant the three of us went straight to my room. I rang for a waiter and asked him to bring us coffee and rolls. My travellers' cheques had been changed by one of the resident foreigners who had means of securing a realistic rate of exchange. He had no scruples of conscience because the official exchange operation was legal robbery—the official rate for one pound sterling was twenty-five roubles. The best way of translating that into terms of real value is to say that a kilo of butter cost twenty-two roubles and a kilo of tea one hundred roubles. The waiter brought us a splendid meal which, of course, included generous portions of caviar. Before Lola made her way back to the university I begged her not to run the same risk again and explained that Allie and I as foreigners ran no risk at all. I also told her that the Orthodox churches were so full on Sundays that in future she could easily lose herself in the crowd when she wanted to go to Mass.

After breakfast Allie and I went to Z.A.G.S., the Bureau of Inscription of Civil Statutes. It was more or less what in England we call a Register Office. The Soviet system of civil marriage is less complicated than ours. There is no formal declaration of intent. The marriage ceremony is no more than the registration of marriage. The communist theory was that marriage is essentially bourgeois. It is not in the best interest of the state for a couple to marry. If it gives them comfort they may declare that a state of marriage exists between them but there is no legal obligation to register a state of marriage. When children are born of a union a state of marriage exists whether or not the union has been registered. This has significance in the event of a break-up of the union. During the early days of the revolution the institution of marriage was despised as a relic of religious superstition. Free love was a sign of Marxist liberation. Children were regarded as belonging primarily to the state and not the sole responsibility of the parent. Crèches were attached to all factories so that parents would not be hindered in discharging their duties towards the state. If couples had registered their marriage there was no difficulty or delay if either wanted a divorce. It could be obtained free of charge on application to Z.A.G.S. with or without the consent of the other partner.

This theory had not been successful when put to the test. Resuming my role of psychologist I asked for an interview with the superintendent of Z.A.G.S. Allie armed with shorthand notebook and pencil acted as my secretary. I soon found that the Soviet outlook had radically changed. Although religious marriages solemnised after December 1917 were not recognised, merely casual unions were no longer advocated. Nobody was forced to register a marriage but it was very much in the interest of the parties—especially the woman—to do so. Legal marriage had acquired respectability. Concurrently divorce had fallen in esteem. The first careless rush of freedom was being officially slowed down. Gone were the days of free divorces. Now there was a rising charge for each divorce. A third divorce cost the applicants five hundred roubles. No man would be granted a divorce without agreeing to pay alimony for his wife and children. Speaking as a progressive psychologist I suggested that the Soviets were being unfaithful to communist principles. By making it more difficult to obtain a divorce the state was endangering its own position. Children would look to their parents before looking to the state. The family would in the end become more important than the state. The superintendent, a woman, looked at me with a mixture of pity and exasperation. "Don't you realise," she said, "that the family is the centre of the state?" I had not expected in a Soviet institution to hear this simple affirmation of Christian philosophy.

It was not only on divorce that the Soviets had already begun in 1936 to revise their social legislation. Their whole attitude towards women and morality had undergone a marked change as a result of experience. The communist revolution violently rejected not only the Czar and the Orthodox Church but all the moral taboos associated with Christianity. A quarter of a century later a liberalising campaign against Christian morality was to be waged in the West. Its objective was the establishment of the permissive society. In Soviet Russia the experiment was seen to have failed by the middle thirties. Hence the tightening of standards which even as a visitor to the U.S.S.R. I could easily observe. Since 1917 women in the name of liberty had been ostensibly treated as the equals of men. They had now learned that emancipation is not the same as freedom. The women on factory night shifts or sweeping the streets would gladly have repudiated emancipation. They would have had nothing to lose, so to speak, but their chains. It was attractive in theory for women to be given equal status with men in everything. In practice the old principle "Expel nature with a pitchfork . . ." was proved true. If motherhood is reduced to prosaic production of new bodies its mystique disappears. Family life is destroyed and the state is in danger of disruption. The Soviets were discovering that the old bourgeois (Christian) morality had its value even apart from pie in the sky.

Take as an example the Soviet attitude towards abortion. Until 1936 every clinic had an abortorium which performed thousands of operations every month. The importance of a woman lay in her capacity as a worker. Her position as mother or prospective mother of a family was overlooked. Many factories insisted that women seeking employment should produce a doctor's certificate to show that they were not pregnant. When they discovered that their condition precluded them from a job they naturally applied at the nearest abortorium in order to become eligible for employment. Facilities for abortion naturally led to an orgy of free love. Even if a woman had not the courage to face what in other countries used to be an illegal operation, she always had the comforting knowledge that in Russia there are no illegitimate children. The prospect of destruction of domestic life and the prevalence of disease, coupled with the ever-growing desire of the Soviet Union to provide cannon fodder, led to an alteration in the abortion laws.

Abortion was now permitted only in special cases. The law worked well. Official statistics published by the Department of Public Health, enabled me to compare the figures for the quarter July to September for 1935 and 1936.

	1935	1936
Minsk	1303	90
Rostof	3140	474
Saratov	2978	107
Svedlovsk	2129	109

But this decline in abortion did not satisfy Kaminsky, People's Commissar for Health. In a trenchant article in *Izvestiya* of 18th October, 1936, he complained that doctors were allowing too many loopholes to women seeking operations. "Such doctors," he said, "must understand that they are acting against the interests of the state. Some look only at the profit motive. They are acting not from humanitarian motives, but from gain. We must not blind ourselves to the presence of such as these, but we shall speak to them in the language of the criminal code. They must not expect mercy . . .

"Mrs. J. is given permission for abortion because her husband has tuberculosis. Another suffers from hysteria, another from loss of appetite. Illness of husbands is becoming quite a usual motive. If the wife cannot complain of illness she uses her husband. He drinks too much. 'He is melancholy,' she says, 'give me an abortion.' So true is this that one would think that in modern Russia, the husbands gave birth to the children and not the wives . . . We are going to spend 750 million roubles above the plan on maternity homes and crèches. We should remember the words of Stalin: 'We must think of humanity and work for the life and health of the young generation.'"

After visiting Z.A.G.S. I went with the Intourist party to the Palace of Pioneers. This mammoth youth club was included in the itinerary of every tourist. Materially it is the kind of youth centre which every local authority in Britain would like to provide. It contains facilities for recreation, study and cultural activity of every kind. Unlike youth centres in this country the Palace of Pioneers is open to children of every age. Provision is made even for those still in the kindergarten stage. The advantage of making this provision is evident in a community where mothers as well as fathers have to work. The only reservation I had concerned the actual use to which the Palace was put. It seemed too perfect to be true. The Assistant Director who acted as our guide said in answer to one of my questions that the building was open to the children of all workers irrespective of party membership. Thousands of children, she said, came every day. I found this hard to believe for two reasons. In the first place there were at the time of our visit no more than twenty or thirty children in the whole building. Since school attendance was in shifts the child population would have been free at any time of the day. The second reason for suspicion was the state of the children's play rooms. Everything was uncannily in order. I pointed out to our guide a huge fort surrounded by hundreds of toy soldiers. They were in ranks according to size and colour. Tanks, aeroplanes and army trucks were similarly displayed in regular order. Foolishly I gave way to the temptation of demonstrating to my fellow tourists that we were being misled, I said that although the time was now past twelve o'clock I was quite certain that no small children could have been playing in the room that day.

I would gladly have withdrawn my words as soon as I had spoken. Our guide was very angry indeed. She asked our group to excuse her while she went to fetch the Director. He was very stern. He had been informed, he said, that I had made hostile remarks about the Palace of Pioneers. Tourists were entitled to ask civil questions but enemies of the Soviet State were not wanted in Moscow. He then asked my name, profession and the name of my hotel. I already regretted having so needlessly drawn attention to myself. I felt however that having blundered it would now be better to take the offensive than make an apology. I told the Director that my remarks had been misunderstood. My attitude, I said, was neither hostile nor favourable to the Soviets. I was interested only in facts. I repeated that as a psychologist with much experience of children I was certain that this playroom had not been used by children that morning. If I were going to be misinformed by the guide I had no further interest in the Palace of Pioneers. I proposed therefore to return at once to my hotel.

I was nevertheless very afraid of what might happen as a result of my indiscretion. I assumed that the Director would make a report. The result might well be that Intourist in London would be instructed to examine my credentials more closely. If their enquiries went no further than 45 Reddington Road, Hampstead, the address of the Eyres, I had nothing to fear. But if the Soviets were really determined it would not be difficult to find out all about me. There were probably not half-a-dozen families of my name in the whole of England. Making my way back to my hotel I learned by experience what it is to think furiously. My best plan, I thought, might be to return home without delay. But this would not be easy. My passport had been taken from me on my arrival at Leningrad. With the notoriously slow movement of Soviet bureaucracy it might take some days to retrieve. Suddenly a solution came to mind. It was the passport which gave me the idea. The more I considered it the more certain I was that it was likely to succeed. Like most good plans it was simple and blindingly obvious. Instead of waiting for the Director to report me I decided to report him. I hurried to the Intourist office and complained that I had been insulted by the Director of the Palace of Pioneers. Despite documents from Intourist in London requesting all assistance to be given me as a psychologist I had been treated as an enemy for asking simple questions from a psychological angle. Since the promised co-operation was not forthcoming I requested the immediate return of my passport.

The Intourist manager asked me to reconsider my request and added that it would be impossible to produce my passport in less than forty-eight hours. I threatened to seek the help of the British embassy if my journey home were unduly delayed. He then promised to do his best to expedite the return of the passport. Though beginning to breathe more freely I knew that I would not feel really safe until I was beyond the borders of the U.S.S.R. But before the day was out all my fears were set at rest. The manager of Intourist came to present the apologies of the Director of the Palace of Pioneers. The unfortunate man, he said, had not been informed of my speciality (the term used indiscriminately in Russia for a person's interest, profession or hobby). If I would withdraw my request for the return of the passport Intourist would undertake that this unpleasant experience would not be repeated. They would arrange for me to visit any institution I cared to name and all concerned would be informed of my speciality. I was gracious in my acceptance of the apology. I withdrew my request for my passport. I asked if on the next day a visit could be arranged to the law courts where I would like, if possible, to interview a judge.

That evening I gave a party in my room at the National Hotel for my new friends. To my sorrow I had bidden goodbye that day to Jack Ross returning home via Kiev. There was a large Jewish community in that city and he had reason to hope that he would not find any of his family in such pitiable conditions as those of the niece we had visited. Henry Ware was my chief guest. He was Allie's 'contact' and it was through him that we had been able to visit the students' quarters in the university. A theoretical Marxist in college in the U.S.A., Henry had come to Moscow for expert tuition. Being a particularly bright young man he had naturally become cynical. In the year 1936 the inefficiency of Russia's technicians was more obvious than the Soviet potential for producing sputniks. Good plumbing is part of a modern American's religion. The squalor of the students' quarters had no doubt contributed to Ware's cynicism about the Soviet Union.

The party had an international flavour. Henry and Allie were Americans. The Russians were Lola and her friend Julius. This was my first meeting with Julius. We took to each other immediately but almost at once began an argument about Stalin. He took for granted that I was an atheist. Since I wanted to engage him seriously on the subject of Stalinism I allowed the religious issue to go by default. Julius was a Jew. Like most of his race he was a man of great compassion and generosity. That is why Lola was so devoted to him. She was, in fact, anti-Jewish but in her case this had nothing to do with anti-semitism. She was resentful of the privileges which at that time so many Jews were able to enjoy. When Julius was not present Lola spoke to us about the growing anti-Jewish feeling in Russia. This in no way disturbed her affection for Julius. I do not know if Lola intended to marry Julius. I was at no time alone with her and so had no opportunity for any really private conversation with her. She told me more about herself in her letters after my return to England than in our talks in Moscow. That evening Henry offered to become a postbox for Lola and Julius to enable them to write to me after my return to England. Letters from abroad were in danger of being opened if addressed to Soviet citizens. Henry as a foreigner was safe. Lola and Julius exchanged correspondence with me for several months. After that it became hard to find topics of mutual interest. I shall give some extracts from the first letter I received from Julius. It reveals his staunch loyalty to Stalin.

To understand the letter it is necessary to know that after a glass or two of vodka the party in my hotel became by Russian standards quite hilarious. I contended that although he called himself an atheist Julius was in fact a pious believer. His faith was in Red Fascism and his god was Stalin. There was little to choose between the German and Russian Fuehrers. I had purchased a small bust of Stalin and I began to play the fool with it. I ended up by lathering Stalin's face and shaving him—while carrying on a kind of barber's patter of insult and ridicule. The two Russians laughed to the point of tears. Lola was delighted because she hated all Stalin stood for. Julius was laughing for the opposite reason. He was fascinated by the very blasphemy of my words and actions. His was a fearful joy. By the time he wrote his letter to me he had obviously regretted his sin of omission. That night he merely enjoyed himself. Now he must make amends by defending Stalin's authority. His letter is dated 4th December, 1936. I take it out of sequence since it is really part of the story of the hotel party.

I give the exact text with its quaint syntax and spelling. I omit some sentences in which the language is unintelligible. Julius knew much less English than his friend Lola.

Dear Jhon [he wrote]
First of all excuse me my barbarian English, but you must suffer if you want me to have as a correspondent. All right? If something will be not understandable for you, you must tell me about this. Good?

You write in your letter 'It was such fun to watch your face as I performed the tonsorial offices for X in the hotel.' Of course it amused me very much but it does not mean that I don't recognise the necessarity of an authority. Especially in our time of hartless social struggle and civil wars. [The Spanish civil war was in progress and the toilers were working 'voluntary' overtime without pay as a contribution to the war effort.] Dear Jhon you must understand masses can be lead only by two means. By their psychology which is old, as old is the religion. We abolish the religion but it is impossible to change social consciousness of the masses radicaly and rapidly. So we must use the authoritative way by an unusual personality whose word rings authoritatively. The history teaches us that only troght the lead masses can be solved great historical problems: The quiker runs social events the louder must sound the authority of a certain personality 'fürer'. The social struggle now is so decisive and our enemies are so heartless it is impossible to wait to change them by educational methods. So we are forced to use the authoritative mutation of the masses. Our social ideals can be solved only by power, by struggle, by numberous masses for the fight. May be tomorrow we must have millions of masses to fight our enemies. [Since 1935 Nazi Germany was recognised as the chief enemy. The U.S.S.R. and Germany were already virtually at war in Spain. Within a few months Tukachevsky and the other generals were to be executed for alleged conspiracy with the Nazis.] Tell me Jhon would it be possible to win such a number of people without the power of an authoritative personality? So good-bye. I would be very glad to see you next summer. I think we can have a very good time. J.

P.S. Don't forget to answer me. All right?

The letter naturally did not carry the name or address of the sender.

The next morning I kept my appointment with the law. Accompanied by Allie, who was armed with a reporter's notebook, I waited on the chief judge of the Moscow People's Court. His name was Smirnoff. He had been a baker before becoming a judge. He patiently explained the procedure of a people's court. It is a court of first instance. Above it are the regional courts and, of course, the supreme court. There is, nevertheless, no category of crime excluded from its competence--not even murder. Much of its business is concerned with what Smirnoff described as banditry. This in England would, I assume, be known as petty crime. Trials for counter-revolutionary activities might pass through this court in their first stage but would end up in higher courts. In Moscow at this time there were over a hundred people's courts. They were presided over by a judge and two social representatives. The judge is elected for three years. The social representatives (assessors?) remain in office for twelve months. At that time in Moscow the panel from which the social representatives were chosen contained twenty-five thousand names. Of these seventy-eight per cent were Stakhanovite workers. If elected these men and women were given six months' legal training. This, if true, would be an improvement on the English system which provides little training for lay justices. An accused person who wants a particular counsel to defend him must pay the fees either personally or through his trade union. Otherwise, as in England, a dock brief is available without charge.

The quality of justice dispensed at the people's court depends almost entirely on the ability of the presiding judge. Decisions are taken on a majority verdict. It is theoretically possible for one of the social representatives to disagree with the judge. In this unlikely event the dissenting assessor must still sign the verdict but may add a proviso of non-agreement. What really matters is how often justice will be obtained at the hands of the judge. That was one reason why I was keen to discover the methods of electing judges. The principle was clear enough. People are likely to elect the most respected and trusted among their fellow citizens. Judge Smirnoff explained that each district is divided into bushes (wards?). A bush contains about fifteen thousand souls. One people's court might look after anything up to seventy-five thousand residents. That, of course, would be one of the larger courts. Most people's courts would be much smaller—similar, in fact, to local police courts in England. I was not very interested in statistics but I pressed the judge hard to discover how he and his colleagues came to be elected. From what I had already learned of communist attitudes I found it hard to credit that the Soviets left the choice of judges entirely to the citizens. I had seen undeniable evidence of fear among the people. Left to themselves they would be unlikely to appoint a Stalin-type judge. Allie took down my conversation with Judge Smirnoff in shorthand. I give an excerpt to illustrate how difficult it was for Smirnoff to give a plain answer to a plain question. Those familiar with Orientals may discern in the Soviet judge's answers an eastern pattern of thought.

Q. Are the people completely free in their choice of judges? If so, how is it possible to secure the verdict of say seventy-five thousand people on the merits of an individual man?
A. Four or five different places, cinemas or halls, are chosen as places of meeting, and, by raising their hands, the people decide on the judge of their choice.
Q. Are there several candidates for a vacant judgeship? If not, I do not understand where the liberty of choice of the people is provided.
A. You do not understand the nature of our country. There is no need for several candidates. All the candidates who are selected are well known to the people as the people's friends.
Q. But who nominates the candidates?
A. The people themselves nominate the candidates and then they elect them.
Q. But when the people foregather, the candidates must have already been nominated by somebody. Is not that somebody the state?

1905: My family.

1913: Maypole dancers (*row*: M. Cremen, J. He... M. Owen, R. Aitken).

1916: Taken just before Jim joined the Royal Navy.

1919: Fr. Bickerstaff's class (*front row, third from right* D. J. Hennessy; *back row, second from right* J. C. Heenan).

Ushaw College, Durham.

SS. Peter and Paul, Ilford, where I was baptised and ordained.

1929: Student in Rome.

A. M. D. G.

John C. Heenan

Ordained Priest

July 5th, 1930

————

Pray for me

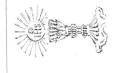

Prayer

"O Jesus, Eternal Priest, keep Thy holy ones within the shelter of Thy Sacred Heart, where none may touch them. Keep unstained the anointed hands, which daily touch Thy sacred body. Keep unsullied the lips, purpled with Thy precious blood. Keep pure and unearthly the hearts sealed with the sublime mark of Thy glorious priesthood. Let Thy Holy love surround them, and shield them from the world's contagion. Bless their labours with abundant fruit and may they to whom they minister here below be to Thy priests a joy and consolation on this earth and in Heaven their everlasting crown."

My ordination card.

1928: Fr. Weaver, S. J., with future priests.

6th July, 1930: The baby is my nephew, Brian Reynolds, F.R.C.S.

1935: My parents.

1948: The last picture of my mother
(aged 82).

1932: St. Joseph's School, Barking (*front row, right* Maggie Lyons; *back row, second from right* Maureen Cremen).

Broadcast se

1938: With my brother Frank.

1936: Passport photograph.

1936: Lola.

: Political prisoners near
Moscow.

1938: Manor P
- altar servers

1939: Manor Park
- First Communion

1940: Manor Park - outdoor procession.

1941: Ecumenical Service for A.R.P. workers.

1949:
The mobile chapel.

1949:
With Fr. Dwyer, C.M

1950: Rome - my sister
with Dr. King and
Helen Courchaine.

1949: Royal Albert Hall - rally to support Cardinal Mindszenty.

Val Elwes by Simon Elwes, R.A

12th March, 1951: Leeds Cathedral.

A. You must know that in our country the state and the people are one, and therefore when a man is selected to be a judge by the state, he is selected by the people. We do not in this country select a man just because of his parents or of his social standing. We do not want to have a highly educated judiciary out of touch with the common people. But we want men that we can fully trust and who have brains in their head. In capitalist countries you can graduate from your university or law school and remain a fool. In our country a man must be socially cultured. When a man is elected a judge then he may study the law.

Q. But I have not quite gathered yet how exactly names are supplied by the state for selection. Is a list of names furnished by the Department of Justice?

A. No. The social organisations nominate candidates who are approved by the state, and the approved candidates are offered for election to the people.

Q. Can the people refuse the names that are offered to them?

A. Of course they can. But they do not refuse because only the best men are offered for election; citizens who have lived in a particular district and are well known by the people and by their organisations as capable and just.

Q. But do you not agree that any system of election of judges is bad, because if a judge holds his position in virtue of his popularity with the people, his decisions, especially towards the end of his tenure, are bound to be affected?

A. This is not true in our country. In capitalist countries the system is that the state and the people are different. Here the state and the people are one, and the judge, who is the servant of the people, is the servant of the state, and, therefore, would not allow his judicial decisions to be affected by popular sentiment. If he allowed favouritism he would be removed by the state.

Q. But the masses are not capable of judging upon the judicial qualities of any man. He may be a popular social worker, but he may not have the legal mind which will enable him to sift evidence and decide, whatever his personal feelings may be, whether or not a man has been proved guilty in law. It would often happen that, as a man, a judge would condemn, but, as a judge, he will say 'Not proven'. How can ordinary people know if judicial qualities are present in the candidate?

A. In this country our law is written not only on pages in

volumes, dead permits and dead laws. Our lawyers do not follow thick books written during the ages. This is not important. Important it is for a man to have brains and to be able to combine three things together: reasonable concentration on facts, economic experience and political education.

We are shocked by the travesty which is given the name of democracy in Eastern Europe. In communist states—as once in Fascist Italy and Nazi Germany—elections are held without alternative candidates. The almost unanimous vote obtained by unopposed candidates is solemnly promulgated. Having abandoned hope of understanding the free elections for judges in the Soviet Union I decided to sample the actual administration of justice in court. Accompanied by an interpreter I attended part of two trials. I went into each courtroom prejudiced against the whole system. To my surprise—almost to my annoyance—I was favourably impressed. It must be remembered that I was never present at a political trial. I did not attend the higher courts where at that time and for some years to come (1935–1938) the notorious public prosecutor Andrei Vyshinsky terrorised those who by Stalin's decree were to be found guilty and liquidated. A most pleasing impression was given by the very atmosphere of the court rooms. There was none of the legal panoply which so bewilders anyone making a first appearance in an English court. I have twice been present at trials in American courts. On each occasion I felt some nostalgia for the bewigged dignity of our courts at home. Here in Moscow I saw dignity without wigs. The discourtesy so rife in America's lower courts could scarcely be imagined in Soviet Russia any more than in England. Lawyers and witnesses are too disciplined or, perhaps, too well-mannered to show contempt. Whatever be the explanation I found in the Soviet people's courts an admirable mean between the styles of the British and American courts.

The first trial was that of a Red Army officer accused of forging party membership cards. There were apparently no political implications. I did not stay long enough to hear the whole story. Whatever offence the prisoner was alleged to have committed it was evidently not regarded as very serious. Neither he nor his friends sitting in the front row looked unduly worried. He had probably done nothing more than hand out party cards to people who were not registered. (It was not difficult to come by a membership card. I still have one in my possession.) There were very few people in court and the proceedings were monumentally dull. Neither counsel spoke a word while I was present. The judge conducted the trial talking continuously to the prisoner. It seemed to be a friendly dialogue. The judge never raised his voice. He said that he did not wish to exaggerate the fault of the accused. The officer agreed to everything the judge suggested. Yes, he had been rather foolish but, after all, he had not been guilty of any real crime. I did not wait to hear the verdict. After half-an-hour I had seen enough to gauge the atmosphere of one people's court. The two social representatives might as well have stayed at home. All they had to do was keep awake. This difficult task they carried out without apparent strain.

In the other court a young woman was on trial for the alleged murder of her husband. The case was nearing conclusion when we arrived and I was therefore able to await verdict and sentence. The presiding judge was prosecutor, defence counsel and philosopher. While I was present no one but the judge and prisoner said a word. The judge was quite a young man but he behaved in a fatherly way towards the young woman in the dock. Once again I was struck by the dignity and lack of pomp. It was Comrade Judge and Comrade Citizen. Listening to barristers addressing uneducated witnesses in English courts I have often thought that the barrier of thought and language can be so formidable that the administration of justice becomes needlessly difficult. This woman and the judge spoke the same language in every sense. She realised that she had done wrong. The court appreciated that the provocation had been enormous. After the briefest of conferences with the lay assessors the judge declared the woman guilty. He said that in view of the fact that she was an excellent engineer and also a good mother he did not propose to send her to prison. She would be on probation for three years. Everyone seemed satisfied with the result. There was no handshaking, no congratulations, no thanking, no smiling. This was Russia not England.

It may seem shocking that a woman who had killed her husband even under provocation should receive no punishment. Yet, in fact, an injustice might have been done by putting that young mother in gaol. In the year 1954 when I was Bishop of Leeds I visited Askham Grange, the women's prison in York. The governor was Miss Size, a remarkable woman who had retired from the prison service as governor of Holloway. She was recalled from retirement to open this first experimental open prison for women. I invited prisoners to come to my room if they wanted to have a private chat. One of my first visitors came to complain that she had been unjustly sentenced to three years' imprisonment. I asked her what she had done. She had killed her mother-in-law. The girl said that the old lady abused her and the children all day long. One evening as the girl was bathing one of the babies by the fireside the mother-in-law began a fresh attack. After the day-long nagging this was more than the young mother could stand. She hit the old lady with a poker. According to her story it was a gesture more than a blow but her mother-in-law took fright, fell off her chair and hit the back of her head on the stove. This, the girl said, was what killed her. I asked if her husband believed her story. Yes, he did and never missed a visiting day. Meanwhile her three small children were pining for their mother. I told Miss Size that at the risk of being thought ingenuous I fully accepted the truth of the girl's story. "So do I," replied Miss Size. She then told me she was so convinced a miscarriage of justice had taken place that she had just written a report to the Prison Commissioners. She suggested that since I was a completely independent observer a letter from me would carry weight with the Home Secretary. It did.

The day following my visit to the people's court I came near to being much more personally and painfully involved in the court scene. I was arrested. I was taking a morning stroll near the Bolshoi Theatre when I noticed a woman in rags begging in the street. Begging was, of course, an offence and I waited to see if she would be moved on by the police. It struck me that her photograph might prove useful as proof that poverty had not been entirely abolished in the U.S.S.R. as its supporters claimed. I had become careless and over-confident. With a snapshot of the well-guarded Lubyanka prison already in my camera it should not be difficult to take a shot of the old lady. As soon as I had taken the picture two men accosted me with angry gesticulations. I did not realise that they were members of the secret police. I was not left long in ignorance. One of the men speaking in English told me that it was an offence to take photographs and insisted that I must accompany him to police headquarters. Once more I had needlessly made myself an object of suspicion. This time I was not only disgusted with myself but really alarmed. Although the police had not actually laid hands on me I was clearly under arrest. One man ordered me to follow him while the other walked behind to make sure that I did as I was told.

I was taken to a splendid building known to me as the Moscow Hotel. Passing by this fine new building I had more than once wondered why it was not used for tourists. It was described as a hotel probably because it contained suites for official guests as well as government offices. The picture I had taken of the old lady worried me less than the rest of the undeveloped film in the camera. I decided at all costs to keep possession of that film. When we arrived at the Moscow Hotel the police took me to an office where a civilian of military appearance sat at an imposing desk. Listening to the story of the two men he looked at me with growing distaste. I could not follow the conversation but evidently this man decided that the matter must be dealt with by his superior officer. The latter when he arrived began to question me in excellent English. He said firmly that he must confiscate my camera. The capitalist press, he complained, was interested only in hostile news about Soviet Russia. It was evident that I had taken a picture of the beggar woman in order to publish false propaganda concerning social conditions in the U.S.S.R. Once more he demanded my camera. While he was speaking I was pondering how to play for time. I protested that it was uncivilised to arrest a visitor for taking a picture in the open street. To a foreigner the old lady looked picturesque in her peasant costume. Nobody had warned me that it was against the law to take photographs of Soviet citizens. The Bolshoi Theatre was not a prohibited area and, indeed, I had taken several photos there. Intourist had warned us not to take pictures of the Kremlin or of military barracks. Since I had disobeyed no regulations I refused to have my camera confiscated. The police chief was very calm. He did not want to use force, he said, but he must insist on taking possession of the camera.

By this time a plan had formed in my mind. I agreed to hand over the camera on one condition. My camera must be confiscated in the presence of the British consul. I asked the police to telephone the consul and ask him to come to the Moscow Hotel without delay. This did not please the police at all. They said that they did not want this to be blown up into an international incident. (Relations between Britain and the U.S.S.R. at the time were fairly good.) They would prefer to settle the matter in a friendly manner. They decided not to confiscate my camera after all. They would be satisfied to have the film. This gave me my cue. If that was all they wanted, I said, I would make no further demur. I quickly opened up the camera thus exposing the film. I pulled it out and threw it on the desk. They were satisfied because the offending picture could not now be published. I was even more satisfied because the rest of the film could not be inspected. We all shook hands and I was allowed to go. I made a firm resolution to be much more circumspect during my few remaining days in Soviet Russia. Thoroughly chastened by my latest experience I had no difficulty in keeping this resolution. I wish I could say the same of all the resolutions I have made since that day.

Time was running out but there was still one institution in Moscow which I was most anxious to inspect. Many years earlier when the Webbs were preaching the Soviet gospel they were uncritically supported by George Bernard Shaw. Despite his brilliant mind he was in some ways as simple and stubborn as a child. He never retracted his foolish praise of Soviet despotism. After the equally brilliant Frenchman André Gide had written *Return from the U.S.S.R.* he brought out a second book to show how he had been hoaxed by the Soviets. This book he called *Adjustments to my Return (Retouches à mon Retour de l'U.R.R.S.).* After visiting the Soviet Union Shaw wrote a panegyric of Soviet penology. Criminals were regarded, he said, as patients to be cured not as delinquents to be punished. His account of Bolshovoi, the experimental prison outside Moscow, had aroused my interest and I was hoping to visit it. Preliminary enquiries were not encouraging. Intourist informed me that no foreigner had been allowed to visit Bolshovoi for some years. It would require a special permit from the Commissar for Internal Affairs (Home Office). Since my interest was psychological my best hope would be to approach the Commissar through V.O.K.S. (International Commission for Cultural Affairs). The problem was to make out a convincing case in higher quarters than Intourist. Once again Garry Bostock lent his support.

He telephoned the director of V.O.K.S. and told her that as vice-consul he was particularly anxious to arrange for a distinguished young psychologist from England to visit Bolshovoi. He proposed to bring me to her to explain in person the purpose of my proposed visit to the prison. When we arrived at V.O.K.S. Garry introduced me with great deference and gave the impression that I was a very important person indeed. The director, as might be expected, was a lady of high intelligence. She questioned me at length about my qualifications and the purpose of my visit to the prison. I had to use a certain verbal dexterity in giving my answers. She was interested, for example, in my doctorate of philosophy but it would have been unwise to let her know that it was awarded by the Gregorian University in Rome. Nor when I mentioned school inspection did I think it necessary to disclose the fact that I was concerned with the religious inspection of Catholic schools. I gave as my chief reason for wishing to see Bolshovoi our growing anxiety over juvenile delinquents. I told her that I had read Shaw's description of Bolshovoi and felt that we might have a great deal to learn from the Soviets. The director was very gracious but could hold out no strong hope that permission to visit the prison would be granted. She undertook to approach the Ministry of the Interior on my behalf and promised to recommend my application. I left V.O.K.S. feeling fairly satisfied. Although the prospects of receiving permission to visit Bolshovoi were bleak, at least I had not aroused suspicion by asking to go. I went back to the Bostocks' home for a dinner party which had been arranged to give me the opportunity of meeting some of the non-diplomatic English residents. Among them were the Vickers engineers and their families to whom, of course, my identity was not disclosed. From them I learned something of the difficulties encountered by foreigners doing business with the Soviet government. In addition to the delays of bureaucracy they had to contend with the inability of Russians to behave like normal clients on account of the suspicion attaching to anyone in contact with foreigners. Entertainment, a normal part of business practice in the rest of the world, was barred in the Soviet Union. Russian clients simply could not risk their liberty by becoming friendly.

It was after midnight when I returned to the National Hotel. As soon as I entered the door the clerk on duty told me that a gentleman from the Ministry of the Interior had been waiting for me for several hours. This was alarming news. I wondered which of my misdemeanours had been reported. Above all I feared that the clever director of V.O.K.S. might have grown suspicious and sounded the alarm. The name of my patient visitor was Einstein (he claimed no relationship with the mathematician). Einstein had brought the surprising and very welcome news that the Commissar for International Affairs had agreed to make an exception in my case. I would be welcome at Bolshovoi the following morning. My surprise was only equalled by my relief that I had not once more landed myself in trouble.

Bolshovoi is called not a prison but a labour commune. It was started in 1924 by Felix Georgenski, who had a vocation for reforming young criminals. After the Russian famine thousands of young people roamed the country. Given the name *bezprizorniks* they were not what we now call hippies. They were not, in other words, drop-outs in the modern sense. They were children who, having begun to wander in search of food and security, ended up by becoming gangsters. Georgenski, although a former head of the dreaded Cheka, had a genuine love for children. He was convinced that punishment and physical violence could never be a way of salvation for these unfortunates. The Soviet government appointed Georgenski and his assistant Yagoda (later head of O.G.P.U. and, still later, liquidated by Stalin) to organise the commune. It was centred on the house of a former chocolate king named Kraft. The colony started with fifteen young jailbirds. By 1936 the experiment had proved itself. The commune had no less than twelve thousand inhabitants at the time of my visit. It contained factories, workshops, schools and theatres. A hundred and forty hectares of land were under cultivation. The factories specialised in the production of sports goods and produced nearly fifty per cent of the national needs. The annual turnover of the commune was the impressive figure of forty-seven million roubles.

It is difficult to know how much of the information given to me was true. I was put on my guard against accepting everything without question by a curious incident which occurred half-way through the day. The officials at Bolshovoi had been instructed to allow me to go freely wherever I wished—evidently the story of the Palace of Pioneers had been faithfully reported. Einstein, my guide, was no ordinary Intourist official but a Man from the Ministry. He was able to speak and act with authority.

The incident occurred in one of the women's blocks. I pointed out at random a block I would like to visit. Entering the first room on the ground floor I found the place in some disorder. The girls were naturally embarrassed to receive a visitor without having had a chance to tidy their room. I talked to them for a few minutes with Einstein interpreting. While we were talking a young woman came into the room, spoke to Einstein and pointed upwards. When she had finished Einstein replied with a curt *'Nyet'*. I immediately asked him why he had refused. I had sensed from her gestures and demeanour that she wanted me to be taken upstairs to her quarters. I had also heard her say something about speaking English. (This naturally was one of the Russian sentences I had learned.) Einstein was perplexed and indignant. If I didn't speak Russian, as I pretended, how could I have followed his conversation with the girl? I reassured him at once. I told him that although I knew only a few words of Russian I did understand young people. It had been only a guess on my part that the girl had invited us to her room. Einstein smiled again and agreed to come upstairs. The girl led us to the room she shared with three companions. It was a most attractive room, well lit and tastefully decorated. In the corner there was a girl sitting in an invalid's chair. She was the English speaker whom her friend was anxious for me to meet. We chatted for a moment or two and I congratulated her rather insincerely on her English which was, in fact, very poor. She replied that she knew I was only flattering her because she had been studying English for only a few months. The one foreign language she spoke really well was Italian since her family had originally come from Italy. This gave me a wonderful opportunity. "*Allora*," I said, "*parliamo Italiano!*" I had been told by Einstein that the commune catered for all prisoners irrespective of their record. Criminals were no longer put into penitentiaries but given a genuine chance of rehabilitation in places such as Bolshovoi. The young lady could speak freely to me because neither Einstein nor anybody else in the vicinity understood Italian. She told me that she had been in prison in Kiev for two years before coming to Bolshovoi. She gave me to understand that the commune was in the nature of a reward for good behaviour. After this incident I listened to whatever I was told with some reserve.

Despite the inaccuracy and exaggeration of the official claims made on its behalf there can be no doubt that Bolshovoi was a remarkable experiment. The commune not only taught trades to the young people but created in them an interest in art and music. The illiterates were taught to read and, according to the story I was told, about a hundred each year were prepared for university. I could easily have been deceived but responsible Russians, including Maxim Gorky, have written in admiration of the achievements of Bolshovoi. The institution is greatly to the credit of the Soviet Union.

When I asked what means of correction were used I was informed that sanctions were rarely needed. The heaviest crime, drinking, was dealt with by fines and detention. The heaviest punishment was expulsion from Bolshovoi. This is not so incredible as it sounds. It is true that in the West a prisoner would hardly fear expulsion but in the Soviet Union to be expelled without documents is equivalent to a sentence of starvation. There would be neither work nor shelter. Bolshovoi is run on the enlightened principle that those leaving must be fitted to take their place in society. They are treated more as graduates than as ex-prisoners. Before leaving, each prisoner is made a member of his trade union or enrolled in the Red Army. After a period of satisfactory work in a factory or, alternatively, successful completion of military service, a prisoner's criminal record is destroyed. Technically there is no stigma attaching to an ex-prisoner. He may even be a member of the party. This is the Soviet equivalent of canonisation.

I was amused by the refusal of the officials in Bolshovoi to admit the existence of any slight imperfection in the system. I asked, for example, if they had much difficulty with homosexuality. The men and women are, of course, living in separate quarters. The reply was that Soviet citizens are not subject to the weaknesses of capitalist society. Homosexuality was a monopoly of the aristocracy in Russia. The worst crime these young people committed was drug-taking Despite the concentration of thousands of delinquents I was assured that there is no contamination. In Bolshovoi nobody learns bad habits. Everyone profits by the example of the good. Despite such nonsense I came away convinced that both in principle and practice Bolshovoi is excellent. Today's young people in England are immeasurably more sophisticated than the young Russian delinquents I saw in 1936. Bolshovoi could not be transplanted to Britain to replace our approved schools. I am quite certain that a commune is sounder than any juvenile prison. Father Flanagan of Boys' Town, Nebraska, U.S.A. has shown how this can be achieved.

I spent my last day in Moscow saying goodbye to the friends of assorted nations I had acquired since my arrival. I had been in the U.S.S.R. less than a month but I felt a lifetime away from the Barking curate. England seemed remote in time and space. The expression 'Iron curtain' had not yet been coined but any traveller felt that Russia and England were in different worlds. During the final few hours in Moscow I bought papers and books to use in rebutting denials of religious persecution. I did not need to know much Russian to make my selection because illustrations gave a sufficient indication of the text. The anti-religious journals were unbelievably brutal. At that time I had not seen the Nazi anti-Jewish paper *Der Stürmer*. I realised later that *Der Stürmer* and *Bezbosnik*.

(*The Atheist*) could have come from the same publishing house. Substitute popes, priests and believers for Jewish rabbis, lawyers and writers and the messages of the two obscene journals were identical. Scurrility and blasphemy filled every page. I bought also some children's books which are crude and direct in their approach. Priests are depicted killing babies. Fat men in shiny top hats crucify workers. One infants' reader tells a story in a series of pictures. In the first drawing a young mother and her baby are kissing a cross held by a bishop wearing a tall mitre and a wicked leer. By the end of the series of pictures the faces of mother and child have become disfigured with spots and sores contracted through kissing the cross. Children with the lowest I.Q. would be able to grasp the lesson that religion is bad for health.

I had little opportunity of studying the religious situation in the Soviet Union. Even if I had been able to talk in Russian to the Orthodox clergy they would have been afraid to speak to a foreigner. Father Braun told me a great deal of what was happening in the Soviet Union but his information, though doubtless true, was second-hand. My mission had been to collect first-hand information. The one thing I saw daily was the deep fear of the people. Had I been in touch with Russians in public life I would have seen far greater fear abounding. The Stalin terror had been in progress for some months at the time of my visit but was little known in the outside world. In the autumn of 1936 all eyes were on Spain where the loyal workers supported by the toiling masses of the U.S.S.R. were fighting Franco and his Nazi and Fascist confederates. It was only after repeated trials and interminable legal assassinations that English people realised the frightful reality of Soviet democracy. The following is a *Times* report of 22nd March, 1938. This was published a year and a half after my Moscow visit. It is significant because it shows how long a time elapsed before citizens in this country were able to see what I—and presumably any diplomat or journalist—could see so plainly in 1936. The Soviet Union in 1936 was still being presented by left-wing propagandists and 'intellectuals' as a workers' paradise.

So far as the Russian masses are concerned the most recent, though not necessarily the last, of the series of great treason trials has been a complete and unqualified triumph. Lincoln's aphorism about the limits of popular credulity has lost much of its value in those modern States where the central authority control both Press and wireless. All the people have been told only the Government truth and now believe it to be the whole truth.

To estimate the real effect which the executions and trials since 1935 have had on the country it is important first to study the lists of victims and the offices they held.

Among the men near the top of the Central Government, two Deputy Prime Ministers (Rudzutak, Mezhlauk) have been 'removed'; the Ministry of Defence has lost by suicide and the executioner three Deputy Ministers (Gamarnik, Tukhachevsky, Orloff), who were 'unmasked' as traitors, and three others (Yegoroff, Alksnis, Viktoroff) have disappeared to unknown fates; the Ministry of Defence-Industry has lost both its Minister and Deputy Minister (Rukhimovich, Muklevich); Posts and Telegraphs have been for many a kind of condemned cell; Smirnoff, Rykoff, Yagoda held this post for brief periods before going to the dungeons of the G.P.U., their successor Khalepsky and his Deputy (Prokofieff, friend and assistant of Yagoda) have followed them. Stalin's police have removed, shot, and otherwise handled or mishandled so many high officials that their names make a long and weary list. In fact, they have been the chiefs in almost every Ministry, including envoys to almost every country. The purging of the 11 constituent 'Republican Governments' of the Soviet Union has been even more thorough than at the Centre. To mention a few, the R.S.F.S.R. or Russia proper has this way lost the Ministers of Education, Finance, and Justice; the Ukraine its Premier and Director of Education; White Russia its Premier and Minister of Agriculture; Tajikistan its President and seven Ministers; Turkmanistan its President and four Ministers; Georgia its Premier and six Ministers; Armenia its President and five Ministers, and Kirghizia its President (Shamurzin). Some 40 chairmen of Territorial (Oblast) Executive Committees, the 'Mayors' of Kieff, Kharkoff, and Rostoff, more than 500 directors of trusts, factories, and big industrial undertakings have also recently paid the penalty of 'enemies of the people'. Havoc among Communists engaged more particularly in high party posts than in the Administration has been on a similar scale. They include Bukharin, Zinovieff, Kamenyeff, Rudzutak, all former members of the *Politburo*, the highest organ of the party, and many of the highest officials in the constituent 'Republics'.

The blow delivered to the Red Army last June, when Marshal Tukhachevsky and General Yakir, Uborevich, Kork, Eideman, Feldman, Primakoff, and Putna were shot without the formality of an open trial, has been followed by the wholesale 'removal' and disappearance of senior officers. In most cases they are taken by an unknown hand and no announcement is made. Nothing definite was known about Admiral Orloff, Deputy Minister of Defence and Commander-in-Chief of the Red Navy, who represented the Soviet Union at the Coronation in London last year, until Voroshiloff in his speech on February 22 mentioned that Orloff had been 'wiped off the face of the earth as a traitor and a spy'. Among others who have disappeared from the highest posts in the fighting Services are deputy political chiefs of the Army, generals, commanders and deputy-commanders of the Kharkoff, North Caucasus, Ural, Transbaikal, Leningrad, and Moscow Military Districts, and the Tank Corps; Tkacheff, commander of the Civil Air Force; Tupoleff, the famous head of Soviet aeroplane construction; Admiral Sivkoff, Commander of the Baltic Fleet; Kozhanoff of the Black Sea, and Kireyeff of the Pacific Fleet; and nearly all the political chiefs of all the military districts and the Red Fleet. In 1935 the newly organised Military Council attached to the Ministry of Defence consisted of 80 men; of these 51 have since been proclaimed traitors.

No unbiased foreign observer of the last trial was wholly convinced that the prosecution had justified these assumptions, but for the purposes of the trial itself that was beside the mark. The prosecution did not seek to convince foreigners. What it wished to do—and did—was to reduce ideological oppositionists like Bukharin to their lowest terms as the Soviet public saw them, to make a simple, easy, childish identification, which the masses could understand, of theory with practice, of anti-Kremlin discussion with treason, rebellion, sabotage, and espionage, of all aims and methods to overthrow the Kremlin's authority with murder, counter-revolution, restoration of capitalism and every other crime in the Soviet calendar.

The greatest shock of the year was in June, when the executioner began killing the heads of the Red Army. These were not given an open trial. Since last summer the formality of a public trial has become the exception rather than the rule. In December Yenukidze, member of Stalin's Constitutional Commission and

Secretary of the Central Executive Committee since 1918, Karakhan, Deputy Minister of Foreign Affairs, and six others were shot without trial as traitors and spies, the names and fate being recorded in the Soviet Press. In this month's trial, of the 21 men in the dock 18 were shot. The Constitution as a whole since the end of last year, though in practice it is a mere caricature of what the Stalin Commission worked out, is a shell without a kernel. Many of the members of the new 'Parliament' elected without opposition candidates last December as men then in full favour have since been relegated to the rank of traitors and disappeared. The constituent republics have not yet had their elections of local parliaments, but plans have been published to hold most of them in the summer. As the national republics have suffered most in the purge, extremely few of the men who worked out and passed their particular Constitutions will be present at the elections.

How far these trials have affected the morale of Soviet enterprises or of the Red Army time alone can tell.

I was glad to be going home. The strain of acting was beginning to tell. It is one thing to take part in a charade for half-an-hour but quite another to keep up a pretence for weeks without a break. Amateur dramatics are not an adequate preparation for serious masquerading. In a play everyone knows that you are Joe Bloggs not Richard III. The only rehearsal for my marathon performance had taken place more than five years earlier in Rome at carnival time. Impersonating a fictitious Mr. Traynor of Chicago, I had been shown round the English College by an unsuspecting student against whom I had a grudge. Bernard, the student concerned, had played a successful and humiliating practical joke on another young student. Painstakingly we planned a reprisal. We knew that Louis Dolan, a close friend of Bernard, lived in Chicago. This led us to invent Mr. Traynor, a character from Chicago on a European tour. Our first step was to obtain possession of writing paper from the Grand, one of Rome's luxury hotels. Mr. Traynor duly wrote to inform Bernard that on the advice of his friend Mr. Dolan he proposed to pay a call. He was interested in the Catholic faith and hoped that Bernard would be able to solve some of his religious problems. In order to forestall enquiries Mr. Traynor's letter was followed immediately by a second letter, delivered by hand. The second letter said that Mrs. Traynor and her daughter were dissatisfied with the poor service at the Grand

Hotel and Mr. Traynor was taking them to Naples. He himself however would return to Rome in time to keep his appointment at 11 o'clock on the following day (Shrove Tuesday).

We assembled a wig and a wardrobe. For two busy hours on the Tuesday morning the make-up man of our student dramatic society worked on my face. A beard to match the grey wig was built hair by hair. Then elegantly attired I was smuggled to the reception room to which in a few moments Bernard was summoned by the hall porter. Bernard conducted me round the college giving me a comprehensive history of that venerable institution. The moment of purest joy came when he took me into the library. I was in my seventh year and nearing the end of my theological course. Bernard was only in his first year of divinity. Taking down from the shelves volumes of the Fathers of the Church I asked Bernard to explain certain passages. They were, of course, all controversial texts. Poor Bernard was completely out of his depth. With sadistic pleasure I plied him with more and more questions. Then, almost inevitably, I overplayed my hand. I asked if he would join me and my wife that night for dinner. He replied that he would have to ask the rector who, he added, in any case would want to meet me. I pleaded shyness of ecclesiastics to no avail. To my chagrin Bernard insisted on bringing the rector into the library to meet me. Instead of pulling off my wig there and then I was foolish enough to allow myself to be interviewed by the rector, Mgr. Godfrey, who kindly invited me to stay to luncheon. I made my excuses and left the college with all possible speed.

My troubles were not quite over. The rector told Bernard that he must take Mr. Traynor to see the rector of the American college. Since for a Protestant layman Traynor was amazingly well-informed on Catholic theology it would be best to put him in touch with an American priest. He could then continue instructions in the faith after his return to Chicago. Then came an almost incredible quirk in events. Bernard came to me to ask a favour—would I accompany him to visit a Mr. Traynor who had spent the morning in the college? Naturally I assumed that the game was up. But no. He went on to explain that this American gentleman was well read and Bernard had been unable to answer his questions. The rector had therefore suggested that one of the theologians should accompany him to answer the insatiable Mr. Traynor's questions. I had planned the denouement for that evening—carnival traditionally ended with a smoking concert in the common room. The end came, in fact, more quickly. Bernard came to my room to give me final instructions. When he opened the door he found not only me but, scattered all over the room, the finery, wig and beard of the morning's visitor. There was some delicate discussion with the rector later in the day. He took it all in the spirit of the carnival.

Impersonating the American was something of an ordeal but it did not last long and was undertaken for fun. My Russian performance was easier in that I did not assume a false name and accent. It was much harder because it was unremitting. It would incidentally have carried more unpleasant consequences in the event of failure. On that last day in Moscow I was therefore happy in the knowledge that before midnight I would be safely on my way to Poland. Some of my friends came to see me off but Lola was not among them. Julius was perturbed by her absence. There was always anxiety for the safety of Russians who had been seen in the company of foreigners. I was also sorry but for another reason. Although our group had spoken of future meetings I wanted to tell Lola that in all probability I would never return to the Soviet Union. Never having seen Lola alone, there had been no opportunity of giving her any idea of my future activities. It was most disagreeable to have to mislead all these new friends. I would have much preferred to take them into my confidence but the risk would have been too great. Now that I was about to leave it might have been possible to have given Lola some hint of my position. It would have been impossible to have had a private word at the station but it was unsatisfactory not to have said goodbye. The reason why she was not on the platform came to light later. She had come to the station but could not find the platform for the Warsaw train. She must have hesitated to ask directions for fear of disclosing that she was in touch with foreigners. Thus my last few minutes in Moscow provided another example of the prevalent fear.

Before describing my adventures in Poland and Germany it will be convenient to close the account of my relations with Russian friends. I never heard from Ross or Levett. I wrote a Christmas note to Jack Ross but received no reply. Julius replied to my letter—I have given extracts from his answer. He did not write again. Lola wrote on a number of occasions. I think of her still with great compassion. This secret believer whose gentle nature was bruised by the crudities of Soviet communism was overcome by her brief encounter with people from the West. She was left longing for the civilised social life we are at liberty to enjoy. Freedom for her did not represent a chance for political action but an opportunity to practise her religion and to make friends irrespective of race and ideology. I have often wondered how many young Russians shared Lola's longing. I did not know during my visit that within the Kremlin itself there was another young lady, Svetlana, Stalin's daughter, whose ideas were not unlike Lola's.

I shall give only a few short extracts from Lola's letters. I do not know if she survived the perils of Stalin's purges and the hazards of the second world war. I never knew her family name or, of course, her home address. It would be insensitive even after all these years to quote her letters in full. A few sentences however will reveal something of the gentleness of her character. It will also show how I tried to make amends for having had to conceal my true identity from my Russian friends. In her first letter (30th November, 1936) Lola explains why she did not see me off. "I waited for half-an-hour at the station to see my friend off. The lights were out and I could see nothing. So I went home. You can't imagine I was so sorry. With sadness in my heart I came home and could not speak with anybody. That night I was with Allie and she told me you had looked for me." Because of its unconscious humour I give another short extract from the same long letter: "When I received your letter I was so glad that I lost my appetite. So if you want to make your little friend be happy please write to her as much as you can."

I did not write again for nearly three months. I felt that Lola was entitled to be told something more about my position but I shrank from hurting her. I did not know how to explain that for security reasons I had been obliged to deceive her, Allie, Julius and all my new friends. Since I was unable as yet to think of any solution, my next letter was of the ordinary conversational kind. To this Lola sent a six-page reply. Her letter, dated 25th February, 1937 begins "My dear John". Towards the end of the letter she refers to this: "I hope you are not angry with me that I call you 'my dear'. Maybe you think it is too soon to call you in such a way. But my feelings tell me that I can do it. If it is not pleasant for you write to me please." I was rather alarmed by both the tone and content of this second letter. I regretted all the more that it had been impossible to tell Lola exactly who I was. I realised that, in the old phrase, absence makes the heart grow fonder. I decided that for her own good I must risk giving her pain. I rejected as too hurtful the obvious course of merely breaking off correspondence. Once more I consulted my playwright friend, Wilfred Eyre. After much thought and discussion we decided it would be best to tell Lola that I intended to give my whole life to the Church. Thus, we thought, the correspondence would peter out without any offence being given. My only consideration was how to tell this to Lola without humiliating her. She might feel slighted if she were to learn that I had deceived her about my identity. The final wording of my letter was left to Marney Eyre. We felt that a woman would know how to put the matter tactfully. The following is the relevant part of my letter:

> ... Now, Lola, I'm going to tell you something which will, I know, be a great surprise to you. I had meant to tell you the day we missed each other at the station. I had no other opportunity as we were never alone together. I am going to become a priest (minister of the spirit). It will be soon because I have already studied philosophy and other subjects. This means I shall never visit the U.S.S.R. again. I may be sent to the middle of Africa. A Catholic priest, like a soldier, must obey orders always. Unlike a soldier he may never marry. I shall always remember with pleasure our meeting in Moscow and will pray constantly for your happiness.

This promise I kept. I used to pray for Lola as the Stalin purge grew more widespread. Nor did I forget her when the German armies invaded Russia.

Lola replied, by return of post, on 18th March, 1937. Her letter began "My devout friend John". At first glance I feared that my news had made her bitter. She was, on the contrary, merely incredulous. "Henry and I have spoken about it and we are at a loss. Is it seriously?" Lola does not think that my being a priest is a good idea. "It is not fit for you." But her generosity conquers her disapproval. "Of course I like such people who gives his life for some business. So I can say that I wish you to come off with flying colours and to be well known priest in London." But Lola remains sceptical about my vocation: "John, maybe you will change your decision and will choose another speciality." She feels I am throwing away my life—as some Catholic parents do when their sons and daughters want to become priests or nuns. "But what is to be done?" She adds: "Somebody must be a priest and you were chosen by the fate." But

Lola does not at all like the note of finality in my letter: "I think it will not be a reason for finishing our correspondence. I hope you will write to me. P.S. John! write Mockba not Mocha."

I wrote only once more. I have no copy of this letter. Judging from her long reply I must have tried to explain that the priesthood meant more to me than just a 'speciality'. I must also have reminded her again that there had been no opportunity in Moscow of telling her my plans. This evidently gave Lola comfort. In her final letter (17th April, 1937) she sounds more reconciled "My devoted friend John," she begins, "I was very glad to have such a true letter. Now I have a clear idea about everything. When I met you for the first time you made a great affection on me. Your aspiration to do good for the people astounded me. Your attitude was very simple and good. If you want to know, it is very difficult to meet such a man as you are. You tried to do something good for me." But, womanlike, she does not leave the matter there. Two pages further on she comes back to the idea of my unsuitability for this 'speciality'. " . . . I cannot imagine that John who was so jolly in Moscow (a reference to the jolly party during which I shaved Stalin to shock Julius!) would be a priest. Tell me please, of course if it is possible for you, did you ever love anybody before?" Lola ends as she began: "Well John, I shall not write more. I think now it is everything clear. We shall not write more about it. The weather is nice. It remembers me when you were in Moscow. Well goodbye, your friend, Lola."

CHAPTER
SIX

THE TRAIN FROM MOSCOW WAS WARM AND COMFORTABLE. I FELT TIRED but relaxed. I need no longer fear trouble with the Soviets. My next problem—a very small one—was how to cross the Polish border without forfeiting all the Russian literature I had bought. At that time the whole Polish government and people were fiercely anti-communist. I had been warned in Moscow that the Polish customs would examine baggage for communist propaganda. I packed most of the papers and booklets inside various articles of clothing. I did not propose to declare them. I would have been sorry but not inconsolable if they were confiscated. Other Russian papers I left in the railway carriage under the seat. The one document I really wanted not to lose was my copy of the new Soviet Constitution. This, I had been told, was like a red rag—or should I say a red flag?—to Polish customs officers. To double my chances of smuggling it through customs I bought two copies of the document. One I put just inside my suitcase. If the case were opened it would be at once exposed to view. The other copy I held rolled up in my hand. This simple stratagem was even more successful that I had expected. The official swooped on the copy of the Constitution, assumed that I had no other literature and looked no further. He did not notice what I was carrying in my hand. When I returned to my compartment the Russian papers had been removed.

It was raining heavily when the train arrived in Warsaw. The train was met by a car from the Polonia Palace Hotel. It was an expensive hotel but I had decided to give myself a luxurious rest after the anticipated hardships of my Soviet excursion. (In fact I had encountered no hardship of any kind.) After a bath and a cup of coffee I went for a walk in the city. The sight of goods in shops and of sophisticated advertisement was stimulating after the drabness of Moscow. Although fascinated by the display in shop windows and the ingenuity of rivals fighting for customers I felt a certain nostalgia for the Soviet commercial system. I had spent a few weeks in an atmosphere free of commercial exploitation and in a way I was already missing the freedom from hidden persuaders. (It was a similar experience thirty years later after the peace of a newspaper strike to find myself back among screaming headlines.) It took some months after leaving the Soviet Union to become reconciled to the world of commercial competition. There can be no doubt that many communist ideals would be acceptable to men of good will if only they had not become tarnished by the intolerance of those who exercise power in communist countries. The inequalities and injustices of the capitalist system can best be seen from the outside. I was never subjected to what later came to be called brainwashing but I left the Soviet Union with some appreciation of what Soviet Russia might now be had it not fallen into the hands of such ruthless men as Lenin and Stalin. Of the two Stalin was probably the more humane, though by civilised standards he was beyond the pale. The ideal of abolishing exploitation of man by man is highly attractive. The tragedy of Russia is that one kind of exploitation has been substituted for another.

Fascinated by what in contrast to Moscow seemed a lavish display of merchandise in the main shopping centre of Warsaw, I could not take my eyes off the shop windows. I was taking no notice of what was going on in the street when suddenly I heard a shout and I felt a sharp blow. My hat was knocked off and an angry officer rushed at me flashing his sword in a most ferocious fashion. It did not in any way alarm me but it made me extremely angry. I had no idea of the motive of his onslaught. Knowing no Polish I shouted back at the soldier in Saxon expletives. It was heartbreaking to have come unscathed from the hands of Soviet atheists only to be attacked by Christian soldiers. My evident anger so surprised the young officer that he ran off to rejoin his troops. Someone in the crowd who spoke a little English then told me that when a regiment is passing by all cars must stop and pedestrians must stand to salute the flag. This explanation did little to mollify me. I was so disgusted that I decided to cancel my stay in Warsaw and proceed at once to Berlin.

This may seem a peevish decision to have made but it is easy to imagine the bitterness I felt at my reception in Poland. In Italy I had grown scornful of the frequent parades of pirouetting Fascists carrying standards. I have always had a reverential admiration for the brave Polish people and the morning's incident was so utterly out of character that I felt a shattering disappointment. The contrast between this reception and the courtesy I had received in the Soviet Union hardened my resolution to leave Warsaw without delay. (Reading history backwards it is easy to see that Poland in 1936 was in a pathological phase. Colonel Beck was playing Hitler's game— unsuccessfully as it turned out. Fear and hatred of Soviet Russia had led Polish politicians to seek Nazi friendship. It was a kiss of death or, to vary the metaphor, it was the smile on the face of the Nazi tiger.) I returned to the Polonia Palace Hotel and cancelled my booking. I had not slept in my room. I had spent only enough time in the hotel to have a bath and a cup of coffee. I told the booking clerk of my experience with the troops and asked him to look up the time of the next train to Berlin. Before giving me the key of my room the clerk insisted on sending for the manager. The latter was not at all co-operative. He agreed that I might leave at once if I wished but my baggage would not be released until I had paid for the two days' stay for which I had contracted.

We argued at great length. I was determined neither to stay nor to pay. I contended that this was no longer the kind of Warsaw to which a foreigner would want to come. Having been attacked by Polish troops I argued that it was the Poles not I who had broken the contract. The manager replied that he had no control over the political situation. Clients had no right to demand the hotel management to look after them anywhere except in the hotel. This was clearly a reasonable point of view but I was not in a reasonable mood. Garry Bostock, knowing that I was to spend a few days in Warsaw, had given me the name of the British consul whom he knew well. I was about to convert the soldier's offence into an international incident when our altercation was interrupted. An important-looking man (he was soberly dressed, wore rimless glasses and carried a dispatch case) walked swiftly up to the manager and held a whispered conversation. He then gave me a deep bow, introduced himself as a government official and asked me to come with him to the manager's office.

In excellent English he told me that the incident had been

reported and he had been sent to apologise officially. I had been followed to the hotel by a police officer in plain clothes. The soldier who knocked off my hat did not know until I spoke that I was a foreigner. He was under the impression that I had kept my hat on my head when the flag was passing because I was a Jew. There had been an anti-Jewish riot at Warsaw University that morning. The detachment of troops were, in fact, returning from the riot when I was accosted. That was the reason why the young officer had behaved in such a regrettable manner. Already excited, he had been provoked by what he took to be the sight of a Jew insulting the flag. My anger was not appeased by this explanation. I said that if a Jew was in peril through failing to take notice of a detachment of soldiers marching up the street there was little to choose between Poland and Nazi Germany. I was even more determined to leave the country. This official said that there had been a genuine mistake, the Polish authorities were sincerely sorry and wished to make amends. He then ordered the manager to produce my baggage. Since there was no train to Germany until midnight I would be the guest of the government for the rest of the day. I might order whatever I wished free of charge. I was given a private dining room and I took particular pleasure in ordering a splendid dinner at the expense of Colonel Beck. I left Poland without having spent a single zloty. I had no sympathy for Polish statesmen that night. Three years later the world learned of the anguish they had suffered. It was more than a political joke which later described Poland as crucified between two thieves. When the courageous Polish people were suffering their agony I wished that I had not been so young and impetuous on my first visit to Warsaw.

I thus arrived in Germany two days earlier than expected. Originally I had intended to spend only one night in Berlin before keeping my promise to be the guest of Herr Wilhelm in Dresden. My brother Jim who worked in the bank of Thomas Cook and Son had booked a room for me at the Central Hotel in the Friedrichstrasse. He had also opened a registered mark credit account in my name at the Deutsche Bank und Gesellschaft. To my surprise I found a letter of welcome awaiting me at the Central. It was from the foreign department of the Berlin Official Tourist Association in Unter den Linden. It was a personal and signed letter. I give the text of the letter because it provides an example of the attention to detail given by the Nazi government in its desire to make a good impression on foreigners.

Berlin, 31.10.36.

Dear Sir,

In extending to you the welcome of the City of Berlin we have the honour to inform you that we lend assistance to foreign guests visiting our country who desire to get detailed and personal information about the life and the various institutions of this country, such as Hospitals, Public Welfare Institutions, Labour Service Camps, National Motor Highways, Industrial Plants or anything of special interest to you.

We also like to call your special attention to our Commercial Department which is at your service in giving you expert information on anything relating to Import and Export trade.

Our services are rendered *entirely free of all charges*. Members of our Association speaking your language will be pleased to return the hospitality experienced in your country and assist you in any way during your stay.

Very sincerely yours,
Berlin Official Tourist Association
Foreign Department
I.V. Krovelhe.

John Heenan Esq.,
BERLIN
Central Hotel.

I would have liked to put the Nazis to the expense of providing a car to take me to a labour camp—at that time we had not heard of the notorious concentration camps—but I decided that I could employ my time better without official guidance. I would be given the party line ad nauseam during my stay in Dresden with Herr Wilhelm. I had the name and address of a non-establishment couple in Berlin. They were Elsa Jacobi and her fiancé Hans Shroeder. Elsa was a typist. Hans, a zoologist, was deputy director of the Tiergarten (three hundred). Both were anti-Nazi. They were especially bitter about the treatment of Jews and told me of the brutalities inflicted on their unfortunate Jewish friends. In England at that time we knew that Hitler had attacked Jews but we did not appreciate the extent of his savagery. Elsa and Hans told me that anti-semitism was part of the Nazi creed and was fast becoming the creed of German youth. Educated people were still unenthusiastic about Hitler but, like Henry VIII's friends who grew rich on the spoils of the monasteries in sixteenth century England, many gentiles were the beneficiaries when Jews were toppled from high places in commerce and the professions.

Most Germans realised by 1936 that the anti-Jewish drive had gone too far. But, according to Hans, it was immensely difficult to retreat. An ideological dogma cannot lightly be denied. Nazi propaganda had identified world Jewry with world communism. In the beginning there was some evidence to support this view. Russian Jews, Polish Jews and German Jews having been victims of recurrent pogroms, it was small wonder that they were the raw material for revolutionaries. In the early stages of Soviet evolution Jewish influence had been considerable. This made it more easy for Goebbels to propagate the canard that Bolshevism was the tool of Jewry. The Nazis claimed that immorality was its other tool. The Jews, according to this myth, planned to control world finance in order to deprave and corrupt the morals of the gentiles. Hollywood and the whole world of entertainment were said to be in the hands of the Jews. The obscene and spurious Protocols of the Elders of Sion were reproduced as valid history. Persecution of the Jews was part of the civic duty of all true lovers of the German Fatherland. Mixed marriages between gentile and Jew were regarded as acts of treason by putting in jeopardy the purity of the so-called Aryan stock. Elsa and Hans pointed out the ubiquitous anti-Jewish notices and slogans. I made a note of some of them: *Eintritt für Juden verboten* (No entry for Jews). *Dieser weg geht nicht nach Palestinien* (This is not the way to Palestine). *Nur tote Juden sind hier willkommen* (Only dead Jews welcome here).

Some of Hans' Jewish friends had escaped with their lives but without their money. One woman whose husband had been killed took her children to France. She had been collecting foreign currency against the day of her liberation but when her permit arrived it stipulated that she must take no money out of the country. She had given it to Hans and Elsa for safe keeping. They produced a large envelope crammed with French, Swiss and American banknotes and asked me to smuggle it through the frontier currency control and send it to the poor Jewish family from England. Apart from my distaste for the actual smuggling operation I had a special reason for wanting to avoid currency offences. The Nazi regime, which hated Catholicism only a little less than communism, had arrested a number of priests for alleged currency offences. (They were all priests belonging to international religious orders with headquarters outside

Germany.) As a priest in disguise I would provide ammunition to the Nazis in their fight against the Catholic Church if I were caught smuggling money out of Germany. I could not explain all this to Elsa and Hans who did not know that I was a priest. I felt no moral scruple in breaking the Nazi laws in order to restore its money to this poor Jewish family and a few days later took it across the German/Dutch border without mishap. In those days foreign currency was confiscated on entering Germany and returned on leaving. If, as in my case, the traveller entered and left at different frontier points reclaiming currency could be a lengthy transaction. When we stopped at the frontier I placed myself at the end of the queue and reached the cashier only a few moments before the train was due to continue its journey. I showed every sign of alarm that I would not have my money returned before the train left. The cashier had some difficulty in calming me down and forgot to ask if I had any other foreign currency in my possession. The money was duly sent to Paris and I assume that the Jewish family received it. The habit of fear doubtless prevented them from acknowledging receipt.

My arrival in Berlin coincided with the tenth anniversary of the foundation of the Nazi party. Not incongruously I went to a beer-hall and asked for a stein-krug (pint) with Munich sausages. My chief impression—according to my notes—was that the men who served the beer were the fattest waiters in the world. Perhaps they sampled their own goods too often. They may have been unconscious disciples of FitzGerald —

> I often wonder what the vintners buy
> One half so precious as the goods they sell.

Whatever the explanation they were all heavyweights. In this beer-hall and in each restaurant I visited alms were solicited from the guests by men dressed in khaki with armlets bearing the letters S.A. This campaign was described as Winterhilfe which means Winter Help. The collection was not so much a charity drive as an additional tax imposed on both employer and employed. In direct taxation in the Third Reich allowances were made according to the number of children. This, of course, is common practice in all countries but in Nazi Germany irrespective of income a man with ten children paid no taxes at all. This was part of the effort to raise population for the good of the Fatherland. Almost all economic planning and legislation took into consideration the likelihood of war. Winterhilfe and the rule that on one day in the week every restaurant must serve a one-course meal (*eintopfgericht*) were part of the massive effort to husband resources and pay for the build-up of Germany's military strength.

On Sunday morning I went to Mass at St. Hedwig's Cathedral. I called at the clergy house to discuss the situation of the Church under the Nazis, but the priest I saw was non-committal. It would have been boring to explain that I was a priest in disguise so I spoke just as an English Catholic anxious to hear how the German brethren were faring under Hitler. I was given no information. In dictator countries, whether of the left or right, freedom does not exist. His own security and that of his family or the institution he represents requires a prudent citizen to hold his tongue. I was about to see the German scene through Nazi eyes. I took the train to Dresden to be the guest of Herr Wilhelm whose acquaintance, it will be recalled, I had made in the Moscow lathe factory. He was at Dresden station to meet me with his powerful motor car. He immediately explained that the programme he had prepared for me would demonstrate the difference between Soviet Russia and Nazi Germany. In Moscow the visitor is so completely in the hand of Intourist guides that he will probably come away from Soviet Russia having seen only what will leave a good impression. Wilhelm was determined to leave me free to see whatever I wished. He explained that next day his car and driver would be at my service so that I could tour the whole city to satisfy myself of the truth of his claim that Hitler had abolished all slums. I accepted his offer and made a thorough tour of Dresden. I had not visited that part of Germany in pre-Nazi days and was therefore unable to judge whether the neat streets and the invariably good condition of even the smallest houses were a Nazi creation or the legacy of a race which has always loved cleanliness and order. I had to agree at the end of my tour that the material boasts made by Wilhelm were fully justified. It is sad that only a few years later this beautiful city was made a holocaust by Allied bombers. It is even sadder to remember how many of its inhabitants were to become victims of our fight for human dignity.

Herr Wilhelm had invited some of the local citizens to meet me the following evening at a dinner party in my honour at the Ratskeller, a splendid restaurant in the city centre. Among them were his two closest friends Bartholomaeus and Hübner. The two were completely different in outlook. Apart from being Germans all they seemed to have in common was that, like Wilhelm himself, both were obviously very prosperous. Bartholomaeus was one of Hitler's economic advisers. His province was the production of synthetic rubber. At the beginning of the meal he was reserved to the point of suspicion. I had no idea in what terms Wilhelm had described me to his friends. I am not sure that he had been completely taken in by my pose of psychologist. Having seen me in Moscow using two different cars with diplomatic registration plates he probably assumed that I was in some way connected with the British government. But he knew from our conversations that I was intensely critical of Soviet communism and apparently that was all he needed to know to give me his confidence. I formed this view as the result of an amusing incident during dinner. I had asked some question or other about his factory which I had inspected that morning. I think I had enquired whether it could easily be converted to the production of munitions in the event of war—the conversation having turned to the possibility of war between Germany and the U.S.S.R. My question alarmed Bartholomaeus who turned to Wilhelm and whispered the word *vorsicht* ('watch it'). To his intense embarrassment a sudden silence made his whisper audible to all. "Don't worry, Herr Vorsicht," I said quickly, "I'm a friend." We all laughed noisily and Wilhelm assured the company that it was quite safe to speak frankly in my presence.

The following day I spent some hours with Herr Hübner, Wilhelm's other friend. To my surprise he frankly told me that he was completely out of sympathy with the views of Wilhelm and his friends at dinner the night before. We shall return to Hübner, but first it may be of interest to give some account of the outlook of Wilhelm and his Nazi friends as revealed to me that night in the Ratskeller and on the following day at luncheon and dinner. I cannot reproduce the actual words spoken during those two days and it is only fair to say that my recollection is naturally coloured by all that happened during the next few years. I therefore propose to transcribe without comment the notes I made in Dresden on my last night in Wilhelm's house. To make them credible it is necessary to bear in mind that in 1936 few in Germany or in England thought that our two nations would soon be engaged in another war. Hitler was still consolidating his position within the Reich. His only foreign adventure at that time was in Spain where Nazis were confronting communists. We may assume that the opinion of Nazis in the position of Bartholomaeus and Wilhelm would reflect the world outlook (*Weltanschauung*) of the Nazi leaders. The following account was written without the benefit of what with scant respect for euphony we have come to call hindsight.

We began, naturally enough by exchanging views on what we had observed during our time in Russia. Wilhelm's friends were full of questions about factories and mechanical equipment in the Soviet Union. He gave them technical information which was rather out of my range. I gave some account of what I had seen in the homes I had managed to visit. The story of our tour led to general agreement that war between Germany and Russia is inevitable in the fairly near future. Britain is regarded with annoyance because Anthony Eden is allowing himself to be made a fool of by the Soviets. They thought it a great joke that the Russians had played our national anthem for a British delegation. The Soviets would not want God to save anyone—especially not a king. It is important for the Western powers not to make too long delay before dealing with the Russians. If they are not attacked during the next ten years they will have established a hegemony in Europe. The smaller countries will all become communist and the Soviet Union will establish a great empire.

Germany is not yet ready for war but is preparing at high speed. By developing synthetic products (petrol, oil, rubber) it will become self-sufficient for long enough to win the war against Russia. As soon as Germany is ready she intends with the help of Austria and Italy to provoke an issue which will justify an attack on the U.S.S.R.

The salvation of England depends on her seeking an alliance with Germany. The only obstacle is the question of colonies. Germany must expand to live (lebensraum). It is essential for her to have colonies. Great Britain has far more colonies than it can control. If only the English are reasonable they will see that their interests coincide with those of Germany. Italy should have taught Britain a lesson. The Italians did not negotiate but went straight for their objective. Other countries protested and pretended to apply sanctions but, of course, Italy won. Fascism is the doctrine of force. Only the language of force is understood by the nations of the world. The League of Nations is futile in attempting to restrain great nations. Germany does not intend to be told what to do by the League. The U.S.S.R. possesses one sixth of the world's surface. Germany must have part of it. The only way to obtain it is to take it.

Poland is allied to Germany for motives of self-interest. The Poles understand that Germany must expand and have made an alliance only to prevent the German army from marching. Because of the Polish hatred of Soviet Russia she can only look to Germany for support. What is needed in Europe is not a series of pacts for mutual assistance but a pact entered into by all the Western powers to hold Russia in check. This should not be a defensive alliance but a militant pact of mutual mistrust of communism. There should be a universal crusade to liberate the Russian people from their communist masters and to rescue the world from the international dictatorship of the Jews. The German people are becoming more and more exasperated by the activities of the communists. The only logical end is a war of extermination. This war will be long and bitter. It will be a war to the death. Both sides will have to be ruthless with all enemies both external and domestic. No dictatorship can afford to trust anyone. It must rule by fear until its objective is achieved.

The coming war will be a civil war between nationals of opposing ideologies as well as a war between nations. There will be no neutrals. Britain will no longer be able to live in splendid isolation from the rest of the world. Its empire involves it in every dispute throughout the world. Germany has discovered that its ideals and methods are shared by the Japanese. Germany, Italy and Japan are united in their hostility to world communism and their belief that force is the only method of gaining prestige among the nations. The Japanese are war-minded and use their traditional ideology to create an army of fanatical fighters. They are trained never to surrender. Those who fall fighting for their country are assured eternal bliss. The alternative is to surrender to the enemy and this is abhorrent to the Japanese warrior. They have now developed a human torpedo guided by its pilot who, of course, will commit suicide when the weapon hits its target. Even children are conditioned to a militarism which finds its chief glory in self-immolation. In every Japanese school there are pictures or statues of the three young soldiers who first became human torpedoes in the Manchurian war. Each morning as well as bowing to the Emperor pupils bow to the images of these three young heroes.

Nearer the Fatherland are the small countries on the Soviet borders. They fear and hate the Russians and will rush to arms as soon as Germany gives the signal. Finland's army though small is immensely efficient. It is so well organised that it can be mobilised within two hours. It is capable of powerful resistance to the Red Army. Each soldier on completing his military service takes home arms and knows exactly where he must go on the outbreak of war. There will be no waiting for call-up papers or posting. The whole civil organisation in Germany is co-ordinated with the military machine. Roads are planned not only for the convenience of travellers but for army requirements. These roads are constructed in concrete with deep foundations in order to support tanks and armoured cars. These autobahns are the admiration of international tourist agencies. They do not realise that the roads leading to Czechoslovakia were designed to ensure rapid transit for German armoured divisions.

The military preparations are disguised as social and economic measures. Young men are trained ostensibly to achieve physical fitness. In fact they are being given discipline which will fit them to become soldiers after a brief enlistment. Prohibitive expenditure on building autobahns is avoided by recruiting a vast labour force. There is universal conscription of labour. The wages are nominal and the labour camps are constructed at minimal cost. These conscripts provide cheap labour but by living together develop a spirit of comradeship and national pride. No exemptions are granted except on grounds of health. No distinction is made according to social class, education or professional status. Thus the whole German community is being welded into one great community dedicated to the Fuehrer and to the building of a greater Germany. It is true that many members of the middle classes are reluctant to go to labour camps. There is still opposition to the Nazi ideals among the aristocracy. The Party however has survived its days of peril and nothing can now destroy it apart from the defeat of Germany in a world war.

There is no longer any fear of revolution in Nazi Germany. The enemies of national socialism have lost their chance. The system of internal security has now been perfected. In every apartment house there is an agent of the secret police (Gestapo) who supervises security in the building (hauswart). His duty is to report any strange behaviour or disloyal comment among the residents. He also takes note of the visitors who come regularly to each family. He must if possible listen outside each apartment to discover if the occupants listen to the foreign radio. At regular intervals the hauswart hands in a report to the strassewart who has a whole street or section of a large street as his territory. The reports are studied at police headquarters and in this way the manner of life, the views and associates of every family are known.

My notes contain no comment on this account of Nazi outlook and activity. I need only add that Wilhelm and his fellow enthusiasts did not regard any of these anti-democratic measures with disfavour. Mentally they were already men at war. They were proud that the leaders were taking such precautions against their country being attacked unawares. In some ways Wilhelm was like a child. His pride in Nazi thoroughness was certainly more childish than malicious. One evening he took me to a smart establishment which served drinks, light refreshments and provided a cabaret. It is the only place in which I have seen the system of table telephones so popular in Scandinavia. The patron may dial the table number of a friend sitting at a distance or if he is lonely may telephone an invitation for a drink to an attractive stranger. My knowledge of German did not enable me to follow the jokes of the cabaret comedian but I understood enough to realise that they were not unduly subtle. I heard him retail, for example, the old story of the Chief Rabbi who accepted the Pope's challenge to eat pork on condition that it must be served at the Pope's wedding breakfast. Suddenly Wilhelm flushed with rage. The comedian apparently had made a joke about Goering's habit of acquiring new uniforms and decorations. He rushed off to complain to the manager. Since jokes about Goering's uniforms were as common as those about Goebbels' speeches this incident showed me what a childish fellow Wilhelm must be.

Herr Hübner was of a very different calibre. He was a gentleman and also very rich indeed. One morning Wilhelm had important business at his factory and took me to Hübner's house to spend a couple of hours before lunch. As soon as we were alone Hübner suggested a walk in the grounds. His house was built in a small park containing a miniature zoo. He took me out of the house, I now realise, so that our conversation could not be overheard. When we were comfortably seated in a small pavilion Hübner opened his heart. He had a great love for England, spoke English without an accent and had his suits made in Savile Row. He was delighted to be able to talk freely to an Englishman. Hübner described Wilhelm as essentially simple and good-hearted. Apart from his engineering ability which had given him his fortune he was without talent or culture. Wilhelm's political views he held in abhorrence. He declared that national socialism was communism by another name. World revolution was Hitler's ambition no less than Stalin's. The army was apprehensive but the younger officers had fallen under the Nazi spell. He thought that a revolution in Germany was still possible. It was the only way of saving the country from continuing its headlong march to war. He thought of war only in relation to Soviet Russia. He evidently thought that revolution or even war would be better for Germany than living under Hitler.

Herr Hübner told me several political jokes. I confess that the only impression they left on me was that Germans are more easily amused than ourselves. I remembered how in Rome the German students used to be incurably jocose. Walking up and down between lectures they were liable to say: "Narrabo tibi fabulam iocosam" (I am going to tell you a funny story). I made a note of a few of Hübner's stories not because I thought them worth recording for their humour but because they illustrate the political preoccupation of the middle classes during the early Nazi years. An occasional political joke is acceptable in any country but politics become the sole topic of conversation only in a sick society. Political anecdotes were usually a conversation piece. The protagonists were always Goering, Goebbels and Hitler. Here are two of Hübner's stories:

The three Nazi leaders in a boat safe from eavesdroppers were discussing what they would do in the event of a revolution.

Goering said: No problem for me. I would only have to change my uniform.

Goebbels said: No problem for me. I would only have to make a different speech.

Hitler said: It wouldn't make the slightest difference to me. After all, I'm a foreigner. (*Ich bin ein Auslander*).

In another story the three stalwarts are appearing before St. Peter at the gate of heaven. Hitler comes up first for judgement and is sentenced to walk ten times round the world as a punishment for all his lies. Goering comes next and is condemned to a hundred trips for his lies. St. Peter then notices that the third man has disappeared. Goebbels has gone to buy a motor cycle.

A different note is struck in a Jewish joke. Goering, the story goes, was trying to persuade Hitler to relax the Jewish persecution. He contended that only Jews are any good at business. Without their help Germany would face economic ruin. To prove his point he took Hitler to buy a box of matches. In the first shop Goering asks for a box of matches. When they are produced he looks into the box and says to the shopkeeper:

"The heads of the matchsticks are on top. I want matches with the heads on the bottom."

"Sorry sir, these are the only ones we have in stock."

The same performance is repeated in two more gentile shops. At last they enter a Jewish shop. Goering repeats his request for matches with the heads at the bottom. The Jew pauses for no more than a moment.

"You're lucky, gentlemen," he says, producing exactly the same brand of match-box from under the counter but presenting it upside-down. "These came in only yesterday."

A final example of Hübner's jokes is the story of the Nazi who fished a stretch of river all day without success. Towards evening a boy came along with a home-made rod and within half-an-hour caught six fish. The astonished Nazi asked the boy why he had caught nothing:

"You'll never have a bite dressed like that," the boy replied. "When the fish see your uniform they are afraid to open their mouths."

I left Dresden after a farewell lunch at Hübner's. At this final gathering the talk was less serious. In bantering fashion I asked Wilhelm why he wasn't married—I had not realised at first that the mistress of the house was not his wife. He said that he preferred things as they were. Bartholomaeus coming to Wilhelm's aid said, "Why doesn't your king marry Mrs. Simpson?" The lady's name was unknown to me. The Germans were at first unable to believe that I had heard nothing of l'affaire Simpson. Used to the rigorous censorship of the German press they had enviously imagined that the press in England was free. Continental papers at that time were freely reporting the King's romance. Until the Bishop of Bradford made his famous protest our papers conspired to keep the British public ignorant of the monarch's antics which were the table talk of the rest of the world. On my return to England I wrote to Herr Wilhelm but never again heard from him. Shroeder, on the other hand, kept in touch until the war. In 1937 he spent a holiday in England as the guest of my sister and her husband, Sydney Reynolds.

CHAPTER
SEVEN

BACK IN BARKING IT DID NOT TAKE LONG TO SETTLE DOWN IN THE OLD routine. For a few days a certain anxiety remained. My lawyer told me not to take night calls except from the hospital or from parishioners known to me. I received a letter threatening my life. At the suggestion of the Cardinal I took it to a Catholic friend of his in the Foreign Office. He declared it to be a hoax. The only echoes of my excursion were a private dinner I gave at Pagani's restaurant and a public meeting at the Albert Hall. The dinner took place in December when the Bostocks came home on leave. I invited all those who had been involved in the preparations for the trip—Mgr. Elwes, the Eyres, the Dixeys and the Stevens. The guests of honour were, of course, the Bostocks.

The public meeting was arranged at the request of Cardinal Hinsley. It was advertised under the title of 'The Church and Social Justice'. It created enormous interest. The public was excited at the prospect of hearing the true facts about communism from a priest just back from Russia. Ill feeling on a wide scale was caused by the impossibility of satisfying thousands who applied for tickets of admission. The meeting itself was not a success. The programme had been carefully arranged so that the second half would be devoted to the Russian revelations. Unfortunately nobody kept to his allotted time. The chairman spoke for forty minutes and the first speaker for nearly an hour. By the time the Credo had been sung and a collection taken, little time was left. I therefore abandoned my prepared speech and spoke for just over ten minutes. I tried to make amends by a series of articles in the *Catholic Times* which I wrote anonymously as Our Special Investigator.

England by the winter of 1936 had become more settled than in the early part of the decade. The Spanish civil war provided the chief contrast to the comparative peace of domestic politics. King Edward VIII abdicated just before Christmas 1936 and his brother George was crowned in the spring of 1937. The royal crisis in no way shook the institution of kingship. It had the contrary effect of making the British feel even more superior to foreigners who in the absence of a monarchy had to put up with dictators such as Stalin, Hitler and Mussolini. The former King was packed off quietly and scarcely heard of again. Baldwin at the height of his power was universally acclaimed for his handling of the situation. Winston Churchill, who had supported Edward VIII, was shouted down in the House of Commons. He had reached his political nadir. The economic depression was now passing. The divisions in political life were between left and right and almost entirely concerned with foreign affairs. Politicians of the left shelved their internal quarrels to unite in opposition to Hitler and Mussolini. Most people were anti-Fascist but nobody wanted to fight a war. What Nazis did in Germany was their business not ours. Nor were people any more disposed to fight for Spanish republicans or German Jews than formerly for Abyssinians. Nor later would they be prepared to fight for the Austrians or Czechs.

Cardinal Hinsley found himself becoming more involved with domestic politics as these were increasingly affected by events abroad. Hitler liked to choose weekends for springing surprises on the democracies. Until the war broke out and the full horror of his treatment of the Jews was disclosed to the British public Hitler was a much less hated figure than Mussolini. Influential statesmen were working for a German alliance. Geoffrey Dawson's *Times* became almost a publicity organ for Hitler's Germany. In these circumstances Cardinal Hinsley, who had never fully regained self-confidence since his Golders Green sermon on the Pope and Mussolini, made another attempt to bring me to Westminster. This time he acted with finesse. He did not approach me directly. He asked Mgr. O'Grady, the Vicar General of Brentwood diocese, to persuade me to agree to leave Barking and become his secretary for—so to speak—external affairs. The Vicar General sent for me and, although approving the fact that my heart was entirely in parish work, told me that it was nevertheless my duty to help 'the poor old man in Westminster' (shades, I thought, of Golders Green!). I gave a most reluctant consent. A few days later Cardinal Hinsley called on Bishop Doubleday in Brentwood to ask for my release. The cardinal pointed out that he already used me a great deal unofficially and now needed my full-time services. The bishop said that he could not release me without consulting the chapter of canons. This was his way of refusing—bishops are not in the habit of consulting chapters about the appointment of junior curates. In due course, Mgr. O'Grady later told me, the bishop put the matter to the chapter. He told the canons that the diocese was desperately short of priests, while there were plenty of priests· in Westminster who would make better secretaries than I. The bishop had my full agreement.

The approach made to Bishop Doubleday for my services had an unforeseen effect. It did not lead to my transfer to Westminster but it was responsible for my removal from Barking. Bishop Doubleday in his official letter to the cardinal after the meeting of the chapter said that owing to the shortage of priests in the diocese I was indispensable. The shortage of priests was indeed acute but the idea that I was indispensable must have surprised even the bishop himself. Being an honest man he decided to give substance to an otherwise unconvincing statement. He appointed me parish priest of Manor Park. This was in April 1937 when I was just thirty-two years of age. It was unusual for a priest to be given a big parish at such an early age but there is much to recommend the appointment of parish priests while they are still energetic. Unfortunately it is seldom possible to put young men in charge of parishes without doing injustice to middle-aged men who may still be curates twenty years after ordination. One day the whole system may be changed on the model of religious congregations. A religious is appointed superior for a limited number of years. He may be the rector of a community or the major superior over a whole province but when his term of office is over he retires. Returning to the ranks is not considered an affront to his dignity. Most priests would probably regard a curacy as much more attractive than the office of Superior General.

Father Carthy who was some years my senior had recently become parish priest of Custom House, a dockside area. Poor Canon Cameron felt desolate at losing both his curates in so short a time. The canon had come to rely on us both so completely that he had learned extremely little about the parish. During my last few days in Barking

I did everything possible to put him in touch with affairs. I also had to leave my personal pastoral concerns in good order. The converts I was instructing, the marriages I had been arranging and correspondence of all kinds had to be handed over to my successor. One of the material advantages enjoyed by celibate clergy is that they can exchange homes in a matter of days. A clergyman with a young family must face many problems when moving. The most painful part of leaving a parish is bidding goodbye to the sick and old who have come to rely on at least a weekly visit. With priests, as with all professional men, it is against the code to return to visit former parishioners or clients. That is why taking leave of the sick is so hard. Those who are well can, in theory at least, visit the priest in his new parish. Since the priest is loved precisely because he is the priest his successor is, in fact, given the loyalty and love of the people. The outgoing priest is soon forgotten. Former parishioners will not wear out the trail to his new parish. When I became Archbishop of Westminster it was the fifth time I had been told to move by those in authority. Going from Barking was to be the pattern of leavetaking. I ran through the list of families whose problems I had come to understand but not to solve; people who had entrusted me with their personal problems, looking for guidance which I was not spiritual enough to give; families on whom I should have called more regularly and often; school-leavers, converts and young married couples with whom I had meant to keep in touch; souls in which with more pastoral care the love of God would have been enkindled. It was humiliating to leave so many tasks undone. There was, above all, the bitter realisation that my neglect could not now be repaired. I could think of homes which had I visited more often might have been won back to the faith. I thought of all the time I had wasted during my six years in Barking. The only—rather doubtful—compliment I could pay myself was that I had made no enemies. I was on excellent terms with priests, people, officials and non-Catholic clergy. Barking was an exceptionally friendly town. Mr. Frost, the Director of Education, used to say that wherever a town has grown up round an abbey the tradition of friendliness is always found. As I left Barking I remembered my many failures. One such failure pressed on me so heavily that I called on the man concerned on my very last morning in Barking. The story is worth relating. It is not a success story.

Each year during Holy Week I used to preach a parish retreat from the evening of Palm Sunday until Maundy Thursday. This custom I kept up in Manor Park and, when I became a bishop, in the three cathedrals—Leeds, Liverpool and Westminster. One parishioner who never missed a single night of the retreat was a yeoman of the guard. He was a man of over seventy with a well trimmed white beard. He walked upright with the pride of a regular soldier. He was precise in a military sort of way in everything he did. He attended the ten o'clock Mass on Sundays and was always in his place fifteen minutes before Mass was due to begin. He prayed with great recollection. He had brought up his family in the faith. They, in turn, had brought up their children as excellent Catholics. There was only one black mark in the yeoman's record. He had not received the sacraments within living memory. His children could not remember ever having seen him at the altar rails. They knew the reason. In the army he had become a freemason in the belief that this would promote his career.

In these ecumenical days it is probably only a matter of time before the general ban on masonry will be lifted. There are, as the members of the Grand Lodge of England know, excellent reasons for the Church's ban on masonry. English masons themselves are forbidden to have dealings with the Grand Orient and other atheistical sections of the masonic movement. The whole question of Catholic membership of masonic lodges has been under consideration by the Holy See since 1968. Whatever happens in the future, the ban on masonry has hitherto been absolute. When I used to visit my friend he would be in tears as he spoke of his longing to receive Holy Communion once more. He was under the almost certainly false impression that he would have to cease to be a yeoman if he resigned from his masonic lodge. Since there was no question of seeking permission for him to receive Holy Communion while remaining a mason I used to urge him to resign. He always declared that he would resign after some big event had been celebrated. He was going to resign, I remember, after King George V's jubilee, after the next coronation, after the wedding of the Princess. But his resignation was always postponed. When visiting missioners came I would send them to talk to him. He would unfailingly promise to leave the masons after the next royal occasion.

During the Holy Week retreat of 1937 I gave a talk on the forgiveness of sin. Neither on that nor on any other occasion have I preached a sermon with one member of the congregation especially in mind. I could not have suspected that the story of the Phoenix Park murders would have affected the yeoman in any personal way. I told the story of Joseph Brady, one of the 'Irish Invincibles' who had stabbed to death Lord Cavendish and Burke, the permanent under-secretary. Brady, though about to be executed, would not make his peace with God because he could not find it in his heart to forgive Carey the informer. The chaplain brought into Mountjoy prison many holy priests to pray with Brady and try to persuade him to forgive Carey. Brady's answer was always the same: "God himself would not expect an Irish patriot to forgive an informer." The day before the execution was due a nun appeared at the prison gate. She begged to be allowed to see Brady. Leave was granted when she said she had the secret of reading Brady's heart.

Entering Brady's cell the Sister apologised for her intrusion but said that she was in desperate need of help. As one about to face God Brady would be the most likely man in the world to give her the right advice. She explained that she hated a certain person with all her heart. It had become an obsession with her. She now asked Brady if she should throw off the veil and leave the religious life. Brady replied without hesitation: "For God's sake, Sister, don't do that. Try to forgive." "Very well, Mr. Brady," the nun replied, "I forgive you for killing Burke in Phoenix Park. He was my brother." Brady, of course, begged her pardon, forgave Carey, made his confession and received Holy Communion the next morning before he was hanged.

Immediately after the retreat service the yeoman came into the sacristy to see me. Thank God, I thought, he had made up his mind at last. He was bubbling with excitement but its cause was not the one for which I had hoped. He had come to tell me that as a young soldier in his teens he had been on guard duty outside Brady's cell the day the Sister came. Naturally I used the occasion to urge him once more to return to the sacraments. Again he gave a promise but delayed all action. It was to his house I went on the morning I left Barking. I told him that this would probably be our last meeting on earth. He was more distressed than I had ever seen him. He said that he must remain a yeoman of the guard until the coronation of George VI in June. It was only a matter of weeks and he said that this time he really meant it. I am sure that he did. Unfortunately he did not live to see the coronation. He died suddenly a few days later. He was a fine man. I hope he had a great reunion in heaven with Brady and Burke's sister.

I learned from the Vicar General that the bishop had originally intended to send me to Canning Town which at that time was the largest East End parish in the diocese. On reflection he decided that I was too young to be in charge of a parish with three curates. He therefore appointed Father Sloane, my senior by nearly twenty years, to Canning Town. I replaced him as parish priest of Manor Park. I found the finances in a precarious state. There were bills for forty pounds awaiting payment and, hardly by coincidence, forty pounds in the bank. The presbytery was newly built and had not been paid for. I mention money first in this account of my years in Manor Park because it was money which made the greatest impact on me in my early days as parish priest. I had never handled money before. In Barking Canon Cameron had counted the collections, banked the money and kept the accounts. The parish was free of debt. Money was rarely mentioned in church and almost as rarely in the presbytery. I had never been told and had never asked the income or the cost of running the parish. Before many days in Manor Park I realised that the school would have to be enlarged and St. Stephen's church rebuilt. St. Stephen's, a converted army hut bought in 1919, adjoined the school and presbytery. The church of St. Nicholas, officially the parish church, was at the extreme end of the parish. It had been dedicated to St. Nicholas, the children's saint (Santa Klaus) because originally it had been the chapel of an industrial school. It was now used mainly at weekends.

Lack of money coupled with the prospect of a large building programme threatened to give me an obsession about money. I was saved from this fate by the visit of my friend Father Atkins. Tommy, as inevitably he was called though his name was Alban, was a close friend from seminary days. He had come to stay with my mother every year since ordination. This year for the first time I could invite him to be my own guest. He stayed for three days and when he was leaving offered me three pound notes. He said he was sorry that I was so worried about money and promised to send me more. This was the lesson I badly needed. It shocked me into seeing that I was thinking and talking continually about money. I gave Tommy back his three pounds. I thanked him both for the gift and for the lesson. I decided that it was the business of the laity as well as the priest to keep the parish solvent. The steps I took would be considered normal today but in 1937 the Second Vatican Council was a quarter of a century away.

I was blessed in having as president of the St. Vincent de Paul Society a Scot who was as shrewd as he was spiritual. Mr. Thomson's chemist shop was opposite the bank and every Monday he would bank the parish money and give me a sheet showing the details of each collection. These weekly sheets together with the stubs of the cheque book were all the accountant needed when he came each quarter to make up the books. The accountant was a friend from schooldays. One Sunday each year I gave a talk on the parish finances at every Mass. I gave an account of all income and expenditure. I gave the weekly cost of lighting and heating two churches. People familiar with a weekly fuel bill of a few shillings were astonished that the parish bill was for several pounds. Until that Sunday when first I gave a talk on finance there had been a second collection at every Mass. I now announced its abolition. Since they had heard what the parish—their parish—cost to maintain I said that I expected parishioners to make payment to the church part of their normal family budget. I asked them to take the material burdens from me to leave me free for spiritual duties. The following Sunday the income was exactly doubled. By coincidence the total collection from both churches was to a shilling twice that of the previous week. I realise that this sounds unlikely but it is a fact. It is astonishing but true that halving the number of collections doubled the receipts. The explanation of this dramatic rise in fortune, however, had little to do with the number of collections. The explanation is that for the first time people knew exactly how much money it took to run their parish. The men in particular were gratified at being trusted with exact figures which hitherto had been regarded as part of the mystery of religion. From that time I always devoted one Sunday in the year to parish finance. No longer was money allowed to become a preoccupation.

Manor Park resembled two parishes in one. One part was typical of London's East End. It was the densely populated section which lay on each side of the Roman road which runs from Aldgate pump to the Essex town of Colchester. The other section took in the middle-class houses built around Wanstead flats which were originally part of Epping Forest. The school was in the area of the parish served by St. Stephen's church. The Wanstead end of the parish regarded St. Nicholas's as their church. The parishioners thus formed two congregations which, while not in any way opposed, scarcely knew each other because they rarely attended the same church. The parish was within the borough of East Ham and this fact emphasised the bias towards London rather than the county of Essex. It was not an easy parish to weld into one community. Unity was eventually achieved not by my efforts but, as we shall see, by the perils of the second world war. The London blitz wrought immense material havoc in Manor Park but brought all the Catholics together and, indeed, resulted in a magnificent comradeship of the whole town without distinction of creed and class.

The first problem which faced me was an overcrowded school. In 1937 the Butler Education Act was still several years away. Children who did not win a scholarship to a grammar school—and they were the overwhelming majority—had to stay in all-age schools until they had reached the age of fourteen years. Despite the debt on the parish it was obvious that provision of further places in the school was urgent. Among the documents awaiting attention on my arrival in Manor Park was a report from His Majesty's Inspectorate containing what practically amounted to an ultimatum. If the school buildings were not extended the head teacher would be forbidden to admit new pupils. After the war the government required dioceses to establish schools commissions to negotiate with the Ministry of Education and the local education authorities the planning of all school building. At this time the initiative still lay with the local parish priest. My first duty therefore was to raise a loan. In the days before decentralisation had been introduced by the Second Vatican Council the canon law demanded a complicated procedure for borrowing money. The parish priest applied to the bishop, who in turn had to seek permission from the Holy See before a loan could be sought. Within a few weeks of taking office as parish priest I had given an undertaking to the Board of Education (known later as the Ministry of Education and, later still, as the Department of Education and Science) to extend the school. I appointed an architect, put the plans out to tender, applied for leave to borrow money and patiently awaited permission from Rome.

My patience was severely tried. Months passed and I received no word from the bishop. The architect, the contractors and the local education authority began to grow restive. Due to rearmament steel prices and other building costs were rising and the architect warned me that it would soon become necessary to re-negotiate the building contract. I telephoned my friend Father McKenna, the bishop's secretary, to ask if there was any news from Rome. He told me not to worry. Permission had been received and the bishop would soon forward it to me. Overjoyed, I told the architect that although I could not sign the contract until I had received the formal permission of the bishop he could safely give the contractor word to proceed with the building. The letter from the bishop would arrive by the time the work was under way. The workmen began to dig the foundations but no letter came. They started to build the walls. Still no letter. The contractor was in a small way of business and needed the money to pay his men. I therefore wrote to the bishop to enquire if permission to borrow the money had yet come from Rome. To my consternation he replied that permission had been received but owing to rising costs he could not now allow me to build at all. Panic ensued. I dared not give the contractor the bad news. I had to write to the bishop and explain that, although I had not yet signed the contract, the new school building was approaching completion. I explained that I had gone ahead on the advice of the architect precisely because of the rising costs. In the event the building would be erected at the price originally agreed. I awaited an answer from the bishop with trepidation. When next day I received an envelope with a Brentwood postmark I thought it must contain a request for my resignation. Instead it was the Roman document together with an episcopal compliment slip but without comment.

The extension to the school put new heart and life into the parish. The parents breathed more freely because the danger of school places being denied to their children had passed. The added debt was an incentive to greater effort. The two years intervening before the outbreak of war were pastorally blissful. The school staff was enthusiastic, attendance at Mass was increasing, there were never less than a dozen converts under instruction, the laity had taken all financial worries as their province and I had a splendid assistant in Father Hibbert. Despite the responsibilities of being a parish priest I was just as happy in Manor Park as I had been in Barking. The love of Catholic people is so genuine that the heart of a priest would have to be of stone not to be warmed by their devotion. In those days nobody had begun to question the function of the priest. He was the father and servant of his people. He was made welcome in every home even by families which had grown careless in the practice of the faith. We had not yet begun to talk of community in the selfconscious way which later became fashionable. The joy of priests and people as the parish developed was palpable. Then came Munich.

The year from September 1938 to September 1939 was probably the most miserable year of the century. The tension was less bearable than the stress of the war years. The shadow of war grew deeper with the passing months. Hitler had displaced Mussolini as the terror of Europe. People no longer believed his protests of desiring peace. Some attempted to deceive themselves but their efforts were dismissed by most citizens as 'wishful thinking'—an expression which enjoyed a vogue until after the war. Hitler declared after each new venture that he had no further territorial claims but most informed Europeans were convinced that the Nazis were bent on world conquest. The threat to Czechoslovakia was widely regarded as the test. On the eve of Munich the British people were sick at heart. They had never yearned more for peace but few were prepared to buy peace at the cost of self-immolation. It had become clear that if no stand were taken against Germany she would eventually attack France and Great Britain. Hitler for our generation had become what Napoleon was to our forefathers. As an earnest of its determination to avoid war this country had virtually disarmed in the preceding decade. Stanley Baldwin, upbraided for having allowed Britain to become powerless to withstand dictators, would later reply that to have told the facts before 1935 would have lost his party an election. The tragedy of 1938 was that peace-loving Britain had become by its weakness a major incentive to aggressors.

The Czechoslovakian crisis did not reach a climax until September 1938 but for months beforehand the fear of war afflicted the nation. Neville Chamberlain flew to see Hitler in Berchtesgaden on 15th September. He repeated his journey on 22nd September. When he returned from his second unsuccessful peace mission he found that the mood of the public had hardened. Peace moves were now described as appeasement. The small state of Czechoslovakia had suddenly begun to remind the British public of gallant little Belgium of 1914. Even the trade unions which had formed the spearhead of the fight for peace called for resistance. With troubled hearts we saw men digging trenches in Hyde Park. The anti-aircraft defences of London were manned. Forty-four guns were deployed to defend the capital against the mighty Luftwaffe. Thirty-eight million gas masks were produced and emergency plans for evacuating schoolchildren were completed. Over eighty per cent of parents opted for the removal of their children from London in the belief that within minutes of the outbreak of war London would lie in gas-filled ruins. At this point the Prime Minister made his third and most dramatic flight to meet the Fuehrer and the Duce. It was the triumph (or betrayal) of Munich.

On the evening of 30th September, 1938, for the first and last time in my life I saw a prize-fight. A few weeks earlier I had held a bazaar in the parish hall at St. Nicholas in aid of the school-building fund. It is thought—probably wrongly—that the success of a bazaar depends on having it opened by a celebrity. Only a film star or a sportsman was felt to have the power to attract a crowd. In East London prize-fighters were more popular than film stars or even footballers. I therefore invited the British Heavyweight Champion, Len Harvey, a recent convert to the faith, to open our bazaar. When he came to Manor Park he told me that he was about to defend his title against Jack Doyle at the Harringay Arena. That is why I found myself at the ringside on the night of 30th September. Len Harvey had supported me and I was returning the compliment. The stadium was three-quarters empty. The prospective fight in Europe was too great a counter-attraction to the Harringay contest. The crowd was enjoying the minor bloodshed before the big fight when suddenly boxing was held up for a dramatic intervention by the Prime Minister relayed on the loudspeakers. Mr. Chamberlain had returned from Munich bringing 'peace with honour'. "I believe," he said, "that it is peace for our time." Adolf Hitler had graciously consented to sign a piece of paper which declared that the people of Germany and England desired "never to go to war with one another again . . . The method of consultation will be adopted to deal with questions concerning our two countries." This announcement filled Len Harvey with such encouragement that he knocked Jack Doyle clean out of the ring half-way through the first round. The crowd jeered Doyle, thinking he had dived out of the ring to avoid being hurt. If indeed this is what he had done he was obviously more intelligent than he looked. We all went home rejoicing that the champion had knocked out his challenger and Chamberlain had floored Hitler.

The year before the war has left little mark on my memory. We did not willingly drift into war but every international incident seemed to make war inevitable. Citizens though not bellicose were despairingly preparing for the worst. British statesmen were searching desperately for defensive alliances in the forlorn hope of frightening Hitler. We gave a guarantee to Poland which everyone knew was tantamount to a kiss of death. While we were half-heartedly negotiating a non-aggression pact with Soviet Russia, the Nazis and communists were actually working out the details of an agreement. Hopes of peace were finally extinguished on 23rd August 1939 when

Molotov and Ribbentrop, the Russian and German foreign ministers, signed the Nazi-Soviet pact. This made it only a matter of days before the second world war must begin. Chamberlain even at this late hour was reluctant to abandon all hope of restraining Hitler. Together with Lord Halifax, on 2nd September he was still attempting to arrange a withdrawal of German troops from Poland. As late as 7.30 that evening he told the House of Commons that there was still some prospect of a conference with Hitler. Arthur Greenwood, acting leader for the Labour Party, rose to reply. Before he had said a word Mr. Amery from the Conservative benches shouted: "Speak for England, Arthur." And Arthur did. At 9 a.m. on 3rd September the British ultimatum was delivered in Berlin. At 11 o'clock Germany and Great Britain were at war for the second time in a quarter of a century.

During the month of August most people in responsible positions had been making contingency plans. The government sent secret communications to doctors, parish priests and head teachers. We were given the strongest reason to believe that Armageddon was at hand. The grotesque provision of gas masks for babies was made less realistic by the fact that millions of papier-mâché coffins were to be provided for their parents. These paper coffins for some reason were especially macabre. We realised that there would be neither time nor material available for the provision of wooden coffins if most Londoners were to be killed. Pronouncements about paper coffins were nevertheless needlessly alarming. Most corpses, we felt, would have been prepared to forego the comfort of a stout wooden coffin in the national interest. Considerations of psychology as well as logistics doubtless played their part in these government bulletins. It was evidently thought necessary to make clear that the civilian population was preparing not for a picnic but for an encounter with the brutal and bloodthirsty Nazis. All this brought back to mind the first world war. I remembered being told as a small boy of the shortage of chaplains in August 1914. The British Expeditionary Force, sent to France at short notice, suffered terrible casualties. There were not enough priests to tend the wounded and dying. Early in August 1939, feeling certain that war would come before the end of summer, I asked the bishop if I might put down my name for immediate call-up on the outbreak of war. I told him that I was thinking of what had happened in 1914. The bishop refused. He said (wrongly) that there would be no war and added (rightly) that if war were to break out I would be of more use in Manor Park than in France. I told the bishop that Father Hibbert, my assistant, was also anxious to volunteer. In that case, the bishop replied, there was even less question of my going. In the event Father Hibbert did become a chaplain. My brother Frank, also a parish priest, when he heard that I had volunteered went immediately to the bishop on the same errand. To his surprise and my annoyance his offer was immediately accepted.

Everyone of my generation has personal memories of 3rd September, 1939, when Britain found herself unwillingly at war. It was a Sunday morning. The Prime Minister was standing by to address the nation as soon as the ultimatum to Germany expired. This was to be at eleven o'clock—the time of the last Mass at St. Stephen's church. I waited in the presbytery to hear the declaration of war and went immediately into church to inform the parishioners. Although almost everyone had been expecting bad news there was a gasp from the congregation at my announcement and one or two people rushed out of church. I told the congregation that there was no need for panic. Even if the Luftwaffe took off at once there would still be time for everyone to reach home before the bombs began to fall. Immediately after Mass I set off on my bicycle to visit the sick and housebound who would obviously have special need for comfort and protection. My first call was to Nellie Coleman of Fifth Avenue (a street in no way reminiscent of the opulent thoroughfare of that name in New York) who was dying of tuberculosis. Just as I reached Fifth Avenue the sirens began to wail. We learned later that this air-raid warning was given in error, but that morning it was regarded as a confirmation of the prophecies of doom on which we had been nurtured. Before I arrived at Nellie's home a young man in shirtsleeves rushed out of his house to ask if his wedding, due at 2 o'clock, would have to be cancelled. I assured him that it would take more than Hitler to make my friend the vicar break his engagements.

Poor Nellie was terrified. I told her that almost certainly there would be no air-raid. I explained that unless the German planes had been actually on their way before war had been declared it was a practical impossibility for them to have arrived so soon within range of our air-raid warning system. This was an uninformed guess but it had a calming effect on Nellie. If a raid had taken place Nellie would have died of shock. Within a few weeks she was dead from natural causes. I stayed with Nellie longer than I had intended but eventually I was able to complete my calls. Long before I had finished the round of visits the All Clear sounded and all the patients recovered their calm. Some were predicting that "Hitler will never get through." Others were comforting themselves with the thought that air-raids were not, after all, as bad as they had feared. I was already witnessing the remarkable resilience of the sick and old which continued to astonish me when the raids began in earnest. By the end of the war there was not a house in the parish undamaged but, with the exception of some very old and very young people, few lost courage. Towards the end of the blitz people began to take joyful pride in the tribute paid by the rest of the nation: "Londoners can take it." Londoners, of course, had no choice. They had to take it or leave London. I often reflected that sirens were used in the wrong order. The despairing moan of undulating sound which announced a raid added to the terror. It would have been better to use the firm defiant note of the All Clear as the warning.

Priests and doctors form a partnership in poor parishes because their work constantly takes them into the same homes. I was on friendly terms with all the doctors in the town. By coincidence there were three Catholic doctors with surgeries within a few hundred yards of my presbytery. On the day after war broke out one of them, Dr. Michael O'Dwyer, telephoned to invite me out for a drive. I was astonished. He was a hard-working doctor and I had never known him desert his practice except on his free day. I asked him who was going to look after his patients in his absence. "There aren't any," he replied. "They're all cured." On that Monday Michael and his colleagues all had the unique experience of empty surgeries. Both chronics and hypochondriacs had either forgotten their pains or left London in search of safety. For some days London resembled a health resort. The population was too preoccupied with fear of violent death to look for symptoms of disease. Housebound old people, geriatrics as we now call them, who had been unable to move from their beds were metaphorically leaping into cars to be taken to the safety of the seaside or country. Even poor Nellie Coleman who had scarcely been able to breathe summoned her reserves of strength to travel to a safe area.

Then came the so-called phoney war. Apart from the inconvenience of the black-out the country suffered few discomforts. The older generation began to compare these conditions very favourably with those of the first world war. There were no casualty lists, the system of rationing was—and remained throughout the war—tolerable and fair. It was popularly supposed that Hitler was already regretting his attack on Poland and would never be so foolhardy as to attack the French behind their impregnable Maginot Line. Soldiers returning on leave spoke of the confidence and strength of the French army. Those who had seen enemy scouts who had fallen into Allied hands reported that their regimental badges carried the motto *Gott mit uns* (God with us). So perhaps the Nazis were not after all so wicked as we had been led to believe. Almost everyone listened to Lord Haw-Haw (William Joyce) on the radio. Such was our British phlegm and ostentatious nonchalance that the press advertised the times of Joyce's daily broadcasts. He constantly called on the British public to rid itself of Churchill and its Jewish masters (was not the Secretary of State for War, Hore-Belisha—Joyce called him Horeb-Elisha—a Jew?) There was still time to save ourselves from the coming holocaust but if we did not accept the generous offers of the peace-loving Fuehrer his patience would run out and we would be taught a terrible lesson.

Life remained uneventful until the phoney war ended and the real war began. The children of St. Winefride's school had been evacuated during the first week of the war. They had gone to Ingham and neighbouring villages in Norfolk. As soon as it was evident that air-raids were not imminent I went down to visit the teachers and children in their billets. Two amusing memories of this first brief evacuation survive. I went round all the billets to meet the 'aunties' who were kindly looking after our children. In one cottage three small girls burst into tears of self-pity at the sight of a face from home. Like most of the children they told me they wanted to go home. In addition to seeing Mummy their reason for wanting to go home was that auntie's husband (oddly enough not usually called uncle) would not let them say their Catholic prayers. When I tactfully reproached auntie's husband he declared that he had no objection to the other Catholic prayers but insisted on the children saying the following grace before meals: "Thank God and the Fighting Forces for what we are about to receive." He was a patriotic, God-fearing ex-serviceman. The other incident illustrates the pre-ecumenical atmosphere of those days. The headmaster of our school wrote for the parish magazine in Manor Park a description of conditions in the evacuation area. His excellent motive was to reassure parents that their children were being well cared for spiritually and physically. He ended his message with an account of my visit to the diaspora: "To our great joy Father Heenan called at every home to see that the children were comfortable and to thank the kind people who are fostering our children. The next morning Father Heenan offered Mass in the schoolroom and gave Holy Communion to the teachers and the children. Thus our Lord came back to Ingham for the first time since the so-called Reformation."

The Christians of Ingham not surprisingly felt affronted.

Despite warnings from the government, parents refused to suffer continued separation from their children when after a few weeks there was still no sign of enemy action from the air. By the spring of 1940 all the children had come home, school was reopened and parish life was more or less normal. The chief contrasts with peace-time were the absence of men who had been called up and the restriction on social life caused by the black-out. Otherwise there were few signs of war beyond the barrage balloons in the sky and the occupation of part of the school buildings by the Auxiliary Fire Service. Bored civilians in uniforms manning first-aid posts and A.R.P. (Air Raid Precautions) depots gave the town an air of unreality, but life went on peacefully enough. Then came the shattering outbreak of real war. Belgium and Holland were invaded in the early hours of 10th May, 1940. On 14th May the Germans in France broke through at Sedan and within five days had reached the sea. On 15th May the Royal Air Force bombed industrial targets on the Ruhr. Before the month ended the Dutch and Belgians had capitulated, the French were in disarray and the evacuation from Dunkirk had begun. The stage was set for the Battle of Britain. The new Prime Minister, Winston Churchill, told the nation to prepare for 'hard and heavy tidings'. The British people were alone in the fight. In Manor Park we felt frightened but wonderfully elated. The uniforms, balloons, A.R.P., casualty clearing stations and even the paper coffins at last began to make sense.

The story of the London blitz has been often told. It was a time of extraordinary misery and happiness. Misery came through casualties, the destruction of homes and the constant interruption of water and fuel supplies through enemy action. Happiness flowed from the comradeship and genuine charity which bound the whole community together. There was also the literal joi de vivre. It was good—and often surprising—to remain alive after a night of bombing. This joy in being alive was not a sense of superiority over the killed but a recognition that the countless pleasures we enjoyed were bounties—a night's uninterrupted sleep, light, warmth, food and drink. Before the war neighbours might remain strangers for years, but suffering broke down all barriers. As soon as a neighbour's home was struck the survivors, regardless of personal danger, rushed to comfort the afflicted. Before official help had time to arrive the rest of the community gave succour. Homes which survived attack were thrown open to the homeless. Far more remarkable than the courage of Londoners was their loving care of casualties.

I became skilled in tracking bombs to their targets. The clergy had been issued with special A.R.P. armlets which indicated our function. Clad in siren suit and tin hat we could command access to every stricken building. With masterly understatement the landing of a bomb was described as an incident. In the pocket of my siren suit I carried a tiny address book containing just street numbers—I knew the names. Parishioners would tell me when they could stand no more bombing and were taking their families to safe areas. Thus if their homes were involved in an incident I need not waste time looking for them in rubble. As the raids increased in frequency and intensity more and more homes were left deserted. But I soon dispensed with my book of addresses because it ceased to matter which houses belonged to Catholics. When a non-Catholic home was hit I was just as welcome. My nightly routine was to visit the incidents, the first-aid posts and the hospital. When casualties were especially severe I would go first to the hospital and visit the bombed homes later.

One terrible night the raiders flew at great height and were over the outskirts of London before the sirens sounded. It was the first occasion on which they dropped land-mines fixed to parachutes. These could not be heard until they exploded on impact. I was still in the presbytery unaware that a raid was in progress when the land-mines began to fall. The telephone bell rang and was answered by Mary Henry, my housekeeper. The call was from East Ham Memorial hospital which was just outside the parish boundaries. I was wanted urgently by a man who was seriously injured. Before passing the call to me Mary, as usual, asked the patient's name. The name was Joseph Henry—her only brother. Joe had fought in the battle of Mons during the first war and returned to Belgium after the war to marry the girl whose family had befriended British Tommies. He had been on holiday in England when the unexpected invasion of the Low Countries cut him off from his home. Poor Joe was badly injured and the surgeons had to sacrifice his leg to save his life. I urged Mary to leave Manor Park for a safe area. She refused. Her father had been a professional soldier and she said he would not have been proud of a daughter who deserted her post in face of the enemy.

The most distressing incident of the whole war in Manor Park was the bombing of an air-raid shelter. It was an underground shelter in the main road opposite the Three Rabbits public house. This incident was distressing not only because of the number killed but because many were trapped beneath the debris. The water pipes were broken and the unfortunates who were trapped faced the double hazard of bleeding to death or drowning. They were buried under such a weight of masonry that there was little we could do to help them before the demolition squad with their heavy equipment could release them. The doctors had to amputate limbs to free some of the victims. There is nothing more distressing than being powerless at the scene of suffering. There were three doctors present but they were unable to operate or even make contact for several hours. The raid meanwhile continued with unusual severity. Manor Park is virtually part of London's dockland. Quite often we escaped serious damage because the Luftwaffe was seeking more valuable targets in the city and West End of London. We were most vulnerable when, as on this memorable night, the raiders were driven off target by the R.A.F. night fighters and had to empty their bombs on the suburbs to lighten their load as they sped home.

During the grimmest nights there was almost always some quirk of events to turn tears to laughter. This night was no exception. The doctors had instructed the proprietor of the Three Rabbits to keep the saloon bar open as a casualty station. At about two o'clock in the morning only two doctors were left with the heavy rescue squad— Michael O'Dwyer and John Sullivan. It was clear that it would take at least another hour before we would be able to make contact with the casualties. Dr. Sullivan said that it would be best to wait in the comparative comfort of the Three Rabbits. We would thus conserve our energy for later effort. When we entered the saloon bar John decided that the licensing laws must be suspended for the occasion. Our throats were choked with dust and all three of us were near exhaustion. Sullivan had no difficulty in persuading the publican to break the regulations. He ordered three double whiskies. The dialogue which took place was often gleefully recalled by all three of us in later months. That is why I am able to reproduce it with some accuracy.

> John: This is an emergency, Manager. Give us three double whiskies.
>
> Me: John, make it two.
>
> John: For God's sake, Father, take your time. Have one now and another later.
>
> Me: No, John. I mean two. One for you and one for Michael. I don't want a drink.
>
> John: But you *need* a drink. You've been on duty for hours.
>
> Me: It's nearly two o'clock in the morning. I'm saying Mass at 8 o'clock and I have to fast from midnight.
>
> John: That's damn nonsense. That's not religion. As a doctor I order you a stimulant. To hell with fasting.
>
> Me: (Sententiously—Dr. Sullivan at that time had no reputation for being Gospel-greedy. He had never been seen at Mass—at least in Manor Park.)
> John, you wouldn't understand. I'm perfectly free to have a drink. I can either have a drink or say Mass. Which would you do?
>
> John: Manager, make it two whiskies and give the priest a packet of cigarettes.

Before the doctors had been given their drinks the bombing suddenly started again. There was a tremendous crash. A bomb demolished the shop next door to the Three Rabbits. The glasses in the saloon bar were shattered. We ran out to deal with fresh casualties. The three of us stayed together until about six o'clock on that Sunday morning. Then I went home to have a bath, shave and gargle to clear my throat of the dust from the rubble. When I arrived at St. Nicholas' church for the eight o'clock Mass John Sullivan was already there. Subsequently John was at Mass every Sunday morning.

I had my own personal and private joke in the saloon bar of the Three Rabbits that morning. The Germans were in the habit of dropping their small bombs in sticks of five. We soon became expert in judging the likely places where the last three bombs of a stick would fall. The bombing had restarted, as I have said, at the very moment that Dr. Sullivan ordered the drinks. I shouted to him and Michael O'Dwyer to throw themselves on the floor as soon as I heard the second detonation. I judged that the third or fourth bomb could hit the Three Rabbits. I miscalculated by only a few feet. The bomb landed next door. After the explosion and while the glasses in the bar were still falling I could not keep myself from laughing. The doctors were shocked because they thought it out of character for me to become hysterical. But mine was no case of hysteria. I had suddenly thought of what would have happened had the bomb landed on the Three Rabbits. I saw the story as it might have appeared in the local press. What would the public have thought of the priest and two doctors who met their death in a pub while across the road their poor parishioners and patients were drowning in an air-raid shelter? No witnesses of my abnegation would have remained alive. My best friends would have shaken their heads and wondered why I had not had enough sense to keep out of public houses during air-raids.

Pastoral life was dictated by the air-raids. It was impossible to go far from the parish when raids were in progress or in prospect. We often heard the warning siren but nothing more until the All Clear—no gunfire and no bombs. On such occasions I had to sit at home and await a call. My own hospital was the Aldersbrook but the East Ham Memorial Hospital on my boundary frequently summoned me. I used the hours of enforced immobility for writing. Early in the war I became involved in broadcasting and journalism. The B.B.C. frequently invited me to speak on the radio. The first contract I signed with the B.B.C. was to give a series of broadcasts on the Forces programme. The B.B.C. had really wanted Cardinal Hinsley, a superb performer, but he would agree to give only the first of the series and recommended me for the rest. Before I gave these talks for the religious department I found myself involved with the American section of the B.B.C. It happened almost by chance.

The B.B.C. at that time was broadcasting a prestigious programme to North America called *Britain Speaks*. I read a report of one of these talks and was appalled by its futility. In 1940 America was still largely isolationist. Many Americans thought that the U.S.A. had been tricked into joining the first world war by the cleverness of the British. Some were not above believing that we ourselves had sunk the *Lusitania* in order to force them into the war. I regarded a speaker who failed to take American suspicions into consideration as inept. I must have written a letter to the Director of the B.B.C. To my astonishment I received by return post a request from the head of the American section to give the next talk in *Britain Speaks*.

Re-reading the broadcast given on 4th August 1940 is for me an almost masochistic exercise. However balanced and objective I thought myself to be at the time, my talk to America shows evidence of the general emotion felt by people in England when our country stood alone and was thought to be on the eve of invasion. In my book *Were You Listening?** which reproduced this and other wartime talks, the preface claims that I was aware of the dangers of using religion as a weapon of propaganda. I wrote:

> The reality of war is the backgound of all these talks. In a word, they are topical. But they are by no means patriotic speeches. There is something undignified about a clerical recruiting sergeant, yet there is always a great temptation for a priest to believe and teach that God is on the side of his own country. Such a statement is likely to be controversial, at least from the point of view of the millions of Catholics in the other camp. What I think of the Christianity of this country appears all too clearly in the talks which follow. I have not, even in my own mind, canonised the rulers of this country, but what I have suggested, and what I believe quite simply, is that the particular kind of totalitarianism which this country is fighting is as hostile to the Church as it is to the British Commonwealth.
>
> No well-informed person doubts the existence of religious persecution in Germany although it is less blatant than that in the U.S.S.R. When we examine the credentials of some of our own leaders and of some of our past, present and potential allies, it is very difficult, without qualification, to call this struggle a Christian Crusade. But it is certainly, to my mind, a Crusade against anti-Christians. In saying this I am saying no more than can be deduced from both the solemn pronouncements of the Vatican and the more or less unofficial broadcasts from Vatican City.

Reading my first broadcast after more than thirty years I realise that I was very naïve. Since nevertheless it helps to recapture the mood of the times, it may be of interest to give some brief extracts.

> Britain is now fighting, in the main, to preserve what we call Christian civilisation. The odd thing is that England, as a nation, is only remotely Christian (something like the United States of America).

* Burns & Oates, London, 1942.

I know that both countries are ostensibly Christian. Deep down in the hearts of both peoples is a strong Christian foundation, but it has been overlaid with corruption, materialism and self-interest. How many people in these Christian countries ever think of Christ our Lord? How many put God first in their lives? How many fulfil the elementary obligation of man to worship his Creator? They will tell you, here and in America, that they worship God in the new way. That God can be found on Sunday morning in the open fields as well as in stuffy churches. Yes, I know those fields. They have eighteen holes for golf and a nineteenth for cocktails. Yet, knowing all this, I say—forgive me for insisting—England really is fighting for Christianity. Just as a man, suddenly realising that he is in danger of going blind, begins to value and to protect his eyesight, so England is now determined to protect with her life's blood that which she had almost lost—the decency which we call Christian culture . . .

When we talk about fighting a Christian crusade, intelligent critics may be pardoned for observing that there are millions of Christians fighting for the Reich and for their Fuehrer. To them we certainly owe our prayers and sympathy, because the struggle between religious and national allegiance must rob them of all peace of mind, since the scales are so heavily weighted against the balance of conscience. But do not tell me that the millions of Catholics in the Reich, with every Catholic university, college and school closed down, are content. Do not tell me that the Christian parents of Germany are happy in the knowledge that their children, almost from infancy, are forced into the ranks of the Hitler Jugend with its ridicule of religion and its Sunday parades, so timed as to make worship of God impossible. Do not tell me that such parents are content. Well might the Fuehrer complain in his latest speech of the elements in Germany itself who are dismayed at the prospect of a German victory.

I am not concerned tonight to examine the motives or the Christian credentials of the leaders of Britain who protest in the name of Christianity that they are waging a holy war. I am merely telling you that, humanly speaking, a Nazi victory would mean the temporary extinction of the Church in Europe. This is recognised even in Ireland. I wonder if this story has crossed the Atlantic? A young Royal Air Force pilot developed engine trouble over St. George's Channel and made a forced landing in

Greystones Harbour. The harbour master, a typical County Wicklow man, brought in the pilot and gave him a glass of hot punch, sending a mechanic, meanwhile, to look at the engine. It turned out that the trouble was no more serious than an airlock in the petrol feed, and was soon put to rights. The harbour-master shook hands with the pilot and sent him away happy. But a couple of hours later, when the story had reached Dublin, two officials from Dublin Castle came racing down to remonstrate. "Don't you understand," they asked the harbour master, "that Ireland is a neutral country and the pilot, as a belligerent, should have been interned? They are the rules of war." "I don't know anything about the rules of war," was the reply, "but I know something about the rules of hospitality. I knew we were neutral, but nobody told me who we were neutral against. How do you expect me to be neutral against these young men who are fighting the Nazis condemned by our Holy Father?" . . .

Before bidding you goodnight I want to address a special word to youth in the New World. It is simply this: We in Europe look to you with eyes full of hope. Twenty years of irreligious easy-going life has left Europe weak to resist the forces of evil. You have not yet been called upon to make supreme sacrifices. One day, perhaps soon, you may have to take up the struggle. If, by that time, the Nazi spectre has been laid, atheistic communism and other obscenities are lurking everywhere to entice and enslave the generous spirit of youth. We shall refuse to allow soured age to tarnish our ideals . . .

When this struggle is over the youth of Britain may stand weak and materially impoverished. Its ranks may be thinned. Youth of the New World, you are our trustees! May I humbly and with deep respect say to you with St. Paul to his disciple, "Oh, Timothy, keep that which is committed to thy trust, avoiding the profane novelties of words and of false knowledge."

Pray, meanwhile, for the youth of Europe that by God's grace we may be strong and worthy defenders of all that you and we ourselves hold dear.

In my talks on the Programme for the Forces I used language which would probably make little appeal today to the children of those who were young men in 1940:

To the youth of the Forces I want to say this. If you have no interest in religion it is because you have been robbed. I know that many influences have combined to destroy your interest. Soured and cynical men may have told you that religion is all humbug. We all know Scrooge of *A Christmas Carol*. These men are the Scrooges of the four seasons. Don't let them depress you. Above all, don't let them impress you. We priests are not all that we should be. We ought to be saints. But however unworthy we are, He whom we represent *is* worthy of your friendship. Ask of Him the grace to know Him. If you are looking for Christ you will find Him. You will find Him everywhere. He is in your friends. He is in your enemies. He is in the persons with whom you work—yes, and in the person with whom you sin. Learn to know, love and serve Him. That is the reason why God made you. The story of Christ is not a fairy story. If you don't know it learn it now. Your chaplains will tell you about our Lord if you give them the chance.

Youth, today, is looking for a better Europe, is fighting for it, is dying for it. That better Europe can come only when youth has found Christ. At present, youth is not looking for Christ. If we pretend otherwise we are deceiving ourselves, and, still worse, we are deceiving youth. Why do I say that youth is not looking for Christ? Let St. Paul provide the answer: "How then shall they call on him in whom they have not believed, or how shall they believe Him of whom they have not heard, and how shall they hear without a teacher?"

In another talk I asked the Forces to face the prospect of peace. This, on 18th August, 1940, was really asking the impossible:

Then how will peace come? Not by a mere cessation of hostilities. We have already suffered twenty years of unenduring and unendurable 'peace'. Peace can, must and will come only when the world finds the Christ for whom it is now groping. When the world finds Christ the battle will be over. "Have confidence," He has said, "I have overcome the world" (John xvii:16).

Saint Paul, on his journeys, discovered that the Athenians were so anxious to find Christ that they had built an altar to the unknown god. "Ye men of Athens," said the apostle, "what you worship without knowing it, that I preach to you" (Acts xvii:23). Saint Paul was preaching Christ crucified—Christ "who was in the world and the world was made by Him and the world knew Him not" (John i:11). There was some excuse for a pagan world. There is less excuse for a world paganised.

The responsibility of Christians to help the world to find Christ is tremendous and urgent. Talking will help very little. The world is feverish. It demands action. Only the example of practical Christianity will arouse the world's curiosity about Christ. "So let your light shine before men that they may see your good works and glorify your Father who is in heaven" (Matthew v:16).

Whether the change is in me, in young people or in the atmosphere of a country now at peace, I cannot imagine that I would adopt the same tone if I were to address a radio audience today. It is difficult to know what I might say now because monologues are no longer in fashion. Dialogue is the fashion. No matter how gifted the speaker he is now believed to need an interviewer. If there are two speakers they are thought to need a chairman. In the unsophisticated nineteen-forties speakers were allowed on the radio without chaperons. We spoke plainly enough but there was more emotion and more reliance on a common acceptance of religious principles than would be possible in the second half of the century. I would not today speak on the radio in quite the same way as I did on 25th August, 1940.

Don't think that members of Churches are smug, superior people. The Church is anxious to have all men enter. She is not exclusive. She is humble as befits the Spouse of Christ. Today, thank God, there is more unity of purpose and good-will among Christians than there has been for centuries. Bigotry is dying fast. Believers in God, the world over, are uniting to overcome the powers of evil—strong in every country. But remember that Christianity cannot be delegated to boards and committees. Christianity means Christ in the soul—in your soul and in mine. Our Lord is a quiet, unobtrusive guest, but we should not keep Him waiting too long.

Men of the Forces, I leave you with this thought. Whoever you are, you can pray . . . War places all men, but especially fighting men, in a cruel position. To plan destruction is a dismal task. All true Christians desire the peace of Christ. It will come when Christ is given free entry into all nations and into the hearts of the men of all nations.

None of you doubts, or can possibly doubt, that if all men were true Christians, peace, the fruit of justice, would soon be restored to an unhappy world. Now realise this: you cannot speak for all men, any more than I can, but you *can* speak for yourselves. Be true Christians. I suggest respectfully, that each day you might say this little prayer: "Son of God, teach me to know and love Thee." Let me repeat it: "Son of God, teach me to know and love Thee." A sincere prayer is always answered. "Ask and you shall receive, seek and you shall find" (Matthew vii:7). But we must pray, not like the self-righteous, as if we, as a nation or as individuals, had never sinned, but humbly and with real sorrow. "A humble and contrite heart, O God, thou wilt not despise" (Psalm 1: 18).

During 1941 I gave a series of talks which were published the following year under the title *Untruisms*.* On succeeding Sundays I took as a kind of text some expression so hackneyed as to have become a truism. My intention was to prove that these alleged truisms are in fact untrue. The titles of the first two talks indicate the nature of the series: 'We'll all soon be dead' and 'Nothing matters anyway'. These talks attracted a far larger audience than was usual for a religious programme. It was not their excellence that attracted the audience but a happy accident which occurred during the opening talk. It is important in a radio talk to arrest attention in the first few seconds. Otherwise a listener switches off or turns to another programme. With the object of making people stay on the wavelength (my talks came immediately after the one o'clock news) I began in an original way. I set out to shock and startle listeners. I succeeded only too well. Here are the opening words of the broadcast: "He's going to talk about religion—turn him off. Were you just going to say that? I'm not trying to be funny. I'm suggesting that a large number of people will turn me off just because I'm going to talk about religion."

It happened that on that day a large-scale rehearsal of defence tactics in the event of invasion was taking place. Every building of strategic importance in London was under special guard. Broadcasting House was being guarded with particular caution. Somewhere in the cellars an officer was manning a control switch to cut off all radio in the event of a successful landing by the Germans. He was

* Burns & Oates, London, 1942.

probably bored by hours of listening and may have been half asleep when suddenly he heard the words "Turn him off". I described the incident in the introduction to *Untruisms*.

> It is not always a joy to be taken at your word. I started my first broadcast in the series *'Untruism'* with the words "Turn him off"—and turned off I was! I could scarcely complain. I had asked for it. No doubt some technician mistook my opening phrase for an order from Authority.
>
> This hitch, in itself, would not have mattered if the few minutes' delay before my voice was heard again had been made good. But, later, the unfortunate speech was again cut—this time in favour of a dance band. Next day the B.B.C. was a target for almost every newspaper in the country. 'Priest faded for Crooner' was a typical headline. One London daily permitted itself to describe the fading out as 'the most graceless blunder in the history of British broadcasting'. Nothing less.
>
> From my point of view, as a broadcaster, this was all splendid. It attracted a much larger audience for subsequent Sundays. The B.B.C. had my sympathy. It was awkwardly placed. My broadcast immediately preceded 'Music while you work'—a feature for factories. Music alone comes through factory loud-speakers unless a special notice has to be given to the workers. The living voice, in other words, is the sign to cease work. That is one reason why the B.B.C. was unable to allow the first talk to be concluded."

The style of the broadcasts in this second book is much the same as that of the first. Most of the talks were given on the Forces network with occasional contributions to the Home and Overseas services of the B.B.C. My method was very direct and, so it now seems to me, self-consciously straining for effect. I had not yet learned that what your supporters cheer is unlikely to appeal to your opponents. I was trying to reach the lapsed Christians but probably only annoyed them. Here is a fairly typical extract which makes use of the government regulation that church bells must be silent throughout the war except in the event of invasion:

> You've all met the kind of fellow who says to you, "I've got no use for religion myself, but I don't interfere with those who have."

You'd almost think that not interfering with others lets him out. It makes him feel broadmainded—like a teetotaller who says, "I don't drink myself but I don't mind giving a glass of beer to my friends." The difference is that while there is no law of God, so far as I know, which tells a man to be a total abstainer from alcohol, there happens to be a law of God which commands a man not to be a total abstainer from religion.

I must admit that a total abstainer from worship practises a very comfortable doctrine. It doesn't require much strength of character to stay in bed on Sunday morning. But suppose that the church bells were to ring out next Sunday—just think how men and women would spring from their beds. It would mean that the invasion had started. Everywhere people would be on their toes ready to fight and die to defend Christian civilisation. In other words, church bells ringing for Hitler would galvanise the nation. When they rang for God it didn't seem to matter.

I did little radio work after 1942. By that time the country had emerged from the hazards of the months immediately following Dunkirk. Religion had become essential to morale only when England was threatened with defeat (the phenomenon was repeated even in Soviet Russia in its months of peril). Religious broadcasts reverted to the anodyne mixture of hymns, prayers and uplifting talks. Clergy were no longer invited to speak in ordinary programmes. Cardinal Hinsley had been in great demand when the country was in danger. He had gained a formidable reputation as a broadcaster. I made reference to this in my memoir of Cardinal Hinsley:

The war situation was easier. Most former neutrals were either safely in the war or well disposed towards the prospective victors. Cardinal Hinsley reverted, in the eyes of the B.B.C., to the position of Roman Catholic Archbishop. Throughout 1942 he was heard by the British public on only two occasions—the addresses to youth and to Malta. Neither address was spontaneously suggested by the B.B.C. The first was arranged on the representation of certain Catholics, the second under pressure from Monsignor Elwes, the Cardinal's secretary.

The time when his postscripts would be welcome for the courage they infused into the souls of his grateful fellow countrymen had passed. The question of arranging for him to give a talk had become complicated in the mind of the Corporation by the fear that if he were allowed to speak, the leaders of all religious denominations might demand an equal share. Hinsley had served his turn.

Within a short time I became involved not only with the B.B.C. but with the Kemsley Press, Reuters and the Ministry of Information. It is extraordinary how quickly a reputation can be established in the mass media world. Mercifully it can be lost almost as quickly. Names which for months appear in every edition of *Radio Times* disappear without warning and are never seen again. I was not the first nor the last clerical charlatan to be awarded the pretentious and rather absurd title 'Radio Priest'.

I cannot recall the boundaries between the Ministry of Information, the B.B.C. and Reuters. They were working so closely together that it was difficult to know with which one was dealing. For a long time at the request of Mr.—later Sir Christopher—Chancellor I wrote scripts to be read in Spanish and Portuguese to audiences in Latin America. The idea must have been to demonstrate that, unlike Nazi Germany, Great Britain was interested in the things of the spirit. I doubt if the hearers, if any, were very deeply impressed. I found it frustrating and uninspiring to address, at one remove, an audience of whom I knew nothing. The experiment was eventually abandoned. At that time all sorts of unlikely plans were being examined for use in the British war of words. Everything was so hush-hush at this most critical period of the war that nothing that could possibly disclose our intentions to the enemy was put in writing. I have therefore no documents but only memory for my guide.

Two encounters stand out as examples of what but for the fever of war would even then have been recognised as part of a larger lunacy. The first took place at luncheon in the suite of Reuters' managing director. All the directors were present and the meal was of almost peace-time proportions. Surprised and rather flattered by so much attention I had to wait until coffee was being served for my hosts to reveal the motive for their hospitality. In general terms, they explained, Reuters felt that the Catholic Church was not being given a fair deal in the world of communications. They were disposed to offer all their facilities to the Church's spokesmen—especially to Cardinal Hinsley—for sending messages and presenting the Catholic point of view throughout the world. I was amazed by this ingenuous

—it would be unfair to call it disingenuous—approach. My hosts were sincere men but were doubtless acting on instructions from the Ministry of Information. It was amazing to hear that Reuters were on fire to spread the Catholic Faith. The object of the approach was, of course, to reach the many countries for whom the Church meant the Catholic Church and to whom England epitomised Protestantism or paganism. I smiled and took my leave. I did not see Christopher Chancellor again for nearly thirty years but even after such a lapse of time we were able to enjoy the memories of such wartime follies.

The second recollection is of a visit I paid with Mgr. Elwes to the Man-in-Blue. I was never told his name. He wore the uniform of a rankless Royal Air Force officer and I understood him to be the head of the secret service. He informed me that the most powerful broadcasting station in the world was being constructed in Britain. This remarkable instrument was able to blanket any other radio transmissions and its provenance was undetectable. It was at the disposal of the cardinal to address the Germans, the French, the Poles . . . This time I did not laugh. I waited until we had returned to Archbishop's House, Westminster so that the cardinal, Val and I could all enjoy the laugh together.

Impressed no doubt by my formidable billing in the Catholic papers the features editor of the *Sunday Graphic* asked me to meet him. I invited him to lunch with me at the Authors' Club. I had joined this modest club at the suggestion of Collin Brooks, editor of *Truth*, whom I had met in 1938 after I had given a lecture on communism. I had already begun to use my free time to write and lecture. Collin Brooks persuaded me that it would be a great advantage to have a place where I could meet publishers and press people. He sponsored me and on the strength of having written *Priest and Penitent* I was elected. The features editor offered me a contract to write a weekly article for the overseas edition of the *Sunday Graphic*. When he received my first contribution he telephoned to say that he must see me at once. He came down to Manor Park to explain why my article simply would not do. Its major fault, he said, was that it would make people think. I confess that this article had been written with meticulous care. It was, after all, the first of a series which would bring over a thousand pounds annually to the parish.

The features editor went on to explain the psychology of Sunday journalism. Every writer must keep in mind the mentality of typical readers of a Sunday picture paper. He must imagine a man who after a few drinks had gone late to bed on Saturday night. He would want to prop his paper against the teapot and look for silver linings. This is what I would be paid to provide. I was to write uplifting articles to make people feel that the world was not such a bad place as the rest of the paper might suggest. I could bring in religion in moderation. ("You can give them the Bible and that," he said, "when you want a nice quote.")

My second contribution was printed without alteration on the following Sunday. It was the fastest and most thoughtless piece I had ever written. It was almost a satire of the *Graphic* man's talk to me. It was called 'Too much foolish talking'. My man was charmed. He rang up as soon as he had read it to tell me that my style was just right for readers of the *Graphic* (this paper is now understandably defunct). I had grasped his message so well that he would never need to tell me anything again. I never did see him again but I continued to write for the next two years. I used to dictate the articles in less than half-an-hour. Since the British public never saw them I was not subjected to criticism. I doubt if I could have gone on writing those articles for so long had I been meeting people who actually read them. The only person who knew how little thought went into my articles was my secretary Mrs. Williams. She was too loyal to mind.

The only regular reader I ever met was John McCormack who lived in Ireland. He used to write to me about the articles which he thought full of wisdom. The Kemsley money was useful when I had to rebuild my school which suffered a direct hit during the blitz. But writing regular columns in the press prostitutes the style of a non-journalist. I was heartily glad when the overseas edition of the *Graphic* was suspended by reason of the shortage of newsprint.

John McCormack was more than a pen friend. This big-hearted man could not bear life in retirement. Singers are, of course, famous for the number of their positively final appearances but John's case was rather different. He retired and stayed professionally retired. He returned only as an amateur. The reason was that he loved England. America was the land of his adoption and he was a typical product of Ireland the land of his birth. John McCormack was more at home in England than anywhere in the world. When war broke out he offered his talents to this country. He sang for the soldiers, for the sick, for the old and for anyone to whom he could bring comfort. I asked him to sing one Sunday night during Benediction at St. Nicholas' church in Manor Park. I explained very carefully that my chief object was to bring those parishioners to church who could not be attracted by missioners or special preachers. He very gladly agreed to take part in the plot. It was not a very subtle plot. I merely wanted to let people see the incongruity of coming to church to hear a famous tenor while not being willing to come to church for Mass.

On the Sunday evening the crowds were so great that many could not find even standing room in the church. John sang only two hymns—'Panis Angelicus' and 'Sweet Sacrament Divine'. Unspoiled by success and wealth, John McCormack never lost his deep faith. He had that passionate love for the Mass which is so characteristic of the Irish. There is no country in the world which begins to compare with Ireland for devotion to the Mass. As a visitor to Dublin I have been astonished by the numbers at Mass every morning. Professional and business people make morning Mass a routine practice. That, at least, is what I have always seen. I have rarely been to Dublin since the Council so I do not know if the vernacular and the other liturgical changes have upset the Mass-going habits of a profoundly traditional people. When John had finished singing I told the congregation that I had no mind to thank the singer for his services. I hoped that, on the contrary, the singer would thank me for allowing him the privilege of singing in the presence of Christ in the Blessed Sacrament. I went on to preach my prepared sermon on the value of the Mass. I stood outside the church after Benediction among a large crowd waiting for John to come down from the choir loft. When he came he outshone my pulpit performance with histrionics of his own. "Father Heenan," he cried, "with all my heart I thank you for giving me the privilege of singing in the presence of my Lord and my God."

The vigils imposed by the air-raids gave me time for writing something more durable than radio scripts and newspaper articles. I wrote a comprehensive book on the faith which I called *Letters from Rush Green*.* Unfortunately it is printed in the wartime economy style and the type is not easy to read. After the war it was beautifully produced in the United States under the title *The Faith Makes Sense*.† A great deal of thought went into this book, which was an attempt to show that belief in God is reasonable and that Jesus is the Son of God in the literal sense if the Gospel is authentic.

* Burns & Oates, London, 1946.
† Sheed & Ward, New York, 1947.

The second half of the book is a defence of the claim of the Catholic Church to be the Church of God. There is no attack on other creeds but it contains expressions which ecumenism has shown us to be offensive to members of Reformed Churches. The publishers did everything possible after the war to persuade me to bring out a new edition. They even bound a special copy interleaved with blank pages to make revision easy. I could never bring myself to attempt the task. My reluctance to rewrite the book arises from the fact that apologetics (an argued defence of Christianity) is temporarily out of fashion. Until mental discipline and sharp verbal accuracy are once more in favour there will be no market for such books. The day may come when some young priest will flick through the yellowing pages of *Rush Green* and decide to rewrite it in modern idiom with contemporary examples.

The church of St. Stephen was exactly opposite the old parish church of St. Mary and the rectory of my friend the Rev. H.A.S. Pink (later Archdeacon of Hampstead). Stanley Pink and I were close friends of a Methodist, the Rev. A. Binks, superintendent of the East Ham Central Hall. I doubt if any of us had heard the word ecumenism but we were united in charity. Apart from being welcome in each other's houses we lost no opportunity of bringing our people together. Alfred Binks had the cheerful mien common to fat men. Most important, his was the transparent kind of goodness which those close to God seem to radiate. Alfred was the first Methodist I heard say—and this was before anyone had heard of Cardinal Roncalli, the future Pope John—that he would be happy to lead all his flock to the Pope if it would create Christian unity. I doubt if he was much of a theologian but he knew his Bible and said his prayers. I cannot recall him ever actually speaking of love but he had such evident love for all he met that he had no need to talk about it.

During the war I was able to be of some service to my non-Catholic colleagues through membership of the East Ham Education Committee. I was co-opted in the interests of the Catholic schools at Upton Park, Manor Park and East Ham which were within the borough boundaries. When Mr. Butler began to outline a new education bill (which became the Education Act 1944) it was obvious that the government intended to give religion a more prominent place in the curriculum. It is impossible to be certain of other people's motives but I think the politicians were genuinely alarmed by the paganism of Nazi Germany and felt that the British as Christian crusaders should teach young citizens more about Christianity. The evacuation of city children from state schools to church schools in the country had revealed alarming ignorance of Christ. Under the old system school religion had meant little more than telling children Bible stories. That is why in the new Act it was proposed to include a daily act of worship and an agreed (non-denominational) syllabus of religious instruction. My non-Catholic colleagues of all persuasions held meetings to discuss an agreed syllabus and I undertook to sponsor their findings with the education committee. I attended the first of their meetings in order to assure them of my co-operation and ask for their instructions. I advised them to make the headings of religious instruction few and simple: the existence of God and the incarnation, redemption and resurrection of Christ. I shall never forget the comment of Alfred Binks. "Did you say 'simple'?" he asked, "Let me tell you, Father Heenan, there are as many views on the incarnation as there are clergymen in this room."

Stanley Pink, the Anglican rector, was soon able to repay my efforts by doing me a good turn over the forthcoming education bill. It was the intention of some reformers to use the new bill as the occasion for ridding the country of church schools. The so-called dual system (state schools and non-provided schools i.e. not provided [built] by public funds) would give place to a unified system in which all schools would be county schools. An ad hoc group was formed under the title of the Society for Educational Reform. There were no Anglican, Non-conformist or Jewish non-provided schools in the borough of East Ham. When the Society for Educational Reform organised its first meeting in East Ham only the non-Catholic clergy were invited to attend. As soon as Pink discovered that I had not been invited he informed the organisers that if I were not present no other clergyman would attend. When the public meeting to inaugurate a local branch of the Society for Educational Reform took place Mrs. Brace, the chairman of the East Ham Education Committee, presided. The first business was the election of a chairman and other officers of the new branch. Stanley Pink at once proposed my name. Mrs. Brace seconded the nomination and added that she knew me to be an authority on education. They would be very fortunate if they could persuade me to take office. After such a recommendation the motion was carried by acclamation without further nominations. I took the chair and we proceeded to elect the hon. secretary. I proposed the rector, the Rev. H.A.S. Pink. He was also returned unopposed. The rest of the committee were elected from among church people who were present at the request of the rector or myself. The Society for Educational Reform of East Ham proved to be no menace to non-provided schools.

The rectory had several large cellars. The rector kindly allowed us to use the cellars as an air-raid shelter for our children during the anomalous period when, although the school was officially evacuated, the children had, in fact, come back to Manor Park. Since all children had returned, the teachers had no option but to follow them. They had to report each day to the school but were forbidden to teach. The children had nothing to do but roam the streets and play games on the bombed sites. It was demoralising and dangerous. I therefore decided to re-open the school unofficially. I recruited from among the parishioners a number of women who, though lacking official qualifications, had something to offer the children. One lady taught French. This she was well able to do since she was French and had been well educated in a convent near Cherbourg. My own secretary, Winefred Williams, took classes in shorthand. Others gave needlework or music lessons. In addition to religion I taught history, geography and any subject on which I was able to borrow up-to-date textbooks. I even found myself crossing once more the *pons asinorum* to satisfy the more ambitious children curious about the mysteries of Euclid. All the children in the neighbourhood were free to come whether or not they were Catholics—in fact the keenest and brightest of my pupils were Jewish girls. Just before the limit of my knowledge was reached the local authorities relaxed their rule and allowed the teachers to resume their classroom duties. With great relief I put away my Latin grammar, geometry book and Ballard's Intelligence Tests.

One night the Luftwaffe came over armed exclusively with incendiary bombs. They dropped thousands on London and started fires throughout the East End. What was left of my school (half the building) had a flat roof. During the raid I noticed that some bombs had fallen on this roof and were likely to burn through to the ceilings below. The A.F.S. (Auxiliary Fire Service) quartered in the school had disappeared to fight fires further afield. I had no choice but to become my own fire brigade. In frantic haste I threw off my coat, put an A.F.S. ladder against the wall and dashed up to the roof. I kicked out the incendiaries. (This was an act of crass ignorance. An incendiary bomb might explode when kicked. Nobody had told me that the Germans had begun to drop anti-personnel and incendiary bombs in the same load. The very next night one of my parishioners had two fingers blown off disposing of an incendiary.) From the roof I happened to look down to Mr. Pink's rectory. An incendiary had fallen through the roof but nobody seemed to have taken action. I slid quickly down the ladder and ran across to the rectory. Nobody was at home. The rector was presumably in the parish helping to put out other people's fires. Receiving no answer to my knocking I went round to the back of the rectory and broke open the door. I was battling with the fire when a passing fire brigade (not our local A.F.S.) saw the fire and came charging in. With professional speed they unrolled their hoses. One man meanwhile shouted a question at me: "Vicar, where are the mains?" I had to tell him that I had no idea. The fireman could not credit my ignorance. "Chief," he yelled to the man-in-charge, "this 'ere vicar doesn't know where his own———mains are." It was not the moment to explain that I was not a vicar. Having stayed at the vicarage until the fire was out and the firemen departed I returned to the presbytery and divested myself of my Anglican orders.

After the blitz was called off, the war for Londoners resumed something of the character of the former phoney war except for the daily news of the fighting in the Middle East. We still had the black-out, the barrage balloons, the A.R.P. and all the familiar uniforms and equipment, but the sense of danger had passed. It was not until the second phase of the war when the Allies were ready to assume the offensive that the Germans renewed the aerial war on England. They now possessed much more sophisticated projectiles. Meanwhile we had time to breathe. It was even possible to spend a night away from the parish without feelings of guilt. At the height of the blitz an offer had been made by intrepid clergy in the North to relieve priests in the London area for a week or two to enable them to have a few nights of uninterrupted sleep. There was no lack of volunteers but, to the credit of the London clergy, there were no requests for replacement. No priest would have felt happy to leave his people in a danger area while he went away for a rest and change. When the danger was apparently over many priests were glad to take their first few days holiday since the war. I accepted an invitation to visit Ireland as the special reporter of the *Catholic Herald*. The editor, Michael de la Bedoyère, was anxious to have an objective account of the Irish outlook on the war. By this time we in England had convinced ourselves that we were fighting a Christian crusade. Hundreds of thousands of cardinal's crosses were being worn by soldiers on all fronts. The little plastic crucifix carried the legend THE PLEDGE OF VICTORY, a sloganised translation of the historical words *In hoc signo vinces*. Religion and patriotism tend to fuse in the heat of war. Gallant little Belgium coupled with the butchered babies carried in the knapsacks of Hun soldiers had provided the ingredients for a crusade against the Kaiser. The concentration camps (about which our government had been discreetly silent before the war), the brutal treatment of citizens in occupied territory and, of course, the number of civilians killed in the London blitz were a sufficient warrant for regarding the British as soldiers of Christ. Ireland however seemed strangely unimpressed by the claims we were making. The editor of the *Catholic Herald* asked me to investigate.

CHAPTER
EIGHT

IT WAS PLEASANT IN EVERY WAY TO VISIT IRELAND, BEING A COUNTRY
not at war. The bright lights of Dublin and the unrestricted supplies
of fresh eggs, butter and all kinds of farm produce made Eire seem
like fairyland. To this was added the courtesy and traditional hospitality of the Irish people. From the ecclesiastical point of view I was
among the smallest fry. I was still in my thirties and in Ireland nobody
under fifty years of age was considered sufficiently mature to
become a parish priest. My passport to the Church in Ireland was my
position as spiritual director of the Legion of Mary in England and
Wales. The Legion is an Irish creation. Its function may very roughly
be described as being to those in spiritual need what the Society of
St. Vincent de Paul is to the poor and destitute. It is, of course,
much more than that, but this is its chief distinction. It is a charitable
organisation which forbids its members to use it as a means of
discharging their Christian duty of giving material relief to those in
need. I had been appointed national director almost by chance. When
I came to Manor Park I found the Legion of Mary—which at the time
was not even a name to me—already in existence. I was impressed by
the zeal of its members but horrified by the excesses of their zeal. I
found, for example, that in visiting homes these young men and
women questioned Catholics about the validity of their marriages. I
protested to Legion headquarters in London about this and similar
indiscretions of an otherwise splendid organisation. It happened that
the spiritual director of the Senatus (the ruling body for England
and Wales) was about to retire. Without consulting me the Legion

authorities approached the Archbishop of Westminster (still Cardinal Hinsley) to ask for my appointment. Apparently my criticism had appealed to legionaries as proof that I understood the spirit of the Legion and would be able to guide it well. I never regretted accepting the position of spiritual director, which I retained until I was appointed Superior of the Catholic Missionary Society after the war.

I carried with me to Ireland a letter of introduction to Sir John Maffey, United Kingdom High Commissioner in Dublin and a note from Cardinal Hinsley to Cardinal MacRory, Primate of All Ireland. As soon as I reached Dublin I called on Frank Duff, the founder of the Legion of Mary. A man of infectious zeal—his movement has spread throughout the world—and great intelligence, he saw at once the value of explaining the position of Irish Catholics to the Catholics of England. There was scarcely a family in southern Ireland without relatives either in the Allied forces or engaged in helping the war effort in the factories of Britain. Since the denial of the Irish ports to the Royal Navy was the chief aspect of Irish neutrality known to the British public, Frank Duff agreed that it would be good to explain the position in more detail to English Catholics who regarded the war as a Christian crusade and Ireland as a defaulter. My call on Mr. Duff had been intended to be no more than a courtesy call on the President of the Legion but it resulted in a series of introductions which altered my whole programme and enabled me to gather information of the greatest value to my mission. Such was his prestige in Dublin that after a few telephone calls he arranged for me to see the Prime Minister (Taoiseach), Mr. de Valera, the leader of the opposition, Mr. Cosgrave, the Papal Nuncio and the Archbishop of Dublin. The most useful introduction of all was to Joe Walsh, the Secretary for External Affairs (later, Irish Ambassador to the Holy See), to whom I carried a recommendation from Mr. John Dulanty the Irish High Commissioner in London. For the whole of my stay in Dublin he entertained me in his home or made appointments for me with people who might have something of interest to say.

Public interest in the question of Irish neutrality during the second world war is now considerably below boiling point, but it may revive the atmosphere of those days to give extracts from the Report on Ireland I published in a series of articles during November and December 1941. From remarks in the introductory article it is clear that I did not expect to succeed in my mission to explain the Irish patriots to the British crusaders:

I foresee certain inevitable results from my reports ... The Irish will consider that I have misread their view of things and will attribute it to my English birth and training, while the British will be outraged at the very expression of an Irish point of view and will attribute the indiscretion to my Irish blood.

I soon broached the neutrality topic:

The Irish are neutral without really believing that their neutrality would be respected by a potential aggressor if he thought that the war would be won by an invasion ... They know, however, that to declare war on Germany would mean the annihilation of their towns within a few days and nights. Equally Ireland realises that the fall of England would mean the end of such independence as now she enjoys. True it would mean the end of Partition but in rather a different way to that for which hitherto she has prayed and worked.

Does she regard Germany and England as equally likely aggressors? The answer is a qualified 'no'. Germany would invade Eire with no scruples at all. Great Britain would certainly have scruples but, if the winning of the war depended upon it, would no doubt overcome her scruples if American opinion would agree to such aggression.

I made it clear that there was no hero-worship of Hitler among the Irish:

The Irish view of Hitler is that he is a great man gone wrong. When the Fuehrer was leading his country in a crusade against the injustices of Versailles, Eire wished him well. He seemed to be trying to make Germany a self-respecting nation once again. The Irish would understand that. But when German Lebensraum was seen to include the lands of non-Germanic peoples, Hitler's insincerity was made manifest. Until the rape of Czechoslovakia, Hitler was thought to be a great German. Thereafter he was regarded as a great gangster.

While I was across the water the *Daily Mail* published two articles from the pen of an ill-informed American journalist which claimed that Eire is a hotbed of Nazi intrigue. It would be difficult to know who was more outraged at the stupidity and malice of these articles—Sir John Maffey, U.K. representative to Eire, or Mr. J.P. Walsh, Secretary for External Affairs in the Irish Government. But it is not only the British yellow press which harms our cause in Ireland. There is one Catholic weekly journal regarded in Ireland as class-conscious and imperialist which, they complain, loses no opportunity of attacking the Irish nation and Church. I was assured many times that, with the exception of being refused the ports, the British Government has no serious complaint to make to Ireland. The British Government knows well that Eire's neutrality is benevolent, with a very large B.

I then made specific mention of the delicate question of the ports:

To take over the ports is, in fact, to take over the country. For ports are useless without air bases, and both are a mere embarrassment without communications and military defence. To occupy the ports, therefore, would mean to occupy Ireland, and few indeed of those I met doubt that if the English were once more to gain possession of Ireland they would ever again leave her shores. Thirdly, and this is the most obvious but not the most potent cause of refusal, the ports themselves would be rendered unusable by the Luftwaffe long before the British would have the opportunity of defending them.

The Irish view of England as a Christian crusader then received mention:

It is important to know how the Irish regard Great Britain's role of Christian crusader. To believe in the sincerity of the British Government with the example of the North before them, is to ask the impossible; but of the North I shall write later. The Irish do not believe that religion needs to be preserved by force of arms. They think the spiritual weapons of Christians will, by Divine promise, conquer the malice of the enemy.
Those who consider the dangers of the pagan philosophy which is said to rule Great Britain to be more dangerous to the Church than the Nazi regime, are usually no more anxious for the triumph of Hitler than the average Catholic is thirsting for martyrdom. The point is mentioned only as a corrective to the

[237]

self-righteousness of certain British Catholic propagandists who speak as though any who doubted the Christian motives of Great Britain were resisting the known truth. The Irish Catholics do not understand why, for the sake of England, the one nation in the world which has wronged and still wrongs her, she should be expected to be more Catholic than the Pope by declaring the British cause to be the cause of Christ. The religious aspect of the war is not very evident to observers in Eire. They deplore the persecution of the Church both in Germany and in the occupied territories but they regard it as incidental in the programme of the Nazi regime. They think that the British do Hitler too much credit by describing him as Anti-Christ and in any case, as one Irish bishop said to me, he is by no means the first to have been given the title by the British Government. There is a strange familiarity in the epithets used to describe the Fuehrer and Bonaparte.

With the exception of the Catholics in the six counties, who cannot be spoken of in the same breath as their brethren in Eire, it would be hard to find any responsible people in Ireland who desire a German victory. They have suffered enough and realise that a German occupation would renew their bodily sufferings, however good this might be for their immortal souls. Not only are they determined not to obstruct the British effort, but in their thousands the Irish have flocked to join the British colours.

"It would be kind of our critics in England," a well-known Irish statesman said to me, "if, before they criticised our attitude, they realised that we have allowed more men to join the three services than would provide the quota which would have been expected from us as a colony at war." There are, in fact, more Irishmen on active service than Canadians or Australians, and their record of heroism is not inglorious.

Much more significant for our own times is the part of my report which dealt with Northern Ireland. It is important to realise that these words were written in 1941. At that time nobody wished to give comfort to the enemy, yet it was obviously thought proper both by the editor and myself to give the plain facts about the regime in the North. What happened there thirty years later could not have surprised those who had read and remembered what I had written in my report:

As a cause for dissension the fact of partition is as nothing compared with the actual rule tolerated by the British Government in the six Northern counties. Religion is made the criterion of politics and a premium is set on religious discrimination. Protestantism is identified with loyalty and Catholics are regarded as tolerated outlaws. Lest this description seem exaggerated, it will be useful to give some quotations from speeches made by six county statesmen. Here are some excerpts from utterances made by Viscount Craigavon, the late Prime Minister in the North:

> "We are a Protestant Parliament and a Protestant State. I suppose that I am as high up in the Orange Order as anyone, being Grandmaster of loyal County Down. I prize that far more than being Prime Minister. I have often said that I am an Orangeman first and a member of Parliament afterwards."

Mr. Andrews: "Another allegation was made against the Government which was untrue—that of 31 porters at Stormont, 28 were Roman Catholics. I have investigated the matter and have found that there are 30 Protestants and only one Roman Catholic there temporarily."

It must be remembered that in the six counties over one third of the inhabitants are Catholics. Unless it be presumed that no Catholic has intelligence or education, it should follow that a fair percentage of public officials should be Catholic. Yet here are some figures which should be pondered and, indeed, are bitterly pondered by Irish Catholics:

The Cabinet contains no Catholics.
The Houses of Parliament contain no Catholic Officers.
Secretariat—no Catholic.
Ministry of Finance—no Catholic.
Ministry of Home Affairs ⎫
Ministry of Labour   ⎪
Ministry of Commerce   ⎬ not one Catholic
Ministry of Education   ⎪
Ministry of Agriculture ⎭
Royal Ulster Constabulary—Among the higher ranks there are no Catholics and even in the lower ranks there are very few. Of 34 District Inspectors only 4 are Catholic.

It is interesting to notice that the only department where Catholics have good representation is in the Post Office which is a reserved service controlled from London. Candidates are chosen by examination and no religious test is applied. That Catholics have secured good representation in the Post Office suggests that it is not lack of ability which excludes Catholics from high appointment in those services controlled by the six counties administration.

The Judicature resembles the Public Departments with a single exception that there has been one County Court Judge appointed in the fairly recent past. For the rest, a community one third Catholic has no representation on the bench. The Court of Appeal, High Court of Justice, King's Bench, Criminal Appeal, etc., comprising 40 judges, registrars and officials, have no Catholic among them. Of the 21 Crown Solicitors and Counsel, only one is Catholic.

What is true of the national administration is true of County and Rural Councils. Even in those places where the population is predominantly Catholic, the representation is mainly Protestant. The greatest complaint of nationalists (those opposed to partition usually but not always Catholics) is that the elections are unfair. Voting areas are so arranged that it is impossible for nationalists to receive anything approaching their share of seats. Gerrymandering produces the same result in local government as it does in the Belfast Parliament. A glaring example is the parliamentary constituencies in the County of Fermanagh. A population of 32,000 nationalists is entitled to one seat in the Belfast Parliament whereas the rest of the population, numbering 25,000, secures two seats. To keep to Fermanagh (because it has a Catholic majority) the 32,000 nationalists are able to secure seven seats while the 25,000 obtain thirteen in the local government.

It is noteworthy that Protestant ministers of religion in the South were unable to give me a single instance of discriminatory action against their co-religionists on the part of the Eire Government. In Dublin the Government has not even attempted to regain possession of the two Catholic cathedrals stolen from their forefathers, now being used by dwindling Protestant congregations while the teeming millions of Dublin Catholics have no cathedral of their own.

I ended my account of the Irish Catholic outlook on Northern Ireland with a reminder that I was giving the viewpoint expressed to me in Eire. It had not been my intention to provide a full account of the situation.

It may be objected to this sketchy account of the border question that it is one-sided. It is not intended to be anything else. I went to Ireland to seek the views of our fellow Catholics whose support we value but whose official friendship we would value still more. There is much to be said on the other side. If the Orangemen are un-Christian, some of their violent opponents have no greater claim to be called Christians. The activities of the I.R.A. in so far as they were carried out by Irishmen (it is well known that communists and other non-Irish elements were concerned in their nefarious work) could in no circumstances be justified. I am glad to say that I found no Irishman who did not repudiate the murderous activities for which the I.R.A. has been responsible.

In 1941 the word 'credible' had not acquired its present misleading connotation but the need to present evidence in a way that would carry conviction was present to the minds of writers. In order to make my testimony credible I had to avoid giving the impression that Ireland was a modern Utopia with inhabitants who were all saints and scholars. I therefore added some criticism of the Irish at the end of my series of articles. This gave as much offence to certain Irish readers as my account of Irish thinking on the war had given to some English readers. The following passage, for example, was not read with any enthusiasm in Dublin:

Impressions would be neither faithful nor complete without noting some features of Irish life which make an unfavourable impression on the visitor. The first and most obvious is the appalling poverty of Ireland's capital city. Allowing for the impoverished state of Eire and for its dependence upon foreign currency, it is hard to believe that a Catholic Government could not in 20 years have done more to put into operation the principles of Rerum Novarum. While it is extravagant to object to charity as something degrading in itself I find it hard to forget the shock I received during my first week in Dublin from the advertisement for the Flag Day being held in aid of the

Society of St. Vincent de Paul's work for the poor. If half they said about the miserable conditions of the Dublin poor is true, the poor of Dublin are a living reproach to its citizens. Poverty seemed to be regarded in too many circles with complacency. I was amazed to find a Medical Mission to Roman Catholics in Dublin. This institution exists for proselytising the Catholic poor. They receive medical attention on condition that they first attend a religious service in the clinic hall. That poor Catholics go regularly to such a place suggests that there is something wrong with the social services. It is true that the Legion of Mary pickets every Tuesday, Wednesday and Friday but this, after all, is not a soup kitchen but a medical clinic. It is hard to believe that such places could attract so many poor if there were a sufficiency of medical services available to them. The London slums are a living reproach to the richest country in the world. But, as Catholics always point out, in other days the monasteries and convents looked after the poor. Desperate poverty in the midst of plenty is one of the results of national apostasy. Ireland is a Catholic country and it is disturbing that in Catholic Ireland degrading poverty should be tolerated. Many times late at night I saw small boys selling newspapers, and in certain sections of Dublin it was hard to go many paces without being accosted by beggars. Allowing for the easy-going ways of Irish administration one must not expect the neat and tidy parcelling up of beggars that takes place in other countries. But my impression was that the poor are too numerous and too miserably poor.

I also detected what I regarded as the beginnings of a cleavage between young people in Ireland and their clergy. My observations may be of interest now because after more than a quarter of a century the symptoms I detected in Ireland have everywhere become a feature of the Catholic landscape:

It is remarkable that not only the priests but also Protestant ministers were at one in naming dances as one of the great curses of modern Ireland. I therefore lost no opportunity in seeking the views of the young people themselves. I found, as I had suspected, that they were sullen and resentful of the attitude of the clergy. The days of the docile laity gladly accepting the dictates of the soggart aroon are surely numbered in Catholic Ireland. For an earlier generation it was enough for the priest to disapprove for the people to refrain from action. In Ireland there is far less loyalty to the clergy than in England. It is not for me to allocate the blame. In general the clergy denied that there is any lack of love and co-operation between priest and people. The younger laity almost always affirmed it.

The clergy, in season and out of season, denounce what are called all-night dances. I asked young people many times why they could not be satisfied with a Cinderella dance ending at midnight and they always replied that boys would not think of coming to a dance until 11 or 12 o'clock at night. One need not be of a suspicious nature to fear that young Irishmen coming to a dance at that time of night will, in all probability, have had a number of drinks to put themselves in the right mood. So far as I could gather, the complaint of the clergy was not against the actual dancing but the drink which preceded it and often followed it, and the inevitable loosening of restraint in the early hours.

I concluded the series in the journalistic tradition by striking an eirenic note:

My last words are a quotation from a conversation I was privileged to have with Dr. McQuaid, the new Archbishop of Dublin, whose sanctity and humanity are applauded by Catholic and Protestant alike. "Hatred," said the Archbishop, "is un-Christian. We must all work together. Irish, English or German, we are all the children of God. The war is an incident. It will pass. The Church will go on. Non prevalebunt—the gates of hell will not prevail if only we preserve charity."

The reactions to my articles are no longer of interest. The editor of the *Catholic Herald* was brave to publish the severe criticisms of a friendly neutral country. What in retrospect seems more significant is the liberty permitted at the height of a war for national survival. It is a powerful tribute to the British love of freedom. The only criticism of the articles now worth recalling was in the *Jewish Chronicle* of 28th November, 1941. It provides a suitable introduction to the story of an earlier encounter between this paper and myself. Under the heading IRELAND AND NAZISM a short paragraph drew attention to my articles:

The *Catholic Herald*, to whose kindly references to the *Jewish Chronicle* centenary a word of sincere recognition is due, publishes this week the first of a series of articles in which the Rev. Dr. Heenan records what war-time Ireland is thinking. The writer is careful to emphasise that the articles do not contain his own views but only his impression of the views of others, and this denial in advance one must, of course, fully accept. Whether the publication by our contemporary of the pro-Nazi, anti-British, and anti-Jewish sentiments attributed to Irishmen is calculated to help or impede the national war effort is, however, another matter; and some might think that whatever gain it might bring by way of explaining the puzzling war attitude of Eire to Catholics nearer home would be exceeded by the damage done through the spreading of jaundiced views and mischievous falsehoods, and the stirring of ill-feeling at this critical time.

Shortly before the war I had been invited by Dr. Downey, the Archbishop of Liverpool, to give a lecture in the Picton Hall. This was a memorable occasion because it was my first experience of the warmth of Liverpool Catholics whom in later years I was to come to love and serve. I was pacing the floor of the green room when my friend Tommy Atkins interrupted my rehearsal. "You don't have to feel nervous," he said. "The hall is full of good old Biddies. They won't understand a word of what you say. They'll just look at you and say to each other 'Isn't he lovely?'"

Immediately after the meeting was over I hurried to the station to catch the London train. There were few passengers and I found a carriage empty but for one man. My travelling companion was destined to become a life-long friend. He was reading a book on the Russian Politbureau but he soon put it aside and we fell into conversation. His talk was fascinating. He was a widely travelled man and an orthodox Jew. He had visited Germany and Austria before the war with the object of helping to rescue some of his persecuted brethren. He was one of the many Jews I have met who deserved to be called citizens of the world. In the best sense he was a cosmopolitan.

The journey to London passed all too quickly. When we arrived at Euston I told my companion with great sincerity how sorry I was that the journey was over. I asked him to honour me one day by coming to stay with me. He readily accepted and gave me his card with one address in Rodney Street, Liverpool and the other in Harley Street, London. He had consulting rooms in both cities. I discovered later that his services were in demand abroad as well as in this country. Until I saw his card I did not realise that Jackson-Lipkin was a medical consultant. He said that he was 'in medicine'. Thinking him to be a traveller in pharmaceutical goods I had been amazed by the range of his knowledge. I was glad that I had invited him to be my guest before learning that he was a distinguished physician. Acquaintanceship on trains is more casual than that between fellow passengers at sea. Although even shipboard friendships are notoriously fleeting, many of my closest friends I first met on my travels. Clerical dress attracts most people in need of consolation. Drunkards make straight—or as straight as they can—for the man in the clerical collar. According to their condition they pour out confidences, abuse or blasphemy. But mercifully most travellers are not intoxicated. Sober people with problems also feel that they have some right to unburden themselves on the clergy. The magnetism of the Roman collar (or the Sister's habit) is a tribute to earlier generations of priests (and nuns). It is not by chance that almost everyone takes for granted our approachability and willingness to listen. Even when feeling tired I have resisted the temptation to conceal my priesthood because being always on duty has a high spiritual value. What is true in the English-speaking world is said not to hold good elsewhere. Some clergy and nuns on the continent (and in recent years in Canada and the U.S.A.) say that they go into disguise to gain the full confidence of ordinary men, women and children. The Sisters of Charity—the most beloved group of women in Europe—will have none of this concealment. Nor, I believe, do English Catholics want to see their priests and nuns in disguise. In my personal experience the Roman collar has been a passport into the hearts and homes of hundreds. I would not have come so close to Dr. Jackson-Lipkin had I been dressed as a layman.

Three or four months elapsed before my new friend and I found a free evening. He came to stay in the presbytery at Manor Park the night before one of his Harley Street sessions. Preparing for my guest was a matter of some anxiety. He had mentioned on the train that he was an orthodox Jew, but at that time I did not know that 'orthodox' is patient of several interpretations. My interest was, of course, in what food to offer him. I telephoned a Jewish neighbour to ask

[245]

advice. I knew that he was an orthodox Jew but not that he was a fanatical observer of Jewish minutiae. He told me—what I already knew—that the food must be kosher. He went on to say that I must provide kosher wine for dinner but on no account was I to open the bottle. This would render it undrinkable to an orthodox Jew. My Jewish neighbour then gave me a list of instructions about the cooking of the meal. When I relayed all these to my housekeeper she said that my Jewish friend would have an omelet or she would take the night off and leave me to do my own cooking. I asked one of my parishioners to go shopping in Whitechapel for Jewish delicacies and, especially, for a bottle of kosher wine. He brought me back a hock-type Palestinian wine not incongruously named Karmel. When the doctor arrived we met as old friends and without delay resumed the conversation begun on the railway journey. I would have offered him a glass of sherry before dinner but my Jewish neighbour had applied a veto to anything non-kosher. Mary's omelet was delicious and after a few minutes I invited Dr. Jackson-Lipkin to flavour it with a glass of Karmel. I handed him the bottle and corkscrew. He seemed rather surprised at being asked to open the bottle but proceeded to do so without comment. I noticed that he pulled the cork with his left hand.

It was then that curiosity overcame courtesy. I told him that I fully understood that he had to have kosher wine and that he must open the bottle himself but, I asked, was it also part of Jewish orthodoxy to open the bottle with his left hand? At first he looked startled. Then he began to smile. He assumed that some Jewish friend with an advanced sense of humour had provided me with an impossible set of rules for entertaining the orthodox. When he heard the details of the instructions given by my neighbour he realised that I had fallen into the hands not of a practical joker but of a man suffering from religious scruples. He pointed out that ritual observances are practised in Jewish households but few are regarded as obligatory in mixed company.

Our friendship was still firm when many years later I returned to Liverpool as Archbishop. Soon after my arrival I was officially entertained by Dr. Jackson-Lipkin, now President of the Liverpool Athenaeum. But Jackson-Lipkin did not have to wait twenty years to give public proof of his friendship.

I had been interviewed by a paper about the morale of the East End of London under the battering of the Luftwaffe. Newspaper interviews are almost always tendentious. For this reason experienced people always insist on seeing the report of an interview before passing it for publication. Otherwise the public may be given a completely false version of a man's views. This does not involve printing a single word which is objectively untrue. Although the exact words of the person interviewed may be given, balancing words may be omitted. It is the classical distinction between *assertio falsi* and *suppressio veri*. The only publicity venture more perilous than a newspaper interview is a recorded interview on radio or television. This is sometimes edited beyond recognition before transmission. On one occasion a television team asked to be allowed to come to Archbishop's House, Westminster to record a twelve-minute interview. Half-a-dozen subjects were covered by an able and, indeed, famous interviewer. Later in the day the interview was shown to the public. It lasted for two minutes. The only subject touched was contraception. Viewers may have been left with the impression that with me contraception was a personal obsession or that it is the chief doctrine of the Catholic Church. A further disadvantage of interviews whether printed or on the air is that the interviewer can manipulate ideas without falsifying words. Interviewed about Mozart the conductor of the Hallé orchestra might suddenly be asked if despite the number of musicians it has produced did not Germany also produce poison gas in the first world war? There is only one answer to that question but the public will assume that the conductor of the Hallé must be pathologically anti-German when it reads a headline in the newspapers next morning:"NEVER FORGET GERMANS USED GAS" SAYS FAMOUS MUSICIAN.

The interview to which I am about to refer appeared in the *Catholic Herald*. I have kept no copy of the published interview but in the course of it (judging from *Jewish Chronicle* clippings which I have kept) I must have agreed that there was a certain amount of anti-Jewish feeling arising from two rumours current in the East End. The first was that when the bombing became severe, Jews left for safe areas. The second was the alleged monopolising of shelters in underground stations by those who had remained at home. I was also quoted by the *Jewsih Chronicle* as having said "For Catholics to be anti-semitic would not only be un-Christian but unpolitic."

Small wonder that the *Jewish Chronicle* pounced. Almost certainly I had repeated the offensive rumours and said the words quoted above. There was probably no *suppressio veri* or any sort of manipulation by the *Catholic Herald*. By unpolitic I must have meant to convey that anti-semitism would be for Catholics not only wrong but self-destructive. Persecution is always evil, but when it is carried out by one minority against another it cries to heaven for vengeance. That must have been what I had in mind but it is evidently not what I actually said. The *Jewish Chronicle* rebuked me thus:

> Dr. Heenan sums up his remarks with the conclusion that "for Catholics to be anti-Semitic would not only be un-Christian but unpolitic." Unpolitic—note that word. One recoils at its intrusion into the realm of pure spirituality. It conjures up the art of politics and demagogy and of ecclesiastical plotting and strategy. It would have been unpolitic, thought Hitler, not to use the Jew as a stalking horse to power; and imitators nearer home think likewise. It would have been unpolitic, in the view of pre-war conversionists, not to bribe poor Jews into apostasy by material gifts, and richer Jews, perhaps, by more subtle ways. It is 'politic' to brand the war as Jewish—the lie which, together with others, Dr. Heenan regretfully publicises. It is 'politic' in Hitler's eyes, to sell his so-called convictions to the Bolshevist devil; 'politic', according to Mussolini, to stab Republican France in the back for the sake of the dream of a Catholic Latin Bloc; 'politic' for Laval and Petain to betray their country and adopt the execrable Nuremberg laws. History is saturated with the tears that have been shed through emphasis on this tragic word, with the sordid cruelty it has so often connoted. If Dr. Heenan had said that Catholic anti-Semitism would be un-Christian, and instead of adding 'unpolitic' had had a word to say for justice, fair play, and Christian mercy, and the expression of that selfless love which the Jew, Paul, praised. perhaps criticism of Jews would not, in the future go on, to use Dr. Heenan's phrase, 'definitely increasing'.

I was embarrassed by this (justified) criticism but not sufficiently wise to write to the *Jewish Chronicle* to make clear that I had not volunteered information about attitudes towards the Jews in the East End but had merely answered questions of my interviewer about the rise of anti-Jewish feeling. My immaturity led me to write instead a letter which though formally and ostensibly an apology now reads more like a fresh attack.

ANTI-SEMITISM — A CATHOLIC VIEW
From the Rev. Dr. John C. Heenan
To the Editor of the *Jewish Chronicle*

Sir—In a recent leader the Editor of the *Jewish Chronicle* took me to task for my opinions, expressed in the *Catholic Herald*, which he judged to have an anti-semitic bias. If my statement gave this impression (as obviously it did) I apologise immediately and without reserve. Curiously, the remarks complained of were inspired by regard for Jewish people, rather than hostility. I said—and say—that criticism of the Jews is increasing and in a Jewish paper I am prepared to be much more outspoken than I was in a Catholic paper. Anything in the nature of anti-Jewish propaganda would be unworthy of a priest and most distasteful to me personally. But let us face facts. There is a great similarity in the position of Jews and Catholics and of both it may be said, in the words of the Scriptures, that the enemies of a man are those of his own household. The biggest enemy of the Church is a lapsed Catholic or a practising Catholic notably un-Christian in his way of living. We know the harm being done at the moment by lapsed Catholics. Men like Hitler, Goebbels, and Mussolini, to name but a few. It would be stupid to blame the Church for the activities of such as these, but the fact remains that they are Catholics and that they are outstanding examples of evil influence in the Europe of today. My point in writing is to say that the lapsed Jews are the real enemies of the Jewish people. There are far too many Jews who are Jewish by race but not by religion. There could be no case made out for the persecution of Jews if the majority were living up to the high principles of their religious code, just as it would be harder to sustain persecution of the Church if all the members of the Church were real Christians. I want to give an example, to illustrate my point, from the leading article to which I have already made reference. The Editor took me to task because I said that many of the leaders of communism in this country are Jewish and pointed out that Stalin has 'bumped off' practically all his Jewish supporters. Of the anti-Jewish purge in Russia I am well aware. I arrived in Moscow soon after the execution of Kamenev, Zinoviev, and the rest, and I remember reading lists of Jewish names in *Pravda* which were being changed to Christian names for reasons of security. I saw how Jews were persecuted for their religious beliefs by the communists. But all this does not alter the truth of my statement that the majority of the leaders of communism in this country are Jewish. *Corruptio optimi pessima*, and Jews who, having forsaken the law of Moses, leave God to serve tables, do happen often enough to drift to the communist party. If anyone doubts it let him go to communist meetings and judge for himself the race to which the majority of the leaders belong. Hard-working minorities nearly always achieve unpopularity in a community and I have always felt that the root cause of Jewish persecution has been the industry of the Jews themselves. In Russia (at least before the purge) many of the executives were Jewish. The reason presumably is that the Jews suffered so many restrictions under the Tzars that they made the most of the small chances they had received of education. When the Soviets came to power and had rid themselves of the educated elements in the old Russia they found that in the main only the Jewish sections of the population could stand up to the new tasks. Later, non-Jewish communists became jealous and wanted members of their own family to displace the Jewish executives.

You may think I am trying to have it both ways; that I am blaming both Jew and anti-Jew for persecutions. I admit that there seems to be a paradox. The solution, in my mind, is this. That while persecution of the Jews is usually founded upon jealousy, Jews who do not practise their faith or live up to its principles, often provide specious reasons to justify the intolerance of the anti-Semites. Pope Pius XI, of happy memory, set a lead for all Catholics in his protestation against anti-Jewish propaganda. No good Catholic can have hand or part in anti-Jewish activities. Yet I repeat that just as the lapsed Catholic is the real enemy of the Church so the disproportionately large numbers of men who are Jewish by race but not by religion are the real enemies of the Jewish people.

I am, & c.,

JOHN C. HEENAN

The Presbytery,
Little Ilford Lane, E.12.
December 18th 1940.

The response of the *Jewish Chronicle* was astonishing. Far from attempting to rebut my arguments the editor devoted the first leader of the next number of his paper (December 27th) to supporting what I had written. Here is the relevant part of the article:

THE PRICE OF BETRAYAL

SOME criticisms were recently passed in these columns on certain references to Jews made by the Rev. Dr. John C. Heenan in the course of an interview printed in a Catholic contemporary. The reverend gentleman, an active worker in East London, now writes to say that if his statement gave the impression of anti-Semitic bias on his part he apologises immediately and without reserve. Anything in the nature of anti-Jewish propaganda, he points out, would be unworthy of a priest and most distasteful to him personally, and adds further the important reminder that "Pope Pius XI, of happy memory, set a lead for all Catholics in his protestation against anti-Jewish propaganda." This obviously sincere disclaimer will be readily accepted by Jews, who will also welcome his forthright declaration that "no good Catholic can have hand or part in anti-Jewish activities."

Dr. Heenan goes on to say that the remarks complained of were inspired by regard for Jewish people rather than hostility. He urges that, of the Jews, as of the Catholics, the saying holds true that "the enemies of a man are those of his own household. The biggest enemy of the Church is a lapsed Catholic or a practising Catholic notably un-Christian in his way of living ... the lapsed Jews are the real enemies of the Jewish people. There could be no case made out for the persecution of Jews if the majority were living up to the high principles of their religious code, just as it would be harder to sustain persecution of the Church if all the members of the Church were real Christians." Jewish persecution, he admits, is usually founded on jealousy, but "Jews who do not practise their faith or live up to its principles often provide specious reasons to justify the intolerance of the anti-Semites."

There is, it will be admitted, more than a grain of truth in this analysis. Has not, indeed, the same diagnosis been made again and again by many thoughtful and anxious Jewish observers? Dr. Heenan tells us bluntly that there are far too many Jews who are Jewish by race but not by religion. That is a palpably true indictment of a way of life much too common in our midst.

Historically, it is a dangerous contradiction. To our people it offers a treacherous foothold on a slippery pedestal. To the Gentile who is understandably mistrustful of and puzzled by a religionless Jew, it is an unforgivable offence, an object of suspicion and fear, and indirectly a source of weakness to the Christian daughter Church of Judaism.

The next week's issue and several following issues carried letters to the editor condemning him for what was regarded as his supine attitude. It seemed that every Jewish lawyer and doctor as well as the whole rabbinate in England wrote to attack the unfortunate editor. The letters were civilised but none gave the editor (or me) much comfort. Unless he was a man of altogether exceptional humility I feel sure that the editor would have published a selection of supporting letters had any been received. I assume that his correspondents were all hostile. Pages of letters appeared during ensuing weeks. To these I evidently must have felt it my duty to reply. It now seems amazing that the editor should have allowed me to inflict yet another letter on the suffering readers of the *Jewish Chronicle*.

A CATHOLIC'S VIEW OF ANTI-SEMITISM
Dr. Heenan Replies
Money a Danger to Jews
From the Rev. Dr. John C. Heenan
To the Editor of the *Jewish Chronicle*

Sir—My critics provide remarkable testimony to the courtesy of Jewish people. All wrote to correct and even chastise me, but with no word of bitterness or personal invective. In this they followed the lead given by yourself in your generous appreciation of my own good will. Such controversy, without vindictiveness, is almost unique, and for this, if for no other reason, worth pursuing.

In less than a column it was possible for so ungifted a pen as mine to trace exhaustively every symptom and cause of anti-Semitism. I was content, in effect, to say: "I am writing for Jews, not for their enemies, who, in any case, will not read my words. May I, therefore, humbly suggest that irreligious Jews provide specious reasons for the persecutors." The reasons being admittedly specious, obviously I did not consider persecution to be thereby justified.

I am not unaware of countless other motives for anti-Semitism. Having put down jealousy as a root cause, I left it at that because, as I have said, I was addressing not the Jew-baiters, but their victims. Let us again speak frankly. Jews do seem to 'arrive' both in business and in the professions. They are industrious people. It is not surprising that less successful rivals are jealous. Again, Jews are not nationalists. Although, as for example the last war showed, they can be good Germans, or good Englishmen, as well as (and perhaps because of being) good Jews, they are international-minded and both intellectually and emotionally out of sympathy with that exaggerated nationalism so prevalent in the Europe of today, and, incidentally, condemned by the Popes. This is another fruitful source of persecution. Yet again Jews, like all other peoples, have racial characteristics, some of which are good and some bad. Thus the Prussians are methodical, painstaking, and physically clean, but among their vices are to be race-proud, bullying, and anti-European (in the sense of being, as yet, incapable of absorbing European culture). Jewish virtues, to mention few among many, are family loyalty, kindliness, and industry. Notable among Jewish vices—critics sharpen your pencils!—is avarice, in the sense of straining moral principles to justify good business. I am not suggesting that most Jews, or only Jews, are unscrupulous in business, but I do say that money is a danger to the Jewish people in a somewhat similar way that drink is a danger to another race, which, in order not to extend the present controversy, I shall refrain from naming.

To return to my original contention, I believe that if more influential Jews were sincerely devoted to their religion there would be less opportunity given to malevolent anti-Semites of making dupes of decent Gentiles. There is, for example, important Jewish influence in the cinema world. All who wish that this powerful organ of public education should be used in the cause of morality would be happy to know that those who choose films do so with an eye to the decalogue rather than the box office.

Let me repeat, finally, that I speak plainly—at the risk of being thought unconsciously anti-Semitic—because I am writing in the Jewish Press and not in the *Strürmer*. I am well aware that accusations brought against any section of the Jewish people could be proved against innumerable Gentiles. Since sweet reason will never convert the persecutors, let me, turning a scriptural allusion in an original direction, suggest that we make friends of the mammon of iniquity. Let us remove from our lives those things which provide both anti-Jew and anti-Christian with premises, however insignificant, upon which they may erect a monstrous, though illogical, case for racial and religious persecution.

As I do not intend to participate further in this correspondence, I gratefully take the opportunity of expressing deep satisfaction at the kindly treatment accorded me by the editor and correspondents of the *Jewish Chronicle*, and of reaffirming my sincere good will towards all my Jewish friends.

I am, & c.,
JOHN C. HEENAN

The Presbytery,
Little Ilford Lane, E.12.
24th January 1941.

Thirty years or so later the letter sounds patronising but perhaps in those emotional wartime days it was tolerable.

The whole controversy was brought to an end by an editorial note. Dr. Jackson-Lipkin had evidently not forgotten his kosher dinner at my presbytery before the war:

Dr. I. Jackson-Lipkin of 48 Rodney Street, Liverpool 1, writes:

Dr. Heenan is, I am sure, well able to deal with his critics, but the words 'bias' and 'prejudice' have been introduced, and I think that in fairness to Dr. Heenan something should be said against this suggestion which has no basis in fact. I happen to know Dr. Heenan, and I am glad to think that I enjoy his friendship. I have personal knowledge and practical experience of the fact that in a quite recent publication of his he took great pains and care to avoid anything that might reflect unjustly on Jews. He has done this not only as a matter of sincerity as a writer, but also because he belongs to that select band of people which is the avowed enemy of injustice and oppression. He is thus naturally an enemy of Jew-baiting and Jew-hating. If this letter will help to eliminate the element of 'bias' and 'prejudice' from any further controversies with Dr. Heenan, I will, with your aid, Mr. Editor, have fulfilled my plain duty.

Once the air-raids became a routine and the suffering of injured and homeless people part of our daily experience I felt myself becoming more and more the father of a family. I was grateful not to have been accepted as an army chaplain. I might also have found myself a prisoner in Germany or Russia if events had developed in a slightly different way. During the early part of 1940 when the phoney war was still in progress I was invited to lecture in Denmark. A very keen convert was anxious to promote what in those days was called Catholic Action. He came to Manor Park and pressed me to return with him to Denmark. I declined the invitation on the grounds that a parish priest could not leave his parish in war-time. I suggested that a member of a religious order would be more likely to feel free to travel. Eventually he secured the services of Father C.C. Martindale the celebrated Jesuit preacher and writer. Poor Father Martindale was in Denmark when the Lowlands were invaded and was interned. I often thought of him during the London blitz. I thanked God that I had resisted the temptation to lecture in Denmark.

Even more narrowly I escaped the misfortune of becoming a prisoner of the Russians. It seems now like a fairy story but in the winter of 1939 when the Soviet Union overran Lithuania, Latvia and Estonia the small but gallant Finland refused to accept the same fate as the Baltic States and resolutely fought the invaders. To the astonishment of the whole world—and, especially of the Russians— Finland drove back the Soviet troops and inflicted heavy casualties. Such was the admiration and enthusiasm of the Allies that an Anglo-French expeditionary force of 100,000 men was recruited. Volunteers were called for early in 1940 and a detachment of the guards was sent to Scotland to practise skiing. Major Green, a very gallant soldier and a zealous Catholic, was most impressed when he heard that the Finns were bombing Moscow with Bibles. These Bibles were probably as fanciful as the Russian troops in London with snow on their boots during the first world war, but they created a good impression among the devout. Major Green decided that a Catholic contingent should be raised to go to the rescue of the Christian Finns. He was told by Cardinal Hinsley to discuss the project with me. On the strength of my few weeks in Soviet Russia I was evidently regarded as an authority on Eastern Europe. I had rarely met anyone so enthusiastic as Major Green. He was convinced that Catholics had a duty to aid the Finns. He wanted to persuade the Duke of Norfolk to be the commander of the Catholic contingent and prepared a list of Catholic junior officers who would be prepared to serve. I was to be chaplain, and as a first move was to write a letter to the Catholic papers seeking volunteer doctors and nurses. At the request of Cardinal Hinsley I went with Charles Green to the Finnish Aid Bureau in Smith Square. On the following morning (25th February 1940) I received a letter from the Deputy Director agreeing to the proposals we had put before him:

24th February, 1940.

With further reference to your call on me this morning with Major Green, I am glad to be able to confirm that the Committee of the Finnish Aid Bureau have agreed to the formation of Catholic companies, with their own priests, for service in Finland.

As far as possible arrangements will be made for them to proceed as separate platoons to Finland, but you will appreciate I am sure, that the number which can proceed in any one ship must depend on the accommodation available, and any limit which may be set for diplomatic reasons on numbers travelling at one time. However, this should present no difficulty, as they could reassemble at the base on the other side.

I hope this information will allow you to start your campaign in the Catholic Press, as mentioned this morning. I would like to assure you that, as far as lies in the power of this Bureau, every possible help will be given to you, and on behalf of my Committee I express to you in advance our sincere thanks for your efforts.

Major Green was indefatigable. His main problem was to secure from the War Office the release of himself and other suitable officers. On March 1st he sent me a memorandum giving an account of his activities:

55th Army Training Regt.,
Pinehurst Barracks,
Farnborough,
Hants.

March 1st 1940.

My dear Doctor,

1. Many thanks for yours. Between us we seem to be wading through the difficulties. I went to town yesterday to get as

many answers as I could to the questions in my own memorandum.

Here is the result:

2a. What do the Finnish Aid Bureau (hereinafter called the F.A.B.) mean by Companies?

Answer: Nothing particular. They only used the word because they don't expect us to raise much more. Let's hope we can show them different!

2b. Do they expect recruits to be soldiers and/or skiers?

Answer: No.

2c. Have the F.A.B. any objection to our recruits undergoing a preliminary period of training in England?

Answer: None whatever. I have full leave to go right ahead with the war office, both over that and over getting officers released, BUT he does not think they will play. In fact he has been instructed to definitely refuse all applications from serving officers or soldiers.

3. The pay problem:

Better than I could have dreamed possible. They will pay us at British rates, whatever the rank we are given. (I happen to know that this is new, and I suspect the hand and pocket of Kermit Roosvelt, our future C. in C.—good luck to him!)

So much for the F.A.B. I was shewn straight in to Gibson this time—a grand chap—and delighted with our effort. Said he thought I should be released if H.E. asked for me, as he had been so good!

4. My adventures with the W.O. were not so immediately productive but hold hope for the future.

I first saw Martineau, the man at the W.O. who runs the office side of the 5th Scots Guards (the mystery ski Battalion at Bordon). I told him what I wanted and asked him how to set about getting senior officers released, likewise juniors from the officer training units. He replied—"I don't think they can play much, but certain people can be 'decommissioned'. I have the doing of it. I fancy you will only get your heads."

Then to my delight he said "You had better go and see the A.D.C. to the C.I.G.S." i.e. Ironside. This I had wanted but had never dreamed of hoping for. I worked directly under Ironside in the last war, on rather a peculiar job, and I know he will remember me well, but I couldn't for the life of me see how to get at him. Here it was—handed to me on a plate! ...

Now as to my own domestic problem. I think it would be easy to get Ironside to order me out, and no more bother about it, but unfortunately that is ruled out, owing to my promise not to go without my wife's consent. It would be unfair. Therefore I am afraid it becomes a question as to whether the Cardinal would be kind enough to ask for me, and write a letter to me asking if I would like him to do so. After a good deal of thought I have decided to send a rough record of my service; first because I don't see why he should be expected to buy a pig in a poke—I might be the most utter dud for all he knows, also because it justifies a certain sentence which I have marked for easy reference, which would certainly impress my wife. I hate doing this but it seems the fairest way. I shall just hand the letter across the table, and say what about it. If she won't agree that's an end of it.

This is the sort of letter that I think might work the oracle. As far as I can see it is all gospel truth, except that it is put far more flatteringly than I deserve.

> Dear Major Green,
>
> The appeal for Catholic volunteers seems to have had a good send-off in the press and I hope it will bear fruit. Should it result in a Catholic contingent, I feel that it is only fair that you should be offered a command, as you have been so helpful in pushing the plan.
>
> I have taken the liberty of informing myself as to your military record, and will be happy to apply to the War Office for your release. Would you please let me know if it is your wish that I should do so.

Perhaps it would be as well to show the whole of this letter, so that he may know how we stand up to date. When shall we meet next? Saturday would suit me best as the C.O. doesn't like me taking leave in the middle of the week.

Yours ever
CHARLES GREEN

In January 1940 the Allies had approached the governments of Norway and Sweden for permission for the passage of the Anglo-French forces. These neutral powers not only refused this request—

which would certainly have made a battlefield of their territories —but also were unwilling to have staff talks which might have given the Germans an excuse to invade. In these circumstances it is hard to see how the dispatch of an expeditionary force to Finland could remain feasible but at this stage of the war the Allied leaders were without experience. The Germans had made no military moves. It does not seem to have occurred to anyone that our volunteer forces would have had no chance of reaching the Bay of Finland. In early March the decision to go ahead was taken by the Chiefs of Staff. Commanders were officially informed that their troops need anticipate no opposition before arriving in Finland to engage the Red Army. On 12th March Finland accepted the peace terms of the Soviet government.

CHAPTER
NINE

AFTER THE LONDON BLITZ ALL REMAINED QUIET IN MANOR PARK UNTIL the resumption of the German air offensive during the second half of the war. Life was far from normal but gradually the usual parochial and diocesan activities were resumed. There was renewed interest in social questions arising from the accepted belief that a new order would be introduced after the defeat of Hitler. The strange fact is that despite the overwhelming victories of the Germans few in Britain felt any doubt about the ultimate success of our arms. Everyone was thinking in terms of reconstruction. Sir William Beveridge was at work on his plan for universal social security and Mr. Butler on his new education bill. In May 1941 the golden jubilee of Rerum Novarum (the monumental encyclical on social justice by Pope Leo XIII) was celebrated at meetings in all the great cities of Britain. I was invited to speak at the Opera House in Manchester. From my speech, published a year later, I quote the opening paragraphs to illustrate the light-hearted spirit of the times:

> I was a little dismayed when I learned what subject I was expected to discuss with you this afternoon. When I agreed to come to Manchester I did not know the title of my proposed speech. Here is the text of the telegram sent to me in the name of the Bishop of Salford: 'Will you talk at Manchester May 18th?' Presuming that this meant a speech on one or other of the five peace points of the Sovereign Pontiff, I sent the following reply 'Yes, I'll speak, but what about?' I want you to notice the gay

nonchalance of my acceptance. For this was despatched in March and, at that time, land-mines were falling so freely all around my parish in the East End of London that I thought it extremely unlikely that I should be alive today and so have to redeem my promise. Life seemed so insecure and the possibility of existence in May so remote and joyous, that I think that had the telegram read 'Will you appear at the Opera House, Manchester, May 18th?' I would have replied 'Yes, what shall I sing?'

We have come together at a time when a new world order is being evolved. I am not suggesting that this new order must necessarily be the new order of the Third Reich, but I do say that whatever be the issue of the present conflict, or however long delayed, it is quite certain that the after-the-war-world will be quite different from the one that we knew before.

In the world of yesterday and, to a lesser extent, the world of today, finance was the ruling force, but this is not now true of every country. Our present enemies have a genius for the strategy of the by-pass. To by-pass in battle is spectacular, to by-pass the economic field, if skilfully achieved, need attract little notice. Germany has by-passed the money lenders and in great measure based her external commerce upon a system of barter. That is a considerable contribution to the breakdown of mere money-power. The United States of America at the other end of the scale, and for different reasons, has also struck a blow. Feeling her way of life to be in mortal peril, she discovered that it was almost of no importance whether or not Britain had any money. With or without money Britain must be given the means to resist. Democracy, she decided, does not live by money alone.

So, in different ways, both friends and enemies are beginning to say the same thing—that it is absurd to regard money in itself as of supreme importance. Imponderable human values and the very goods of the earth—the importance of these had been obscured by financial tyranny. That, in effect, is what Pope Leo XIII was saying fifty years ago when he put his finger upon 'rapacious usury' (as he called it) so often condemned by the Church as one of the major causes of injustice. This aggravated the helpless misery of the labouring masses until a small number of rich men had laid upon them a yoke little better than that of slavery itself.

Once the blitz was over and we no longer lived day and night in a state of tension, life in Manor Park became blissful. Shortages of what we had been accustomed to regard as the necessities of life served only to accentuate the pleasure of being able to eat a normal meal or buy a pair of shoes (coupons and supplies permitting). It was not easy for me to look after the parish alone. Father Hibbert, my curate who had become an army chaplain, was never replaced. I was fortunate in having as neighbours in Forest Gate the Franciscan friars who throughout the war sent a priest to Manor Park each Sunday and whenever else I needed help. Without the Franciscans it would have been impossible to provide four Sunday Masses in my churches. In those days the rules for the Eucharistic fast were still rigorous except for members of the Services. Priests with the Forces could say Mass any number of times each day when visiting troops. No special concessions were made for priests doing duty on what was called the home front.

The whole Manor Park community, irrespective of social, religious or political divisions, had been united by common danger in a way that prosperity could never have brought about. Here, for all I know, may be the germ of a solution to the problem of evil. Nobody knows why the good God allows pain but all who lived through these dark days of war in London had actual experience of the joy born of sorrow. During the interval between the blitz and the dropping of the V1 and V2 missiles pastoral activity was uneventful. Normal priestly duties were resumed. Two or three times a week I would take classes in the school. The rest of the day would be spent calling on the sick and in pastoral visits to people's homes. The sick had not stayed away long. They preferred danger among friends to safety in the midst of strangers. Resuming the peacetime routine of house-to-house visitation I found that the parish register had changed considerably between 1939 and 1941. Some mothers whose husbands were in the Forces had given up their homes to live with their children in the evacuation areas. They would probably never return. Their homes had been taken over by bombed-out families. A favourite myth among clergy is that those who move away are always the best people while only the lapsed move in. It was my good fortune, on the contrary, to acquire new parishioners of exceptional zeal. They more than made up for those lost from the parish.

Civil life also resumed a fairly normal pattern. As a member of the East Ham Education Committee I was on close personal terms with most of the town councillors and the officials in the town hall. They were splendid people to work with. I remember, in particular, Mr. Garrard, the Director of Education. An exceptionally public-spirited man he was elected national president of NALGO (the National Association of Local Government Officers). He was also the leading layman of the Methodist flock of my friend Alfred Binks. Mr. Garrard was near retirement at this time and his assistant John Dyer succeeded him while still in his thirties. Dyer had an exceptionally quick mind and among many cultural achievements had a wide knowledge of music. He had a large family and all of them inherited his talent. Two became members of the National Youth Orchestra. Arising from the deep personal affection I had for John I undertook a singular responsibility towards his family. Many people—especially those whose children were evacuated—worried about what would happen to orphans whose parents were killed in an air-raid. Some parishioners asked me to become the guardian of their children 'if anything happened'. As parish priest I would in any case have looked after their children so I had no hesitation in accepting. By the end of the war I had in my desk a number of do-it-yourself documents (adapted from Last Will and Testament forms obtainable from the local stationer) appointing me guardian to potential orphans.

After much thought John Dyer and his wife Barbara invited me to become guardian of their children in the event of their being killed in an air-raid. At this time there were, I think, four Dyer children all under twelve years of age. This was something of a dilemma. There would have been few problems with the other orphans I had agreed to inherit. Kind nuns and teaching brothers would doubtless have provided free places in their boarding schools for my adopted children. But what would I do with the young Dyers? I explained to John and Barbara that having no money to pay for their children's education I would have to throw myself—or, rather, their children— into the arms of monks and nuns. Would they turn in their graves if their children ended up by embracing the Catholic faith? They had given full consideration to this possibility. They knew that I would not proselytise and if of their own accord the children chose to become Catholics they would be quite happy. On this understanding I agreed to become their guardian. This time there was no do-it-yourself document but a properly drawn up legal contract. In the event I did come very near to adopting the whole Dyer family. Their house was blasted by a rocket towards the end of the war. Fortunately John was in an air-raid shelter in the garden while

Barbara and the children were with relatives in the country. By the mercy of God none of the flock was killed during air-raids and I therefore inherited no children.

Education was under constant discussion once the stress of air-raids was over. The public was scarcely aware of the war during the long pause in the European fighting. The Middle East seemed a long way off. It is true that our forces were engaged, but desert warfare seemed to produce relatively few deaths. We heard more of pockets of prisoners—they always seemed to be in pockets—than of long casualty lists. Nobody could ignore the war entirely but politicians spent most of their time planning the future of Britain. They were careful during the second world war to avoid making references to a future Utopia. They were even more careful not to boast that they were building a land fit for heroes. They did not even call the second war the war to end war. The jargon in the early nineteen-forties was based on Hitler's promised new order—without realising it we took from Hitler a great deal more than his bombs. The Youth Service was really an imitation of the Hitler Jugend in theory though not, of course, in method. As part of the new Britain after the war there was to be an entirely new system of social security. The comradeship of joint service, shared danger, evacuation, rationing and the virtual disappearance of domestic servants led optimists to dream of a Britain without class, snobbery or social distinctions of any kind. As part of the reshaping of society the whole educational pattern was to be reviewed. For two years before the Education Act of 1944 the future of schools was a topic only second to the conduct of the war. It is remarkable that a country could give itself seriously to refashioning its educational system at a time when national survival itself was far from assured. It is even more remarkable that the plan was not essentially altered by post-war conditions. The Butler Act was a most intelligent combination of guesswork and planning.

Whenever education is under discussion the Catholic community comes alive. It is one of the mysteries of life that even those Catholic parents who neglect their religious duties are usually passionately determined to send their children to Catholic schools. When discussions on the new bill began, Catholics saw that the proposed reorganisation was going to present them with an impossible task. The age range of most parochial schools was from five to fourteen. The proposed division between primary and secondary schools and the raising of the school-leaving age would call for new buildings in almost every parish in the country. Under certain conditions the bill offered a fifty per cent grant towards the cost of building a church school. These conditions, however, were so complicated that not even the experts could always agree on which buildings qualified for grant. There would be a difference between a new school, a transferred school and a substituted school. There were to be independent schools, aided schools, special-agreement schools and direct grant schools. Depending on its category a school would attract (the civil service term for being entitled to) grants varying from zero to seventy-five per cent. Primary schools of every kind were denied a grant but a subsidy could be claimed in respect of children whose families had been displaced from another area. If governors of Catholic schools were prepared to surrender their right to appoint teachers and be content to have one or two 'reserved' (Catholic) teachers on the staff and to reduce religious instruction to a minimum, the government was prepared to pay practically the whole bill. To nobody's surprise the Catholic authorities did not so much as look at this carrot.

There was great confusion in educational circles. The Catholic Education Council worked out the probable cost to the Catholic body and reached a figure which bore no resemblance to the modest sum forecast by Whitehall. After the war, when all the theory had to be reduced to practice, the Catholic Education Council had as its chairman Bishop Beck, who had once been the headmaster of a Catholic school. He was very good at sums and confirmed the accuracy of the Catholic Education Council's earlier calculations. After a battle lasting many years, successive governments did their best to remedy the defects of the original Butler Act by giving what Catholics called—neither contemptuously nor ungraciously— instalments of justice. All this was in the future. In 1943 I was very involved in the educational battle. My work with the education committee of East Ham gave me opportunities of reading the documents being circulated at that time to provoke discussion. I soon had a fair grasp of the probable future shape of education. I quickly realised that despite its excellent proposals the new Act unless amended could destroy the dual system and put non-provided schools out of business. Only those parents who could afford to send their children to independent schools might be able to give their children a Catholic education. Although 1944 was still many months away, the Church opened a campaign to inform Catholic parents of the issues involved. It had been proved beyond peradventure that unless a state school happened to have a number of convinced Christians on the staff, children would receive virtually no religious instruction.

As the time for the debate on the bill in Parliament drew closer the number of public meetings increased. Some were to explain and invite support for the bill. Others organised by such bodies as the Catholic Parents and Electors' Association were called to urge a radical revision of the bill so far as it affected church schools. I was in some demand as a speaker but unfortunately I had once more fallen out of favour with my bishop. He resented my public activities which had grown steadily from 1941 to 1943 under pressure from Cardinal Hinsley. Broadcasting and writing had caused my name to be known to a fairly wide circle. At the request of the cardinal I had on more than one occasion become the spokesman for the Church. Understandably this gave little joy to the Bishop of Brentwood. My own dilemma was baffling. I could not refuse to speak or write when asked to do so by Cardinal Hinsley, but to obey the cardinal involved displeasing my bishop. My first controversy with Mr. H. G. Wells provides an example of my being pressed into service as defender of the faith. On 30th August, 1942, Mr. Wells, whose mental powers were no longer at their peak, wrote an article in the *Sunday Dispatch* entitled THREE YEARS OF WAR AND STILL WE DO NOT BOMB ROME. Mr. Wells called upon Catholics to depose Pope Pius XII:

> He is in open alliance with the Japanese; he is the declared enemy of our ally Russia. He outdoes both Mussolini and the Quirinal in its implacable hostility to the new world . . . Malta asks why the Allies do not bomb Rome? Canterbury has been bombed, and the Archbishop has been within an ace of death; Lambeth has been bombed, Athens murdered. Italy is the most vulnerable of all the enemies of the freedom-loving peoples, and yet mysterious forces restrain this necessary counter-attack. It is not a question of religious faith but of forthright warfare.
> What mysterious influences or what diplomatic imbecility is it that prevents this clear and decisive action? Why not a 2,000lb bomb in the Vatican garden as a warning now? . . . Why should the allied nations refrain from a thousand-plane raid upon the Eternal City? There would be no real vandalism in that. The

charm of Rome has always been its ruins. Modernisation has vulgarised it. It could be devulgarised so easily. St. Peter's is architecturally inferior to St. Paul's, and the Axis raiders did their best to get St. Paul's.

Northcliffe House, realising the risk of losing readers by publishing this anti-Catholic tirade, sent a proof copy of the article to Cardinal Hinsley offering equal space for reply in the following week's issue. The cardinal asked me to write the article. I agreed to do so but not on the terms proposed by the editor. I pointed out that thousands who read the attack on the Pope would not see the answer. I urged Cardinal Hinsley to insist that the reply must appear on the same page on the same day as Wells' piece. Most reluctantly the editor agreed. Underneath the offending article he printed the following explanation:

> In view of the reference to his Holiness the Pope and the Roman Catholic Church in Mr. H.G. Wells' review of the war, the *Sunday Dispatch* felt that an authoritative reply to Mr. Wells should be made, and submitted a proof for this purpose. The member of the Roman Catholic Church selected to answer Mr. Wells was the Rev. Dr. John C. Heenan. Here is his article:

The following are a few excerpts from my reply. At the time they seemed amusing:

> I cannot fail to observe the similarity in utterance between Wells in the *Sunday Dispatch*, Goebbels in *Das Reich* and Farinacci in *Regime Fascista*. All are agreed that the Pope is the enemy of the New Order.
> But if he must do Goebbels' work, why doesn't H.G. finish the job? He refers to the Pope's crusade against Russia. Why not give chapter and verse. Goebbels badly wants it. Hitler's greatest complaint against the Pope is that he won't play ball . . . H.G. excels himself when he talks of bombing the Vatican. (By the way, why only the Vatican *gardens*—2,000lb bombs cost money—and why drag in Malta? Are the Catholic Maltese more likely to be sustained by the cardinal's burning words of encouragement or Mr. Wells' slanderous suggestion that they want to massacre the Holy Father's household?) H.G. should

leave it to the R.A.F. to select their targets. Thousands of Catholic airmen would, I feel sure, bomb Rome if the order were given. But must these Catholic boys be asked to denounce the Pope as the enemy of Christian civilisation before being given their wings? Is that fair to the memory of Paddy Finucane or young Garland, V.C.?

But if the Vatican is bombed, who will be the victims? The British Minister? The Belgian or Polish Accredited Representatives? Someone should have told Mr. Wells that the hospitality of Pope Pius XII is reserved for diplomats of the United Nations.

I congratulate H.G. on his Mediterranean plan. It's time we started a Fifth Front. (Things aren't going too well on the other four, H.G.) 'Deal austerely with Franco'. That's the offensive spirit we want to see. We haven't enough on at the moment. And why not have a smack at Salazar at the same time? He is only a dirty dago . . . But the invasion of Italy sounds good to me, though I'm as ignorant of strategy as H.G. himself. Admiralty, go to it! But there's always a snag . . . Admiral Harwood is a loyal son of Pope Pius XII. Tell us, Harwood: Can England and H.G. Wells trust you? No answer? He doesn't hear. The admiral is too busy sinking Italian ships.

Nobody took any notice of Mr. Wells' attack in the *Sunday Dispatch*. Subsequently he made a more sustained but equally futile onslaught on the Catholic Church in a book called *Crux Ansata*. For the second time I was drawn into controversy with Mr. Wells. This time it was not Cardinal Hinsley but the reviewer of *Crux Ansata* who involved me. The review was severely critical of the book but spoke kindly of the author. It suggested that if Mr. Wells really did believe the libels he wrote about the Church it could only be because his sheltered life had kept him from contact with the Church. Since Mr. Wells had an honest and open mind, the reviewer said, he ought to meet a priest to discuss what the Catholic Church really teaches. In a footnote to the review the editor of the *Catholic Herald,* Michael de la Bedoyère, offered to book a private room at a London restaurant and pay for a dinner at which Mr. Wells could meet either Father Martin D'Arcy, a Jesuit scholar, or Father Heenan, a parish priest. H.G. Wells published a letter of acceptance in the next issue of the paper. Father D'Arcy declined on the grounds that he was a scholar not a controversialist. Since Mr. Wells would not be meeting Father D'Arcy, one of the greatest minds of the century, I accepted the invitation, though I rightly regarded myself as a very poor substitute indeed. The editor then wrote to Mr. Wells to arrange a convenient time and place for the dinner. Suddenly Mr. Wells became less amenable. He told the editor that before he would settle a date for dinner I must send him a copy of *Crux Ansata* marking the pages I found unacceptable. He also required me to furnish him with the arguments I proposed to use in challenging his accusations against the Church. It was obvious that the dinner would never take place. I therefore proposed to the editor that H.G. Wells and I should have a debate under the chairmanship of a public figure who should be neither a Catholic nor a notorious anti-Catholic. I suspected that Mr. Wells did not really want to discuss his book either in private or in public, but I did not want to give him any easy excuse for refusing. I offered to debate any pages of the book to be selected by the author himself or, alternatively, to take as the title for our debate the conclusion of the book i.e. the Catholic Church is the enemy of civilisation. The debate was to be in a large hall and proceeds would go to the Red Cross. ('Crux Ansata' means literally 'the cross with a handle' but the implication of the title is that the Catholic Church has betrayed Christ and carries a twisted or crooked cross.) In a letter to the editor of the *Catholic Herald* Mr. Wells declined to debate on the grounds that in a shouting match he would not be able to make the voice of reason heard. The outcome of all the negotiations was a paperback edited by Michael de la Bedoyère and called *Chuck It, Wells*. This told the whole story of H.G.'s attack and subsequent refusal to debate the issue.

I had not spent much time in sporting activities since ordination. I owned a tennis racket but no golf clubs or fishing rod. Half-a-dozen games of tennis were about my average for a season. If I had been important enough to appear in *Who's Who* I would have listed my hobbies as reading and writing. During this period I might well have added public speaking to my list. It may have been a hobby but it was certainly not a recreation because it required great effort on my part to write a speech and learn it by heart. Then and at all times I suffered considerable strain in delivery. The time needed for composition which could have been better spent visiting homes in the parish made me reluctant to accept speaking engagements. Unfortunately I was plagued with invitations to speak. A little talent for oratory can be as dangerous as a little learning. To have been heard on radio was taken at the time as a sign of rare ability. The odd phrase 'B.B.C. personality' had not yet been coined—that was the creation of television—but publicity was difficult to avoid. I might make a speech only once in three months but there was little exciting war news and the press quoted me so often that I gave the impression of being always in the public eye. At the beginning of the campaign for the Education Bill I was invited to address many meetings of parents and teachers. Bishop Doubleday felt that it was time to apply the curb. He began by requesting me to submit my B.B.C. talks for censorship. Since most of my talks had been given at the request of Cardinal Hinsley I had been in the habit of sending the text to him. For a time I sent my scripts to Bishop Doubleday but eventually he told me to deal once more with Westminster. He probably found the strain of reading my scripts too much to bear.

The Bishop of Brentwood was convinced that for my own sake and that of the Church it would be best for me not to be seen and especially not to be heard outside the parish. To say that he silenced me would suggest ruthlessness, but he was not a harsh man. He was a conscientious bishop suspicious of a priest who seemed to spend too much time in extra-parochial work. Without issuing an actual ukase he let me know that he did not wish me to undertake any more outside engagements. For many months I refused all requests for my services on grounds of parochial duties. This was no hardship—public speaking may be thrilling but it exacts a high price from sensitive performers. I was not ungrateful for the respite I enjoyed through the bishop's intervention. Through obedience to his wishes I was destined however to be led into further trouble. One day I received a telephone call from an old friend, Canon Dick Earley. He was speaking from a meeting of Manchester priests which had been called by the Bishop of Salford to discuss education. The meeting decided to open the Salford campaign with a monster rally in Belle Vue, Manchester, a favourite site for large-scale productions from prize-fights to evangelistic revivals. All the parishes would march with bands and banners to Belle Vue one Sunday afternoon. The clergy were waiting to know on which Sunday I would be free to address the rally.

I simply said that I would not be free on any Sunday. When Dick pressed me I explained that I was without a curate. He brushed that excuse aside and undertook to send down a priest from Salford to supply for me. I next pleaded that I had been told to rest my voice. He assured me that the meeting would not take place for at least three months by which time my voice would be fully restored—this was to be the biggest rally ever held by Manchester Catholics and would need a long time to organise. In the end I had no alternative but to tell Canon Earley that my bishop preferred me not to accept any more speaking engagements. He asked me bluntly if I had been silenced. I replied that, while I had not been silenced, the bishop had made his wishes absolutely clear. I therefore repeated quite firmly that I was not available for the Manchester rally and thought I would hear no more of the affair. I was astonished the following afternoon when Dick Earley and another priest appeared at my door in Manor Park. On the instructions of their bishop they had gone down to Brentwood to make a personal appeal to Dr. Doubleday to lift the ban. My bishop was puzzled and rather cross. He said, quite correctly, that he had never put a ban on my speaking in public. The canon then asked if it were true that he did not wish me to accept any speaking engagements. Yes, the bishop said, this was true, but I ought to have known that on such a special occasion as this he would not have objected to my accepting the invitation. As the priests were leaving the bishop told them that I was free to go to Manchester on condition that I did not speak at any rally except the one at Belle Vue. The Salford priests apologised on their arrival at Manor Park for going to Brentwood without asking my leave. Having talked to the Bishop of Brentwood they now knew what I meant by saying that although the bishop had not actually silenced me he was not enthusiastic about my making public appearances.

I used to wonder why the bishop was so ungracious towards me. It was not, I felt sure, the result of personal antipathy. It did not occur to me at the time that he might resent the modest reputation I had acquired through broadcasting and writing. I did not think that he could be envious because it seemed to me that an old man has to be singularly stupid to object to the success of his juniors. It is, of course, possible for a man to envy another his youth, but even this is unlikely among men who have fought the good fight. Few would want to fight it all over again. They are more likely to say with Saint Paul "The time of my departure has come. I have fought the good fight, I have finished the race, I have kept the faith. Henceforth there is laid up for me a crown of righteousness which the Lord, the righteous judge, will award to me on that day, and not only to me but also to all who have loved his appearing" (2 Tim. iv). If purely personal feelings came into it at all the Bishop of Brentwood may have felt aggrieved that the archbishops of another diocese (Cardinal Hinsley and his successor Cardinal Griffin) had been making so much use of one of his own priests. There was also his conviction that I had been spoiled by Canon Palmer and given ideas above my station. For my part I did not at any time feel hostile to Bishop Doubleday. At times I felt frustrated and angry but I never thought the bishop guilty of malice and did not bear him any grudge. I thought that his judgement was poor but I did not realise that he had become prematurely senile. Although I did not know it I was dealing with a superior who was in grave need of help. Later the Holy See appointed George Andrew Beck to be co-adjutor Bishop of Brentwood with right of succession, but by that time I was no longer living in the diocese.

The characters of some men are moulded and strengthened by adversity. Others are broken by suffering—especially if they believe themselves to be victims of injustice. Priests of my generation (young men at the outbreak of the second world war) were able to withstand hardship and injustice more easily than the young priests who came later. We were not made of finer clay but we were less vulnerable. We were perhaps more capable both of inflicting and suffering pain. In God's providence I learned a great deal from Bishop Doubleday about the exercise of authority. He helped me to avoid at least some mistakes in the three dioceses of which I was later to be bishop. It is likely that through insensitiveness or bad judgement (but not, I hope, malice) I have given offence to priests within my jurisdiction. Bishop Doubleday's treatment of me doubtless prevented me from giving much more. To illustrate the point I shall describe one or two further encounters with the bishop. They are worth revealing because they form an essential part of my evolution. Our characters are formed by all who exercise influence over us.

From Bishop Doubleday I learned how to suffer injustice from a Father-in-God without developing a grudge against the Church of God. Serving under a senile superior also taught me that unquestioning obedience can sometimes be a positive dereliction of duty. It became fashionable many years later to regard all obedience as weakness. At the time of which I write, the accepted doctrine was to obey superiors even if they were misguided. That outlook did not seem odd to a generation brought up on Ignatian spirituality. It later became unacceptable even to young Jesuits. The Charge-of-the-Light-Brigade-mentality became rare during the nineteen-sixties. The obedient-unto-death outlook was insistently deprecated by Jesuit and Dominican theologians after the Council. Such enlightened mentors were not available in my early days in the priesthood. Hence my spiritual struggles when faced with unreasonable orders from my bishop.

As a co-opted member of the education committee I was the spokesman for all the Catholic schools in East Ham. This exemplary borough gave to non-provided schools (all of which happened to be Catholic) the same careful attention as to its own. It was never necessary for me to fight for the rights of our Catholic children. They were given more than their rights through the generous interpretation by the local officials in East Ham of ministry regulations. Membership of the education committee was a great help to my pastoral work because it led to acquaintance—and often to friendship—with many councillors and town officials.

Local authorities annually request bishops to nominate members to serve 'in the Roman Catholic interest' on certain statutory bodies. Towards the end of the war instead of renewing my nomination the bishop named Mgr. O'Grady the parish priest of Walthamstow to serve on the East Ham education committee. This astonishing action caused much embarrassment. The director of education rang up to ask why I had resigned and also wanted to know why it was necessary to go outside East Ham to find a Catholic representative for the education committee. My friend Mgr. O'Grady was the most embarrassed of all. He knew nothing about East Ham and would find it hard to take an intelligent interest in its affairs. He was already a member of his own education committee in the borough of Walthamstow. The other priests in East Ham naturally wanted to know what I had done to cause the bishop to dismiss me. It did not occur to Mgr. O'Grady—although he was Vicar General of the diocese—to warn the bishop of the problems his action would create. Still less did the Vicar General think of refusing the impossible task of replacing a local man on a committee of a local authority. For my part I accepted the humiliation as a deliberate and conscientious contribution by the bishop to my spiritual good.

The bishop was determined to chasten me. Soon afterwards he gave me another rebuff which, by comparison, was no more than a passing blow. The Association of Convent Schools is a national body of superiors and headmistresses, one of whose functions is to hold an annual conference. A conference was to be held in Brentwood and the president of the association Mother Dympna Fox F.C.J., invited me to lecture on teaching the social encyclicals to sixth-formers. The lecture, which was in no way noteworthy, was based on the premiss that to secure the interest of the young it is necessary to show that religion has a bearing on people's daily life. If I had known the jargon of the future I should doubtless have told the nuns to make religion relevant and meaningful. I suggested that the nuns might combine a certain amount of civics with religion by taking their girls to see factories, offices and hospitals, and to visit the local town hall and even Parliament. This kind of approach, combining social study and religious instruction, was still fairly novel but by no means revolutionary. The object was to gain practical experience for discussion of Christian duties towards the whole community. The Bishop of Brentwood was in the chair for my address. He had been invited to preside only at the opening session but the poor man, by now partially deaf, thought he was expected to attend every meeting of the conference.

As soon as I finished my lecture the bishop gave the nuns a sharp warning. He told them to dismiss from their minds what they had heard from me. The children for whom they were responsible must not have their minds filled with dangerous ideas. They should be taught to keep their religion as they had learned it at their mother's knee. Dr. Heenan, he assured them, was not an authority on religious teaching but fortunately there were good theologians available to guide them. The good nuns were stunned by this attack. For my part despite embarrassment I was only sorry for the bishop. His hearing had been failing for some years and I felt fairly sure that he must have picked up a misleading version of what I had said. I had kept to the subject of the social encyclicals and their practical application. I had not entered any of the wider fields of theology.

When the bishop had finished speaking the five hundred nuns in the audience sat in puzzled silence. Mother Dympna Fox then rose and spoke no less emphatically than the bishop. She found his lordship's attack incomprehensible, she said, because I had done exactly as I had been asked. For her part she wanted to thank me for a lecture which was informative, inspiring, etc. etc. but she could not speak for the other Sisters. This was (and was intended to be) an invitation to the nuns to demonstrate. For several minutes they behaved like angry penguins. It was brave of Mother Dympna to contradict the bishop so forcefully in that period of history. Today it requires no special courage for a nun to attack a bishop or, for that matter, for a priest or layman to denounce the Pope. In those hierarchy-conscious days Mother Dympna's act merited a decoration for valour. Bishop Doubleday, deaf though he was, could not misunderstand the nature of the demonstration. With great humility he stood up at once to express his sincere regret. He admitted that he must have misunderstood most of what I had said. He had not known, he added, that I was speaking to a brief provided by the nuns. After the meeting the bishop expressed his regret to me personally. He was a confused man who had only done what he saw as his duty. If, as he thought, I was misleading the Sisters it was for him as my bishop to rebuke me publicly. I was not in any way offended because I understood his motives. The nuns came from every part of England and did not know Bishop Doubleday. They were not edified.

It may puzzle future historians that Britain devoted so much attention to education and social security while the war was still very far from won. Some will attribute the phenomenon to the kind of exhibitionism which led householders to display notices forbidding mention of defeat since the possibility did not exist. Other historians may decide that the British were merely whistling in the dark. When the Wehrmacht was at its most formidable England was singing 'We're going to hang out our washing on the Siegfried Line (. . . if the Siegfried Line's still there)'. When our cities and ports were being reduced to rubble a new record was put on the national gramophone: 'There'll always be an England'. The true explanation of the interest in social legislation before victory was that the deplorable social conditions following the first world war had never been forgotten. The Jarrow hunger march and the means test were still vivid memories. The public and the politicians were equally determined that this time no attempt would be made to deceive returning warriors. As early as 1942, when all effort was still needed to ensure national survival, the Beveridge Report and the Education Bill were being drafted. If the war were to be lost, England, together with the rest of Europe, would be under the heel of Hitler, but nobody was so unpatriotic as to make preparations for such an unlikely eventuality. England simply does not lose wars. After winning the war everyone was determined, in the current slogan, to win the peace. That is why so much energy was devoted to social planning from the end of the blitz until the reconquest of Europe began on D-Day, 6th June, 1944.

Once again a false peace was shattered. Our island people had almost forgotten that while we were living in comparative peace the people on the continent had suffered without respite since the summer of 1940. The shooting had stopped but citizens in the occupied territories were entirely dependent on the enemy for survival. They had also been subjected to air-raids from the R.A.F. and the American flying fortresses. Europe was blanketed by silence but the war remained a grim reality for our friends abroad. As for the Middle East, we had known all along that war was going on in those parts but it seemed a *Boys' Own Paper* kind of war. Names like Sidi Barrani and Tobruk had a friendly magic about them. Italian soldiers were not to be taken very seriously. Rommel was no cad but rather a sport who would much rather have been fighting on our side than Hitler's. Montgomery was the greatest military genius since Napoleon—or was it since Wavell? In the absence of heavy casualty lists the war in the Middle East hardly made itself felt in England. As for the Far Eastern theatre of war, that was being kept in mind mainly by those whose unfortunate relatives had been captured by the Japanese at the fiasco of Singapore, which had suddenly been discovered to be defended only from the sea. Just when the war seemed farthest away the onslaught from the air began all over again.

During the quiet years the German scientists had not been idle. The blitz on Britain had failed but they did not plan to attempt it again just with larger bombers. They had devised and produced pilotless planes and rockets. These were the secret weapons with which Hitler had often boasted he would bring Britain to its knees. If D-day had been delayed much longer it is likely that he would have succeeded in making the towns of this country uninhabitable. To the pilotless planes (flying bombs, doodlebugs) some sort of answer was quickly found. They were shot down in large numbers at sea or over the hinterland of the South-east before reaching London, their main target. Large numbers nevertheless were able to penetrate our defences. Flying bombs, being jet propelled, moved at great speed. At a calculated point the engine cut out and the device dived steeply to explode on impact. It was providential or lucky, according to taste, when it hit an open space instead of a row of houses. The few seconds from the stopping of the roar of the engine until the bomb exploded were the most nerve-shattering moments we had ever experienced. It was even more terrifying than in the old days of the blitz when we listened to the whistling of approaching bombs. Although a partial defence was mounted against the flying bombs, no answer was found to the rockets. Since their speed was greater than sound their approach was silent. The first perceptible sound was the actual explosion of the rocket on impact. Until the rocket sites were destroyed by the air force or overrun by the army London and the towns of eastern and southern England were defenceless. The timing of D-day was perfect. If it had been attempted earlier—as Stalin and his ideological supporters in Britain persistently demanded—the invasion would have failed. Until the U-boats in the Atlantic were completely mastered it would have been impossible to supply an army invading the continent. Civilians, of course, did not know the strategy of General Eisenhower's campaign. We followed eagerly the advances of the Allied armies but for us they represented not so much conquered territory as captured rocket sites.

Although the rockets were more devastating than the flying bombs or any of the 1940 missiles except land-mines, they were somehow more tolerable. There was, for instance, no wailing siren as harbinger. Once the air-raid warning had sounded on the approach of a flying bomb, nerves were taut until it had passed over. Nothing was heard of the rocket until it had exploded elsewhere. Those in the target area presumably heard nothing. The flying bombs came so frequently that general warnings had to be abandoned in the interests of production. The government introduced a new warning system operated by a look-out man on the roof of an office or factory who at the latest possible moment sounded his rattle if the building was in the bomb's trajectory. At the sound of the rattle people took cover until the bomb had passed over or had exploded. A great deal of damage was done to the houses of Manor Park parishioners but no lives were lost. The parish church of St. Nicholas narrowly avoided destruction when a rocket landed a few yards from the front porch. Fortunately this happened when the church was empty. All the windows were blown out by the blast which also severely damaged the fabric. We were able to patch up the building sufficiently to keep it in use until the end of the war when permanent repairs were made. We did not know at the time that this damage to our parish church was the last the parish was to suffer from enemy action. The war still had several months to run but the Germans no longer had rocket sites within striking distance of London. The Luftwaffe meanwhile was too occupied defending the Fatherland to renew conventional bombing raids. Nor by this stage in the war would they have had any success because the R.A.F. and the American air force had complete mastery of the skies.

The period between D-Day and VE-Day (the end of the war in Europe) was eventful in Manor Park apart from the raids by flying bombs and rockets. There is in the parish a large open space known as the Wanstead Flats. It is not an enclosed park but, as its name implies, just a flat piece of land. Originally part of Epping Forest this land was restricted by provident county councillors to recreational use. It is the lung of the congested borough of East Ham. During the spring of 1944 the whole of Wanstead Flats was taken over by the army. It had been in partial occupation by the forces operating anti-aircraft guns and barrage balloons since the beginning of the war. Civilians were now totally excluded from the area and the Flats were covered with tents ranging from small bell tents to vast marquees. During the month of May the camp filled up with soldiers. We did not need to be very clever to deduce that D-day was near at hand. The distance from Wanstead Flats to Tilbury docks is little more than twelve miles. The troops were strictly incommunicado—not only were they not allowed to leave camp but no civilian was permitted to approach within shouting distance. During the night of June 3rd the soldiers disappeared. They had been taken to the docks to embark on their perilous journey. (After the war I learned that some of my young parishioners had been among those troops and must have suffered a double nostalgia leaving Manor Park on that summer night.)

For the next two or three weeks a continuous stream of tanks, guns and soldiers arrived in Manor Park to spend a few hours or days in the camp on Wanstead Flats before leaving to reinforce the troops now established on French soil. These young soldiers straight from country camps had not heard the sound of a bomb. Now with no protection beyond the canvas of their tents they were exposed to an intensified bombardment of flying bombs (the rockets were not put immediately into service because Hitler was reserving them as his ultimate weapon to force the Allies to capitulate). We hardened campaigners paid little attention to passing doodlebugs—we took interest only if they were coming in our direction. Then there was nothing to do but look brave and say our prayers. I found it difficult to compose a suitable prayer. I naturally wanted the doodlebug to keep going but it seemed selfish to pray it on its way when it might fall on someone indispensable like the mother of a family. The soldiers trapped on Wanstead Flats were longing for the security of the battlefields.

It was about this time that I had an accident which might have been fatal. I fell asleep driving my car. Until this happened to me I would not have believed that such a thing was possible. I have since learned that falling asleep at the wheel is a recognised hazard of long-distance lorry drivers—hence the strict rules limiting their hours of duty. One Saturday afternoon I had been in Highgate attending a meeting of the Legion of Mary hostel for young girls who had been rescued from the streets. On my way home the North Circular Road was crowded with army traffic returning from the docks. The vehicles, empty except for the drivers, had been carrying stores and equipment to the boats. It was a beautiful June afternoon, the sun was blazing and I was tired after a sleepless night during which flying bombs had kept me busy in the parish. The clop-clop of the tyres on the huge wheels of the army trucks acted as a lullaby. I fell asleep for perhaps no more than two or three seconds. I awoke to find my car on its side at the foot of a tree which it had apparently tried to climb. The rubber-covered steering wheel was badly bent and my chest was severely bruised. A modern plastic wheel would have broken my breast-bone. The car was wrecked beyond repair.

I had practically reached home when the accident happened. The ambulance had to take me only a few hundred yards to the Aldersbrook Hospital. This was the hospital I visited every day and, during air-raids, every night. When I arrived not as chaplain but as a casualty there was much fussing and clucking among the nurses. We had been through so many hard times together that we were like one family. The matron had me taken to her own apartments near the hospital gates while a room was being made ready in the hospital. I was fully conscious though dazed and in some pain. A policeman came for particulars of the accident and the matron advised me to see him at once to avoid being disturbed once I was in bed. On condition that he would ask the fewest possible questions the police sergeant was allowed to see me. He apologised for bothering me and asked me to tell him briefly how the accident happened. I told him that I had fallen asleep. Notebook in hand the police officer looked incredulous. "That can't be true, sir," he said, "because it would mean you were driving without due care and attention. When you come out of hospital you would have to be charged. You weren't asleep at all. The sun was in your eyes and blinded you." I must have been very dazed indeed because I began to argue with the sergeant. I pointed out that I had been driving due east and at five o'clock in the afternoon the sun is in the west. The splendid sergeant nodded and explained that 'sun in your eyes' was only a manner of speaking. The sun was, of course, really behind me but was shining into my driving mirror and hence dazzled me. He wrote down his version of the accident in his book. "When you wake up," he said as he left, "try to remember you didn't fall asleep." The policeman had been on duty during air-raids and had seen me often at 'incidents'. That is why he could not accept that I was driving without due care and attention. Dog doesn't eat dog.

I was then taken into the hospital. A sister and nurse were busy prettifying a little room with flowers borrowed from the other patients who, of course, all knew me. The sister told the nurse to give me a drink before allowing Dr. Cohn, a refugee and a gifted, compassionate man, to look for broken bones. Then took place a piece of dialogue which for all its absurdity I have never forgotten and still find attractive.

> Sister: Nurse, give Father some orangeade and put some glucose in it.
>
> Me: Sister, what is glucose?
>
> Sister: Never you mind. Take it from me glucose is good for nursing mothers.
>
> Me: But, Sister, I haven't come in here to have a baby.
>
> Sister: That's true, Father, but you never know what you might go out with.

Just as I was settling down a nurse came in to say that two gentlemen wanted to see me urgently. They were my old friends Tom and Will Fitzgibbon. Driving down Aldersbrook Road they had seen a small crowd round a battered car which they recognised at once because they had only just finished overhauling it in their garage. They rushed up to the policeman and told him who they were. The policeman immediately took them aside and told them as friends of the reverend gentleman to go to the hospital to make sure that in his dazed state he had grasped the fact that he had not fallen asleep driving his car. After further brainwashing by the Fitzgibbon brothers I was now ready to believe that I had not fallen asleep nor hit the tree. It was now clear to me that the tree had behaved in a disgraceful fashion. It had obviously uprooted itself and made an unprovoked attack on my defenceless car which was blinded by the sun.

I spent an uncomfortable few days in hospital. The pain was bearable and the nurses were charming but I found it a terrible strain to be in bed while flying bombs were falling. Until then I had not realised how easy it was to be brave during an air-raid by keeping busy. Dodging bombs was more tolerable than waiting for them to fall. I soon left hospital and went into the country for two days, but it was impossible to stay longer while my parishioners were still in danger. It happened that no bombs fell on the parish during my short absence. This led my beloved sacristan Elizabeth Woiwod to welcome me back with these ambiguous words: "Thank God you're back, Father. I prayed that nothing would drop on Manor Park while you were away." That very night Sixth Avenue, the street in which she lived, was badly damaged. I wondered if it might have been safer for the parish if I had stayed away.

Once the British and American forces had established themselves in France they began to send back German prisoners of war. The camp on Wanstead Flats which had been used for the invasion troops now became a prisoner of war camp. The day after the Germans arrived I visited the camp to ask if I might be allowed to say Mass for the prisoners on the following Sunday. The commandant gladly gave me leave to speak to the prisoners and find out if any were Catholics. I discovered that the majority of the prisoners were from the Rhineland and they undertook to build an outdoor altar for the Sunday Mass. The camp commandant was most enthusiastic that I should do something for 'the poor devils'. He remarked that Latin made it easy for me to hold a service for foreigners and regretted that without a clergyman to read the Bible and say prayers in German he would not be able to arrange a Protestant service. In abandoning Latin the Church has given up more than a language.

On the following Sunday I arrived at midday to find that even if Germans contrive to lose wars they remain masters of methodical preparation. The prisoners had built a magnificent altar for which I had sent from the church all the necessary furnishings and linen. Before Mass I gave a short address prepared with the help of a local

teacher of German. I welcomed the men to England and expressed
the hope that for everyone's sake they would soon be restored to
their families. I told them that so far as I was concerned they were
not prisoners of war but new parishioners. We were not enemies but
friends. I explained that since they were in danger of death I would
give General Absolution so that they could all receive Holy Communion—I did not stress that they were in danger chiefly from their
own flying bombs. I was amazed at the numbers who received Holy
Communion at the Mass. I had expected a hundred or so but I had to
keep breaking the hosts into smaller pieces to provide for nearly a
thousand communicants. The singing was magnificent. Evidently
they had spent much of their time since my previous visit practising
hymns and motets. After Mass I congratulated the prisoner who had
conducted the singing. He replied that for him this was a great and
unique occasion. He had never before performed at a Mass because in
civilian life he was choirmaster of the Protestant Cathedral in Berlin.
An excellent example of early ecumenism.

One of the Germans was a very keen convert. He was proud to tell
me that he was a lay oblate of St. Benedict. He spoke English well
and was a great help in organising and interpreting. I first made his
acquaintance when he came to confession on the Monday morning
following the great open-air Mass. I had a book which gave the
formulae for confession in many languages. It was easy enough to
learn to say: Wann war ihre letzte Beichte? (When was your last
confession?) Nor was it difficult to tell the penitent what prayers to
say for a penance. It was not important that I could understand
only a part of their actual confession. If they spoke slowly I could
understand enough. I discovered that some of them were not
Germans but foreigners pressed into service by the Nazis. Thus a
prisoner might begin by asking if he might make his confession in
French or Polish. It was one of the Poles who gave me both a surprise
and a shock.

He told me that he was a parish priest from Lwow in Poland. He
had been conscripted into the Wehrmacht when the Nazis overran
his parish. He had a burning hatred of Germans. To have been forced
to fight on the side of the conquerors of his country had embittered
him to an extent that I would not have thought possible in a priest.
It is difficult for those born and brought up in the comparatively
unemotional atmosphere of England to appreciate the intensity of
national feeling elsewhere. Our lack of strong sentiment may come

from living on an island without pressure of aliens on our frontiers—I hope it is not because we regard other nationals as lesser breeds. Whatever the reason the British do not easily become passionate in their patriotism. The singing of 'Land of hope and glory' is more likely to be a frolic than a battle cry. I told the Polish priest that I would arrange for him to hear confessions in another tent. He replied that he was unwilling to hear the confessions of German soldiers. I was dumbfounded. I was at a loss how to explain the priest's refusal to the German convert. I could have saved myself embarrassment because the German fully understood and agreed with the priest's attitude. He said that the Polish priest would have put himself in an impossible position by agreeing to hear confessions because no German soldier would have gone to him. I was depressed that political differences could poison the relationship between priests and people. Mine was a typically insular attitude resulting from inexperience. The same kind of situation must have arisen in Ireland during the civil war in which bishops, clergy and whole families were bitterly divided. Members of the I.R.A. may not have been willing to confess to priests who upheld the Free State. So perhaps the Polish priest's view was not strange. I reflected that in modern England we have lived sheltered lives.

Although several months were to pass before the collapse of the German army the war was now almost over for us in Manor Park. The rockets which succeeded the flying bombs enjoyed only a brief triumph. The R.A.F. concentrated their attack on the rocket sites and with every advance of the Allied troops the menace grew less. It was fortunate that the Germans had not had time to develop rockets with a longer range. If they had been able to fire them from the Black Forest during the later stages of the war London would have become a city of ruins. After the rockets we had a blissful danger-free period which took us to VE-Day (8th May, 1945). It was a wonderful day for the British but especially for the longsuffering Londoners. We celebrated it in Manor Park with a parish social in St. Nicholas' Hall. We offered prayers of thanksgiving and had Benediction of the Blessed Sacrament in the church. We then went down to the hall, played the Fifth Symphony, drank tea and sang songs until nearly midnight. Lights were blazing everywhere to celebrate the ending of the black-out. During the evening my car was stolen but I did not let that spoil a happy occasion. Hundreds of cars were borrowed by revellers on VE-Day. The police found my car abandoned at the other end of East Ham the following morning. It was dented and full of scratches. Philosophically I regarded them as the scars of peace. A small price to pay.

As soon as the war in Europe ended my first thought was to rebuild the bombed school. Here I had the invaluable help of John Dyer, the director of education. We both realised that it would be some time before the government could tackle the rebuilding programme. Assuming that with the end of the war there would be a relaxation of controls we had plans drawn up at once. We did not foresee that rationing would be reimposed after the war. Backed by the East Ham education authority our plans were approved by the Ministry with little delay. We were lucky enough to forestall the fresh restrictions. Before the Far Eastern end of the war was over the rebuilding of the bombed school had begun. It was a heartening sight. I was not worried about paying for the building because war damage claims would eventually cover most of the cost. I merely had to borrow a few thousand pounds to keep the contractors happy until 'the war damage' (the colloqualism for the government department concerned) paid the bill. I wrote happily to the bishop for leave to borrow five thousand pounds. He refused on the grounds that I should not have begun to rebuild the school without having submitted the plans to him. He would not authorise me to borrow any money. The building must be stopped forthwith. I wrote in great alarm to the bishop to explain that the building was only a replacement of the damaged section of the school. Strictly speaking there were no new plans to submit. The bishop was not moved.

It is hard to exaggerate my dilemma. If I obeyed the bishop it might prove impossible to bring back the contractors when the bishop had seen the light. There was in addition the devastating effect on public relations with East Ham Borough—as well as the blow to the morale of the teachers, parents, children and the neighbours who after all the bombing were delightedly watching a building actually going up instead of down. I did not know what to do, I had never defied the bishop despite all trials but this time I could see no alternative. Reluctantly I took the bishop's letter forbidding me to borrow the money to the Apostolic Delegate whom I had known both at Ushaw and in Rome. I asked him quite simply to tell me what I must do. I was aware of the principle that it is always safe to obey but I did not see how in this case the principle could apply. I had come to the Apostolic Delegate because I was genuinely in doubt about my duty. To my relief—and somewhat to my surprise since Mgr. Godfrey was an ultra-cautious man—the Delegate's reply was unhesitating. He told me to proceed without scruple in building the school. He added that for some time he had been receiving reports of the bishop's increasing loss of contact with affairs.

It was true that I could now go ahead without scruple. I could not however go ahead, without money. No bank would lend money without security i.e. unless my application for a bank loan were supported by the diocese. The Alliance Assurance Company, the normal source of borrowing, acted only through the bishop. I did not know where to turn. Bernard Griffin, formerly Auxiliary Bishop of Birmingham, was now Archbishop of Westminster. He had been in his last year when I arrived at the English College in Rome. When he was appointed to Westminster to succeed Cardinal Hinsley I kept out of his way. Unlike the old cardinal he would not need my help. Some months after his arrival in Westminster Archbishop Griffin telephoned me in Manor Park. Knowing what I had done for Cardinal Hinsley, he said, he wondered why I had not offered to help him. I replied that I had made up my mind to keep away from Westminster because my relationship with Hinsley had been entirely personal and I did not want to be an embarrassment to the new archbishop. He said he understood and much appreciated my motives. But, Cardinal Griffin went on, he also was a stranger to London and advice from an old friend might be most helpful. Then he asked me directly to resume my visits to Archbishop's House. I demurred because my connexion with Westminster had made relations with my bishop so difficult that I really hoped never to have to enter Archbishop's House again. With a rather testy reference to Mohammed Bernard Griffin said that he would have to visit Manor Park instead. This seemed an absurd reversal of positions so I suggested a compromise. I invited him to meet me that afternoon at the Authors' Club in Whitehall only five minutes distant from Westminster.

As a result of that meeting I resumed in modified form my service to Westminster. This entailed giving occasional advice on public policy and on exceptional occasions helping with speeches and pastoral letters. As in Hinsley's time I was never consulted nor ever gave advice on diocesan matters. Now that I was in financial difficulties I decided to seek help from Westminster. When I showed Archbishop Griffin the letter I had received from Bishop Doubleday he began to think that the bishop must be going out of his mind. It was obvious that the building of the school could not be stopped. I pointed out the impossibility of borrowing money without the bishop's fiat. The archbishop, who rarely regarded financial problems as insoluble, went to his desk and wrote a cheque for the required sum. Thus, at last, my problem was solved. I wrote at once to the bishop telling him that an anonymous benefactor had let me have the money interest free pending the government grant for war damage. The building went ahead and was completed before the complicated system of licenses for post-war building came into effect.

The summer of 1945 was memorable mainly for personal reasons. My old friend and former parish priest Canon Cameron had been seriously ill for some time. He was a shy man and had few friends. Whenever I visited him in his presbytery at Barking I came away feeling miserable. Canon Cameron was a dying man but nobody seemed aware of his condition. I therefore persuaded him to let me arrange for him to be nursed in the Aldersbrook Hospital which I visited every day. Several rules had to be adjusted to enable a hospital in Manor Park to accept a patient from Barking, but with good will and determination most regulations yield to gentle pressure. So far as I remember, Canon Cameron first became a guest in my house and thus qualified for entry to the Aldersbrook as a resident of East Ham Borough. He had advanced cancer of the stomach but it gave him little pain. He deteriorated so gradually that it was easy to forget that his illness was fatal. On more than one occasion I attempted to broach the subject of death but each time he turned away from the subject. Death was so far from his conscious mind that one morning I found him in angry mood because a priest had written to promise prayers for his peaceful end.

So many summer days passed without my being able to prepare my old friend for his last journey. It was not that I was afraid of telling the canon he was dying nor that the canon himself was afraid of death. It was simply that some psychological mechanism enabled him to avoid discussion of his condition.

On 14th August, 1945, the Japanese capitulated in the wake of the atom bombs on Hiroshima and Nagasaki. During the previous week Canon Cameron had grown perceptibly weaker. August 15th was VJ-Day. (The official date was 2nd September but naturally VJ-Day was celebrated as soon as the surrender of Japan was known.)

That morning when I went to see the canon I was determined not to be put off. As soon as I entered his room I said to him: "Do you know what day this is?" He did not. He did not even know about Japan's surrender. He had probably forgotten all about the war. I told him that it was August 15th, the feast of the Assumption of Our Lady, and that I was going to bring him Holy Communion. In preparation I would bring a friar from Forest Gate to hear his confession. All went perfectly. The canon suddenly became more alert than he had been for some days. He made all the Latin responses when I gave him Extreme Unction. He had only one complaint—that nobody had told him sooner that he was dying so that he could have made a better preparation. For me the V in VJ-Day will always stand for Vincent Cameron. My old friend died the following week.

The months immediately after the war passed quickly and happily. The men began to return from the Forces and the few children who had remained in the evacuation areas came home. Apart from the debris (which was not completely cleared for several years) the only reminders of the war were the casualties. The men who had been prisoners of war—especially under the Japanese—remained gaunt and haggard for a long time after their release. Some of our young men did not return. Among them was Fred Lowe, who before the war had been outstanding among the youth of the parish. He seemed to have been given all the gifts of nature and grace that any young man could possess. He was deeply spiritual without any kind of display. His mother was a saintly woman whom everyone loved. His wife Renee, whose twin sister had become a nun, was a gentle smiling girl who was as popular as her husband with the other young people. Fred was killed soon after D-Day. His wife, who was awaiting the birth of a baby, was being looked after during her confinement by her mother. With an instinct that the news was bad she had intercepted the message from the War Office and brought it to me. Renee lived only a few hundred yards from the presbytery but it took me half-an-hour to reach her. I took out my cycle and went up and down several side roads rehearsing what to say. It would have been bad enough at any time to break such news but it might be dangerous to give her a shock in her condition. But how was it possible to 'break it gently' I simply did not know. At last I summoned my courage and went to her house. Her mother opened the door and pointed upstairs to where Renee was in bed. To be visited by the priest creates no surprise in a normal parish. I did not therefore have to find an explanation for my visit. I asked Renee if she had heard from Fred recently. She said that she had not heard since D-Day. I then told her I had heard that he had been very seriously wounded. I had decided— partly for the sake of the unborn child—to return later with a second message after the news of the grave wounding had prepared her. Renee looked at me quite calmly. "Fred's been killed, hasn't he?" she asked. Fred's absence was one of the saddest features of post-war Manor Park.

The great slogan of those days was 'winning the peace'. We were told that it was easy enough to win wars—it was a natural thing for our country to do—but difficult to win the peace. We had lost it last time and must not do so a second time. The key to winning the peace was thought to be fair treatment of the beaten foe. This time there would be no blockade of a starving Germany. We would do everything possible to help the Germans rebuild their towns and restore their economy. The damage and death resulting from air-raids by the Luftwaffe were small compared with the devastation and slaughter inflicted on German industrial towns by the British and American bombers. The Rhineland was the most afflicted area and to this the British government gave early attention. The Rhineland is one of the most Catholic parts of Germany and many of the bombed schools belonged to the Church. Archbishop Griffin was approached to send out a civilian priest—an army chaplain might arouse suspicion—to act as a liaison between the army of occupation and the German bishops. The Foreign Office suggested that I would be acceptable as my name was known in educational circles on account of my speeches at the time of the Butler Bill. The archbishop replied that he would have to approach the Bishop of Brentwood but there would be no difficulty in appointing me.

The next day Archbishop Griffin telephoned to tell me what was proposed. I was not keen to leave Manor Park just as we were doing our own post-war reconstruction but he assured me that there would be no need to resign my parish. He thought that no more than two or three months in the Rhineland would be required to smooth the path between the occupying power and the Catholic authorities.

The archbishop went down to Brentwood that afternoon to explain to Bishop Doubleday what was wanted. He asked me to dinner at 7.30 that evening when he would give me further details about my task in Germany. I was at Westminster soon after 7 o'clock but the archbishop had not yet returned from Brentwood. At 7.30 he still was not back. It was after eight o'clock before he came home looking flushed and tired. He had been given a very cold reception. On no account would Bishop Doubleday agree to give me leave of absence. He had no confidence in my judgement and was sure that I would make a hash of the Catholic schools question in Germany. Nor would he agree to make me an honorary canon. (Taking the bishop's agreement for granted, Archbishop Griffin had suggested that it would facilitate my dealings with the German hierarchy if I were given some ecclesiastical title.) Bishop Doubleday was convinced that to be given a position of authority would be bad for me. So once again I was beholden to him for being allowed to remain parish priest of Manor Park.

My good fortune was not destined to last much longer. During the annual meeting of the hierarchy in Low Week in 1947 one of the items on the agenda was the future of the Catholic Missionary Society. This is a company of priests from various dioceses (i.e. not members of religious orders) founded by Cardinal Vaughan early in the century to preach the faith throughout England and Wales. Its chief function was to be the provision of lectures on Catholic theology for non-Catholic audiences. It was intended to attract converts but even more to correct the grotesque notions common early in this century regarding Catholic belief and practice. Eventually, and perhaps inevitably, conversion became its main objective. The lectures commonly took the form of missions to non-Catholics. Each summer the C.M.S. priests organised what was called the motor mission. A mobile chapel was taken to villages and country towns where ignorance of the Catholic religion was hereditary. Among its members the Catholic Missionary Society had counted Herbert Vaughan, nephew of the cardinal, John Arendzen, a notable theologian and scripture scholar, Richard Downey, golden-tongued orator who later became Archbishop of Liverpool, Owen Dudley, the most eloquent speaker of them all, whose novels had been translated into every European language. Like those of Robert Hugh Benson fifty years earlier, these novels had a religious theme. Dudley's books were thrillers which held the reader's imagination while the problem of evil and other lesser obstacles to faith were solved by the characters he created. Father Dudley could have become a rich man but, of course, his very considerable royalties went to the support of the C.M.S.

The second world war—unlike the first—had brought the activities of the Catholic Missionary Society to a halt. The black-out and the disinclination of people to congregate while air-raids threatened made the preaching of missions impossible. Soon after the outbreak of war most of the C.M.S. priests were recalled to their dioceses or became chaplains for the Forces. The mission house at Brondesbury Park was commandeered by the government. After the war it proved impossible to regain possession of the Brondesbury mission house. De-requisitioning of premises proved to be a much slower government operation than requisitioning. Parliament had voted the government absolute control of all property early in the war. Without a mission house available it seemed likely that the C.M.S. would fade away. The bishops doubted the wisdom of buying a new property. After forty years the original objectives of the Catholic Missionary Society seemed far less urgent. True the conversion of England had not made any spectacular advance but much of the old prejudice had disappeared. A further consideration was that Father Dudley was obviously too old to build up a new missionary society. The bishops had almost decided to let the C.M.S. die when Archbishop Godfrey, the Apostolic Delegate, pleaded with them to grant a reprieve. The Apostolic Delegate said that the Holy See would never condone the action of the hierarchy if it let the Catholic Missionary Society disappear. It would be assumed that evangelical zeal was cooling and that the Catholics of England had abandoned hope of winning this country back to the Old Faith.

Impressed by the plea of the Apostolic Delegate the bishops decided to save the C.M.S. Cardinal Griffin was instructed by his fellow bishops to invite me to become Superior of the C.M.S. He telephoned early one evening to give me this astonishing information. I was astonished because I had convinced myself that while Bishop Doubleday lived I would be safe in Manor Park. When the cardinal had given me the bishops' message I naturally asked him about the attitude of my own bishop. He said that Bishop Doubleday was so deaf that at the meeting he did not know that my name was under discussion until the rest of the bishops had agreed on my nomination. In view of the unanimity of the choice he gave reluctant consent to my being approached. Some of the bishops had thought that I might not want to give up parish work and that it would be unfair to press me. So I was to be allowed to think over the proposal and give my decision the following day. I told Cardinal Griffin that I needed no time for reflection. I was quite sure that the more I reflected the less willing I should be to leave Manor Park. If the whole body of bishops had made the request I would have no peace of conscience if I were to refuse.

My last few months in Manor Park were so busy that I had no time to pine. Apart from leaving everything in good order for my successor I had to devise means of resurrecting the Catholic Missionary Society with no members and no mission house. On the evening of the fateful telephone call I had retained my presence of mind sufficiently to make my acceptance of the post of Superior conditional upon the bishops releasing priests to join the C.M.S. staff. The bishops agreed to release suitable priests if available, but such a promise is not always easy to honour in practical terms. Clearly I would ask bishops to release priests with special gifts. They must be good speakers and even if not theologians in the technical sense would need to be well read in theology. Above all they would have to be full of zeal for souls and willing to work hard. At that moment it looked as if they might also have to bring their own food and sleeping bags. The bishops were as good as their word. Most generous of all was Dr. Downey, Archbishop of Liverpool. He had been a member of the C.M.S. for fifteen years and had never lost his love for the society. Although they were not all free to join immediately, he promised me three priests by the end of the year.

My first recruit was a volunteer—the others were approached either by me or by their bishops. Father John Coyne, although a Liverpool priest, was at Oscott, a seminary in Birmingham, where he taught fundamental theology and Church history. Having taught students for many years he now wanted to make direct contact with the public. He was to prove a great asset in rebuilding the Catholic Missionary Society. In addition to presenting Catholic doctrine with persuasive eloquence he made his wide knowledge of Church history available to other C.M.S. members preparing lectures or articles. The second recruit was Father George Dwyer. Although he had studied in Rome for eight years and was a sound theologian, he had been sent to Cambridge to study modern languages. He was now teaching French and Christian Doctrine at St. Bede's college, Manchester. He had been a priest for fifteen years and was more than ready to exchange the teacher's gown for the preacher's stole. The third early recruit was Father Frank Thompson, the university chaplain in Newcastle-upon-Tyne. He was a gentle, witty, erudite man but, although I did·

not know it when I asked his bishop to release him, he had a severely damaged heart. He died after he had been with us only a year.

I now had three recruits but no headquarters. During my last few months in Manor Park I spent all my spare time house-hunting. Since we were looking for premises large enough to house a dozen men with domestic staff and to provide large rooms suitable for a chapel and library we were not in competition with house-hunting families. Speculators had not yet begun to buy large houses for conversion into flats. We were therefore reasonably hopeful of finding a suitable building. Our search was mercifully short. One day a Miss Nora Keary telephoned to offer her assistance. She had heard from a mutual friend that I was looking for a suitable property to turn into a mission house and since house-hunting was her hobby it would give her genuine pleasure to lend her aid. Nora Keary found a house almost at once. It was only the second one she 'viewed'. The first house which an agent sent her to view was, incredibly, the old mission house at Brondesbury Park! The Hampstead house was perfect for our purpose. Nora became a cherished friend and helper of the Catholic Missionary Society. The property in West Heath Road was on offer freehold with vacant possession. It has remained the headquarters of the C.M.S. with modern extensions called the Catholic Enquiry Centre.

Before we had taken possession of the new mission house Father Dwyer showed that his ability was practical as well as academic. He was severely material in his approach. He wanted to know once we were installed in the mission house how we proposed to keep alive. The question he asked with some persistence was "What are we going to use for money?" I was able to supply no very satisfactory answer. I had assumed that since the bishops had given us a task to perform they would see that we would not lack the means. George Dwyer thought that I had a great deal to learn about human nature. He explained patiently that any body of men—not only bishops—customarily solve a problem by appointing a man to do the job and leaving him to sink or swim. When we took possession of the mission house we had no money, but prodded by Father Dwyer I approached Cardinal Griffin, who gave us generous housekeeping money. The furniture and household effects had been put in store by Father Dudley. Much of it was now in a poor state but through the charity of friends—especially the Ursuline Nuns—we were able to make the house in Hampstead habitable. All this was in the future. Meanwhile

I remained in Manor Park with something of a split mind. My attention was divided between leaving affairs in order for the next parish priest and negotiating with bishops for likely recruits.

My recollection of the last few weeks in Manor Park is indistinct. Once more, as in Barking, there was the painful leave-taking with the old and the sick who would not be able to visit me in Hampstead. (Not that many parishioners do in fact visit their former priests. The relationship between a priest and his people though personal and warm is professional on both sides. I had not returned to visit any Barking family during my ten years in Manor Park and few had called on me.) Leaving Manor Park was less painful than leaving Barking because I was not exchanging old parishioners for new. I would not have to transfer my affection to a new flock. A priest of the Catholic Missionary Society has the whole country for his parish. I would be preaching missions in the Brentwood diocese—perhaps in Manor Park itself—so the parishioners knew that we need not lose touch with each other. But, of course, I would lose the joy of being the father of that devoted family.

At the time it was not possible to appreciate all that leaving Manor Park would entail. I did not realise, for example, that I was making a final break with the utterly satisfying way of life I had known as curate and parish priest. As a missioner and later as a bishop I was still to have people to care for but I would never have quite the same relationship with them. In Barking and Manor Park I knew the parishioners, whether or not they were practising their religion. When I was a bishop my flock became too numerous for me to know so intimately. Happily—although at the time I did not have the consolation of knowing it—one relationship was to remain unchanged. This was my partnership with Sisters in work for souls.

There was no convent either in Barking or in Manor Park but in both parishes nuns were always at hand. The Ursulines who had been my teachers when I joined the babies' class were still my guardian angels. I turned to them whenever I needed help for my poor children. Before the 1944 Education Act few poor children had any opportunity of higher education. Whenever an able child was in danger of being deprived through poverty the Ursulines would give her a free place in their convent high schools in Ilford or Forest Gate. They would also discreetly provide clothes so that a poor child would not look or feel different from other girls.

Nuns also helped me to solve problems with the old and the sick.

If any of my old people were destitute the Little Sisters of the Poor or the Nazareth Sisters would give them a home and a loving welcome. The incurably sick were cherished by the Irish Sisters of Charity in St. Joseph's Hospice for the Dying in Hackney. It is not surprising that nuns make special efforts to meet the wishes of a bishop, but it is immensely gratifying to know from experience that a curate could approach nuns with equal success on behalf of the young, the old, the poor and the sick. I did not need to approach nuns on my own behalf. They overwhelmed me with gifts when they heard that I had to set up a new mission house. The Chigwell nuns provided beds and blankets. The ever-faithful Ursulines made curtains and provided crockery, cutlery and vestments. They even organised squads of cleaners to scrub the building before we took possession. I was destined never to lose the charitable help of Sisters, but I did not know this as I was preparing to leave Manor Park. At that moment I was conscious only of all that I was leaving and losing.

Leaving the bomb-scarred school was especially hard. St. Winefride's school had been a source of consolation and sorrow. It had twice led me into conflict with my bishop and shortly before my departure the head teacher had died in tragic circumstances. My relationship with the staff and children was exceptionally close. We had campaigned together in hard times. The two experiences of evacuation, in East Anglia and in Cornwall, had brought us together in a way which would not have been possible in peace-time. The school gave me a farewell concert for which Miss Schooling, a young teacher, wrote a three-act play. I reproduce the short finale because it is amusing and rather touching.

ACT III

THE RESTORATION OF CHRISTIANITY IN ENGLAND
(The children form a semi-circle)

GIRLS:	The Faith was strong in England for hundreds of years.
BOYS:	Till men grew careless and greedy, and did the devil's work instead of God's.
1st speaker:	"Do not obey the Pope. I am the head of the Church,"
All:	said Kings and Queens, and —
2nd speaker:	"Down with the Mass,"

All:	they said; for England was no longer Catholic.
3rd speaker:	But still the Mass went on,
4th speaker:	'though many priests were killed for saying it,
5th speaker:	and England kept the Faith
All:	in spite of dungeon, fire and sword.
6th speaker:	Today the Faith still lives in England.
7th speaker:	But many people here do not know or love God.
8th speaker:	so, like Gregory of old,
9th speaker:	who sent out St. Augustine,
10th speaker:	the cardinal now sends out
All:	OUR FATHER HEENAN. Leave all your friends in Manor Park, and help the whole of England back to God.
11th speaker:	Choose other holy men,
12th speaker:	and, like the twelve apostles,
13th speaker:	pray and preach,
14th speaker:	until this land becomes again Our Lady's Dowry.
All:	Bring back the Mass to every village in this isle.

THE WHOLE SCHOOL NOW JOINS IN:

So we, your children, are here to bid you God speed. We are sad that you must leave us, but we know that you have other work to do for God and England. We shall often think of you, and pray for you, and we shall always love you. May Our Lady help you through all the years to come.

CHAPTER
TEN

A FEW DAYS BEFORE LEAVING MANOR PARK AND THE DIOCESE OF Brentwood I wrote to the bishop. I thanked him quite sincerely for the happy and fruitful years since my ordination seventeen years earlier. Despite his frequent disapproval of my attitude and actions he had given me appointments in the kind of parish to which I was most suited. He had saved me from less congenial posts in Westminster and elsewhere.

As a young man on a walking tour of the Umbrian Vale I had found myself one day in Perugia, where the Good Mother of the Little Sisters of the Poor was an old friend. I had always had a special admiration for these nuns. My first literary venture was a short history of the Little Sisters of the Poor. It was not good enough to publish. On the day I called at the convent a young French nun lay dying. Good Mother told me that Soeur Valerie was in every sense very close to God. She was in the last stages of consumption, which, was still common in the Europe of the nineteen-twenties. The doctor had expected her to die a week before but the Bishop of Perugia had asked her not to die during the week of the Eucharistic Congress in Perugia. He wanted to preside at her Requiem Mass and this would have been impossible during the Congress. Good Mother wrote to Rome a few days later to tell me that immediately after the Congress the bishop returned to the convent. Soeur Valerie meekly asked leave to die. The bishop gave leave and before the end of the week he celebrated her Requiem Mass. I am aware that this story sounds fanciful but it happens to be strictly true. I still treasure the letter which gives the account of the young nun's death.

I had called at the convent of the Little Sisters in the middle of the week of the Congress. Good Mother (that is the title used by superiors in this order) told me about the saintly Sister Valerie and asked if I would like to see her. With charming simplicity she said that Sister Valerie would soon be seeing God and would make sure that any wish of mine would be granted. My constant prayer at the age of twenty-two was that nothing short of death might prevent me from becoming a priest. This is what I told Sister Valerie when I was taken to her bedside. To speak to this young nun or even to see her was a spiritual experience. She had the burning flush on her otherwise pallid cheeks common among tubercular patients. But it was not the pallor which gave her a spiritual look. It was her smile, her joy, her whole demeanour. She could speak only in a whisper but in no way resented my intrusion. Soeur Valerie said that of course I would be a priest one day but was there nothing more I wanted from God? I was not prepared for this question. What other things could I want? Health? I could hardly ask for that with the example of the happily dying Sister Valerie before me. Her sufferings had sanctified her and would soon take her to God. Wealth? It would have been indelicate to ask a Little Sister of the Poor for riches even if I had wanted them. Then I became suddenly conscious that the source of Sister Valerie's happiness was her vocation to give her life for the poor. So I told her to ask God to let me work among the poor once I was ordained. I must confess that I had no noble motives for this request. It was simply that I had always hoped that I would not be put in a bishop's curia after ordination. Soeur Valerie promised that my requests would be granted. We prayed for a few minutes and bade each other adieu.

The bishop's reply was warm and gracious. It confirmed the view I had always held that he had so frequently chastised me only for my own good. In his letter of farewell Bishop Doubleday expressed his good wishes for my future work with the Catholic Missionary Society. That was to be expected. What followed was most surprising. "I have always regarded you," he wrote, "with particular affection. I have watched your work and I am sure that you will do much good in your new sphere. I thank God that it was my privilege to lay hands upon you." The cynic might think that this kindly mood of the bishop was occasioned by his relief that I was leaving the diocese. In fact I had always known that the bishop was fond of me. That is why I had never felt any bitterness at his apparent hostility. I felt sure that he was training the pup in the only way he knew. The

R.S.P.C.A. has now educated ·dog owners to realise that pups are better trained by kindness than by cruelty. Under God's providence it may be that Bishop Doubleday gave me the treatment necessary to prepare me for the infinitely harder tasks awaiting me in later life. The bishop and I parted good friends. I saw him only twice during the next three years. On each occasion he was expansive and demonstratively friendly. He died in January 1951. The following week I was appointed Bishop of Leeds.

I had never had any dealings with the Catholic Missionary Society and had not even met Father Owen Dudley the Superior. I did not know if he would be pleased or disappointed that the post-war Catholic Missionary Society was to be under new management. He was, in fact, pleased. Although mentally as alert as ever, he was too old to begin his C.M.S. apostolate all over again. He had lost his old companions and the mission house at Brondesbury Park was closed. He was glad to retire from active work and stay on in the house in Northwood in which he had taken refuge when the Brondesbury Park house was requisitioned. Father Dwyer and I went to Northwood to see him and ask advice about planning the future of the Catholic Missionary Society. He was most helpful. He loved the Missionary Society and would have been desolate if the C.M.S. had been allowed to die. He courteously offered all the help we might need and professed himself well satisfied with the decision of the bishops. This is what he wrote in a subsequent issue of the *Catholic Gazette*:

A number of new priests will shortly be joining the Catholic Missionary Society under the leadership of its new Superior, Dr. John Heenan.

When His Eminence, Cardinal Griffin, accepted my resignation from the office of Superior, and put the matter of· a new Superior before the Bishops, I had no notion who would be chosen. There was a considerable wait, and then one day His Eminence sent for me to have tea with him. He told me the new Superior had been chosen, and gave me three guesses. I guessed wrong three times. He then told me—Dr. Heenan.

I managed not to drop my cup, but I was frankly amazed—I suppose simply because it had never occurred to me that a prominent man like Dr. Heenan, already up to the neck in well-known activities for the Faith, could be spared for the job. I was not only amazed, but overjoyed that the work I had been doing for nearly thirty years, would be in the hands of the zealous apostle whose great labour for souls I had admired for so long.

Having no experience of the work of the Catholic Missionary Society nor of the problems of community life, I devoted most of my time after leaving the parish to gathering information from missionary societies elsewhere in the English-speaking world. There is no society of priests exactly comparable to the C.M.S. but the Paulist Fathers in the United States seemed to be the nearest equivalent. The Paulists' society whose official title is the Society of Missionary Priests of St. Paul the Apostle was founded in New York in the middle of last century by a Father Hecker. Their original purpose was the conversion of non-Catholics with special care for the coloured. Their rule of life was based upon the constitutions drawn up by St. Alphonsus for the Redemptorist Order. Technically they were not members of a religious congregation but secular clergy. I thought it likely that their rule of life and missionary methods might serve as a guide to me and my future colleagues, of whom none had previous experience of missionary work. I therefore wrote to the Father General, who kindly invited me to visit the U.S.A. to study the work of the Paulists. He told me that there were other communities such as the Vincentians (also secular clergy) who specialise in missionary activity.

The Catholic Missionary Society was founded in 1901 by Cardinal Vaughan, Archbishop of Westminster. The cardinal was a member of a distinguished Catholic family which had produced an astonishing number of priests and nuns. This was due, under God, to a saintly mother whose practice was to spend an hour each day before the Blessed Sacrament praying that all her sons and daughters would be called to the priesthood or the cloister. So efficacious was her prayer that her five daughters took the veil, six sons were ordained priests (including the renowned preacher Father Bernard Vaughan S.J. of Farm Street) and of these no less than three became bishops. Cardinal Vaughan was enthusiastic for the missions. He founded the Mill Hill Fathers for the foreign missions and the Catholic Missionary Society for missionary work at home. The apostolate of the C.M.S. was "to bring back the Faith to England and Wales by means of sermons in churches and public lectures in halls". The cardinal laid down no rule of life for the priests of the society but drew up constitutions governing their recruitment and activities. Religious conditions in 1947 after two world wars were very different from those of 1901. That was the main reason why I felt the need to study the constitutions and methods of other missionary societies before taking up office as superior of the C.M.S.

My tour of the United States provided little in the way of guidance, but it produced material help which was to prove invaluable when we set up house in Hampstead. Rationing continued for a considerable time after the war—in fact for certain commodities it became even more stringent. After the war even bread was rationed. Not only food but materials of almost every kind were unobtainable without coupons. For the first time in my life I had to give thought to sheets, blankets, furniture, carpets, curtains, crockery, pots and cookers. My many relatives in the U.S.A.—especially my nun cousins—shamelessly begged from all our friends. Convents and rectories were raided for clothes, towels, altar linen, vestments and even tinned food. Some of my bewildered benefactors must have thought that I was about to embark on a round-the-world voyage of exploration or possibly a polar expedition. I was astonished to discover on my voyage home how many portmanteaux and packing cases I had acquired for the conversion of England. When eventually I stood on the quay at Southampton and saw my luggage stretching as far as the eye could see, I felt more like the Queen of Sheba than St. Augustine. A friendly transport agent took me under his protection. When I explained what I was carrying in all the suitcases and boxes he told me to wait until he found the right customs officer. He disappeared and was so long absent that I was afraid I would miss the last train to London. This apparently was part of his strategy. At the last moment he arrived panting in company with his favourite customs officer. He waved his hand over my vast possessions. "Nothing of any value here, mate," he told the officer. "This is all personal for Father's mission." I was then bustled into the train. There was great rejoicing when the luggage eventually arrived and the treasures were displayed. It is difficult to describe our elation at the sight of secondhand sheets, used curtains and even dishcloths. It is less difficult to recall the thrill of finding six shining white nylon shirts.

I stayed a few days with Walter Briggs in Detroit. I was invited to stay by his wife, a Scot, whose sister lived near Manor Park. The firm of Briggs makes the bodies for Ford's motors. My object in visiting

Walter Briggs was to secure a car for the mission house. At that time there was a wait of a year before being able to take delivery of a new car. Though knowing little of the C.M.S. I was aware of the Motor Mission run during the summer months by priests of the society aided by volunteers. The pre-war motor chapel was in storage with the mostly decaying household goods of the old mission house and would never take the road again. Nor would it have suited our purpose. What we now needed was a car which, serving as ordinary transport during the year, would take a trailer chapel during the summer campaign. I had no trouble in persuading Mr. Briggs to send a note to Fords in Dagenham requesting priority for a small car (Ford Prefect 10 h.p.). I am not a good beggar. I am sure that if I had asked him Mr. Briggs would have presented a car to the C.M.S. Perhaps I was a little nervous of him on account of a contretemps which occurred during the first day I spent as his guest. It arose from my ignorance of baseball etiquette.

Walter Briggs owned the ball park of the Detroit Tigers. He was a baseball fanatic, which is a species several degrees more alarming than a baseball fan. Walter went to the ball park every afternoon during the baseball season to cheer his Tigers. As his guest I had little choice but to accompany him although I had little knowledge of the game and no interest in it. On this day the Tigers were playing the Chicago Cubs (or they may have been the Boston Red Sox). Without understanding the finer points of the game it is easy enough to discern who are the star pitchers or batsmen (if these are correct terms). To score a 'home run' a player must be either very efficient or very lucky. Hitting the ball out of the ground is a feat which merits the plaudits of the crowd. So, at least, I thought until the day I accompanied Walter Briggs to his ball park. During the course of the game one of the Chicago Cubs (or the Boston Red Sox) hit a gigantic home run. No cricket-loving Englishman could help knowing that this was a splendid act of gamesmanship and accordingly I applauded heartily. Walter Briggs was affronted. "In my box," he said severely "we root only for the Tigers."

My journey to America was well worth while for material reasons and, of course, for the joy of reunion with my many relatives and friends. During the worst of the bombing in London it had seemed unlikely that I would ever see them again. In the event it was one of my cousins, Kieran Pilkington, who did not survive the war. He had joined the U.S. navy and was killed in the landing at Salerno. It is impossible to exaggerate the warmth and generosity of American friends. After the stress and deprivations of wartime, this period of relaxation gave me renewed strength to face my task in the Catholic Missionary Society. I was disappointed, however, in my hope of learning a great deal of missionary techniques or pastoral strategy from the American clergy. Despite the predominantly Irish tradition and common language, Catholics in America and England are remarkably dissimilar. If the Channel has made us unlike continentals, separation by the much wider Atlantic has also made us different from our American brethren. It must be remembered that I am giving impressions received in the year 1947. A quarter of a century later these differences had become immeasurably greater. (The Church in America used to be comparable only to the Church in Holland for slavish adherence to everything traditional and Roman. After the Vatican Council American Catholics were encouraged by theologians to adopt a radically different outlook towards the religious life and, indeed, towards the Church. In the name of spiritual renewal some religious orders relaxed all rules. The diocesan clergy were more moderate in their reforms. The American laity for the most part were bewildered rather than renewed by the unfamiliar attitudes. They were particularly depressed when the Sisters whom they had idolised began to abandon their religious dress.)

The Paulists and the Vincentians demonstrated their missionary methods but with one exception I did not think that these would be productive in England. The only new and potentially useful instrument of conversion was a correspondence course conducted from New York, St. Louis and other great cities. I brought back samples of the literature used in the advertisements and the postal courses of instruction in the Catholic Faith. The Centre in St. Louis had been very expensive to set up. Cardinal Spellman, an enthusiastic supporter of enquiry centres, had contributed a million dollars. Each of the thousands of prospective converts was given individual treatment. This was made possible by the use of automatic typewriters. Thus the questions asked by enquirers were reduced to numerous categories for which the priests prepared stock answers. There are perhaps a dozen questions customarily asked, for example, about confession, the Virgin Mary or papal infallibility. Skilled clerks ticked the appropriate number of the paragraphs which the typewriter would set out automatically in letter form. If enquirers raised personal problems or asked unusual questions they would be answered by one of the priests on duty at the centre. It was obvious that sophisticated methods of this kind would be far beyond our resources for a long time to come. Some years later, after I had left the Catholic Missionary Society, an enquiry centre was set up at the mission house—but without automatic typewriters.

Apart from this world-wide postal apostolate (it was world-wide because many of the prospective converts were in the U.S. armed forces overseas) there was little in the American Church which could serve as a model for the work awaiting me in England. The relationship between clergy and people seemed much closer to the continental than to the British style. Priests usually worked in and from offices to which parishioners were trained to come. They went to the people only if they were sick. At that time this seemed to be the most striking difference between the pastoral methods in Britain and elsewhere. Clergy of all denominations in this country are expected to make regular visits to parishioners in their homes. The old saying "A house-going priest makes a church-going people" remains the guiding rule for priests in a parish. This has led to close relationship between clergy and people. Affection for the priest and reverence for the priestly office were not missing in America but, so far as I could judge, the priests were expected to make social calls rather than pastoral visits. I had already decided that in the Catholic Missionary Society we could achieve results only if we were assiduous in visiting the homes of the people to whom we proposed to preach. It seemed unlikely that the people who needed us most would come to our mission services unless we called on them with a personal invitation.

The four new members of the Catholic Missionary Society took up residence in Hampstead on 5th November 1947 without even noticing that it was Guy Fawkes Day. The *Catholic Gazette* was our sole link with the associate members of the C.M.S. who had remained faithful to Father Dudley during the war years when the society had been unable to function. Despite having no activities to report and although rationing of newsprint killed off most small magazines, Father Owen Dudley and his dispersed members managed to keep the *Gazette* alive throughout the lean years. It was no small feat. Financially the *Gazette* was a liability but as a link with C.M.S. supporters it was invaluable. I invited Father Dwyer to take over the editorship and Father Thompson became business manager. I quote from the issue of the *Gazette* which chronicles our arrival at the new mission house:

The great adventure has begun. The Fathers of the Catholic Missionary Society have at last assembled in the new Mission House in West Heath Road. But we do not feel very much like Missioners. As yet, our activities have not been strictly apostolic. We have been—and still are—furniture removers, electricians, carpenters, odd-job men and scribes. Especially scribes. We have filled in endless forms, signed innumerable permits, written to various ministries, renewed identity cards, become affiliated to butchers, bakers, I nearly said candlestick makers. Candles for the altar are one of the few things unrationed.

I am afraid that the house has not yet that tranquillity of order so rightly advocated by spiritual writers. Our books, for example, are not in the library. They lie, in their thousands, on the floor. We have bookcases, but they are blitzed and mutilated; their shelves are missing, doors are unhinged, sides are bulging. But we are not worried.

All this inconvenience has its own value. I have said that we have not yet engaged in directly apostolic labours. But the first frustratingly material preoccupations are not without their bearing upon the apostolate ahead. If we can now surmount the obstacles cheerfully, we shall be able later on to withstand the positive hardships awaiting us when we begin campaigning in enemy country. That, in the near future, is what we are planning to do. We must coax. We must be patient.

That is why these first few weeks are so valuable. It is wearying to stand at windy street corners and to talk in cold half-empty buildings. Hence the value of this wearying period of initiation.

Picture the scene. I sit at my desk writing, let us suppose, to the Northmet Power Company. I am seeking elucidation of Section 28 (b) of the Electric Engineers Regulations. I am trying to discover if our circuit comprises V.I.R. cable of sections not less that 7/.044. I have found my textbooks no help. I find nothing in the *Dictionnaire Apologétique de la Foi*. Nor, for that matter, do I discover anything in the English dictionary. I am struggling with my letter, when suddenly an agonised voice comes from the stairs: "Quick, it's slipping." Rushing up, I find that one of the Fathers has made a wardrobe from assorted pieces of wood. Halfway up the staircase, he and it are stuck. Yes, the adventure has started.

How does all this help in the conversion of England and Wales? I like to remember that the Apostles were fishermen before Our Lord made them fishers of men. They might well have been furniture removers. Having been that, God will allow us to move far more important things by Faith. We have discovered that Faith does not move furniture. But we know that Faith can move mountains. Our more easy task in the future is to move not mountains but men.

(Catholic Gazette December 1947)

We now had a house and four priests in residence (with several others in prospect) but we had no programme of missions and no domestic staff. Mary Henry, my housekeeper in Manor Park, bravely came to look after us until we could find Sisters but one person could do little in such a large house. We canvassed various convents for nuns willing to co-operate with our missionary efforts. It was easy enough to find nuns to look after orphans, handicapped, blind and deaf children but it was difficult to convince nuns that a community of healthy young priests represented a work of charity. We sought nuns by writing letters and by calling at convents. Neither our literary style nor our personal charm met with any success. So we took to prayer as a last resort. If we had prayed from the first instead of relying on our powers of persuasion we might have found our nuns sooner. It was Cardinal Griffin's suggestion that we should invoke the aid of St. Teresa. I told the story in the February (1948) issue of the *Gazette*:

FRANCISCAN ALLIES

When I joined the great army of house-hunters I had already decided that, eventually, we must have nuns to run the mission house. Unlike most of the homeless—who are satisfied to find any kind of house—I would consider no property not having in its grounds an additional house suitable for a small convent. On the suggestion of the cardinal, the problem was put to St. Teresa. She solved it. The present mission house is ideal for our purpose.

The next and more baffling task was to find the nuns. We wrote to every convent we knew and to a still larger number of Religious Congregations whose existence we had hitherto not suspected. We soon saw that, humanly speaking, we were asking the impossible.

Every convent had more work than it could manage and less vocations than it needed. So we decided that St. Teresa who found the house must finish the job. Accordingly the priests each said a triduum of Masses in honour of St. Teresa. By the first post on the day following the triduum we received a letter of acceptance from the Franciscan Sisters of Littlehampton.

It is fitting that these Sisters should have come to help in the great work for the conversion of England and Wales. They are following a noble tradition. Not the least important part of the sanctity of St. Clare lay in her unfailing encouragement of St. Francis. In her biography we read that she constantly urged him to continue his missions to the people when he himself felt disposed to forsake the world for a life of contemplation. St. Clare, too, it was who courageously faced the army of Frederick the Second when from the Valley of Spoleto it launched an assault upon Assisi. History records that St. Clare took the Blessed Sacrament from the little chapel and held it in the face of the invaders. The dazzled soldiers fell backward and the whole army took to flight. We do not anticipate an armed attack on the mission house. But the example of St. Clare, encouraging the Friars in their mission work, will doubtless spur our own Sisters to emulate their great patron. The mission house will not only be a home to which the Fathers may return between missions for a few days of peace and preparation. It will also be a spiritual storehouse. The Masses and prayers of our Sisters will provide a much-needed support for our apostolic labours.

Great enterprises are sometimes predestined to fail through lack of preparation. Our work in the C.M.S. was in no such danger. For the first few months we undertook no engagements. We wanted to feel our way and prepare our minds before presenting ourselves to the Catholics of England and Wales. Fathers Callaghan and Holland soon joined us from Liverpool and Father Martindale came from Lancaster. As we grew into a community and felt able to exchange ideas with great freedom it became clear that our C.M.S. would have only a superficial resemblance to the pre-war Catholic Missionary Society. The priests under Father Dudley were essentially preachers and lecturers. We did not think that this would be our role. The war had made a great difference to social habits. Radio—and, soon, television—discouraged people from going to halls to listen to speakers. The best speakers could be heard in comfort at home. We also made up our minds to give attention to Catholics more than to those outside the Church. We felt that ignorance of the faith was so widespread within the ranks of practising Catholics that we ought to give plain doctrinal missions to our own people. We would, of course, keep others in mind but we all felt that to explain the truths of faith 'to our own people first was the most likely method of spreading knowledge of the Catholic religion. In our experimental plan we decided to give the first week of a fortnight's mission to Catholics and invite them to bring their non-Catholic friends during the second week. We also resolved to spend our days visiting the homes of the people. Only in this way, we felt, would we have an audience for our sermons and lectures in the evenings.

We had all been busy men before coming to Hampstead. It was a new and unpleasant experience to be out of work. We could have preached a month's course of Sunday sermons or given retreats in convents but we were convinced that it was best to keep rigorously to our chosen pattern of work. We were afraid that if we were to accept casual engagements we might never settle down to the hard apostolate awaiting us. We used to take turns on the Catholic Evidence Guild platform at Speakers' Corner in Hyde Park. We preached regularly in St. Edward the Confessor's, the parish church of our part of Hampstead called Golders Green. One of us would be in the pulpit while the rest were sitting in the sacristy making notes on his sermon. Back in the mission house later that evening we would hold an inquest. It was no fault of ours if we did not become efficient preachers before taking the missionary road.

We did not begin our regular work until the end of February 1948. We then gave missions in Manchester, Liverpool, Glasgow, and London among the cities and in Fleetwood, Hastings, Epsom, Welshpool, Ruthin and Caerphilly among the smaller towns of England and Wales. Once we began to preach missions we never had an idle period.

In order to make ourselves known to the largest possible number of priests we invited volunteers to give up a week or fortnight of their annual holiday to join us in our summer campaign. We now had a motor car (by grace and favour of Henry Ford) and a trailer chapel, but this was largely what is now called a gimmick. We used it in market places but it rarely attracted crowds. The useful work was done in churches and halls. During the summer of 1948 we took Oxfordshire as our mission field. No less than a hundred priests volunteered their services. Our ambition was to have a resident priest in every group of villages throughout the summer. We were not looking for a spectacular rush of conversions. Nothing could have been further removed from the Billy Graham technique which soon afterwards became popular. We wanted only to provide a quiet presence of the Catholic Church in the countryside of Oxfordshire. The people always received us with courtesy and occasionally with interest. The scattered Catholics were delighted to have the Mass brought to them. When the campaign closed we were able to leave one or two permanent Mass Centres, some of which in due course might be erected into small parishes.

The priests who volunteered to help us on the Oxford mission came from every diocese in the country and from several religious orders. We also accepted priests from Ireland and from the United States of America. Two members of the Chicago Mission Band (a U.S.A. version of the C.M.S.) were sent by Cardinal Stritch. They came to help us and incidentally to pick up hints for use in Chicago by observing our missionary techniques. They were highly successful missionaries and taught us a great deal about the most efficient way to run a missionary society. These zealous men, Father Hillinger and Father Hoffman, preached in a style which had gone out of fashion in England early in the century. Apart from their studied rhetoric the sermons included generous doses of emotion and occasionally pure sentimentality. Our own restrained style of preaching did not tempt us to feel superior because the American priests attracted and held the crowds far more successfuly than the rest of us. In Chipping Norton market place, where we spoke during much of the summer, the Americans were particularly effective. The public address system attached to our mobile chapel was almost perfect and threw their voices without distortion (apart from the American accent) a distance of some forty yards. One whole family living in a side street listened to the mission for a whole week without ever seeing the missioners and were so impressed that they took instructions from the local priest after we had gone.

Paradoxically our busiest campaigner was Father Frank Thompson who spent the whole summer in bed. Soon after he had joined the C.M.S. we learned that he had a heart condition so severe as to make him incapable of any active work in the field. He organised our programme, attended to correspondence and, above all, he prayed. He was taken seriously ill one day while visiting friends in Weybridge. The house of the O'Keefe family had always been his second home. He was nursed through a long illness with loving attention by Mrs. O'Keefe. He suffered intense pain which he accepted with perfect resignation as his contribution to our summer campaign. Vicarious suffering, a basic doctrine of the Redemption, is one of the great Christian mysteries. When Father Frank's pain became unbearable he would use our campaign as another sufferer might use a drug. "Quick," he would cry "give me the name of another village." God alone knows how many souls were brought to God through this priest's sufferings. He died in Weybridge but we brought his body back to the mission house. I celebrated his Requiem Mass in St. Mary's Cathedral, Newcastle-on-Tyne. Father Thompson had been with us rather less than a year, had preached only one sermon—on a Good Friday—and written one article for the *Gazette*, on the resurrection of the body.

The Oxford Mission gave us a great experience and, through the volunteer missioners, brought the C.M.S. to the notice of wide sections of the clergy. We knew that in the future we would not lack support for our work or requests for our services. What we did not know was that the success of the Oxford experiment was to lead to an enterprise of far greater scope and difficulty. The bishops decided that during 1949 there would be a general mission throughout England and Wales in preparation for 1950, the centenary of the restoration of the hierarchy after penal days. Having seen the willingness of the clergy to serve under us in Oxford, the bishops instructed the C.M.S. to organise a mission in every parish in the country. We were to have at our command all the regular missioners from the religious orders together with the diocesan priests who were confidently expected to volunteer their services in large numbers. During November 1948 Cardinal Griffin and Bishop Beck, the co-adjutor Bishop of Brentwood, attended a meeting at the mission house to which all the major superiors of the religious orders were invited. As a result of this meeting I sent a letter to every priest in England and Wales to enquire the dates on which he would like missioners to be sent to his parish. He was invited to express any preference for secular priests or regulars (e.g. Redemptorists or Jesuits) but to make our work more easy he was urged to leave the choice entirely to us.

To my surprise and intense gratification most priests were content to leave the choice of missioner to the C.M.S. This was surprising because the experience of one year had already shown me how selective priests were about missioners. ("If you can't send the priest I want let us call off the mission for this year. Please don't write back and say you will send me ' a good man'. I have suffered from good men before.") The circular letter also invited priests to volunteer as missioners. It was obvious that if the whole country was to have a mission within one year we would need hundreds of preachers. The volunteers were filtered through a selection board in their own dioceses. Before sending out a missioner we had to make sure that he was sound, zealous and articulate. There was no lack of volunteers but the services of some were not used. We were completely discreet in not disclosing the nature of the report we had received from the local diocese. ("This priest is excellent in every way but being long-winded would be guaranteed to empty any church before the end of a mission.")

I produced a booklet *Hints to Missioners* which contained brief instructions on how to conduct a mission. It was full of what is called homely wisdom. It was, in other words, an insultingly elementary guide to behaviour in another priest's house and pulpit. Its main object was to guard against strangers giving offence to the locals. All hobby-horses must be left at home. The missioner must never forget that the parish priest will have to deal with his people when the visitor has departed. Under no circumstances must the missioner rant, rave or lose his temper in the pulpit. Nor must he complain at the poor attendance even though he may feel personally humiliated by his failure to attract crowds. ("Never forget that a half-empty church is also half-full. There is no point in attacking those who have not come because they are not present to hear you. Congratulate those who have come and persuade them to bring a companion tomorrow evening and your half-empty church will be filled.") The reports received later showed that the volunteer missioners were mostly popular and successful. Their sermons were freshly prepared and having to give only one mission they did not need to husband their energies. The regular missioners who had to go from mission to mission without respite were completely exhausted by the end of the year.

A mission preached simultaneously throughout the country sounds attractive but is quite unpractical. There are simply not enough first-class men available. To make a national programme possible we had to employ veteran missioners who had retired for reasons of age or ill health and non-professionals who lacked parish experience.

Another argument against a general mission is that it is impossible to have a successful mission unless the parish priest is enthusiastic. Almost everything depends on the preparation that has been made for the mission by the local clergy. In some places the clergy were reluctant hosts and the missioner had to fight the parish priest as well as the world, the flesh and the devil. Of the four he was likely to be the most formidable enemy.

Organising a national mission was a task beyond the powers of the C.M.S. since we were still novices. Providentially Redemptorists—the most expert of missioners—took pity on us and one of their priests joined our staff until we had arranged the complete programme for the country. Since we were meanwhile continuing our normal work the C.M.S. members were frantic with fatigue. It was a long and delicate operation to organise missions at the same time in great centres like Sheffield, Manchester or Liverpool. My method was to write on separate pieces of paper the name of the parish, the missioner available, the preference of the parish priest, the dates requested and the weeks when a missioner would be free. Thus I might have in small piles two or three hundred pieces of paper. Now came the really delicate operation. It was necessary to fit suitable names and times to each place. One day I had spread my pieces of paper all over the library floor. After two hours of concentrated work I had fitted in all names, times and places. Each little pile of paper represented a mission fixed. I looked round the floor with deep satisfaction and went into the garden to clear my muddled mind. Five minutes later Sister Patricia called me in. "You need a cup of tea, Father," she said, "after all your hard work. I've cleaned the library and swept up all those bits of paper."

The admirable Mr. Chuter Ede was Home Secretary at the time of the general mission. Cardinal Griffin at the request of the C.M.S. asked permission to include all H.M. prisons, borstals and approved schools in our scheme. The Home Secretary was not only co-operative but enthusiastic. He sent a circular to every governor authorising a mission and asking for every facility to be given to the R.C. chaplain who would be making the arrangements. The only condition was that the whole operation must be voluntary both for the inmates (awful word!) and staff. The prison missions were especially fruitful. There was no difficulty in finding officers to volunteer for extra duty during the mission. Catholic officers all came forward but there was never any shortage of non-Catholics to make up the number. The sadistic 'screws' are largely characters of fiction—or, perhaps, relics of history. In my considerable experience of prisons I have found that the officers (no longer called warders) are prepared to do anything within reason for the benefit of the men and women under their care. For the most part they regard their work as vocational and give their lives to it if the prisoners are co-operative. Unfortunately many prisoners are psychologically incapable of appreciating the good will of those in authority. They are prisoners not only of the gaol but of the social conditions which warped them in childhood. Not a few are illiterate or mentally backward.

The first prison mission I gave was in Walton gaol (H.M. Liverpool prison). It opened on the evening of 15th May 1949. Liverpool is what is called a local prison. Most prisoners have been caught (in police language 'apprehended') in Lancashire. Only in exceptional circumstances would a man be sent to Walton from the south. Prisoners serving life sentences or a term of several years are more likely to be sent to Parkhurst on the Isle of Wight. The opening sermon in any mission is important but for a prison mission it needed to be a masterpiece. News travels faster and public spirit is more compulsive in a prison than in any other community. By next morning the whole prison would know whether the missioner was worth hearing and whether attending the mission was to be the done thing. The first task was to remove suspicion. No, I told them, this mission wasn't aimed at them. It was a mission to the whole country—and why should they be left out? It would be just the same as any other mission with one difference—the men prepared to nurse a grievance—there would be no collection. "I would be unlucky if I did take up a collection, wouldn't I?" (Laughter and general relaxation.) I gave them one or two incidents in the life of Our Lord almost exactly in the words of the Gospel and found that, as outside (prison is 'inside'), hearers are fascinated by the actual words of scripture. The men had come in fairly good numbers and I hoped they would give good reports to their mates and produce a 'full house' for the second night.

After the service I was called to the telephone to speak to my brother Jim. This was most unusual because my family made it a rule never to make contact when I was giving a mission. The news was bad. My mother had been taken ill and was not expected to recover. She had expressly forbidden Jim to let me know because, she said, the men in prison needed me more than she did. My brother had disregarded her wishes because he felt that I would want to be with my mother. In this, of course, he was right but I felt that my mother was also right in saying that the men needed me more. I therefore elected to stay in Walton and offered Mass the next morning that my mother would still be alive at the close of the mission. Before Mass next morning I told the men about the 'phone call and asked them to join with me in praying that I would be able to finish the mission and still be in time to see my mother before she died. During the day my mother was the chief topic of discussion in the prison. Father Lane the prison chaplain came to me during the day with the news that the men were scandalised that I had not hurried home. They thought I must be unnatural. If anyone belonging to them were dying they would leave under escort without delay. As a good son it was my duty to go home.

Before preaching my sermon that night I put the facts plainly to the prisoners. My mother, I told them, had no fear of death and did not need me. She had expressly forbidden any member of the family to let me know that she was so ill. She had been praying for this Walton mission for weeks—in fact she would be praying for the men at this very moment. She was convinced that this mission must go on because it was going to bring great graces to the prisoners. Who was I to contradict her? That was the position. I assured them that as a son I wanted to be with my dying mother but, also as a son, I did not want to refuse her dying wish. Without any doubt her wish was for the mission to continue. Therefore I asked them to say a 'Hail Mary' every night during the week that I would be with my mother at the end. From that evening it was my mother's mission. As I went from cell to cell the prisoners would say "Father, I didn't forget the Hail Mary for your Mum." My mother's prayers were abundantly heard. This was, so far as I can judge, by far the most fruitful mission I ever gave. The men's prayers were also heard. My mother remained alive for three weeks after the mission and, as I shall relate, I was alone with her when she died in the early hours of 8th June.

The atmosphere of Walton prison, according to the prison officers who invited me to their club one night, was transformed during the mission. The number of Catholics coming to the mission services increased each day and even the non-Catholics seemed to be affected by the mission spirit. Prisoners are emotional people and they were touched by my mother's act of self-denial for their sake. In their cells each night they knelt down before going to bed to pray for her. The numbers anxious to make their confession and receive Holy Communion were so great that it was impossible for me to hear all the confessions in the time available. I had to call in neighbouring priests to help. When the mission was over and I departed from Liverpool I left two priests still hearing confessions. The value of such conversions may be questioned. Men who are so easily moved by emotion are just as easily moved by less worthy emotions on their release from prison. I have had more than one proof, however, that the effects of this mission were lasting. Here, for example, is an extract from a letter received on 24th January 1968—nearly nineteen years after the mission. The writer had seen my name and picture in a newspaper and felt impelled to write. Here, in part, is what he wrote:

> ...I was in Walton Prison Liverpool many years ago and you conducted a mission there. I was deeply moved at the time when you told us how your mother before her death told you not to cancel the mission and return home because we needed you more than she did. You can be sure that we prayed hard for you at that time. My point in writing is that I wish you to know that that mission bore fruit and I have settled down with a good job for many years now. I feel that the mission was the turning point in my life. May God bless you always in the very high office He has called you in His Holy Church...

Another man for whom the mission was also a turning point remains in my memory because he had firmly decided not to attend the mission. Before the mission began he made application to change his religion. It is a fact of life in prisons that men work themselves up (or, more accurately, are worked up by the monotony and confinement) to such a point of frenzy that they must make violent protest. The ultimate protest is to break up their cell. This involves smashing every object in it and tearing their clothes into shreds. Other less violent forms of protest are to demand a different cell, new work or a change of religion. To change religion involves a formal appearance before the governor who has to satisfy himself that the request is genuine. Frequently it is frivolous. Thus a rumour may sweep prison that Congregationalists are given a new overcoat and twenty pounds on release. A wave of conversions will follow. A more common reason for changing is a disagreement between a prisoner and his clergyman. That is why at the enquiry both chaplains—the *termini a quo* and *ad quem*—have to be present. There is no unseemly fight for souls but the chaplain will know if the request is serious. If so, it is never opposed. A prisoner may wish to change a nominal for a real religious allegiance as a result of reading, thinking or praying. Usually however a request for change is a form of protest.

Entering Walton prison I was entrusted with a huge master key on a chain which I was told never to relinquish but to keep fastened to my person (trouser button). This enabled me to go everywhere in the prison and unlock any cell door. Outside each cell there is a card giving the prisoner's name. The colour of the card denotes his religion. Red is for Roman Catholics. Blue, I think, is for Jews and white for Anglicans. There are relatively few Jews in prison (not, I think, because they are too clever to be caught but probably because they are a family-based people who look after their own weaker brethren.) Although criminals are not notably pious it is right to place great importance on a prisoner's religion because it may represent his chief hope of rehabilitation. If a man has become a practising Catholic in prison he will be less likely when he has done his time (or, as prisoners call it, his 'bird') to return to crime. The percentage of those who practised any religion when they were outside is negligible. If nevertheless they have the consciousness of belonging to some church their stay in prison can be a time of grace and opportunity. Prison chaplains are men of faith. They know that prison like hospital can give a man his first real chance of seriously reflecting on his duties to God, his family and society.

Father Lane gave me a list of men who needed special attention for very different reasons. Some might be bitter because of an exceptionally severe sentence, the wives of others might have proved unfaithful, some had been recently bereaved. Father Lane also gave me the name of a man who would still have a red card outside his cell although he had left the Church and was about to become a Methodist. It is this man I remember best. When I opened his cell (the prison jargon is 'open up') I was given an angry reception. He told me in fact, to Be Off. He added that I had no right to enter his cell since he was no longer R.C. I told him that I had to visit every cell with a red card. Once inside I asked him at once why he wanted to become a Methodist. He said it was a good religion. I agreed. I noticed on the wall of his cell the snapshot of a middle-aged woman who, I imagined, must be his mother. That was much in his favour—most prisoners seek inspiration from much less maternal prints. I asked if he had written to tell his mother to join the Methodists. "She'd knock my bloody head off if I done that," he replied. "She never misses Mass and I've just about broke her heart."

It is not difficult to do something for a man who respects his parents and despite the hostile reception he had given me we were soon having a friendly conversation. A keen Catholic lad, he had fallen in with the wrong set after leaving school. His new friends soon persuaded him that religion was 'kid's stuff.' He gave me his whole unsavoury story and ended with an account of the crime for which he was serving a six-year sentence. He had not received the sacraments since leaving school. He said that he felt he would like to start afresh and go to confession but he had forgotten his prayers and did not know how to begin. He told me that he was twenty-six years old. That means, I said, that if you left school at fourteen it must be about twelve years since your last confession. I told him to kneel down and confess anything he could remember in addition to all he had already told me.

This incident reminded me of an experience I had in 1931 soon after ordination. I was making my first trip to U.S.A. in one of the old U.S. Lines steamers—possibly the *American Farmer*—in which the passengers were thrown very much together. One evening a woman came up to me as I was sitting on deck and introduced herself as a lapsed Catholic. She had given up the practice of religion after her young sister had died of cancer ("when God killed my kid sister" were her actual words). She had not however been able to lose her faith. It was for this reason that she had come to speak to me. She had been talking to another lapsed Catholic on board. He was an American colonel who, unlike herself, was troubled about his spiritual condition. He was a very sick man who had to keep to his cabin throughout the voyage. The lady told him that there was a young English priest on board and promised to send me to him. The colonel received me warmly and gave me my first high-ball. This is a drink containing so many cubes of ice that the tongue is effectively anaesthetised and the mixture of bourbon whisky and ginger ale is quite tasteless. He told me he had led a wild life and over the drink he gave me a brief autobiography. He ended up by saying that he was now a very sick man and would like the sacraments but lacked the courage to go to confession. It amazed me that a man could tell me in great detail over a drink what in confession would be related with much greater reticence and, incidentally, be protected by the seal of secrecy. I told him to put out his cigarette and confess in general terms what he had already told me. The next day he had a haemorrhage but was able to receive Holy Communion.

It is small wonder that this prisoner brought to mind my American colonel after nearly twenty years. The difference was that the young man in Walton had no fear of confessing his sins. He did not pretend even to himself to be anything else than a criminal. His difficulty was that he had so completely fallen away from religious practice that going to the sacraments had become unreal to him. We had a long talk and he was given the grace to see that he had been his own enemy by staying away from church during so many years. He said that he would cancel his request to change his religion and be at the mission service that night. He kept his word and, to my great joy, was up for Mass the next morning and received Holy Communion with great devotion. His face was radiant. It seemed incredible that a prisoner with years of his sentence still to serve could be so full of joy. Alas! his joy was short-lived.

Half-an-hour after Mass I received an urgent message to go at once to his cell. I hurried to him and found him sitting on his bed with his face in his hands. "This morning I was the happiest man in England," he said. "I know it sounds daft, Father, me being in here and all. It was fantastic this morning at Holy Communion. Then I was here in my cell. Suddenly it came to me all I've done. You couldn't put all that right in five minutes yesterday in confession. It can't be true."

These were more or less his words which I have often recalled. The sermon he heard the night before had been about the woman taken in adultery. I reminded him how our Lord had washed out that woman's life of crime in a few seconds just by saying "Go in peace and sin no more." I assured him that the mercy of God is so great that no time is needed to obtain forgiveness. He was soon at peace once more. I left him to write a letter which would make his mother a very happy woman.

When I returned from Walton I found Father Dwyer and Father Holland awaiting me at Euston station with a car. They had decided to drive me straight to my brother's home where my mother lay dying. I stayed with her more than a week until her peaceful end. It was a consolation to her and a great grace for me. Like Cardinal Hinsley, my mother was deprived of spiritual consolation in her last days. Her burning faith might never have existed. She held her rosary out of the habit of a long life—she was eighty-three years old—but she could not fix her mind on prayers. Her mind had been quite untroubled despite her pains until the doctor began to give her drugs. The speed with which she developed a dependence was remarkable because I have never known anyone more self-disciplined. She fasted every day and abstained from meat every Wednesday, Friday and Saturday. She had often starved herself—especially during two wars—to have food for others. That, indeed, may have been the secret of her health and longevity. (Napoleon once said he had lost many friends through over-eating but none from under-eating.) My experience of my mother's last illness and of others close to me has made me wonder if a clouded mind is not too high a price to pay for total relief from pain. Fortunately as the week progressed less drastic anodynes were provided and my mother's clarity of mind returned. The consolation of prayer was restored to her.

Sister Elizabeth, one of the nuns at the mission house, was a nurse. She had become a family friend and was devoted to my mother. She was given leave by her superiors to look after my mother during her last illness. Sister used to sleep during the day and stay with my mother through the night. On the evening of 7th June when Sister came on duty about eight o'clock I noticed that she looked extremely tired. She confessed that she had been kept awake by noise all day. I suggested that we might share the night's vigil. I had a few hours' rest and took Sister's place at one o'clock on the morning of 8th June. My mother appeared to be in a light sleep. I sat by the bed watching her and reciting the rosary silently. Although her eyes were closed my mother was not in fact asleep. She gave me her hand to hold and almost at once closed her eyes and gave up her soul to God. There was no death agony. Her departing was effortless and peaceful. I wondered if this grace was the result of those prayers of the prisoners that I should be with my mother to give her the last blessing. As I whispered the litany for the dying I felt the beauty of the ritual prayer: "Go forth, Christian soul, out of this world in the name of God . . . who sanctified thee."

The parish church at Ilford was crowded for my mother's Requiem Mass. There were as many clergy as would have been present at a priest's funeral. This was less a tribute to my priest brother and myself than an act of thanksgiving to a woman who had always kept open house for priests. Young men whose parents lived far away always knew that they would receive a loving welcome from her. All the non-Catholic neighbours and friends attended the Mass. This would cause little surprise in ecumenical days but in 1949 it was remarkable. Few of these neighbours had ever before entered a Catholic church. Sydney Kelly, one of my many Protestant relatives, was critical of the solemn Requiem Mass. It appalled him that the Roman Catholic Church showed so little imagination. Nothing, he said, could have been more out of place than the mournful dirge and the *Dies Irae*. The ministers should have been robed in white and the choir ought to have sung a Te Deum. It would have been, in his view, more appropriate if the ceremony had expressed the victory of a Christian who had fought the good fight and entered into her reward. I tried to explain that the sombre music and solemn words of a requiem are for the benefit of those assisting at the funeral. The Mass is in harmony with the sorrow of the bereaved. He was completely unconvinced. It is a tribute to his Christian instinct that in the renewal of the Liturgy the Vatican Council permits white vestments for a funeral and the motif is the joy of the resurrection. I am sure that white vestments would have been right for my mother. I think that her son might more suitably be buried with purple or black.

The death of husband, wife or children must be the keenest loss anyone can suffer. The death of parents affects nobody more than the priest. My father died in 1937 soon after I became parish priest of Manor Park. It was hard to realise that he was dead because my mother kept his memory fresh. Everything reminded her of him. "What would poor daddy have said?" was her invariable comment on hearing news. She was not in any way morbid and did not depress us with elegiacs. All her reminiscences were of the witty or wonderful things daddy had said when we were small children. In some ways my father came more alive as we listened to my mother's panegyrics. I did not realise what a great character my father had been until I heard my mother talk of him so continuously. When my mother died my sister, Mrs. Reynolds, did everything possible to take her place. She and her family played a much greater part in my life after I had moved away from London. When I was a bishop their house became a second home for me.

A priest has a unique relationship with his mother. I did not have to await her death to appreciate my mother's qualities. Her greatest accomplishment was the ability to give herself to prayer and self-denial without those closest to her suffering the tyranny of her good example. Her spiritual exercises were conducted mostly in private. It was assumed that she was resting upstairs while, in fact, she was on her knees reciting her long prayers. But what made her outstanding was not her practices of piety but the unlimited range of her friendship. Throughout her life my mother gave away to friends and strangers anything of value she possessed. Her death changed my life. I did not mourn her because it was impossible to begrudge her the reward she had earned. I shed no tear for her but often felt inclined to shed tears on my own account. Every week since ordination I had spent some hours with her. With complete trust in her discretion I could tell her all about my work. The stories of failures, disappointments and, above all, successes were for her ears alone. A priest can talk to his mother as to no other living person. She is almost an alter ego. After my mother died there was nobody to whom I was impatient to tell my news. The families of my brother and sister did everything possible to supply my loss but nothing could ever replace the disinterested wisdom of my mother.

When the general mission finished early in 1950 the Catholic Missionary Society was soundly re-established in the Catholic life of this country. It would now be difficult to imagine circumstances in which any hierarchy would allow it to disband. After the general mission, members of missionary communities wondered if they would be out of work for years to come. In fact there was no shortage of engagements and we had to extend the scope of our operations. In addition to missions we began to accept invitations to preach retreats to clergy, seminarians and university students. These retreats called for a different kind of preparation and encouraged us to keep up our reading. One congregation being much like another it would be possible to go from parish to parish with one set of sermons. The sermons would be fresh to each congregation but the preacher's faculties would soon atrophy. We took no engagements during the month of January. This gave us an opportunity to make a retreat and invite scholars to stay with us to lead discussions. Among the most stimulating were Dr. Hawkins, the philosopher, and Philip Hughes the historian. Ronnie Knox gave us one of our retreats and former C.M.S. stalwarts such as Archbishop Downey came to give us useful hints on preaching.

I gave two clergy retreats, one in Durham and the other in Nottingham. I found them much more taxing than parish missions. Although there was no laborious house-to-house visitation there was a far greater burden. Giving the conferences was not burdensome—it is hard to find a more sympathetic audience than one's brother clergy—but it was a most responsible task to give wise advice to priests who were strangers. The clergy naturally use the opportunity of a retreat to consult the Retreat Father on personal and pastoral problems. A spiritual director varies his counsel according to the character of the person seeking help. He does not speak to a nervous or scrupulous priest in the same terms as to a man with a less sensitive conscience. One advantage a diocesan priest enjoys over a member of a religious order when preaching a clergy retreat is that as one of themselves he need fear no resentment if he speaks plainly of their shortcomings. A monk sometimes flatters diocesan clergy for fear of sounding spiritually superior.

The substance of my retreat talks subsequently appeared in a book called *The People's Priest*. Unfortunately it was a success and was translated into German, French, Spanish and, I am told, Hungarian and Japanese. I regard the success as regrettable for the very simple reason that although it was sent to the publishers in October 1950 when I was Superior of the Catholic Missionary Society—it was not printed until May 1951 by which time I was a bishop. Now what a man may say bluntly and acceptably to his fellow priests may be regarded as insulting if coming from a bishop. There are passages in the book which might have provoked a chuckle coming from Father Heenan but not from the Bishop of Leeds. Naturally I had no idea when writing the preface of *The People's Priest* that, when published, my words would be coming from a bishop. The few who read prefaces would have known that this was not the book of a bishop lecturing his clergy but of a fellow priest examining his conscience. The volume was dedicated to 'My fellow clergy of the diocese of Brentwood with affection and respect.' The preface concluded with these words:

> Any priest who talks or writes for other priests must risk the accusation of hypocrisy. This accusation, incidentally, is not likely to be made by his brethren but if he has any self-knowledge they are bound to be made by himself. His words are not likely to be insincere but they may be misleading. He may

lack the spiritual wisdom he needs to make him a safe guide. One priest may be resisting grace calling him to a higher state of sanctity. Another may be resisting an opposite grace which would prevent a fall.

Many aspects of pastoral life will be discussed in the pages which follow. They are concerned largely with failings. It follows that many of the sentiments expressed will sound censorious. In this, above all, the secular priest writes with an advantage over the religious. He knows that his brother priests are, on the whole, sound and pious men. But he does not feel any compulsion to tell them so. The religious, on the other hand, fearing to appear superior, may feel it necessary to intersperse his criticisms with all manner of compliments to the pastoral clergy. The reader will find little enough in these chapters about the deeper spiritual life of the priest. My object in writing is much more modest. It is to give younger priests the results of twenty years' experience in the ministry. I cannot tell them what they ought to do. I know by recalling past blunders what they should avoid.

My last year at the mission house passed busily and happily. By now we had our full quota of priests who formed a completely united family. It was a much-loved haven. Returning from missions we were in need of rest since our unwritten rule permitted us no respite while on duty. Our unwritten rule of life was a guide to our spiritual exercises at home and our programme of work in the parishes. We rose early during a mission to say Mass at a time to suit parishioners who had to be early at work (evening Mass had not yet been introduced). We did not pay social calls and accepted no hospitality outside the presbytery. Following the custom we learned from the Chicago Mission Band, we took no alcoholic drink during the course of the mission. To show that we were not anchorites however we gladly joined any celebration the parish priest arranged after the close of the mission. Following the example of the Redemptorists we always refused invitations to stay on in a parish for a few days' relaxation after a mission. We returned to Hampstead very gladly. It is a tribute to our family spirit that few of the priests ever spent an evening outside the mission house in search of recreation. Our community life gave us all the stimulus and amusement we needed.

During the recess in January 1951 personal sorrow struck my

family once more. I was recovering from influenza at the mission house when I received an unexpected visit from Bishop Beck, who had taken Bishop Doubleday's place in Brentwood. He happened to be passing by and thought he ought to let me know that he had visited my brother Jim in hospital that day and regarded him as a very sick man. My brother had a duodenal ulcer and on the advice of a surgeon had gone into hospital early in the New Year. There was no urgency. He had chosen to have the operation at that time simply because it was not a busy period. His wife and children had no cause for worry. I had not seen him after the operation because I did not want to risk giving him the germs of my influenza. Bishop Beck advised me to go down to Whipps Cross Hospital on the following day. After the bishop had left I began to ponder that it was most unlikely that he had merely happened to be passing my way. I decided that my brother must be seriously ill. So although I felt rather shaky on my first day out of bed I decided to go to the hospital at once. I reached the hospital within an hour of Bishop Beck's visit but my brother was already dead. This was a completely unexpected shock to all the family except my nephew Brian Reynolds, a young surgeon. He had seen his uncle the day before and realised that some surgical error must have been made. A day or two later the post mortem revealed that the intestines had been twisted when being replaced after the operation. This carelessness or incompetence which robbed a young family of its father also lost a valuable worker to the Church. A member of the Essex County Council, my brother was indefatigable in his efforts for education and was also active in the Catholic Parents and Electors' Association.

The loss of my mother and brother considerably reduced my zest for living. I did not grieve because both were outstanding in personal holiness and mourning would have been an act of self-pity. I was soon to have a much greater excuse for self-pity. Preaching a mission in Billingham, Co. Durham the week after my brother's funeral, I received a telephone call from Archbishop Godfrey, the Apostolic Delegate. Speaking in Latin he informed me that the Holy Father wished me to accept the See of Leeds which had been vacant for over a year since the death of Bishop Poskitt. I replied with caution. I said that despite my wish to obey the Pope I could not conscientiously give an immediate acceptance. Certain facts about myself were known only to God and to me. Before giving a final answer I must have time to think and pray.

I wrote a simple statement of the reasons why I thought it would be a mistake for me to accept the episcopate. I did not doubt my ability to organise a diocese nor was I lacking in pastoral experience. It was my spiritual qualifications which were wanting. In a letter which I knew was confidential in the strictest sense I told Archbishop Godfrey of some of my moral failings which hitherto I had revealed only to the priest in confession. I also mentioned my habit of speaking bluntly on matters which I regarded as important even in criticism of those in authority whether civil or ecclesiastical. I knew that prudence was the most highly prized virtue in episcopal candidates and I did not count it among my attributes. Having recited my litany of faults I left myself completely in the hands of the Apostolic Delegate. I did not want to refuse the request of the Holy See but it was my duty to make known facts which might render me unsuitable. When I had sent off my letter I felt at peace because I had not described imaginary failings. My letter had not been an essay in mock humility. In a brief reply the Apostolic Delegate said that he did not regard my reasons as justifying a refusal. He had accordingly destroyed my letter and would convey my acceptance to the Holy Father. On 12th March, 1951, the feast of St. Gregory the Great, Apostle of England, I was consecrated Bishop of Leeds in St. Anne's, the Cathedral church of the diocese.

Index